The Principalship:
New Perspectives

The Principalship:
New Perspectives

Paul B. Jacobson
University of Oregon

James D. Logsdon
Florida Atlantic University

Robert R. Wiegman
Florida Atlantic University

Prentice-Hall, Inc.   Englewood Cliffs, New Jersey

The Principalship: New Perspectives *is the third*
edition of the book formerly titled **The**
Effective School Principal, 2nd Ed.

Library of Congress Catalog Card Number: 72-3689

ISBN: 0-13-700856-2

Printed in the United States of America

10   9   8   7

PRENTICE-HALL INTERNATIONAL, INC., London
PRENTICE-HALL OF AUSTRALIA, PTY. LTD., Sydney
PRENTICE-HALL OF CANADA, LTD., Toronto
PRENTICE-HALL OF INDIA PRIVATE LIMITED, New Delhi
PRENTICE-HALL OF JAPAN, INC., Tokyo

Contents

Preface

In the mid-1930s, the late William Claude Reavis, then a professor of education at the University of Chicago, developed a course outline which he called "The Duties of School Principals." This course outlined the duties of both elementary and secondary school principals, differentiating between them where necessary. As far as we know, this was the first time such an organization of material had been attempted. The "Duties of School Principals" course has been taught at the University of Chicago both by the late Dr. Reavis, and by one of these authors. Two of the present authors have also taught it at the University of Oregon. Significantly, the outline developed by Dr. Reavis became the basis of the first edition of this textbook, which is now in its third revision.

If one reads the literature of a generation ago concerning the school principalship, and then examines the material current today, it is almost impossible to believe that the same subject is under consideration. And when one considers what was written a decade ago, the change is so marked that recognition is scarcely possible.

There are many new problems affecting the principalship today: the use of drugs in school—particularly at the secondary level; the militancy of teachers—a situation in which the principal frequently believes himself to be "the man in the middle"; the newer methods of teaching which make thirty children, a teacher, and a textbook totally outmoded, and forecast the advancement of education toward some form of individually prepared instruction, teamteaching, or the like. Then too, growing student unrest has made the principalship a much more difficult position.

Experienced teachers who have acquired the techniques of managing unruly children and soothing irate parents can no longer be considered adequately prepared for the duties of the principalship, even though at one time these were the main requirements. Today the position requires much more in the way of ability, background, and understanding.

The extent of recorded information concerning the functions of principals is so great that it would take many years of personal investigation to acquire the knowledge needed to meet the many requirements of the principal's position. The personal interpretation of this body of material is too great a task for the practicing principal alone. The authors, in undertaking the writing of this volume, were well aware of the challenge of the task of collecting, selecting, and interpreting all this information, and they pooled their resources to carry it out as effectively and precisely as possible. The results of more than 3,500 studies, investigations, and works on administrative topics form a basis to support the generalizations presented in this book. And where we, the authors, felt we could secure greater competence of knowledge in some of the newer areas such as PPBS, we secured independently written materials which we edited and approved. We have drawn upon our extensive experience as principals, superintendents, and professors of education. And always, throughout the book, we have attempted to maintain a careful and considered balance between theory and successful practice.

It is impossible to acknowledge adequately in this space all the obligations we recognize. Many authors, publishers, and organizations have generously given permission to quote significant materials. Acknowledgment is given specifically in appropriate footnotes. Throughout the volume, citations are made to individual investigations and investigators whose contributions enhanced the value of our discussion. For tireless and painstaking technical assistance in the preparation of the manuscript, we gratefully acknowledge Viola Volkens.

Paul B. Jacobson
James D. Logsdon
Robert R. Wiegman

1

The Principalship
Today and Tomorrow

The principalship today is different and much more difficult than it was a decade ago. There is little resemblance between the duties, responsibilities, and problems of the principal of a few years ago and those of today's administrator. Among the reasons for this difference, mentioned in this chapter and expanded elsewhere in the book, are changes in the curriculum and more extensive teacher involvement in it; dissatisfaction of principals with the failure of training programs to keep current with the many aspects of his job; teacher militancy, student unrest, widespread drug use; the general societal unrest engendered by the war in Vietnam; the belief that the black citizen has not been treated fairly; and the existence of social injustices such as poverty in the midst of plenty.

Changes in the Curriculum

There are many serious students of education today who believe that the thirty children, a textbook, and a teacher in the classroom tradition will disappear within the next thirty years, and that some form of multiunit teaching, individually prepared instruction, computerized learning materials, unit teaching, or some other form of instruction will become the prevailing mode in education. Such changes will significantly affect the relationships between the principal and the teachers of a school. At this moment we do not have very much hard data about what the effects of these changes will be, but we have some. Roland Pellegrin, a Research Associate at the Center for the Advanced Study of Educational Administration, has studied the

1

multiunit schools developed by the Research and Development Center at the University of Wisconsin. His investigation was based on an intensive study of four multiunit schools and four control schools, and he secured his data by questionnaires, individual discussions with teachers, and observation.

In multiunit schools, a group of three to five teachers work together under a group leader, sometimes with a secretary, to guide all the learning functions of a specific group. Pellegrin and his associates asked respondents to list (1) the names of the persons on whom they depended most heavily to perform their jobs, and (2) what job must be performed in collaboration in order to be effective. A sociometric table (see Fig. 1) was later inserted to show the relationships between the teachers in a multiunit school and those in a conventional school. From examination of the sociometric dia-

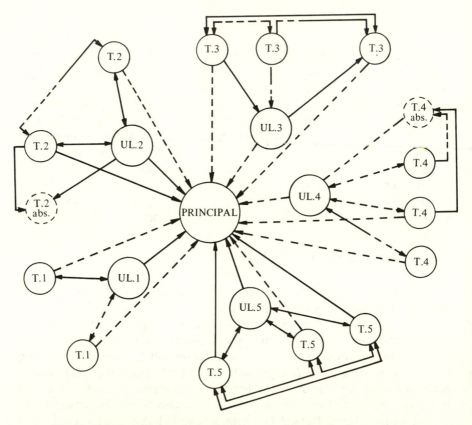

Fig. 1. Interdependent relationships in a multiunit school.

grams, it is clear that the unit leaders are key people, that they have direct relationships with the principal. It is also interesting to note that no unit leader designated another unit leader as a person on whom he was dependent, but the principal received nominations as collaborator from most teachers and all the unit leaders—in marked contrast to the control school. In fact, the principal received all but two of the twenty-five possible nominations.

Pellegrin discussed and explained the relationships of principal to teacher and unit leader in this way:

> Let us at this point make a few generalizations that extend beyond the two schools we have been considering. First, the patterns of relationships in the control school shown in Fig. 2 are almost identical to that of other control schools in our sample. Indeed, the patterns are similar to that of other elementary schools we have studied elsewhere in the country. If anything, the control school shows more interdependent relationships than are usually encountered, owing largely to the presence of teamteaching and other collaborative undertakings not found in the typical school characterized by the self-contained classroom. The fact is that a traditionally organized elementary school in the United States has a primitive division of labor and a differentiation of function in its professional staff. Grade level is the only consistent basis for distinguishing among teachers. Emphasis is on the functions universally performed by teachers, not on the coordination of effort or any form of specialization.[1]

Pellegrin continues:

> These sociometric charts we have discussed map the nomination of teachers and unit leaders. If we examine the responses of principals to the same questions on which the charts are based, we can find the differences between the multiunit school principals and the control school principals. The multiunit school principal reports that his successful job performance depends on a number of people. He lists considerably more names than the control school principal does. The former list of essential relationships is especially longer than his counterpart. Typically the multiunit principal lists the essential relationships with all the unit leaders, and his secretary, and occasionally with another person or two.
>
> The control school principal, on the other hand, lists few essential relationships. They are usually limited to his secretary and the custodian. The multiunit school principal is clearly part of an expanded interaction

---

[1]Roland J. Pellegrin, "Some Organizational Characteristics of Multipurpose Schools," (Eugene, Oregon: Center for the Advanced Study of Educational Administration, 1970), p. 3.

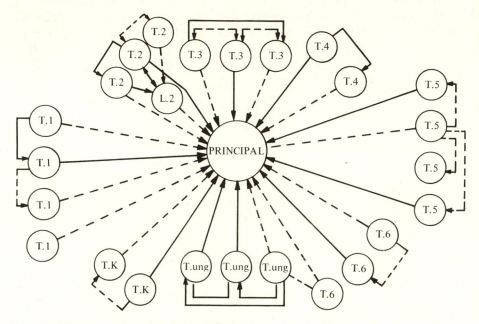

Fig. 2. Interdependent relationships in a control school.

network, in which his relationships to his faculty have changed considerably from that which prevailed in the controlled schools.[2]

In a multiunit school the unit leader, not the teacher or principal, is concerned with the management and coordination of all activities. The teacher's work tends to become more specialized along subject matter lines. For example, one teacher may take math instruction, and another who is good in science may give instruction in that area. Pellegrin continues:

> Some teachers devote most of their time to working with individual pupils, while others work mainly with small groups or class size groups. In two of the schools studied, individualized and small group instruction are heavily emphasized. In these schools some teachers report each spending 75 percent of their time working with individual students; others said they devoted the same proportion of their time to small group or class size ones. A few teachers took special responsibilities for working with even larger groups than usual class sizes, usually at the beginning or end of study units. There is, then, considerable specializa-

---

[2]Pellegrin, "Organizational Characteristics," p. 4.

tion in some multiunit schools for teaching in an individual small group or large group setting. In line of the emphasis given to individual small group instruction in the multiunit system, the development of such specialization is to be anticipated. There are, however, disparities in the amount of such instruction from one unit to another within the school, and one of the schools studied retained class size groups almost exclusively. Individualized instruction in this school consisted almost entirely of routine drill by instructional aid.[3]

Another interesting relationship that emerges is that some teachers serve as expert advisers to their colleagues. Where specialized training is lacking, a teacher may be asked to take the responsibility of learning about recent developments in a subject and of keeping his fellow teachers informed on and about it. Thus, other teachers are assigned to other topics with some resultant specialization.

Authority, Decision-Making Processes, and Influence

In the Pellegrin study, in order to determine authority, decision making, and influence, each respondent was asked to indicate if he (a) had complete autonomy to make decisions himself, (b) had final authority to make decisions after receiving suggestions and recommendations from others, (c) had authority to make decisions within certain limits, (d) had authority to share in decision making with other persons in a group decision-making process, or (e) had no voice in making the decision.

In the control school the distribution of responses presents a picture of a school composed of separate, relatively isolated classrooms where the activities of each classroom are determined primarily by the teachers, and are monitored to some extent by the principal. For the school as a whole, however, the principal is the central authority figure; he is the only person whose activities extend beyond the individual classroom.

In the multiunit school there is evidence that the decision-making pattern is being changed significantly. Even though there are some variations in response, and the pattern varies from school to school, some important generalizations can be made. For one thing fewer teachers see themselves as making decisions individually. Substantial numbers indicate that decisions are shared with others in a group decision-making process. The teachers who indicate that they still make decisions individually stated that at the same time there is a notable shift away from reliance upon the principal for advice and assistance in situations in which colleagues can fulfill those functions. In

---

[3]Pellegrin, "Organizational Characteristics," p. 5.

Table 1

PERCENTAGE DISTRIBUTION OF FACULTY
RESPONSES TO ALL FIVE QUESTIONS

Responses*	Multiunit Schools A	B	C	Control Schools D	E	F	All Multiunit Schools	All Control Schools
a	3.2	11.9	3.0	16.7	7.4	11.4	5.1	11.9
b	28.4	20.9	17.7	32.1	56.9	43.1	21.9	43.9
c	11.6	11.9	18.5	29.8	33.3	40.5	14.7	34.4
d	53.6	50.8	50.0	11.9	1.2	2.5	51.4	5.3
e	3.2	4.5	10.8	9.5	1.2	2.5	6.9	4.5

*Legend:
  a = Respondent has complete autonomy to make the decision himself.
  b = Respondent has final authority to make the decision after receiving suggestions and recommendations from others.
  c = Respondent has authority to make the decision within certain limits.
  d = Respondent has authority to share the decision with other persons in a group or committee.
  e = Respondent has no voice in making the decision (i.e., the decision is made by others).

general, decision making is moving from the individual classroom level to that of the unit level. Unit leaders are making the decisions, usually in a collaborative fashion. It is probably correct to say that in the multiunit school, the unit leader turns out to be the leader, while the principal is the coordinator of all the unit leaders' efforts. This development will, of course, require different sorts of training for the principal, and different activities in the schools.

Job Satisfaction

Ten questions were asked about job satisfaction in the Pellegrin study. In three of the items there was no significant difference between the control and the experimental schools. On the other seven items of those responding the results were as follows:[4]

	Experimental	Control
Highly satisfied in multiunit and controlled schools	26%	15%
Satisfaction with personal relationships with administrators and supervisors	61%	39%

[4]Pellegrin, "Organizational Characteristics," p. 10.

	Experimental	Control
Opportunity to accept responsibility for one's own work and the work of others	61%	43%
Seeing positive results from one's efforts	36%	15%
Personal relationships with fellow teachers	73%	55%
Satisfaction of present job in light of one's career expectations	56%	39%
Availability of pertinent instructional materials	60%	27%

Teachers also believe that they have greater freedom in selecting materials in the experimental schools than would otherwise be true. Three general roles now arise for the unit leader. They are instructional leader, administrator, and teacher. Each one must be performed capably if the unit is to function. Because an appropriate balance between the three is difficult to establish and maintain, however, in this perhaps the principal can serve as coordinator.

Even though in the multiunit system the principal is to be coordinator of the instructional program, his role will be very different from his traditional, conventional school role. Many of the principal's usual duties will be shifted to the unit leader, and the teacher will turn to the unit leader for assistance. The principal will also have the duty of insuring that each unit is properly organized, and that the unit leaders and teachers develop the proper interdependent relationships necessary to carry out the instruction. He may also operate effectively as chairman of the instructional improvement committee.

Professional Satisfaction in the Multiunit School[5]

In another report by Roland J. Pellegrin concerning the professional satisfaction of respondents in multiunit and control schools, the results (on seven out of ten items) were as follows:

	Multiunit	Controlled
1. Satisfaction of progress toward one's personal goals	29%	16%
2. Satisfaction of personal relations with administrators and supervisors	56%	44%
3. Opportunity to accept responsibility for one's work and work of others	58%	47%

[5]Roland J. Pellegrin, "Professional Satisfaction and Decision-Making in Multiunit Schools," (Eugene, Oregon: Center for the Advanced Study of Educational Administration, 1970), p. 10.

	Multiunit	Controlled
4. Seeing positive results of one's efforts	39%	15%
5. Personal relationships with fellow teachers	72%	57%
6. Satisfaction of present job in light of one's career expectations	54%	42%
7. Availability of pertinent instructional aids	58%	32%

The unit leaders also reported higher overall satisfaction than did the multiunit teachers, and, had they been included, the results would have been even more startling. A number of questions on job satisfaction regarding decision making were also asked of the teachers. Their answers are summarized in Table 1. Pellegrin states:

> If we examine Table 1, which summarizes the answers to all five questions, we clearly see the overall pattern. Response a is shown by less than half as many multiunit as control school faculty members. The same is true for response b. Almost two and one-half times as many faculty members in the control school selected response c. On the other hand, response d was chosen almost ten times more often than in the multiunit school. Response e was not often chosen in either set of schools, but somewhat more frequently in the multiunit school. Nonetheless, we can identify the basic decision-making process that prevails. In most instances, the individual teacher makes the decision either alone or in consultation with the principal, or with certain limits prescribed or enforced by him. The teachers in the controlled group and the principal operate within certain limits or guidelines set by the district Curriculum Committee and by central office special subject matter specialists. Thus, both primary decision-makers, the teachers, and principals have limits set on their discretionary authority. In the multiunit schools there are some startling differences for the pattern we have just described. The key factor is that the decision-making process has been fundamentally altered. The evidence is overwhelming. The decision-making authority has been shifted to the unit faculty. When responses b, c, d, and e are chosen as replies to the questions covered in the table, the persons most often mentioned are the members of one's unit. Furthermore, the characteristic responses are to name all faculty members in the unit. The principal figures much less centrally as the decision-maker or limit-setter.[6]

The teachers saw the unit leader as the person to whom they would go if they wanted to make changes in the teaching program or the curriculum.

---

[6]Pellegrin, "Professional Satisfaction," p. 6.

But in the control schools, the influence hierarchy was dominated by the principal. Typically he received three to four times as many designations as most influential as any other individual. The question, "In general, how much influence do you feel teachers as a group have on how your school is run?" was answered as follows. The percentage answering "A great deal of influence" was notably higher than the multiunit school—40 percent in school A as compared with 8 percent in school D, 72 percent in school B as compared with 11 percent in school E, and 22 percent in school C as compared with 11 percent in school F.

> These findings are fully in accord with a substantial body of research in theory and social psychology. For many years certain students of organizational processes have extolled the improvement in morale and work effectiveness that accompanies high rate of peer group interaction and the heavy involvement of people in decisions that bear directly on the work they perform. These writers have contended that when groups actually are given the authority to make and implement decisions that are significant for them, they make these decisions effectively, responsibly and enthusiastically. Unfortunately, the researchers have found few instances in any kind of organization in which there has been a real comprehensive transfer of authority to the work group. The multiunit school is clearly an example of an organization in which group decision-making has become an accomplished fact. This development augurs well for the future of the multiunit concept. We can expect that with additional experience in the operation of multiunit schools, together with further studies of the organization and function of these institutions, it will be possible to increase the effectiveness in which to carry out their responsibilities.[7]

Other Curriculum Activities

For many years the National Association of Secondary School Principals has been interested in improving instruction in secondary schools. For this reason it established a commission in the mid-1950s to seek possible alternatives and solutions. Between 1956 and 1961 this commission worked with nearly 100 junior and senior high schools across the country. The progress of the various experiments were reported by the schools themselves in publications of the National Association of Secondary School Principals in January 1958, 1959, 1960, and 1961. In the 1,134 pages of these reports the teachers and principals of the schools involved provided information on the studies in which they had been involved. Three resultant books outlining experimental approaches to high schools were published: *New Horizons for Secondary School Teachers*, 1957; *Images of the Future,*

---

[7]Pellegrin, "Professional Satisfaction," p. 11.

1959; and *New Directions to Quality Education,* 1960. In addition, an hour-long movie, *And No Bells Ring,* was released in 1960. About the studies J. Lloyd Trump wrote, "These experiments and the studies have led to the formation of a new kind of school basically different from those now in existence."[8]

The development of large group instruction, small group instruction, and independent study was the major goal of the new kind of school to which Trump referred. Recommendations suggested that 40 percent of the time should be spent in large group instruction, 20 percent in small group instruction, and 40 percent in individual study. The advantages of this system are that students are better motivated by contact in small groups with the very best teachers available for a given phase of a subject, large group instruction avoids duplication of teacher effort, makes technological equipment more economically feasible, and by greater economy of time, allows more presentations by outside specialists, university teachers, and community resource persons. Large group classes serve as a transition experience for students. In such situations they learn to take notes, hold back questions until the appropriate time, and develop more responsibility for planning their own learning.[9]

For efficient staff utilization, 40 percent of a student's schedule should be in independent study; this is where many of the problems of the system have become apparent. Central to independent study is the resource center, which may include any or all of the following: a library; a reading room; a viewing room; a listening room; a mathematics laboratory; a science laboratory; an English laboratory; a foreign language laboratory; a social studies laboratory; health, physical education, and recreation rooms; conference rooms; and individual student cubicles or carrels. Teachers are available at all times for individual consultations.

At first teachers and guidance counselors may determine the nature of the student's activities until he becomes independent. (Later we shall discuss a doctoral study of a student's attitude toward independent study in two Oregon schools, and provide an analysis of this study with time and facilities by students in high, average, and low achievement groups.)

Related Literature

Three reports on experiments with independent study conducted at the University of Illinois High School were published by David M. Jackson in the January 1959, 1960, and 1961 issues of the *National Association of*

---

[8]J. Lloyd Trump and Dorothy Baynham, *Focus on Change* (New York: Rand McNally and Company, 1961), pp. 21–22.

[9]Trump and Baynham, *Focus on Change,* pp. 30–31.

Secondary School Principals Bulletin.[10] The authors concluded: (1) That independent study courses proved worthwhile as far as the University High School was concerned. They would remain a regular offering in the science curriculum. (2) That during the two-year trial, only a minimum of supervision had been necessary in the course. (Careful selection of students would be necessary to retain this as a valid conclusion.) (3) That since most public high schools have only a few gifted students, such a course would be a desirable and inexpensive way to allow those students to enjoy special science experiences. (4) That this type of course could be operated with a minimum of funds and teacher time. It, of course, would be highly desirable for teachers to have as much time to devote to independent study courses as they now devote to science courses. (5) That the success of the course would depend not only upon careful selection and early guidance of students, but also upon the willingness of the supervisor to trust students once they had been admitted.[11]

Another extensive survey, conducted by William M. Alexander and Vince A. Hines in 1965, undertook the systemization of information concerning independent study in forty-eight continental states.[12] From a total of 317 secondary schools they selected a random sample of thirty-six schools. Data relating to the characteristics of independent study plans, and to the opinions of students, teachers, and administrators concerning independent study were collected and analyzed. The authors found that, "Independent study is probably more common in educational discussions and literature than it is in the practices of the secondary schools."[13] In the case of the thirty-six schools studied, more independent study projects were found in the English, social studies, and science areas than in any other classes. These projects were responsible for 60 percent of the students engaged in independent study. Only a few schools had programs in business education, industrial arts, home economics, or physical education. Alexander and Hines reported from their sample that independent study seemed to be a way of providing for the very able student, even though this was not the original purpose for which it was established. After obtaining reactions from 300 teachers, counselors, and administrators Alexander and Hines concluded that, "In the opinion of the high proportion of the 300 staff

---

[10]David M. Jackson, "A Search for Practical Means of Improving Instruction by Increasing Students' Responsibilities for Their Own Learning at the University of Illinois High School," *National Association of Secondary School Principals Bulletin,* 43 (January 1959), 233–39.

[11]Jackson, "Students' Responsibilities," p. 201.

[12]William M. Alexander and Vince A. Hines, "Independent Study in Secondary Schools" (Gainesville, Fla.: Cooperative Research Project 2669, University of Florida, 1966).

[13]Alexander and Hines, "Independent Study," pp. 97–98.

members polled, most independent study students are in the top half of the students in the respective classes in the schools."[14] Although this response is only an example of the literature in this field, we think it is illustrative of what exists. Alexander and Hines reported that of the equipment of independent study, the library received the highest rating, and teaching machines a very low rating. Both language arts and remedial teachers gave language laboratories poor ratings. In fact, no facility except the library received an overall rating of much better than fair.

Perhaps we might conclude by saying there is little hard research directly related to independent study activities in secondary schools. A few evaluations have been published that indicate some positive attitudes are held toward independent study practices by teachers who have been involved. The following summarizes the facts and attitudes toward independent study:

1. Independent study is more common in the literature than in actual practice in the secondary schools.

2. More students are involved in independent study programs in the areas of science, social science, and English.

3. Few students engage in independent study programs in business education, industrial arts, home economics, and physical education; the number of students involved in independent study practices in these four areas is relatively small.

4. Independent study is usually seen as a way of providing for the very able students—most independent study students are in the top half of their class. Alexander and Hines hope that independent study opportunities will be extended to all students regardless of academic achievement.

5. With reference to favored facilities for independent study, school libraries receive high scores from all raters. Teaching machines and individual study spaces receive low ratings, while reading improvement devices fare only slightly better than teaching machines. The new electronic media seem to have only a modest impact on the independent study student.

6. Evaluation is a problem. Most schools in the sample had done little to determine the extent to which the goals of the independent study programs had been realized.

7. A total of 82 percent of teachers and administrators involved favored the expansion of the independent study program. The faculty also listed scheduling, finding teacher planning time, providing adequate teacher preparation, and providing means for adequate evaluation as the problems most often encountered with independent study.

---

[14]Alexander and Hines, "Independent Study," p. 33.

Where innovations in study practices and learning techniques occur, the role of the principal is changed. The principal becomes a facilitative figure rather than the traditionally directive one of the past. With the increasing use of new educational methods, such as independent study activities, the problem of the principalship is different and perhaps even more difficult each year.

The Murphy Study[15]

The Murphy Study of independent study activities concerned two schools in Oregon. One was situated in a metropolitan area with an enrollment of over 2,000 boys and girls. The other was located in a smaller city with over 1,000 boys and girls, 25 percent of whom lived outside the city. With achievement test scores available, school counselors identified students who had scored in the high, average, and low ranges. Techniques included an opinionnaire, student diaries, and discussion with administrators, teachers, counselors, and students.

Grade 11 students were selected for the sample, since they had experienced at least one complete school year of independent study. The opinionnaire sample included 476 grade 11 students out of the 864 students for whom achievement test scores were available. The sample, however, included all grade 11 students who were present and available on the day selected for the administration of the opinionnaire in school A, and a random sample of grade 11 students who were present in school B. Of the 476 opinionnaire respondents, 267 returned diaries. School counselors were asked to identify students scoring high and low on the achievement tests used in the school. From this information a sample of thirty-five students from each achievement group was selected from school A, and a similar sample from school B. In all, 210 students were selected; they returned a total of 117 study diaries.[16]

The Murphy study analyzed 461 opinionnaires all together—243 from school A and 218 from school B. Each one was treated as a separate sample. The conclusions of the study are as follows:

1. Most of the students who took part in this study liked the opportunity provided for independent study. Totals of 95.5 percent (school A) and 91.7 percent (school B) expressed this point of view. Forty-two percent of the students who liked independent study indicated they liked it because

---

[15]Gerald Murphy, "A Study of the Relationship Between Achievement and the Use of Time and Facilities by Students in High Schools Using Staff Utilization and Independent Study Techniques" (Ph.D. thesis, University of Oregon, 1969), pp. 35–36.

[16]Murphy, "Independent Study Techniques," p. 44.

it gave them freedom to decide what to do, where and when to study, and gave them the option of studying or not studying.

2. More than 50 percent of both samples agreed that independent study made them want to find out more about their subject matters, that they completed assignments better, and that they spent more time reading materials which helped them to better understand subjects they were taking for credit. Almost 60 percent of the 461 students agreed that they studied more than the subject matter presented by teachers in scheduled classes during independent study time.

3. Approximately 60 percent of the students experienced little difficulty in adjusting to independent study; more than 70 percent found independent study plans easier than small group discussions where teachers helped plan activities and directions.

4. However, problems do exist.

   a. Some students had difficulties in adjusting to independent study. Some 21 percent in school A and 42 percent in school B indicated that they had experienced difficulties. Some students revealed that they seldom received all the help they needed in the library and the resource centers (27.6 percent in school A and 25.7 percent in school B). More than 50 percent in both schools indicated that independent study would be more useful if they knew how to plan their work better, if their reading speeds and skills were improved, and if they were more skilled at note taking.

   b. Students disliked some aspects of independent study. Students who gave reasons for disliking independent study indicated that they disliked it mainly because they did not know how to plan and benefit best from independent study time. Two-thirds indicated that they needed assistance in planning.

   c. From 70 to 94 percent of the students who took part in the study agreed that these conditions were desirable for independent study: that they study where books and materials were easily obtainable; that they study near or in a resource center or library where teachers or teacher aides were available for consultation; that they study with two or three other students who were studying; that they study where audio-visual materials, typewriters, adding machines, and slide rules were available for students' use; and that they study where all lights could be easily adjusted.

5. More boys than girls appreciated the availability of technical aids in study areas.

6. The library, the study center, and the subjects resource center were the three most important facilities which students thought helped them to develop better study habits.

7. The study opinionnaire disclosed few sex achievement differences, although the study diaries revealed sex differences in one school and achievement differences in both schools. Students in the low achievement groups tended to spend less time in the resource centers during independent study time. Level of achievement was an important factor in determining whether or not students used independent time for study or for other activities.

8. Students were asked what they thought could be done to help them improve their study habits. The suggestion offered most often by students was "Learning to organize and plan my work" (27.7 percent).

9. Useful comparisons can be made among independent study programs in various schools.

From the results of this study, it seems clear that students who have had no previous experience with independent study need assistance in learning how to work independently. To effectively maximize the effect of independent study, a creative guidance program must be designed to meet the individual needs of each student. School counselors, librarians, teachers, and teacher aides must become members of teams whose functions and purposes may carry them across professional and specialized lines. Since the objective of independent study is to make the student a self-starter rather than a classroom listener, every student should meet an adviser in a weekly conference group during the first school year. If some form of independent study is to be developed it must be developed as a phased approach in which a great deal of time is spent by particularly adept teachers in planning the program. And many people feel that independent study is growing at such a rate in the secondary school that it will obviously have major effects on the principal's job. He will eventually become a facilitator of learning, dealing with chairmen of learning groups as equals, rather than with lower persons in the hierarchy as was the case forty years ago—or even ten years ago.

The Evans Study[17]

Marvin L. Evans also made a comparative study of secondary school independent study programs. Among his findings are these important conclusions: (1) The literature indicated that teachers in successful independent studies programs had a better understanding of the objectives of their programs than teachers in less successful programs. (2) Teachers in successful programs felt that they had stronger leadership than those in less successful programs. This leadership may come from the principal, from a team

---

[17]Marvin Leroy Evans, "A Comparative Study of Secondary School Independent Study Programs" (Ed.D. Dissertation, University of Oregon, 1968).

teacher leader, or from a specific group of teachers. (3) All of the schools in this study operated under a marginal program, but successful programs made every use of teamteaching. They also seemed to place some restrictions on students' movements during independent study time. (4) Teachers must spend a great deal of time sensitizing young people to independent study so that they can utilize their time effectively, and make the program successful.

Role of the Principal

John M. Foskett's study of the normative role of the elementary school principal[18] was concerned with how the elementary principal perceived his role: Does he perceive it in the same way as he thinks teachers do, as the school board or superintendent do, or as other persons in the community do? To secure data, a role norm inventory of forty-five statements was prepared and administered to a population of principals, community leaders, members of school boards, superintendents, and elementary school teachers. Included were 367 elementary school teachers, 7 members of the school board, 56 community leaders (selected by nominating procedures), and 750 adults living in the community. This sample yielded 607 useable replies.

One result of the study is that there is no complete agreement among principals when it comes to defining their role, although there is some agreement among principals in regards to what they believe other people think their role should be. The average level of agreement among the principals on this subject is less than 50 percent.

Another important finding is that the principals were not definite in their answers. They said "probably should" and "preferably should" rather than "yes" or "no" or "definitely should" or "definitely should not." There is a wide range in the amount of agreement from one norm to another, a range from near zero to complete agreement, with the average around 50 percent. Principals and teachers are in highest agreement, while principals and school boards and superintendents are in lowest agreement, with principals and community member population in median agreement. Probably the basic reason that teachers and principals are closer together than any other group is that principals are chosen from among teachers, are in frequent contact with them, and are therefore mutually reinforcing for each other's ideas regarding norms considered desirable.[19]

---

[18]John M. Foskett, *Role of the Elementary School Principal* (Eugene, Oregon: Center for the Advanced Study of Educational Administration, University of Oregon, 1967), p. 37.

[19]Foskett, "Role of Principal," p. 90.

Probably the explanation for the large differences in views between principals and central administration is that they deal with different matters. The school board is more concerned with budgets, buses, and general problems than with individual instruction in the schools.[20]

Foskett concludes:

A systematic examination of the responses of the principals in each of the populations of others to each of the role norms reveals a degree of ambiguity in the position of elementary school principals. The evidence suggests that the position is not clearly defined. In part, the principal is identified as an administrator, and part as a member of the teaching staff. Similarly, the principals sometimes see themselves as administrators, sometimes as members of their teaching staff. However, there is a tendency for the principals to see themselves as administrators more frequently than do the several populations of others. This ambiguity is heightened by the low level of agreement among the principals themselves and among others for a number of norms that appear to be critical.

The ambiguity of the nature of the position of elementary school principals suggests that the position is interstitial and that it exists between two other positions, that of teacher and that of central administration. As a consequence, it tends to be associated in part with each of the adjacent positions and not completely with either. One is reminded of the classic example of an invitational position, that of a factory foreman who is identified with workers by the top management, and the top management by the workers. This same condition exists for a number of other positions in our society.[21]

The Principal's Problem As He Sees It

Issues and Problems in Elementary School Administration, by Gerald Becker, Richard Withycombe, Edgar Miller, Frank Doyel, Claude Morgan, Lew Deloretto, and Bill Aldridge, under the direction of Keith Goldhammer at the Center for Educational Research and Service, Oregon State University, Corvallis, Oregon published in 1970, was a study of the elementary school principal in all fifty states.[22] It included discussions with people in elementary teacher preparation institutions, state departments of education and regional educational laboratories. The main source of information was elementary school principals in fifty states, including inner-core metropol-

---

[20]Foskett, "Role of Principal," p. 95.

[21]Foskett, "Role of Principal," p. 95.

[22]Gerald Becker, Richard Withycombe, Edgar Miller, Frank Doyel, Claude Morgan, Lew Deloretto, and Bill Aldridge, under the direction of Keith Goldhammer, *Issues and Problems in Elementary School Administration* (Corvallis, Oregon: Center for Educational Research and Service, Oregon State University, 1970), p. 139.

itan centers, suburban schools, intermediate size school districts (15–25,000 students), small school districts (2,500–15,000 students), and rural school districts (fewer than 2,500 students). Chosen from a nominated list of 2,346 carefully chosen by a panel, 291 principals were interviewed. On the basis of these interviews, the authors identified some outstanding educational institutions which they called "beacons of brilliance," and, at the other end of the spectrum, some very poor schools that they called "pot holes of pestilence."

In the "beacons of brilliance" institutions, the principals were charismatic leaders who seemed to instill their teachers with enthusiasm. The teaching staff seemed to work together as teams, and because their morale was high, their service extended far beyond normal expectations. An ongoing process involving teachers and principals, as well as parents, promoted constant appraisal of the effectiveness of the schools, in an attempt to devise new programs and strategies for overcoming deficiencies. Keeping the programs of study adaptable, the emphasis in the instructional programs was placed upon the children's needs. The principals were confident that they could provide relevant and purposeful learning without having to lean on traditional crutches. "Beacons of brilliance" were found throughout the different types of community study, but not in the numbers one would wish to see.

The "pot holes of pestilence," on the other hand, were the result of weak leadership and official neglect. With buildings dirty and in disrepair, these schools were an unwholesome environment for learning and growth. The schools were poorly staffed and poorly equipped. The morale of the teachers and pupils was low and, where control was maintained, fear was one of the main control strategies employed. As for the instructional programs, they were traditional, ritualistic, and poorly related to student needs. These schools were characterized by lack of enthusiasm, squalor, and ineffectiveness throughout, partly because of the principals' attitudes of merely serving out their time, looking always forward to relief and release.[23]

The principals in the "beacons of brilliance" schools seemed to have several important characteristics. First of all, they didn't intend to become principals on their own, but were encouraged by their administrative superiors. Next, most of them had sincere faith in children. And they had an ability to work effectively with people to secure their cooperation. They were aggressive in securing recognition of the needs of their schools, and as such were enthusiastic as principals, accepting their responsibilities as those of a mission rather than as those of a job. Finally, they were committed to education, and especially capable of distinguishing between long and short

---

[23]Goldhammer and others, "Elementary School Administration," pp. 139–40.

term educational goals. These principals were adaptable administrators as well as able strategists.[24]

Critical Issues Confronting the Elementary School Principal—The Ambiguous Role of the Principal

Perhaps the most critical problem faced by the elementary school principal today is the general ambiguity of this position within the school system. There is no viable, systematic rationale for the elementary school principal to follow which provides a basis for determining both expectations of his performance and criteria through which his performance can be measured.

As one reviews the comments of the elementary principals, one gains the impression that they believe they are generally viewed by their superiors and by citizens in the community as subprofessionals rather than administrators with full professional status and prerogatives. Within the texture of the organization the status of the elementary principal probably accounts for many other practices, which the principal considers discriminatory against the elementary schools, in general. Elementary school principals generally are the lowest paid administrative personnel in the school district. They do not have the independence in operation of their buildings which is accorded the secondary school principals. Increasingly, the elementary school principal appears to be cut off from involvement in group decision-making, which affects the manner in which he can perform his duties and determine the operating patterns in his school. As school districts increase in size, the elementary school principal becomes just one more subadministrator in the district. Policies for the allocation of resources, the employment of personnel, and the operating relationships within the district become much more bureaucratic and centralized. The principal feels that it is essential he be given the opportunity to convey the needs in his individual school to the central administration. He is concerned that he has little or no opportunity to participate in district decision-making processes. He deeply resents being thought of as a second-class administrator and attributes much of the frustration as an elementary school administrator to this discriminatory situation.[25]

The inadequacy of preservice training for the elementary school principals is a serious matter. Internship and field experiences are poorly developed, and frequently the program of training for elementary principals, secondary principals, and superintendents is almost the same.

---

[24]Goldhammer and others, "Elementary School Administration," pp. 140–41.
[25]Goldhammer and others, "Elementary School Administration," pp. 141–42.

Elementary school administration principals tend to view their roles overwhelmingly in old-style managerial terms. Increasingly, however, they see groups defying their identification of goals or desirable procedures and meet with difficulties in such matters as gaining acceptance for the introduction of innovations in the school, developing a cohesive approach to common problems within the building, developing cooperative relationships among parents and community groups, and obtaining teacher support for evaluative and developmental programs within the schools.[26]

The Principal and Human Relations

The area identified by principals as the largest source of problems involved difficulty in establishing and maintaining successful and human relations. It was in this area that the preservice program was almost entirely deficient. Principals also felt that they did not have an adequate knowledge of strategies to employ in order to effect educational change in the schools for which they were responsible.

The most severe indication of resource shortage is in the allocation of personnel to the elementary schools. Few elementary schools in the sample and probably throughout the country have any administrative, supervisory, or research personnel assigned to them other than the principal. Although some schools have vice-principals, the general rule is that the principal is the sole administrative resource person in the school. Usually secretarial assistance is below reasonable standards for the efficient handling of the work load. The situation usually requires the principal to spend a large part of his time in routine clerical and secretarial chores.[27]

The Principal and Community Influence

The principals also noted a great deal of community influence on the school, particularly on the part of suburban community parents. In the inner-core cities, apathy tended to be the attitude of parents.

The principals expressed considerable concern over civil disobedience and rebelliousness among pupils in the school. In many parts of the country integration problems and federal government regulations sometimes created difficulties in the schools. Principals noted too that many elementary schools interested in securing aid for the building are not sure how to go about getting it. They felt that the central offices do not furnish them with sufficient guidance.

The principals also cited the following problems and situations as be-

[26]Goldhammer and others, "Elementary School Administration," p. 144.
[27]Goldhammer and others, "Elementary School Administration," p. 146.

ing very difficult to cope with. The problem of public relations was extremely worrisome to elementary school principals. They considered not knowing how to communicate with patrons and other people in their areas or how to build an informed school constituency definite problems. The principals indicated their difficulty in finding enough well-trained teachers to cope effectively with student disruptions and difficulties. The disciplinary problems at school were often enlarged by the negative attitudes at home toward the school. Where there were large numbers of culturally different persons, the principal found unique problems for which he seems to have no adequate solutions. This was particularly true of Mexican-American and black children. Most principals considered supervision and teacher assistance as two of their major responsibilities—a traditional attitude for the past fifty years. One reason that principals are experiencing all these difficulties is that they are not well enough trained in present day methods; they have not realized that the educational situation is changing and with it the principal's role in instruction.

The planning and implementation of innovations in the elementary school are a problem to the elementary principal. Principals do not understand such innovations as curriculum design, scheduling, staffing patterns, or instructional materials very well, and so they do not feel very well equipped, and indeed they may not be, to give leadership in these areas. The Goldhammer study says, "Clearly the quality of an elementary education program is dependent upon the leadership abilities possessed by the elementary school principal. As a principal is, so is the school."[28] The principal *must* be able to discern and utilize the abilities of his staff, to inspire among them an attitude of confidence and cooperation. He must be able not only to identify his responsibilities but also be able to distinguish the relative importance of each of those responsibilities. And he, in turn, must have the training and background in administrative leadership necessary for him to fulfill his responsibilities to his staff, the district administrators, the community, and ultimately to the students of the elementary school.

Principal Preparation and Training

Another important result of the Goldhammer study was the findings concerning training programs in educational administration. Comments made in all nine regions of the United States indicated that the nature of the present preparation program must be changed, that current admissions and screening policies must be reevaluated. Many of the responses implied that many of the respondent principals were really not suited to the posi-

---

[28]Goldhammer and others, "Elementary School Administration," p. 40.

tions they presently hold—regardless of the quality of preparation for the position.[29]

Principals in the study also expressed a great deal of concern about the effects of teacher militancy upon the elementary school principalship. All of those who indicated such a concern tended to think of teacher militancy in historical terms, as though describing a problematical situation which the principal faces now.[30]

Title I and II Assistance to Elementary Schools

A vast array of Title I and II assistance programs administered by the United States Office of Education pour vast sums of money into elementary and secondary schools across the nation. These programs are devoted to (1) improving the quality of education at every level for all persons in the United States, (2) bringing quality educational opportunities to various groups of citizens who have not had it in the past, and (3) helping educational institutions examine themselves in light of society's changing requirements. Some of the specific objectives of these programs are to overcome educational deprivation, to improve library resources, to strengthen instruction, to encourage desegregation, to overcome language difficulties, to reduce the number of school dropouts, to improve counseling and guidance, and to strengthen the personnel who serve in the elementary and secondary schools.[31]

Approximately three-fourths of the Title I money goes to the elementary school, since this is considered the area where help is needed most. The programs are limited to schools selected by the Office of Education on the basis of nominations by state agencies.

Regional Educational Laboratories

There are twenty regional educational laboratories in the United States. Each is striving mightily to improve instruction. But the principals of the Goldhammer study feel that too little attention is devoted to elementary education.

Problems of the Elementary School in the Next Ten Years

Population growth, changes in the socioeconomic level of the community served by the school district, and the effects of these changes upon the school were mentioned the most frequently as areas of principal concern in the study. Urban renewal and industrial growth were given as reasons for

---

[29]Goldhammer and others, "Elementary School Administration," p. 44.
[30]Goldhammer and others, "Elementary School Administration," p. 53.
[31]Goldhammer and others, "Elementary School Administration," p. 64.

some of the expected changes in the socioeconomic make-up of the community. Many of the principals also stated concern for the growing number of disadvantaged children in their districts. In answer to these problems and changes the principals foresaw the introduction of broader community welfare programs within the school system in the form of school health care centers, school meal programs, and the like. Principals also felt that parents and society are demanding that the school take over more social responsibilities; evidence of greater involvement of society in the education of children is expected in the future. Principals were more worried about providing individual attention for the children coming to the elementary schools than they were concerned with finding a place for him to just sit. But in order to accomplish this, the elementary school principals were convinced that the traditional aspects of instruction will have to be changed dramatically. As we have seen and will see later in more detail, this is coming about.

Recommendations

An analysis of the data collected by the study leads to the conclusion that the quantity and effectiveness of present elementary schools is in direct relation to the quality and effectiveness of the elementary school principal. The evidence also reveals that there are significant ambiguities inherent in the principalship that seriously handicap the performance of the elementary school principal. There is considerable concern among principals for the imbalance of authority and responsibility in the principalship. This imbalance must be corrected if the principal is to meet the obligations of his position. Unless immediate action is taken to eliminate these problems, the future of elementary education in the United States is seriously endangered.[32]

A study related to the Goldhammer survey involved forty-seven school superintendents from twenty-two states, and used conferences and individual interviews to gather its information.[33] While this study did not relate directly to the principalship, the problems of the superintendents illustrate very clearly that their concerns in the schools were similar to those of the principals. They may be listed under six categories:

1. *Educational change due to social pressures in the community, in the federal government, and within the school.* All of these create problems of educational administration.

---

[32]Goldhammer and others, "Elementary School Administration," p. 149.

[33]Keith Goldhammer, John Suttle, William D. Aldridge, and Gerald L. Becker, "Issues and Problems in Contemporary Educational Administration," (Eugene, Oregon: Center for the Advanced Study of Educational Administration, University of Oregon, 1967).

2. *Teacher militancy.* One of the most severe problems besetting super-intendents is the growing militancy of teachers and of teacher organizations. Dealing with militant teacher groups who demand a role in decision making has pressed a whole new set of problems upon the superintendent and the principal as well.

3. *Instruction.* Among their other concerns, superintendents emphasize that schools exist to teach the young. The principal may be more intimately involved in instructional problems than the superintendent, but the superintendent is also concerned with curriculum, instructional services of all sorts, and evaluation of instruction.

4. *Administrative leadership.* The number and severity of problems facing administrators mean changes must be made in the major leadership function of the superintendency, enabling him to meet the new demands on his competency. He is forced to consider not only issues and problems and their impact on the school, but also his role in the community and the school organization.

5. *Critical social issues.* After the Supreme Court *Brown* vs. *Board of Education* decision of 1954, the school ceased to be an ivory tower, and has become one of the major centers for the solution of contemporary social issues. The problems of desegregation, ethnic minorities troubles, and the problems of disadvantaged children and adults all have major influence on the schools and their administrators.

6. *Finance.* As might be expected, finance is one of the concerns of school administrators. And school superintendents did not feel their preservice training was adequate for their present positions and the problems they face. In fact, they considered the inservice training they were receiving as nonexistent.

Teacher Militancy

Almost everyone is aware of the increasing militancy among the teachers about salaries, working conditions, and sometimes even about the school calendar. Much of this militancy springs from many teachers' belief that the school board and the superintendent have treated them in a high-handed fashion, telling them to "Take it or leave it." Consequently, many have organized, and in some cases become affiliated with the American Federation of Labor and the Congress for Industrial Organizations. There are now several hundred school districts in nearly all parts of the country where there have been strikes mainly over salary conditions, but also over other conditions of work.

This teacher militancy has made the role of the principal particularly uncomfortable. In general, principals, particularly elementary principals, have been inclined to believe that since they had come from the ranks of teachers, they were still part of the teaching force. Secondary principals have felt this to a somewhat lesser degree. There has lately been great concern at national meetings of the Department of Elementary School Principals and the National Association of Secondary School Principals that principals are the forgotten men in negotiations, and this certainly seems to be true. One of the questions we will deal with later in this book is: Are principals part of management or part of the teaching force? It seems that where there have been strikes and major militant teacher actions, principals as a group are moving toward management and away from the teaching force.

Use of Drugs by Young People

Everyone who is familiar with junior high schools, high schools, and colleges knows there has been a significant increase in the regular or incidental use of drugs. Again hard data are difficult to come by, but the following quotation is significant.

> We resurveyed one of these schools again and found that where previously 20% of the students had used marijuana at least once, that figure was now 57% in the same school. . . . We estimate now that there is about 35% overall usage in all colleges and high schools. . . .
>
> In the first few years of our checking on this, it seemed as though there was an overwhelming number of boys who smoked marijuana rather than girls, but that figure no longer pertains.
>
> There is a very large number of girls, and it is increasing all the time, so that within a short period of time, if this trend continues, we shall have an equal number of boys and girls smoking marijuana.[34]

The leading killer in the 15 to 35 age group in New York City is now narcotics, chiefly heroin. About 25 percent of 950 narcotics deaths in 1969 occurred among teen-agers, and 53 percent among those were under 25 years of age. These percentages are about double what they were ten years ago, meaning that more addicts are now dying at younger ages.[35] Whether the figures in an individual school are higher or lower than the estimates, drug use is a problem which will cause principals and counselors untold anxiety and grief. At this point the problem is mentioned only to indicate it. Solutions, if indeed there are adequate solutions, will be discussed in the chapters which deal with pupil personnel and guidance.

Student Unrest

The problem of student unrest is widespread on college campuses, in secondary schools, and even in some elementary schools. It is rooted in the demand by young people that they have a voice in deciding

---

[34]*Hearings* before Subcommittee on Education of the Committee on Education and Labor, 91st Cong., 1st sess., 1969 (Washington, D.C.: Government Printing Office), Part 1, p. 32.

[35]*The New York Times*, June 21, 1970, Sec. 1, p. 1.

their futures and activities. The precipitants are many—the war in South-east Asia, a feeling that racism is rampant in the United States, that poverty should not be allowed in the midst of plenty, and that present day schooling is not relevant. Protests range from unconventional dress to outright rebellion, riots, and arson. These problems demand action—from calling in the police promptly to more subtle approaches requiring more finesse. All these problems multiply the difficulties of being a principal. We will deal with all of them in more detail and at greater length later in the book, in an effort to help the principal acquire the *new perspectives* he will need.

Selected References

ALEXANDER, WILLIAM M., and VINCE A. HINES, "Independent Study in Secondary Schools," Cooperative Research Project 2869. Gainesville, Florida: University of Florida Press, 1966.

BECKER, GERALD, RICHARD WITHYCOMBE, EDGAR MILLER, FRANK DOYEL, CLAUDE MORGAN, LEW DELORETTO, and BILL ALDRIDGE, under the direction of KEITH GOLDHAMMER, *Issues and Problems in Elementary School Administration*. Corvallis, Oregon: Center for Educational Research and Service, Oregon State University, 1970.

EVANS, MARVIN LEROY, "A Comparative Study of Secondary School Independent Study Programs." Unpublished Ed.D. dissertation, University of Oregon, March 1969.

FOSKETT, JOHN M., *Role of the Elementary School Principal*. Eugene, Oregon: Center for the Advanced Study of Educational Administration, University of Oregon, 1967.

GOLDHAMMER, KEITH, JOHN SUTTLE, WILLIAM D. ALDRIDGE, and GERALD L. BECKER, "Issues and Problems in Contemporary Educational Administration," Eugene, Oregon: Center for the Advanced Study of Educational Administration, University of Oregon, 1967.

Hearings before Subcommittee on Education of the Committee on Education and Labor, 91st Cong., 1st sess., 1969, Part 1. Washington, D.C.: Government Printing Office.

JACKSON, DAVID M., "A Search for Practical Means of Improving Instruction by Increasing Students' Responsibilities for Their Own Learning at the University of Illinois High School," *National Association of Secondary Schools Bulletin*, 43 (January 1959).

MURPHY, GERALD, "A Study of the Relationship Between Achievement and the Use of Time and Facilities by Students in High Schools Using Staff Utilization and Independent Study Techniques." Unpublished Ph.D. thesis, University of Oregon, 1969.

The New York Times, June 21, 1970, Section 1, p. 1.

PELLEGRIN, ROLAND J., "Professional Satisfaction and Decision-Making in

Multiunit Schools." Eugene, Oregon: Center for the Advanced Study of Educational Adminstration, May 1970.

————, "Some Organizational Characteristics of Multipurpose Schools." Eugene, Oregon: Center for the Advanced Study of Educational Administration, May 1970.

TRUMP, J. LLOYD, and DOROTHY BAYNHAN, *Focus on Change*. New York: Rand McNally and Company, 1961.

2

*The Principal
and the Principalship*

The high school principalship as the oldest administrative position in American education antedates both the superintendency and the elementary school principalship. The early high school principalship was not considered a professional position as it is in progressive school systems today. This fact is illustrated by the duties the early principal was called upon to perform.

The duties of master or principal of the early colonial secondary school were extremely varied. In addition to teaching and administering his school, he often served as town clerk, church chorister, official visitor of the sick, bell ringer of the church, grave digger, and court messenger, not to mention other occasional duties. On the whole, however, writings on the development of the public school principalship are meager. The public school system developed so rapidly, as did the people who operated it, and those who were devoted to the study of school administration concentrated mainly on the practical side, so that the study of the evolution of the principalship has been neglected.

But we do have some scattered data on early schools and school administrators. For example, while the Latin grammar school in New England had an important place in the historical development of the American secondary school, its size was not conducive to the development of outstanding administrators. Outstanding teachers, however, were not uncommon; one of the greatest of these was Ezekiel Cheever. Concerning Cheever's administrative achievements, F. C. Ensign states:

And while we look to Ezekiel Cheever as a great schoolmaster and educational authority, he was not, in the modern sense, an administrator. He taught and flogged and wrote. He inspired boys; he stood a worthy type of citizenship in his community, but his administration duties were limited to the routine of a little school and, at most, to an organization requiring but one teacher in addition to himself.[1]

The academy (1828–1860) was likewise a small institution. At its peak it enrolled slightly more than a quarter-million youngsters, or about forty pupils per school, and its staff on the average consisted of the headmaster, or principal as he was sometimes called, and one or two assistants. It is fair to assume that the headship of such a school provided little opportunity for demonstration of administrative or supervisory competence. The academy produced its share of great teachers, but none of them stands out as a school administrator in the modern sense.

Development of the Principalship in City Schools

While the elementary school principalship does not extend backward in point of time as far as the high school principalship, it began to emerge over a century ago. Cities developed rapidly in the United States after 1830, and school enrollments, especially in elementary schools, increased at a very rapid rate. In the fast-growing cities the number of schools and their increasing enrollments made it physically impossible for the superintendent to administer and supervise the work of each individual school in person. It became evident that someone was needed to be responsible for the organization of the school, continuity of teaching materials, and progression of pupils through the grades in an orderly manner. Consequently, the superintendent deemed the head teacher in the local schools the person best qualified to carry out his policies, and so gave him these duties.

As might well be expected because of the haphazard growth pattern of the principal's teacher role, the relations between him and the other teachers were not clearly defined, and so became a potential source of friction. The records of the Cincinnati school committee show their ways of differentiating between the duties of principal teachers and teachers in 1939:[2]

The principal teacher was (1) to function as the head of the school charged to his care; (2) to regulate the classes and course of instruction of all the pupils, whether they occupied his room or the rooms of other teachers; (3) to discover any defects in the school and apply remedies; (4) to make defects known to the visitor or trustee of the ward or district if he could not remedy the conditions; (5) to give necessary instruction to his assistants; (6) to classify pupils; (7) to safeguard school houses and furni-

---

[1]F. C. Ensign, "Evolution of the High School Principalship," *School Review*, XXXI, No. 3 (March 1923), 187.

[2]*Tenth Annual Report of the Common Schools of Cincinnati* (1839), pp. 22–24.

ture; (8) to keep the school clean; (9) to instruct his assistants; (10) to refrain from impairing the standing of assistants, especially in the eyes of their pupils; (11) to require the cooperation of his assistants.

On the other hand, the assistant teachers were (1) to regard the principal teacher as the head of the school; (2) to observe his directions; (3) to guard his reputation; (4) to make themselves thoroughly acquainted with the rules and regulations adopted for the government of the schools.

The committee further pointed out that principal teachers were selected because of their knowledge of teaching methods, children, and the common problems in schools. The trustees felt a lack of firmness in the performance of the principal teacher's duties at times. Many assistant teachers were so well versed in their work that they required little or no working direction. Above all the committee felt that mutual cooperation between principal and assistant teachers was especially important because of frequent changes in the teaching personnel, and because without it order and teaching would suffer.

One of the first elementary schools to supposedly have all its departments united under an administrative principal was the Quincy School in Boston in 1847. John Philbrick, the principal of the school who later became the Boston Superintendent of Schools, is generally credited with this achievement. Pierce, however, has shown that the policy of placing all the departments of a school under the direction of one person was practiced in Cincinnati prior to 1835.[3]

By the middle of the nineteenth century, the status of the principalship in large cities was as follows: (1) a teaching male principal was the controlling head of the school; (2) female and primary departments had women principals under the direction of the male principal; and (3) the principal had prescribed duties which were limited largely to discipline, routine administrative acts, and grading pupils in the various rooms.[4]

Release of Principals from Teaching

In order to carry out their duties efficiently, the principals were frequently released from teaching part of the time. As early as 1857 the principals in some of the schools in Boston were relieved of their teaching duties for part of each day, and in other schools one or two half-days a week were set aside for principals to inspect and examine classes other than their own. A teacher known as the head assistant took charge of the principal's class during these periods. Other cities employed similar plans to

---

[3]Paul R. Pierce, *The Origin and Development of the Public School Principalship* (Chicago: University of Chicago Press, 1935), p. 9.

[4]Pierce, *Origin and Development*, p. 12.

free the principal for the performance of his newly emerging administrative and supervisory duties.

During the period from the mid-1800s to 1900, a shift occurred in the administrative duties prescribed for the principal. Principals were required to perform new duties such as organization and general management, control of pupils, and responsibility for buildings and grounds. School authorities and teachers were beginning to realize that the principalship offered professional opportunities. The individual who merely met emergencies in the local school was no longer an entirely satisfactory candidate.

As the nineteenth century drew to a close, the principalship found its prestige was greatly enhanced. In the large cities the principal had gained the right to decide which pupils should be promoted. Orders to teachers from the central office were now sent through his hands. He gained the right to play a part in the transfer and assignment of teachers. This last responsibility was important to the local school, since the supply of trained teachers in the cities was not always equal to the demand for them. It had often been the case that if a principal wanted to keep a teacher who desired to teach in a better part of the city, particularly if the new school was nearer his or her home, his wishes were likely to be ignored.

Changes in Duties in Recent Years

By 1900 it had become customary for principals in large cities to select their administrative assistants. They had also gained not only the right to choose which cadets assumed full teaching status in the schools, but also to transfer or assign teachers to their duties within the building (except when salary increments were involved).

In large cities the first and second decades of the twentieth century saw the principal's office staffed with clerical assistants roughly in proportion to his needs so that he could be freed to attend to important professional duties. Because it was usually not an easy task to secure adequate clerical help in a public school office, the first clerical relief for the principal came from substitute teachers on a part-time basis. The present practice is that approximately one clerk should be provided for each twenty teachers in the elementary school, or one for each 500 pupils enrolled in the high school.

As the public schools increased in size, the problems of heating, ventilating, and caring for buildings by a custodial staff increased enormously. In most moderate-size and large cities, the principal generally came to be relieved of direct responsibility for the condition of the school plant, except for duties of a general supervisory nature. This development has helped to free the principal for educational leadership rather than burdening him with details.

During the early years of the twentieth century, many principals experimented with various ways of breaking the "lockstep" of the graded system. Whereas their efforts for the past fifty to seventy-five years had been focused on inaugurating the graded system, they now began to try to remedy the defects which had become apparent with its use. Principals tried various plans, often with success, to individualize instruction or to care for individual differences.

The organization and supervision of extracurricular duties in both elementary and high schools have become increasingly important since 1920. How such duties are cared for constitutes a challenge to the principal's competence as a school administrator.

The Rise of Supervision by Principals

The administrative duties of the principal developed before his supervisory function was fully realized. As a result, his administrative duties have often monopolized the major portion of the principal's time. As for the superintendent, he generally intended to improve the instruction in the schools, as was expected of him. In fact, in many of the smaller school systems, his function is still supervision and he performs it if it is to be done at all.

Although it has not been general policy for principals to inaugurate educational innovations in the schools, individual school principals have been responsible for many developments such as cooking classes, sewing classes, manual training in high schools, and constructive activities in the elementary schools. Where boards of education did not support the inauguration of such enterprises, especially in the home and industrial arts areas, individual principals have in some instances subsidized the projects with the help of wealthy citizens until the funds could be obtained from the proper sources.

During the last quarter of the nineteenth century, the principal's position as the supervisory head of the school in large cities became well established. His position of responsibility was recognized and respected both by teachers and by supervisors from the central office. Although principals had the opportunity to exert creative leadership in the improvement of instruction, few did so. But the principal should not be too greatly censured for this lack; his shortcomings in supervisory work were not apparent before 1900 if he maintained proper discipline, kept the teachers covering the courses of study uniformly, and secured reasonable conformity to the methods favored in the central office.

The principal's early supervisory activities were centered on the development of a well-graded system of schools—the ideal for which most superintendents were also striving. Although the principal generally attempted to do what the superintendent requested, in some instances he also opposed the latter's policies, sometimes successfully. It is fair to characterize supervision by the principal before 1900 as inspection. He visited classes, quizzed pupils, paid careful attention to the physical conditions in the room, and attempted to exert a genial influence wherever he went. Unfortunately this conception of supervision has not entirely disappeared from the public schools even today. During recent years the principal tends to be the coordinator, not the figure, of supervision.

Local Leadership by the Principal

The principal's first responsibilities in the local community were to facilitate the discipline of pupils and to protect the central administration from the complaints of citizens. Before 1900 superintendents had shown little interest in what community support for the local school could be or had been generated by the local principal. However, principals in some local schools had already taken the initiative in providing educational leadership for the area in which they worked.

For example, in Detroit, the principal had established a mothers' club —the forerunner of the parent–teacher organization—at the Hancock School. The evidence shows that discussions between parents and teachers in this school had, among other things, reduced truancy and contagious diseases compared with previous years in the same school and with other schools in the same period. Accordingly, similar clubs were inaugurated in the other schools in Detroit. Another initiative action taken was when, as early as 1881, the principals of Boston secured loans of suitable books from the public libraries to supplement the school's collection for instructional purposes. The practice is still followed frequently whenever the local school does not possess an adequate library. Even today it may indeed be one step in the building of a library for the school. Chicago, according to Pierce, was the first city to inaugurate evening entertainments and lectures for parents.[5] This was perhaps the forerunner of the school as a community social center.

In the closing years of the nineteenth and the early years of the twentieth century, individual cities and schools organized penny lunches, school baths, home gardens, school savings systems, and other services which cared for the specific needs of a local area in a city. During the two world wars, principals, teachers, and pupils participated in the support of community activities designed to further the interest of the country in war services. Particularly in the immigrant sections of large cities, local schools undoubtedly influenced adults through their children in a way which no other agency could have.

More recently principals have lent their efforts to such community

---

[5]Pierce, *Origin and Development*, p. 127.

enterprises as neighborhood cleanup campaigns, Red Cross roll calls, and the sane celebration of holidays. The reduction of vandalism at Halloween in districts where principals have built up the proper attitudes among students is very noteworthy. Safety patrols are conspicuous features of school organization in nearly every city in America. This impetus to launch the safety patrol came not from the principals, but from those business organizations which had a direct vested interest in fewer automobile accidents. The principals gave their enthusiastic sponsorship to the movement, and so have promoted training for their pupils in pedestrian safety.

Recently there has been some discussion of the liability of principals in accidents where pupil patrol leaders are involved. So far no court decisions are available to furnish guidance and though opinion differs, there is some evidence that there is considerable legal responsibility on the part of the principal for accidents occurring to patrol members perhaps because of directions given by patrol members.

At the high school level, instruction in safe automobile driving as a part of the responsibility of the schools is currently being provided.

Professional Organizations of Principals

The Department of Secondary School Principals was organized in 1916 at the Detroit meeting of the National Education Association. It has exerted an important influence on the professionalization of the high school principalship. Today it has a membership of over 25,000, the largest of any professional administrative educational group. Another organization formed in 1920 was the Department of Elementary School Principals of the National Education Association. This organization, which now has approximately 19,000 members, has exerted great influence in directing the attention of the elementary school principal to the scientific study of education.

It is now the practice for some graduate schools of education to offer training designed for men and women who intend to enter into or to continue in the principalship as a career. The day has come in many school systems, and is approaching rapidly in others, when demonstrated competence in the classroom is an insufficient qualification for principalship. There is, in addition, a specialized body of knowledge which the principal must know and use, and he does not feel he is being well enough trained in any way (see Chapter 1).

Cooperative Program in Educational Administration

In 1950 and 1951 the Cooperative Program in Educational Administration got under way in eight institutions: Harvard, Columbia Teachers College, the University of Chicago, the University of Texas, Peabody College for Teachers, Ohio State University, Stanford University, and the

University of Oregon. These experimental programs of action-research and inservice training were underwritten by the W. K. Kellogg Foundation of Battle Creek, Michigan, with approximately $3,000,000 in funds. Later a grant was made to the Canadian Education Association and another to the University of Alberta to begin similar programs in Canada. The American Association of School Administrators, the Association of Chief State School Officers, and the County Superintendents Association were represented in the Developmental Committee, which was influential in securing the grant and in shaping general policies.

Most of the programs were concerned with the superintendency. But, as the program developed, more research was conducted concerning the principalship, for it was clear that half of the superintendents were recruited directly from the high school principalship,[6] and considerably more than that had held principalships at some time in their professional careers. Since 1964 nine national centers for the study of education have been generously funded by the federal government. In addition, there are fifteen regional laboratories which are attempting to transfer new findings to individual schools.

Need for Better Principals

More effective ways are needed for identifying and attracting into graduate training programs those persons with outstanding ability who are now in school systems or who can be interested in school administration. To seek out those with the necessary intellectual and leadership abilities, more personalized and systematic procedures are needed than those generally now in practice. Adequate stipends such as those Canadian students have are needed to enable such persons to attend universities for adequate training periods.

The importance of designing programs which will attract talented persons cannot be overemphasized; the finest programs are of little avail unless talented persons enter these programs. The recruitment of even a few dozen persons with outstanding talent who would otherwise enter other fields or who would remain submerged in teaching would be of inestimable value to the future of the nation's schools.

Nationwide Study of Elementary Principals

The findings of a large-scale research project, "Determination of the Criteria of Success in School Administration" (DCS), were published in

---

[6]National Education Association, American Association of School Administrators, *The American School Superintendency*, Thirtieth Yearbook, (Washington, D.C.: The Association, 1952), p. 447.

June 1962, under the title of *Administrative Performance and Personality*.[7] This study, centered at Columbia Teachers College, represents the most comprehensive examination of the administrative behavior of elementary school principals now available. The study, based on a national sample of 232 principals, had three major purposes:

1. To determine dimensions of performance in the elementary school principalship and thus to devlop a better understanding of the nature of the job of the school administrator.
2. To provide information helpful in the solution of the problem of selecting school administrators.
3. To provide materials for the study and teaching of school administration.

A unique feature of the study included the simulation of an actual school district. Thus, the principals in the test situations were able to make decisions in a common situation with a common background of information. Approximately 100 in-basket problems were created which were logically related to the basic information the principals had received. Principals in each test center responded to problem situations raised by the in-basket items, which presented typical problems faced by principals at different times in the school year: the day before the opening of school, the first week in December, and the middle of February. Each problem required some type of resolution. Each principal also had opportunities to demonstrate his communication skill by writing an article for the school paper, by providing an autobiographical sketch for the local newspaper, and by making a tape-recorded speech to the P.T.A.

Principals also analyzed, through the medium of kinescopes, the quality of teaching exhibited by two probationary teachers. In addition, problems presented through tape recordings (an introverted pupil, a parent-teacher conference, discipline in the school, and foreign-language teaching in the elementary grades) were solved.

Factors Affecting the Principalship

In the Griffiths et al. study eight factors were discovered having an apparent bearing on the principalship: Factor A, *Exchanging Information;* Factor B, *Discussing with Others Before Acting;* Factor C, *Complying with Suggestions Made by Others;* Factor D, *Analyzing the Situation;* Factor E, *Maintaining Organizational Relationships;* Factor G, *Responding to Outsiders;*

---

[7]John K. Hemphill, Daniel E. Griffiths, and Norman Frederickson, *Administrative Performance and Personality: A Study of the Principal in a Simulated Elementary School* (New York: Teacher's College Press, Teachers College, Columbia University, 1962), p. 432.

and Factor H, *Directing the Work of Others.* In addition, there are two secondary factors: Factor X, *Preparing for Decision,* and Factor Y, *Amount of Work.*

Undoubtedly we shall find new uses for the Griffiths study materials such as the in-basket testing situation. Simulated materials about the superintendent and the high school principal are also now available. More research is needed in this area, and we shall undoubtedly refine the measures which have been used, eventually developing more precise descriptions of what an individual can be expected to do. Further research will also enable us to write better job descriptions about the principalship, and the desires of the superintendent and the board regarding it.

Concerning mental abilities and knowledge, the study found that there are several noticeable relationships between tests of mental ability and knowledge and six of the primary (and both of the secondary) factors in the study. Those principals who scored high on tests such as (1) School Administration and Supervision, (2) Education in the Elementary School, (3) NTE, General Culture Test (social studies, literature, and fine arts), and (4) a battery of tests on psychological abilities were those whose average performance was characterized more by preparation for decision than by taking immediate terminal action. Factor Y (work output) was also typical of principals with high mental ability. The same tests that predicted high scores on preparation for decision would also be likely to predict high work output.

Implications

Several implications concerning the practice of administration may be found in the Griffiths study. The first is that leadership and administration are not synonymous. The facts of the study indicate that administrative performance was much more than just leadership performance as defined by Factor H—directing others' work—and that stressing leadership to the exclusion of other aspects of administration results in a one-sided, inadequate, incomplete picture. Although control is a major aspect of administration, the principals who were studied failed to demonstrate an awareness of administrative controls such as setting deadlines and planning feedback. The principals did not demonstrate informality toward either superiors or outsiders; there was little or no evidence of behavior indicating informal work with superiors. Study findings hint, in fact, that the principal considers his superior a boss rather than a counselor or an advisor. Study findings also indicate that delegation was seldom practiced in the elementary school; but then delegation should not really be expected until elementary schools are staffed with personnel to whom principals can delegate responsibilities or duties.

Principals tend to use human values and program values to a greater

Fig. 3. Summary of relationships with unique components of in-basket performance with abilities and knowledge, personality, interest and values, professional concerns, interaction performance, biographical data, and evaluations.°

Performance on In-basket Problems	Abilities and Knowledge	Personality, Interest, and Values	Professional Concerns	Interaction Performance	Biographical Data	Evaluations
Factor A Exchanging Information	Has high verbal knowledge and facility; knows elementary education, school administration, and facts about the general culture	Sociable, sensitive, trusting, confident, and relaxed; interests like superintendents, lawyers, or psychologists, unlike policemen	Concerned with teacher and pupil personnel problems, especially with the reaction of pupils to the educational program	Not related	More characteristic of women	Superiors— very positive Teachers— positive Scorers— positive
Factor B Discussing Before Acting	Not related	Mature, self-confident, and relaxed; interests like policemen and public administrators	Not related	Reluctant to participate, regarded as ineffective	Little administrative experience	Superiors— negative Teachers— negative
Factor C Complying with Suggestions	Ability to reason and sees relationships; knows general cultural facts, science, and mathematics; learns new material rapidly	Aloof, shy, practical, skeptical, independent, insecure, unstable and tense; interests like policemen, unlike school superintendents	Not concerned with objectives, evaluation, planning and continuity, curriculum, or child growth and development	Not related	Young, little experience; more characteristic of men	Superiors— very negative Teachers— negative
Factor D Analyzing the Situation	Ability to reason and see relationships; knows general cultural facts, science, and mathematics	Aloof, dominant, practical, shrewd; feels pressure; interests like policemen and public administrators	Not concerned with classroom climate or routines	Participates fully and moderately effectively; talks a lot and suggests new procedures	Has administrative experience; more characteristic of men	Superiors— negative Teachers— negative
Factor E Maintaining Relationships	Slow in seeing relationships; lacks knowledge of science and mathematics	Sociable, lively, sensitive, confident, dependent, and relaxed; interests like superintendents and lawyers	Concerned with instructions, curriculum, personnel, and public relations	Participates fully and effectively	More characteristic of women	Teachers— very positive

Factor			Concerned with		Not related	Superiors/Teachers
Factor F Organizing Work	Not related	Easily frustrated, inflexible, shy, skeptical, insecure, unstable, and tense; interests unlike superintendents, administrators, and psychologists	Concerned with pupil reactions and physical setting of classroom	Emphasizes positive information in interaction; not effective	Not related	Superiors—generally negative Teachers—positive regarding initiating structure
Factor G Responding to Outsiders	Lacks general ability; lacks knowledge of science and mathematics, school administration, and general culture	Submissive, subdued, shy, naïve, stable, and relaxed; interests unlike public administrators and lawyers	Concerned with objectives, planning, evaluation, and effects of teacher performance	Does not participate, regarded as ineffective	Has large amount of teaching experience; older; more characteristic of women	Superiors—neutral to slightly negative Staff members—negative
Factor H Directing Others	Lacks knowledge and ability; unable to learn new material quickly	Sober and stable; interests unlike school superintendents and lawyers	Concerned with objectives but not personnel or pupil reactions	Not related	Has experience in education; older	Teachers—negative
Factor X Preparation for Decision	Fluent, facile with symbolic material, sees associations quickly; good at reasoning; knows school administration, elementary education, science, and facts about general culture; learns new material rapidly	Values educational needs of pupils; interests similar to psychologists and lawyers	Concerned with most areas of teacher performance, especially objectives, planning, methods, teacher personality, pupil motivation, and child growth	Active and effective in group discussion; suggests new procedures	Not related	Superiors—positive Staff members—positive Scorers—strongly positive
Factor Y Amount of Work	Over-all high ability; fluent with words and ideas; knows elementary education, school administration, cultural and scientific material; learns new material rapidly	Not related	Concerned with curriculum, child growth, teacher personality, and personnel problems	Effective in interaction, talks a lot, tries to influence	Not related	Superiors—neutral to slightly positive Staff members—positive Scorers—strongly positive

*Reprinted by permission of the publisher from John K. Hemphill, D. E. Griffiths, N. Frederiksen, *Administrative Performance and Personality: A Study of the Principal in a Simulated School* (New York: Teachers College Press, 1962; copyright 1962 by Teachers College, Columbia University), pp. 328–29.

extent than physical values, such as concern for buildings, property, or equipment. Elementary principals apparently did little that could be called coordination of programs and people.

One of the perennial questions in the selection of principals is: Should women be selected? While less than 10 percent of the elementary school teaching force are men, they account for nearly 60 percent of the principalships. The aspects, according to the Griffiths study, of administrative performance most characteristic of women reflect a unique combination of factors: that of Factor A, Exchanging Information, Factor E, Maintaining Organizational Relations, and Factor G, Responding to Outsiders. On the other hand, the administrative performance of men principals is characterized by a combination of Factor C, Complying with Suggestions Made by Others, and Factor D, Analyzing the Situation. It is perhaps true that women are the forgotten persons in school administration. So far as we know, there are no women superintendents in the U.S.A.

For a superintendent or a school board to decide what they want in an elementary principalship, tests already in use or in the process of being developed could be very useful. Unfortunately, the central office often wants someone who will maintain organizational relationships, use caution in reading bulletins, and carry out central office policies, while the teachers want someone who is adept at dealing with parents, and who can not only assist teachers with learning problems in the classroom but also take some responsibility for personnel problems.

Inservice Training

There is a growing awareness among those concerned of the need for inservice training for school administrators. Such training includes membership in professional organizations; state, regional, and national meetings; and workshops. Some state departments of education provide excellent opportunities for inservice growth. Many universities provide advanced graduate work in summer sessions or through an extension service. There is a need for new types of principal's clinics to keep administrators up to date, as well as a need for more small, informal professional group meetings on a regular schedule to provide for the exchange of ideas and experiences. Inservice training should probably be the joint responsibility of the professional group, the state department of education, and training institutions. Included in such a program will be newer materials on school administration which resulted from the CPEA studies.[8] There is also a growing feeling that some form of internship experience is desirable, and several graduate

---

[8]American Association of School Administrators, *Professional Administrators for America's Schools*, Thirty-eighth Yearbook, (Washington, D.C.: The Association, 1960), pp. 85–115. See this work for a more comprehensive description.

programs include internship experiences. But whether these experiences should be as administrative assistant to a superintendent, assistant to a principal in a school, field experience in the community agency dealing with young people, or a combination of these remains to be decided. Chapter 1 indicated the feeling on the part of many principals that inservice programs are nonexistent.

Qualifications for the Principalship

General Qualifications

It is important that the successful principal have certain personal qualities. A successful principal should (1) be a superior organizer and a skilled administrator; (2) be able to administer his school without allowing it to consume his entire time; (3) have some time for the supervision or co-ordination of instruction—a thoughtful and therefore a time-consuming process; (4) also be a wise and discreet executive who handles parents with tact, firmness, and skill; and (5) be able to make decisions promptly and correctly if he is to be an efficient executive. An executive will, of course, delegate such responsibilities as he can; the others he will assume and effectively discharge.

In addition, the principal must be a good business manager. The financial details of extracurricular activities, the lunchroom, the school store, and other concerns must be cared for in a businesslike manner. The requisitioning of supplies, their proper and prompt delivery throughout the building, and their economical use are problems over which a careless or nonprofessional principal might spend his entire time.

Personal Qualifications

The principal should have demonstrated his own competence to teach if he is to recognize good teaching when he sees it in the classroom. Of course, he should be so well versed in the theory and practice of education that he is able to recognize acceptable forms of good teaching other than the particular ones of which he is master. On the personal side, there are a number of qualities which make success easier; their absence may well cause failure. The newer teamteaching techniques or multiunit schools may alter the principal-teacher relationship a great deal.

Physically, it is important that the principal possess good health and that he be free from physical deformities and serious defects in speech or hearing.

But more important than any set of physical characteristics are the principal's mental characteristics. It is essential that he possess a high degree of intelligence to enable him to acquire the technical training required for the position—this task is constantly increasing. It is important, too, that a principal be broadminded and open-minded, since all types of children in society attend the schools. Some practices that he may find among certain groups of children will require broad-mindedness in dealing with them.

We may mention personal charm as extremely desirable as an attribute of the principal. And certainly an even temper is an asset to anyone who deals with the public and even more to someone who is in constant contact with children. Both patrons and teachers appreciate promptness and regularity, and these assets greatly facilitate the routine management of the school. Fortunately the pompous manners of some educational administrators of the past are passing.

Ability to Enlist Cooperation

Closely related to the lack of regard for the feelings of others, a failure to exercise tact, sympathy, and friendliness is the trait of self-glorification. It is very common for principals to speak of *my* school instead of *our* school. The school exists for the children and belongs to the community. The principal is hired to administer and supervise it in order to improve it. Without the cooperation of the teaching corps—who put into practice the ideas the principal is trying to promote, and who frequently improve them in the process—there would be no advancement in the teaching practices. It is easy and quite human for the principal to take the glory for improvements or innovations in a school system, passing lightly over the important contributions of others. A wise principal should commend his faculty in speech and print for its contributions to educational progress and minimize his own part. In the local community it is important to keep the names of the school and the teachers before the public.

If the principal is qualified to hold the responsible position he does, he should encourage teachers to experiment within the limits which educational science approves. This may take many forms, such as controlled experiments in various methods of teaching supported by adequate testing programs, modification of the curriculum to care for individual differences in abilities or aptitudes, or curriculum construction or revision. It necessarily follows that any principal who stimulates or allows a teacher to depart from traditional practices will support that teacher when and if the necessity arises. There is always a strong likelihood that any new venture will be criticized by some community groups on the grounds of cost, "fads and frills," or just plain difference from what the patrons expected and experienced a generation ago.

It also follows that a wise principal would not implement extensive innovations until he had convinced his superior officers of the practicability of his plans and secured their sanctions. Furthermore, responsible community groups must be interested in and persuaded to be favorable to any extensive revision of the schools. Even if the principal has an intermediate executive officer or superintendent to whom he reports, he is not relieved of his responsibility for community leadership. In a case where the principal is the chief executive officer of the board of education, his neglect in obtaining community support for educational change is almost certain to result in early elimination and a return to traditional, previously prevailing practices.

Development of Criteria of Success in a School Administration Project

A study involving an analysis of the behavior of 232 elementary school principals, each of whom acted for five days as Marion Smith, Principal of Whitman School, provided a problematic test situation. During the five days, each principal handled a standard set of realistic administrative problems. Methods for scoring the records of the principals' behavior were developed, a factor analysis of the scores was performed, and correlations of factor scores with many other measures of ability, personality, interest, and job performance were computed. The findings appear to have significance for theories of administration and leadership and may very possibly influence the teaching of educational administration. Importantly, the materials of the study provide a means of evaluating outcomes of school administration instruction from a variety of viewpoints. The findings raise a number of challenging questions about the usual criteria for selecting school administrators, and provides materials which are potentially useful in the selection process.

Experience of the Principal

The elementary principal has in the past been recruited chiefly from the teaching ranks on the basis of long experience. The traditional line of promotion has been from classroom teaching to a teaching principalship, and then to the supervising principalship. In large cities men who have demonstrated competence as superintendents of schools in smaller cities are sometimes brought in to function as supervising elementary principals. In some school systems, the elementary school principalship is a stepping-stone to the junior high school principalship. Other educational positions which many junior high school principals have held preceding their appointments are senior high school teaching, senior high school principalships, and superintendencies of small school systems. Few principals attain their positions directly from vice-principalships.

The senior high school principal has had a somewhat different background. More persons come to the high school principalship from high school teaching than from any other position. In a recent survey, the positions which high school principals had most commonly held before appointment were high school teaching and another principalship.[9] In many cities the line of promotion is from elementary school principalship to junior high school principalship and then to the senior high school principalship. This practice is defended on the grounds of morale in the system; that such a promotional policy is desirable because of salary differentials. But if salary is equivalent for equal training and experience in a city system, it is probably wiser to leave the competent elementary principals where they are functioning effectively, and seek high school principals elsewhere—outside the system if necessary.

School Principals' Training

A study by Daniel Griffiths of 561 principals indicates that the highest earned degree is generally the master's degree. However, in recent years the doctorate has been gaining rapidly. There is reason to believe that in the future persons who aspire to the most important principalships will probably seek the doctor's degree with greater frequency than they did in the past.

Salaries Paid to School Principals

Median Salaries in City Systems

The data presented in Table 2 reveal the mean salaries paid to different types of principals in cities of the United States in 1969–1970. The range of salaries is naturally very great. In elementary schools in cities with small populations, the lowest salary paid to teaching principals was $7,619, whereas in cities of 500,000 or more people, the highest salary paid to the elementary principal was $24,825. For high school principals, the range in salaries is also great, running from $8,499 in smaller cities to $26,866 in cities of over 500,000 population.

The supervisory high school principalship pays more than any other type of principalship in all sizes of cities, the supervisory junior high school principalship ranks second, followed closely by the supervisory elementary school principal. The teaching elementary principalship, as would be expected, pays less than the other positions. These salaries are for the most part generous, and are higher than those paid to teachers in the same

---

[9]Based on personal correspondence with Daniel Griffiths.

Table 2[10]

POPULATION GROUPS

	100,000 or more	50,000 99,999	25,000 49,999	12,000 24,999	6,000 11,999
Supervising Elementary Principals					
Range Low	13,571	10,801	10,972	9,805	7,619
Median	18,693	16,236	16,215	16,787	15,881
High	26,569	21,600	23,890	23,815	24,825
Junior High Principals					
Range Low	14,180	11,241	11,550	11,241	8,388
Median	19,200	16,675	16,906	19,356	17,215
High	26,579	22,735	24,823	26,197	26,690
Senior High Principals					
Range Low	14,180	14,228	12,788	11,339	8,499
Median	19,982	18,660	18,269	18,883	18,112
High	28,995	25,252	25,554	27,587	26,866

systems. In general, the salaries paid to well-trained principals are enough that the principalship may well be considered a possible career choice by people who have an interest in school administration and are willing to obtain the necessary training.

Methods of Selecting Principals

The Merit System

The superintendent of schools should nominate the principal, subject to ratification by the board of education. Nominations should be made from lists of either eligible persons within the school system or competent persons from outside. The most competent person available, for the salary that can be offered, should be selected. Many cities select the personnel for the principalship in this way, but in recent years some cities have tended to

[10]"Selected Salaries of Principals," *Research Report*, R 2, (Washington, D.C.: Research Division, National Education Association, 1970), p. 9. Copyright 1970 by the National Education Association Research Division.

eliminate persons outside the system from consideration, or have required a specified number of years of teaching experience in a particular system before an individual may become eligible for a school principalship. Obviously, this practice automatically excludes many administrators who have already proven their competence elsewhere. While such practices may be defended on the grounds of improving morale within the local school system, they cannot be defended as methods of securing the best qualified person for the position at the offered salary. In smaller school systems, principals are usually selected on the basis of credentials and experience. In large systems the criterion of some form of service is generally employed in the appointment of principals.

As a means of avoiding petty policies, favoritism, and nepotism in appointments, many cities use some type of competitive examination in the preparation of eligibility lists from which the nominations are to be made. Some cities hold examinations from which the eligible lists are prepared under rigid civil service regulations. Where civil service methods are not followed, cities often require that the nominations represent an agreement among the educational executives of the central office; others require the superintendent to choose from a limited list of available candidates prepared by his associate or assistant superintendents. Still others permit the superintendent to make his nominations from available personnel within or without the system on the basis of the applicant's credentials.

Candidates for the principalship today must at least meet certain standards of academic education, professional preparation, and previous experience before they are even considered eligible. If competitive examinations are given, further eliminations are made from the qualified group. Even in cities in which the responsibility for nomination rests solely with the superintendent, the choice of a principal focuses the attention of professional groups on the standards employed to such an extent that the superintendent is critically judged by the professional merit of his appointments.

The number of principalships in the United States is estimated to be 18,000 for high schools and 23,000 for elementary schools.

Certification of Principals

The special certificate requirement for principals or other administrative officers is a relatively new practice in education, having developed largely since 1930. In 1967, forty-nine states issued certificates for principals. Today about two-thirds of the states require a master's degree for certification as a principal, and they tend to require two or three years of teaching experience before a person is considered eligible for a principal's certificate. As expected, the states paying the highest salaries also maintain the highest requirements. In many better positions, the salary schedules recognize the doctor's as well as the master's degree. Although the requirements are not overly high when considered as a whole, they represent the substantial achievement of over thirty years, and they indicate that the principalship is rapidly becoming a profession.

Conditions of Employment

During the past twenty-five years, teachers as a group have made rapid social gains through carefully prepared salary schedules, retirement provisions, tenure, and provisions for sick leave. The laws are somewhat ambiguous with respect to principals, since the general term used in most laws is *teachers*. It is generally assumed, and administered in practice, that principals enjoy all prerequisite rights of teachers except tenure. Although the laws concerning the tenure of principals and other administration affairs in the schools are not specific, the available court evidence tends to confirm the belief that principals hold tenure as classroom teachers and not as school administrators. But in eleven of the eighteen states that have con-

Table 3

Number of Years of College Preparation or Degree Required	Number of States Requiring*		
	Elem. School Principals	Sec. School Principals	Superintendents of Schools
7 years or Doctor's Degree	0	0	1
6 years + but less than Doctor's Degree	1	0	1
6 years	0	3	20
Master's Degree + but less than 6 years	10	8	10
Master's Degree	34	36	16
Bachelor's Degree + but less than 5 years	4	3	2
Bachelor's Degree	1	0	0
Less than Bachelor's Degree	0	0	0
No certificate issued	2	2	2
	52	52	52

*(Includes D.C. and Puerto Rico).
Adapted from Table 6, *Minimum Degrees and Semester Hours for Administrative Certificates*, p. 64 in *Certification Requirements for School Personnel in the United States* (Washington, D.C.: National Education Association, 1970). Materials in the pamphlet are from T. M. Stinnett, *A Manual on Certification Requirements for School Personnel in the United States* (Washington, D.C.: National Education Association, 1970).

tinuing-contract laws, principals are specifically included. It is reasonable to conclude from this that the conditions of employment for principals are at least as satisfactory as those of classroom teachers, even though the militance of teachers may have tended to make the principal the man in the middle as far as his job position goes.

Opportunities of the Principalship

The principalship varies in attractiveness throughout the United States. Many principals who have administrative assistants and clerical help are still just building custodian-principals, either because of the rules in their particular systems or because their plans have failed to work effectively. When the conditions of the job are such, because of central office policy, the principalship cannot be truly called a profession. Well-trained principals do not care to or need to spend their entire time requisitioning and distributing supplies, doing clerical work, or seeing that clerical work is done; neither do they devote all their time to answering the telephone, disciplining unruly children, or supervising the work of the janitors or custodians, although these duties are important to a well-administered school.

Fortunately it is not necessary for the principal to spend all his energies in such activities. But one thing for which well-trained principals can almost always find ample opportunity is helping to solve the learning problems of children. If opportunities do not exist in the school where he is working, a well-trained person will have little difficulty in finding another position where his talents will be used and appreciated.

Nature of Demands Made on School Principals

Recent data, collected from elementary school principals, indicate that 59 percent of supervising principals think of themselves as educational leaders and that 39 percent consider themselves supporters.[11] The attitude was backed up by the superintendents concerned; over 60 percent of them said the elementary principals were recognized as leaders.[12]

To defend the way they spend their time, principals might claim that they are required to perform so many routine administrative duties that supervision of instruction and other time-consuming professional functions must of necessity be neglected. They might insist that telephone calls must be answered, reports to the central office must be made, callers must be re-

---

[11]National Education Association, Department of Elementary School Principals, *The Elementary School Principalship—A Research Study*, Thirty-seventh Yearbook, XXXVIII, No. 1 (Washington, D.C.: The Association, September 1968), p. 39.

[12]NEA, *Elementary School Principalship*, p. 40.

ceived, mail must be attended to, order in corridors and on school grounds must be maintained, and all the other routine duties of minor importance must receive attention. When he has performed these multitudinous routine chores, virtually no time remains for the higher-level responsibilities.

Delegating Responsibility

If all principals were supplied with an adequate number of clerical assistants capable of performing clerical duties and many of the minor administrative duties, a delegation of work along functional lines might be effected; the principal would personally perform the supervisory duties, major administrative responsibilities, and such other duties as he considered necessary, while he delegated other duties to his clerical assistants. Sadly, however, the available evidence reveals that principals generally do not have adequate clerical assistance.

In an investigation by the same committee which produced the Thirty-eighth Yearbook for the National Education Association, Department of Elementary School Principals, it was found that the functions of elementary school principals have not changed much in thirty years, but that what improvement has occurred has been in the direction of providing more time for supervision.

On the average, the principal spends nine hours each day at school. He spends less time on supervision and pupil personnel and more time on clerical work than he would wish,[13] chiefly because he has inadequate clerical assistance. Twenty-three percent of elementary school principals have clerical assistants; only 58 percent have one or more full-time assistants.[14] Until the enrollment exceeds the 600 mark, full-time clerical help is extremely rare. An investigation directed to more than 500 secondary principals ascertained that about five out of six were provided with some clerical assistance. Since nearly half of the supervising elementary school principals and approximately one-sixth of the secondary school principals have only part-time or no clerical assistance, relief from clerical and minor administrative duties must be accomplished by some plan other than delegating the heavy load to clerks.

Functions of Nonteaching Principals

Principals need suffer no misapprehensions regarding what is expected of them when they are placed on a nonteaching basis.

Some school systems follow the practice of sending out many letters of instructions which make immediate demands on the principals. Some of

---

[13]NEA, *Elementary School Principalship*, p. 98.
[14]NEA, *Elementary School Principalship*, p. 74.

these instructions to the principals are administrative regulations that must be studied, understood, and incorporated into practice at once. Others contain important statements of policy, items of information, and problems for attention. These letters of administrative instructions from the central office make heavy demands on the time of principals. The extent and bulk of such communications may only be appreciated if, during a school year, their number is noted and a tabulation made of the many separate instructions to which the principal must give careful attention.

A survey of over 200 school principals revealed that the approximate weekly time spent on community service ranged from an hour to over fifteen hours, the average being about three-and-one-half hours. The nature of the community services in which principals participate is varied. The study of the elementary school principalship indicated these figures for supervising principals: 91 percent belong to a church; 71 percent to business and professional clubs; 55 percent belong to lodges; and many also belong to recreational, health, and social welfare groups.[15] The pattern for teaching principals is similar. Facts also indicate that principals of today are more likely to belong to lay organizations than they did three decades ago.

Organization of Functions for Effective Management

Organization Influenced by Central Office Policies

The trend, particularly in cities of considerable size, appears to be in the direction of the practice of granting the principal greater autonomy in the management of the local school than has been granted in the past. This tendency is justified on the ground that the principalship is a position of great professional importance in the administration of city schools. In recent years in systems maintaining a number of individual schools, the local school has acquired general recognition as a community institution, organized and administered with special regard for the local constituency. Too much central control may tend to interfere with local initiative and may produce a mechanical uniformity in local administration that sometimes creates a climate of mediocrity. Too much local autonomy, on the other hand, may result in a breakdown of the central system and in a reversion to the ward type of organization now almost universally abandoned in progressive cities.

It is therefore apparent that the relations between the head of the local school and the central administrative officials should be clearly de-

---

[15]NEA, *Elementary School Principalship*, p. 87.

fined. Each should know the locus of his responsibility and should strive to function efficiently. The definition of these relations, moreover, is a matter of such importance that it transcends the personalities involved in any single system. It requires understanding of the principles of administration to control the dealings between local and central administrators in city school systems in general.

Relations of Principal and Superintendent

In cities which provided early (1840–1870) for the selection of the school superintendent, the local school principal and the superintendent tended to develop as contemporary professional officers. The superintendent soon realized his inability to administer the district or ward schools of his city efficiently without the aid of a professional assistant in each local school. He recognized the potential administrative possibilities of the head teacher or principal of the local schools. The head teacher or principal could assume certain administrative responsibilities and at the same time discharge the duties of a regular classroom teacher.

Philadelphia had reached a population of approximately 900,000 before it selected a superintendent for its schools in 1882. Each local community school was controlled by a board of six trustees elected by the local district. The chairman of each local board of trustees served as a member of a central board, which undertook to chart the professional progress of the schools of the city. Under this organization the school principals became the chief professional officers prior to the appointment of the first superintendent. But relatively few of these principals ever attained the status of supervisory officers under their local boards. Despite the fact that the central board of education, which certificated principals and teachers, had adopted a rule authorizing local boards to organize their schools under supervising principals, it was the superintendent who was to take the step which transformed the local school principals from head teachers into supervising principals or professional school officers.

The relations between the local principals and the superintendent in Philadelphia were largely advisory until legislation was enacted in 1911 which abolished the district boards and placed all the local schools under a central board appointed by the Court of Common Pleas. This legislation eliminated ward or district control and made the local school principal an intermediary professional officer between the central office and his school instead of head teacher under a local board.

As a whole, several broad generalizations about the status of the principalship may be made.

Principal directly responsible to the superintendent. The tendency for principals to maintain direct administrative relations with members of the board of education has largely disappeared due to the rise of the superintendent to a position of educational leadership in city school administration. The passing of both the ward system of selecting school board members and administration through standing committees of the board of education has contributed still further to the demise of this practice, although a few vestiges remain.

Principal responsible for carrying out superintendent's policies. The superintendent is recognized as the chief executive officer of the education department, while the principal is the chief representative of the superintendent in the local school. The relation between the principal and the superintendent is, therefore, that of subordinate to superior. According the principal great freedom as the responsible head of a local school does not grant him autocratic power. Through general rules and regulations and by specific instructions and directions, the board of education and the superintendent impose themselves upon the administrative prerogatives of the principal. As a check on the misuse of power, the superintendent requires that local practices conform with general policies and that departures from established procedures receive central office approval.

As a means of unifying practices and carrying on inservice professional training, superintendents hold meetings periodically with the principals to discuss policies and to give instructions. With the exchange of opinions made possible in this way, the principal may exercise considerable influence not only in the formation of new policies and the modification of established policies, but also in acquainting the superintendents with the needs and problems of the local schools.

Relations of principal with intermediary administrative officers. The relations of deputy, associate, assistant, and district superintendents with school principals are determined by the superintendent, invariably clothed with power by the board of education to nominate assistants and to assign powers and duties. The relations are both general and functional, depending on the organization of the central office. Some cities have secondary intermediate officers functioning as district or regional superintendents or supervisory principals. The purpose of establishing this type of position is to secure more aggressive supervision of the local schools by the central office than that possible by the superintendent and his immediate assistants. But, evidence indicates that this plan has failed in its purpose because the tendency of the district superintendents has been to neglect supervision and become subordinate administrators, frequently serving only to interfere with the effective functioning of the principal in his relations with the central office.

The warranted conclusion here is that the relations between the principal with the central office should be made as direct as possible. The establishment of "long-circuit" administrative relations is often conducive both to ineffective central office administration and to the development of weak school principals. If the central office would accept the theory that schools are best administered if the principal is made the responsible head of the local school, then its relation with the principal should be such as to develop initiative, responsibility, and efficiency in local administration rather than mere clerical subserviency.

The intermediary executive officer between the superintendent and the school principal should be endowed with central office power to deal directly with the principal in the functional relations prescribed. If these relations are supervisory, the central office intermediary should function as a supervisor; if they are administrative, the official should function as an administrator, not just as a buffer between the principal and the central office.

Relations of principal with assistants in the school. As schools have grown, thoughtful students of administration have wondered how many assistants a principal should have. The 1952 Yearbook of the American Association of School Administrators offered the following comment:

> In a school which has 40 teachers it is impossible for one principal to be conversant with the work of each teacher so that he can coordinate it adequately with the efforts of all the others (see Fig. 4, Plan A). It would be better organization, and it is probable that better instruction would result, if four or five classroom teachers were made resource consultants, each in charge of coordinating the instruction of a group of other teachers (see Fig. 4, Plan B). In this way the span of control[16] would not be violated and the persons who were doing the coordinating would be recognized by their fellow teachers as superior teachers who could help them. The principal would coordinate the work of the consultants, deal with public relations, and coordinate the individual school with the school system as a whole. The consultative type of leadership proposed is not identical with either the typical department head or the assistant principal as found in many schools. The duties would not be clerical or administrative, but would be concerned exclusively with instructional leadership.[17]

Certainly this recommendation is a goal rather than present practice in school organization. If and when it is realized, the principal will have to reconcile himself to losing his assistants; they will be in demand for administrative and supervisory positions in the local school and elsewhere. When-

---

[16]The term *span of control* has come into the literature of business and civil administration. It means that *for effective administration there is a limit to the number of individuals from whom the executive may personally receive reports and with whom he may discuss and determine programs of action.*

[17]National Education Association, American Association of School Administrators, *The American School Superintendency*, Thirtieth Yearbook (Washington: The Association, 1952), pp. 74–75.

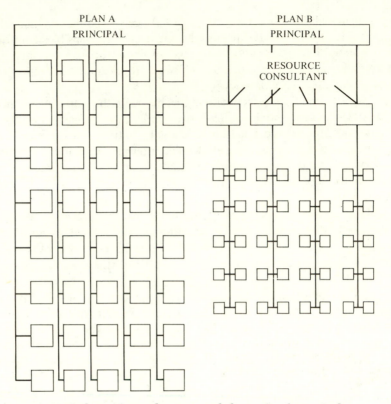

Fig. 4. Typical practice and recommended practice for a single school unit.[18]

ever assistants are available, they will be directly responsible to the principal to carry out the duties he delegates to them.

It is also necessary to have channels whereby matters can be settled when interpersonal relationships go awry. For example, the principal can appeal to an assistant superintendent in charge of instruction if supplies are not furnished on time. Ordinarily he will deal with the business office, unless the personal relationships have gotten out of hand. In theory, a principal has only one superior officer, but he actually acts on suggestions from, and gives suggestions to, dozens of persons in the school system—when personal relationships are at their best.

Democratic Participation

Since neither authoritarian nor laissez-faire management provides the type of control which a school needs to realize its objectives, some other

---

[18]NEA, *American School Superintendency*, p. 75.

type must be maintained which will be in harmony with the major purposes of public education. This type of control has long been recognized in theory, but it has been difficult to find in practice except in certain innovative schools. In recent years most principals have recognized the importance of training their students for participation as citizens in democratic government. Accordingly, they have attempted to organize their schools as laboratories in which boys and girls can obtain, under guidance, experience in self-government as well as an understanding of democratic government through instruction in the classroom. The application of this theory has been difficult in many schools not only because of the reluctance of some principals to try experiments that might bring criticism from the public, but also because of many teachers' inability to cooperate understandingly in order to make their classrooms a part of a school laboratory in which the theory and the practice of democratic government are effectively integrated.

The assumptions which underlie democratic administration are (1) universal respect for an individual's worth and dignity regardless of his race, creed, or social status, (2) increasing emphasis upon ways and means of cooperation for common benefit, and (3) stress on the development of each individual's potentialities so long as they do not conflict with the common welfare. If these assumptions are accepted, it follows that all the personnel of a school must be fairly represented in policy making and appraisal. It follows too that persons should be assigned to tasks where their special aptitudes may be utilized most effectively. And as often as possible, facilities should be arranged to best serve the needs of the entire community.

With respect to the development of curriculum materials, democratic procedure may involve intensive study by a group of teachers and the principal both in the school and in a curriculum laboratory or workshop. The assistance of specialists may be obtained, and an individual may eventually agree to edit the tentative course of study. These then become the basic materials, developed cooperatively. After they are approved by the board of education, they are placed in use in demonstration lessons, conferences, classroom visits on call, and teachers' meetings. There is no dictatory attitude concerning teaching materials on the part of an administrative officer such as often occurred in past years. Rather, cooperative selection by all interested persons is now the case.

Especially in large schools, principals are often tempted to sacrifice the rights of the individual to participate in school management for a type of control by a few highly selected individuals which guarantees efficient administration with little waste motion. When this is done, the control ceases to be democratic, although it may be a benevolent dictatorship. In order to keep the control democratic, the principal must constantly strive to have it exercised both by and for the individuals who constitute the school group.

One form of organization for democratic participation that has been very effective is the Principal's Council or the Building Advisory Committee. Such a committee, elected by the teachers to meet regularly with the principal, may consider school problems. Policies cooperatively developed are then put into practice. Such a council can probably best be inaugurated if it is charged with the responsibility for solving one immediate problem which is of concern to the group. Such a problem might concern conduct in the lunchroom, care of the building, providing suitable recreation, or revising the curriculum to meet the needs of a group of children who are obviously not well cared for—provided the problem(s) really exist. As teachers become more demanding and militant, they want to participate in deciding class size, free lunch periods, payment for extra duties, and so forth.

One matter must be clearly understood: the responsibility for making policy carries with it both the duty of supporting that policy when it has been decided upon by the group and the obligation of personally doing everything possible to make it effective. Policy making without the responsibility of support is dictatorship—the assumption of authority without true responsibility. Too often individual teachers have felt that, because they disagreed personally with a particular policy, they did not need to support it, even though it was agreed upon by their representatives or by the majority of the group. Such procedure is in direct contradiction to democratic action, where support of the majority position is necessary, with the right of criticism restricted to the representative group and not extended to the general public, which may not understand the issues involved. The privilege of freedom of speech does not, nor can it ever, mean the right of unrestricted criticism of that group by a member outside the group's confines. Once a policy has been settled and the opportunity of being heard has been fulfilled, the teacher must either support the policy or, as common decency demands, resign from the group. Thereafter any criticism is legitimate. Perhaps one reason why teachers have been so free to criticize their principals and superintendents is that they have had so little opportunity to participate in making policy.

But support does not exclude the individual from the right to try to have policy changed by the group which formulated it. The right of a minority to change its status to that of the majority is unquestioned. But it should be done in the proper manner. Everyone has an obligation to obey the law; if he disapproves of the law, he has the responsibility to try to have it changed while still obeying it.

Morale in an Individual School

Although no clear-cut evidence clearly indicates that a teacher's satisfaction with his job and his effectiveness of performance are related, it seems logical that some kind of a direct relationship exists. Existing evidence shows that where teachers have freedom to plan their work and opportunities to participate in making policy in matters of curriculum and teacher welfare morale is high. Equally important seems to be consistency in administrative behavior so that teachers know what to expect. Even when behavior is consistent, it must also be what teachers have learned to expect. And the relationships which teachers have with their peers in informal groups in the school are very important. Perhaps the most important ingredient in teacher satisfaction is his attitude toward the principal.[19]

Selected References

AUSTIN, D. B., "The Role of the High School Principal," *Teachers College Record*, 56 (April 1955), 404–11.

BRIDGES, M. EDWIN, "A Model for Shared Decision-Making in the School Principalship," *Educational Administration Quarterly* (Winter 1967), 49–61.

BROWN, R. E., "Humanizing the Role of the Elementary School Principal," *National Elementary Principal*, 49 (April 1970), 24–26.

The Bulletin of the National Association of Secondary School Principals— A Report on the NASSP Administrative Internship Project, No. 333 (January 1969).

BULLOCK, WILLIAM JR., The Relationship of Educational Training and Years of Administrative Experience. . . . School Principals, *Journal of Educational Research*, 63, No. 1 (September 1969), 3–5.

COUNTS, GEORGE S., "The Spirit of American Education," *Teachers College Record*, 59 (May 1958), 450–59.

CROSSFIELD, RUTH, "As Some Kansas Principals See It," *National Elementary Principal*, XLVII, No. 5 (April 1968), 12–13.

CUNNINGHAM, L. L., "Hey, Man, You Our Principal? Urban Education As I Saw It," *Phi Delta Kappan*, 51 (November 1969), 123–28.

EGGERT, C. L., and FLETCHER JONES, "Program of In-Service Training for School Administrators," *National Association of Secondary School Principals Bulletin*, 42 (March 1958), 25–30.

EIKENBERRY, D. H., "Training and Experience Standards for Principals of Secondary Schools," *National Association of Secondary School Principals Bulletin*, 181 (November 1951), 5–62.

"The Elementary School Principalship in 1968—A Research Study," Washington, D. C.: Department of Elementary Principals.

FERREIRA, J. L., "Administrative Internship and Role Change: A Study of the Relationship Between Interaction and Attitudes," *Educational Administration Quarterly*, 6 (Winter 1970), 77–90.

---

[19]Jack A. Culbertson, Paul B. Jacobson, and Theodore Reller, *Administrative Relationships* (Englewood Cliffs, N.J.: Prentice-Hall, Inc., 1960), pp. 414–437.

FISHER, WILLIAM H., "Ends and Means Reconsidered," *Education*, 78 (January 1958), 304–8.

GOLDHAMMER, KEITH, and G. L. BECKER, "What Makes a Good Elementary School Principal?" *American Education*, 6 (April 1970), 11–13.

GORTON, R. A., "Principal's Orientation Toward Participation in School Decision-Making," *Journal of Secondary Education*, 45 (March 1970), 124–29.

GROBMAN, HULDA G., and VINCE A. HINES, "What Makes a Good Principal?" *National Association of Secondary School Principals Bulletin*, 40 (November 1956), 5–16.

HARMON, J. J., "Principal's Role in Changing Power Structure," *School & Community*, 55 (November 1968), 45.

HAWKINS, HAROLD, "The Next Step? Teachers Select Principals," *Clearing House* (November 1969), 169–73.

HERRICK, VIRGIL E., et al., *The Elementary School*. Englewood Cliffs, N.J.: Prentice-Hall, Inc., 1956.

HORTON, BEN JR., "A Study of the Problems of Beginning Principals as a Basis for Improvement of the Program for the Education of Principals at Appalachian State Teachers College," *Educational Administration and Supervision*, 44 (September 1958), 261–71.

"How Should Team Leaders Be Chosen? Teachers' Opinion Poll," *Instructor*, 78 (August 1968), 25–26.

HOWSAM, ROBERT B., "In-Service Education of School Administrative Background, Present Status and Problems . . ." Albuquerque: University of New Mexico, 1966.

HOWSAM, ROBERT B., and EDGAR L. MORPHET, "Certification of Educational Administrators," *Journal of Teacher Education*, 9 (March) 75–96 (June 1958), 187–203.

HUNT, H. C., "Principals, Will You Accept the Challenge?" *National Elementary School Principal* (October 1952), 22–23.

JUILFS, ERWIN J., and ROBERT L. FOOSE, "Are Administration Competence and Democratic Administration Compatible?" *National Association of Secondary School Principals Bulletin*, 43 (April 1959), 79–84.

KEARNEY, NOLAN C., *Elementary School Objectives*. New York: Russell Sage Foundation, 1953, p. 189.

National Education Association, American Association of School Administrators, "The Organization of the Superintendency," *The American School Superintendency*, Thirtieth Yearbook, Washington: The Association, 1952, 65–102.

National Education Association, Department of Elementary School Principals, *The Elementary School Principalship, A Research Study*, Thirty-seventh Yearbook, XXXVII, No. 1 (September 1958).

NAYLOR, DOUGLAS H., and J. V. GRAUGHER, "Changing World of the Principal As We See It," *National Elementary Principal*, 47 (April 1968), 8–12.

PATTERSON, WALTER A., "How to Obtain a Principalship," *Clearing House* (January 1970), 310–14.

"Principalship," *The National Elementary Principal*, XLIV, No. 5 (April 1965).

RHODES ERIC F., and R. P. LONG, "The Principal's Role in Collective Negotiations," *Educational Service Bureau*, 1967, pp. 1–113.

"Salaries Scheduled for Principals, 1967–68," National Education Association Research Division, *NEA Research Bulletin*, 49 (October 1968), 49–91.

SCHWEIKHART, PHILIP A., and HAIVER E. McNABH, "What Is the Role of the Principal in Democratic Administration," *National Association of Secondary School Principals Bulletin*, 41 (April 1957), 204–7.

SECOR, LYNN J., and J. PAUL ANDERSON, "What Adminstration Practices Contribute to Better Principal-Faculty Relationships?" *National Association of Secondary School Principals Bulletin*, 42 (April 1958), 162–64.

SHANNON, T. A., "Principal's Management Role in Collective Negotiations, Grievances, and Strikes," *Journal of Secondary Education*, 45 (February 1970), 51–56.

SINCLAIR, ROBERT L., "Leadership Concerns," *National Elementary Principal*, VLVIII, No. 1 (September 1967), 17–20.

SPLAWN, ROBERT E., "Boards of Education Members' Perceptions of the Role of the Board, Superintendent and High School Principals...."*Annual Publication of School of Teacher Education*, III (May 1969).

3

Planning
the Year's Work

The Nature of the Preliminary Work

The amount of work to be done in the principal's office before the opening of school depends upon the efficiency of the school organization during the preceding year, the familiarity of the principal with that organization, and the care and foresight exercised by the principal in closing the previous year's work.

If a high school has been well-organized, students will have had guidance in selecting courses, schedules will have been made, and the athletic schedule for autumn will have been arranged. In well-organized schools supplies, equipment, and textbooks will have been ordered and inventoried, and repairs and redecorating will have been arranged for and completed. The necessary teachers will have been hired and assigned, so that the principal need not ordinarily concern himself with securing new teachers unless there are last minute resignations or deaths. The permanent cumulative records should show the placement of every child enrolled during the preceding year, and standard test results should be available for guidance purposes, either on the permanent record or in some other easily accessible form. In addition, health records, age-grade distributions, and records of attendance generally will be found. Reports from other schools about pupils who are enrolling should frequently be available.

In particularly well-organized schools the principal, if he is new to the position, may expect to find his predecessor's annual reports to the superintendent, copies of administrative bulletins of the preceding year, certified accounts of extracurricular or petty cash accounts, and complete records on the training of all teachers and their fitness for specific tasks. Information should also be available about ability grouping, if it has been practiced, about serious work with curriculum reorganization, or about other experimental projects in which the faculty has been engaged.

Before School Opens

How long the principal will need to work in his office before the opening of school will depend on his experience in school administration, the size and complexity of the school organization, and the adequacy of the preparation made during the closing period of the preceding year. The period of time will range from a few days to several weeks. The principal new to his position would do well to spend more time than what he considers the essential minimum in order to insure a smoothly functioning school on opening day, even though his predecessor may have planned all the details.

Undoubtedly the most pressing problem in planning the year's work, particularly at the high school level, is scheduling classes. If no schedule is available for the opening of school, the preparation of a suitable one becomes the principal's first task. Because of its importance, scheduling will be treated separately in the following chapter. The other duties incident to the planning and executing of the year's work will be dealt with in some detail in this chapter in the hope that the discussion will be helpful for beginning principals. More experienced executives may wish to compare their present practices with those suggested in order to evaluate critically specific activities they may have evolved over a period of years.

Certainly no one who has had experience in administering a school would seriously claim that all duties are of equal importance. But there are few schools, except very small ones, where most of the practices cannot be applied with profit; there are none where planning the year's work will not prove to be of benefit. Among such duties are planning an administrative bulletin, organizing a schedule for the school, assigning teachers, conferring with other educational officers, inspecting the building, notifying students or patrons of the opening of school, dealing with students who transfer from one school to another or who desire work permits, providing opportunity for individuals to remove academic deficiencies, organizing the extracurricular program, organizing the supervisory program, planning for the second semester (if the school is organized by semesters), collecting material for the annual report, and planning the closing of the school term in such fashion that the next term will begin auspiciously. In the discussion that follows, duties have been considered as though the year consisted of one term. In most large and medium-sized communities, many of these duties occur twice a year, since semiannual promotions are frequently the rule.

Problems of Opening of School

Of all the problems faced by a principal, those connected with the opening of school are probably the most burdensome. Opening the school term is especially difficult for the principal assuming a new position due to his unfamiliarity with local conditions. But even after years in a position, a principal cannot neglect planning activities incident to the successful launching of the new year's work. The way the school term opens will have a profound effect upon students, teachers, and patrons. The ideal is to have the new term open smoothly as though school were merely being resumed after a weekend recess. While it is scarcely probable that a new term can be opened with so little confusion, it is possible to have the school operating on the afternoon of the first day as though it had been in operation indefinitely.

However, in many schools confusion is evident in all parts of the organization. In extreme cases there are teachers without students, classes without teachers, even class sections with enrollments twice the capacity of the room. Teachers are handicapped because of shortage of supplies, lack of books and equipment, and improperly classified students. In many schools it is the custom to close school at noon of the first day to allow the principal and teachers to organize the work so that it may begin properly on the second day. In other cases schools operate on a half-day schedule for the first week, making adjustments during the afternoon sessions, and beginning complete operations at the opening of the second week. In isolated instances, principals who have served for several years in a community may not have their schools properly organized at the end of six weeks. Such a waste of the students' time and tax funds is inexcusable. It is in fact ample justification for releasing an obviously incompetent principal from his position, and securing one who is competent to open the school term with a minimum of delay in organization. Since there are always shifts in pupil personnel due to changes of residence, the principal must be prepared to accommodate a somewhat different pupil personnel from that present at the close of the preceding school term. There also are usually some changes in the teaching staff due to promotions and resignations. Summer activity of the custodial staff may have removed some equipment from customary places, and supplies on hand will in all probability have been considerably augmented since the close of the preceding term. The principal must deal effectively with all these problems.

Orientation Week

During the past decade, orientation week or preschool workshops have become standard practice in outstanding schools throughout the nation. Usually part of the week is reserved for requisitioning books, preparing visual aids for classroom learning, and getting ready for the opening of school. This may include the registration of students. Such a procedure is most important in making new students, particularly at the kindergarten or first grade level, feel at home when school opens. Generally a part of the week—under ideal arrangements a second week—is set apart for conferences between classroom teachers and supervisors, building meetings of principal and teachers, and professional study. Frequently persons from outside the school system are brought in for several days to assist the faculty on an inservice or workshop basis on matters such as child growth and development, curriculum problems, and guidance. Infrequently such workshops, begun during the orientation week, continue study for a semester or a year, either with or without credit. In some parts of the United States, especially on the Pacific Coast, the preschool workshop has become almost standard practice. Such a procedure is a golden opportunity for the principal to organize his work so that school will open on the first day as though it were reopening after a weekend recess. The duties described in the rest of this chapter will be more easily carried out in schools that have an orientation week.

Necessity for a Plan of Procedure

A new principal should anticipate many of the problems that are likely to arise and plan procedures enabling him to deal with them on opening day. If he does so successfully, his administration will have an auspicious start. No doubt a principal will receive certain information from his superior officer, either through conference or through printed or mimeographed bulletins or both. Such information as the names of teachers and the work for which they are best fitted, the time of beginning and closing the school day, the curriculum and materials of instruction to be used, rules and regulations of the local school system, and such other information as the central office finds desirable to place in the hands of the principal must be available.

Information Within the Building

Further information about practices in the local school can be secured from the clerical force and administrative assistants, if there are any. More can be gleaned from the official records in the office. It is usually advisable to keep intact all former administrative practices which are not definitely harmful and to make only such changes in administrative organization as sound educational procedure requires. If the new principal follows a strong executive, he should start with the organization which was in force, changing it only when he is certain that improvement will follow.

Additional information can be secured through a careful inspection of the building with the custodian. The heating, ventilating, cleaning, and lighting systems should be inspected on this tour of the building. It may also prove worthwhile to inspect the fire alarm system and see that exit signs are posted in all rooms. The principal should also inspect the clock signal, check the supplies, and inventory the textbooks, if these things have not already been done. It will be advisable to see that all service facilities, such as lavatories and drinking fountains, are in working order and that the school lunchroom is ready for service.

It is wise to become acquainted with the members of the custodial staff to make sure that they know their duties and that they are prepared for the opening of school. In systems where enrollments fluctuate considerably, the custodians will have considerable work providing seating for rooms with increased enrollments. The equipment in each room should be adequate to care for the number of boys and girls expected on opening day.

In many schools, particularly secondary schools, too, it will be necessary to arrange for students who do not live in the district and who are not entitled to attend without tuition charge. This can usually be most conveniently cared for before the opening day of school.

Assigning Teachers

If each teacher is assigned a homeroom, the teacher's name and his subject or the grade and hours of use of the room should be placed on the door. The principal should also see that the program of work for the school doctor or nurse is ready if the health officers are full-time employees who begin work with the opening of school.

Changes made during vacation in boundaries of the district, in routing of arterial streets or highways, or in building developments, either commercial or residential, which may create administrative problems should be carefully studied to anticipate any problems. These changes should especially be carefully studied in the elementary schools.

In the assignment of teachers to their duties, much information can be obtained from previous office records. Teachers who have extended periods of service in the local school should be assigned to the grade or subject to which they have previously taught, unless there is evidence that they would be more effective or happier in another assignment. New teachers should then be assigned to the remainder of the positions. In a well-organized school, teachers will be appointed to fill specific positions and will be well equipped for the work involved.

Announcing the Opening of the Term

In city systems the superintendent of schools or his subordinates will provide announcements to the press giving detailed instructions to students about the opening of school. In independent schools it will be necessary for the principal to make arrangements for newspaper releases. In isolated cases he may have to send notices by mail to students to notify them where and when to report for school.

The Administrative Bulletin

In order to provide for many of the duties incident to the opening of school, it is good procedure to prepare an administrative bulletin which may be duplicated and given to each teacher before the opening of school. In some large systems this bulletin may take the form of a printed manual or handbook describing for regular and substitute teachers exactly what is to be done under certain conditions.

The following are illustrative of the topics which might be discussed in an administrative bulletin or handbook: teachers' hours, schedule of bells, hall and locker room duties of teachers, mail boxes for teachers in the office, hours at which supplies may be secured, regular requisitioning of supplies, committee assignments (such as the committee on reading, the committee on professional meetings, or the social committee), chaperoning or attending school parties, assignments to extracurriculum duties, dates for group and general teachers' meetings, the official school calendar, a list of assemblies (if they are planned in advance), procedure for teachers in case of personal illness, procedure for teachers if contagious diseases are suspected in children, code for students, and procedure for securing janitorial service in addition to that regularly furnished. The report forms used by the teachers in the school may be illustrated on separate pages, with explanations of how and when they are to be used.

Such an administrative bulletin is invaluable because it furnishes a handbook for new or substitute teachers, acts as a reminder to teachers who have served in the school, and causes the principal to think through the administrative routine for the year. How elaborate such an administrative bulletin should be will depend on the size and complexity of the organization of the local school and the completeness of the teachers' handbook furnished by the central administration.

In some cities the central administration publishes a handbook with space for the local school principal to duplicate a section for distribution to his staff.

It may well be repeated for emphasis that the preparation of an administrative bulletin or handbook serves to focus attention on all the details which need to be faced before and after the opening of school. For a new principal it proves invaluable as a device to help him think through the routine organization of the school and know what reports are to be made, what duties are assigned, and to whom they are assigned. For an experienced principal it will tend to prevent overloading any details.

Preliminary Teachers' Meeting

When an administrative bulletin has been prepared and distributed to teachers in advance of the opening of school, it is the practice in some schools not to hold general meetings of teachers before the opening for routine administrative purposes. In some forward-looking cities, the central administration has replaced the opening teachers' meeting with an orientation program.

If teachers' meetings before the opening of school are policy, they should be made as profitable as possible. Such a meeting is neither the time nor place for a detailed statement of educational aims and objectives. The local meeting should be short, for teachers will probably wish to spend time arranging their classrooms, securing their quota of supplies and books, and organizing their work for the opening of school. At such a meeting, the statement by the principal should be brief and general, with a warm welcome to the new members of the staff and ample time for the questions which some teachers will surely ask about the opening, no matter how carefully the administrative bulletin has been worked out. By placing all announcements in a bulletin, the principal can facilitate the teacher's preliminary work and cause him to begin his duties with enthusiasm.

Teachers' Meeting at the End of the Opening Day

It has been traditional to hold a teachers' meeting at the end of the first day of school to discover what provisions have proved to be unsatisfactory, where there was serious overcrowding, and the like. Such meetings are unnecessary if the principal has undertaken careful planning for the opening of school. Teachers should not be burdened with a routine administrative meeting at the end of the first day. It is far better to deal individually with the few teachers who have problems than to detain the entire group.

Duties Assigned to Teachers

Permanent members of the teaching force who are familiar with the routine of the school should be assigned on the opening day to care for specific duties that the principal cannot conveniently care for in person. In the elementary school, supervision of the playground and the building are such duties. One or more of the specially qualified members of the staff may be assigned to classify tentatively by grades the students who are new to an elementary school. A teacher or an assistant principal may be assigned to registration and program-making for new entrants in the high school. New entrants at either the elementary or high school level should be classified as their reports indicate will be best for them; or, if they appear without reports, as in some cases, they can be classified as they claim they should be with adjustments being made when and if the evidence clearly shows that they are misplaced.

Enrollment Data

Since most school systems wish to know the enrollment on the first day, the principal should make plans to have the enrollment reported at the close of the morning session or at the end of the day, if that will suffice for report purposes. In many systems, such reports are required each day of the first week. In either case a convenient blank sent to the office by all teachers will facilitate in assembling the enrollment data.

Handling Students Who Have Removed Deficiencies

Before the opening of school, provision must be made for reclassifying students who were failed at the end of the year and who have removed their deficiencies by attendance at a summer session or by tutoring. In the latter case they should report or demonstrate their competence by testing. To leave them until after the opening of school will necessitate reclassifying some and rearranging the study programs of others, procedures which waste student time, are conducive to poor morale, and cause unnecessary difficulties for the principal in the opening days of the year.

Delegating Some Duties to Students

The more mature and responsible students may well be assigned to act as guides for pupils who are new to the school. If a student council has been organized, it can be used to help orient new pupils. In some schools "big brothers" and "big sisters" are assigned to all entering students to show them locations of lockers and rooms and to acquaint them with the routine of school procedure. Such an arrangement makes the first day or days easier for entering students, who may be bewildered. It tends to build a wholesome spirit in the school.

Transfer Students

Although the principal may have delegated many duties for the opening day of school, there will still be a multitude for which he is personally responsible. It is entirely possible, for example, that he may need to arrange for substitute teachers because of unexpected illness on the part of some member of his faculty. Even though some permanent members of the teaching corps who are thoroughly familiar with the classification procedure in use in the school take care of most of the transfer students, there will be troublesome cases which must of necessity be referred to the principal's office for decisions. Transfers are likely to cause more work and confusion on the opening day than regular students.

In elementary schools it is good procedure to furnish teachers with lists of boys and girls who are regularly promoted to their rooms. The students normally report to the room to which they are assigned, while beginning students are sent to the kindergarten or first grade room, depending on which one is the initial grade. Transfer students may be classified by the teachers in charge of that procedure, assigned to specific grades for which they appear best fitted, in the understanding that reclassification may be expected later. The class teacher then adds the names of the transferred students to those who were regularly promoted, deletes those names which were furnished her as transfers to other schools, thus making a class roster.

In secondary schools it is a frequent practice to ask transfer students to report to the school before the opening day so that they may be assigned to class before the opening session. This will mitigate, but not entirely relieve, congestion and confusion on the opening day, since there are always some pupils who will not appear as requested. These students will have to be assigned to classes, programs made for them, and their names inscribed on the class lists. It is good practice in secondary as in elementry schools to furnish each teacher with a list of the students who may be expected to appear in his class. The late registrant must be provided with evidence that he is enrolled in a specific class so that the teacher may enter him on the list. He must also be provided with guide service to his first class. It is advisable to have teachers exclude individuals whose names are not on the list, as some will certainly attend classes where their friends are enrolled rather than those to which they are assigned, unless they are prevented from doing so by administrative procedure. The principal, or someone delegated by him, must deal with these stragglers. Details are reserved for the next chapter; they can more conveniently be treated in the discussion of schedule-making.

Opening School

The Opening Day of School

It goes without saying that the principal, and teachers too, should be on duty early on the first days of school. Perhaps an hour before the scheduled time for the opening day will be sufficient. In all probability some students and parents will be there before the principal is. The principal can care more conveniently for them before the rush starts. By doing so the principal will gain respect for the school administration because he has taken care of new enrollees or transfers promptly, even though they have not followed the suggested procedure prior to the opening day of school; besides, he will have cleared the way for the day's business.

In order not to overlook some of the responsibilities which he must discharge on the opening day, the principal should prepare a list where each one can be checked off as it is performed. The list should contain only those duties considered essential to the successful opening of school and those which should not be neglected because of emergency duties perhaps more urgent in nature but less important. The kinds of these duties in a specific school depend on the condition of the building, the philosophy of the principal with respect to school administration, and how well the preliminary planning has been done. Among these duties may be care of transfer students, inspecting the work of teachers new to the school, inspecting lunchroom conditions, observing the halls during intermissions, considering enrollment reports, and supervising transfer of students and equipment. To these, any principal must add those duties which are special to the local school.

Responsibilities of the First Week

During the first week the principal may find it necessary to make many adjustments in individual student programs, balancing class sizes, adjusting classroom equipment and supplies, and checking students expected in school who have not reported. These duties are arduous in schools located in communities which have rapidly shifting populations, and they should not be permitted to take a principal's entire time. In well-organized schools, it is quite possible for the principal to make supervisory or inspection visits as early as the afternoon of the first day. All the new teachers should be observed during the first days of the new session. Making a list of the duties which should be performed during the first week will prevent the neglect of such duties through oversight.

In many schools, locker keys are issued to the students during the first week of school. While it is preferable to have locker keys or lock combinations checked out through the homeroom first thing on the first day, it may not be possible—especially if deposits are required to insure the return of the keys or locks at the end of the term. In such a case, proper procedure should be explained to students by the teachers through a bulletin; provisions should be made for the orderly distribution of keys or locks during the first week.

In schools which do not close at noon for the lunch hour, it will be necessary to announce which pupils are to use the various lunch periods, since very few schools have lunchrooms large enough to accommodate the entire school enrollment at one time.

Some writers have advocated opening the first day of school with a general assembly, and such a procedure has been followed successfully. However, most experienced administrators do not advocate such a procedure. It is entirely possible and very desirable to hold a successful assembly *later* in the opening week. At the high school level, such an assembly may consist of the introduction of the faculty by the principal, or of the new members if the faculty is large, singing songs known by students enrolled during the preceding year, and a brief and friendly welcome by the principal. An assembly like this helps develop the feeling in faculty and students that the school is well-organized and so helps to start the year auspiciously. In schools which have well-organized and functioning student councils, members of the council can help in caring for the details of seating, flag salute, reciting the student creed, or other traditional items. If the assembly committee is a smoothly functioning organization, the opening assembly will be followed by a series of programs.

Other Functions Incident to the Opening of School

After a high school has been in operation for a short time, it will be necessary to organize the activity program for the year. Arrangements must be made for class organizations to meet and elect officers. Sponsors who have been announced in the administrative bulletin should know their duties and see that the properties of elective office procedure are carried out. Homeroom organization must begin to function; this means the election of officers so that the administrative function of the homeroom and the dissemination of information may proceed regularly. Very soon after the opening of school, it is also good procedure to hold a fire drill which has been announced to students and teachers. After that the frequency of fire drills may vary as determined by the need in the school and by regulations imposed by the central office or by the fire department.

Organizing the Calendar

It is advisable to have a school calendar of social and athletic events for the year so that activities will be arranged in sequence rather than allowed to pile up at certain times or fail to happen because of lack of time. A representative committee of teachers and students working under the direction of the principal, or the director of activities if one has been appointed, should carefully log all possible events such as athletic contests, parties, class plays, lyceum numbers, or any other sponsored activities, and arrange a calendar to be duplicated and distributed throughout the school.

After the calendar has been adopted, it should be adhered to except for extraordinary reasons. Planning the calendar during the first month has become an advisable procedure. It is also desirable to plan a means of checking the success of parties and social affairs so that improvements may be made in planning similar affairs in the future. A checkup at the time the social calendar is adopted focuses attention on desirable procedure at social events for both students and faculty sponsors and facilitates the success of such events.

Checking Materials for Teachers

Inasmuch as equipment, supplies, keys, and the like must be issued to teachers at the beginning of the school year, something will certainly be overlooked unless a check list of the items to be delivered to teachers is prepared. In schools which have clerical service, such a list will enable the clerk to do her tasks more effectively. Likewise, in the opening days of school, so many reports are required from teachers that a list should be prepared showing horizontally across the top of the page what items are required and vertically a list of the teachers. It is then a simple matter to check off the items as they are turned in by the teachers. And it furnishes an easy means of reminding those teachers who have forgotten to make the necessary reports.

In schools where a daily bulletin of information is prepared—and this will include most medium-sized and large schools—reminders may be inserted in the daily bulletin that certain reports or records are due at a certain time. Not all teachers perform clerical duties with promptness, so reminders in the bulletin will prove helpful. With a few teachers it may be necessary to deal individually. It is not at all impossible to have a large faculty turn in records and reports promptly, and in acceptable form, if the principal gives adequate instructions as to when and how records are to be delivered, checks up on the reports, and deals with laggards with firmness and tact.

Duties Throughout the Year

As soon as possible during the first month, extracurricular activities should be organized. A bulletin describing these activities should be prepared to assist the students in making selections unless a handbook is available. The extent of the program will depend on the size of the school and its philosophy. The responsibility for organizing the program rests either with the principal or with some person to whom he has delegated it.

It will also be necessary to plan the supervisory program with the teachers so that it may be focused on specific problems recognized by the teachers and principal as being of great importance in improving the instruction furnished to students in the local school. This planning, too, should be done as soon after the opening of school as possible.

Similarly, the guidance service must be organized. Counseling furnished to students by teachers, physicians, psychiatrists, or other workers provided in the school must be coordinated to provide the best possible service for students. Unless the principal provides for coordination and takes an active interest in the guidance program, it will not be as successful as it could be.

In addition, the principal must plan with or for his administrative assistants the broad policies of office procedure, and in some cases the details. He must also plan for inspection of the building and grounds; arrange the details of supplying books, equipment, and supplies; and determine how much time he can or should devote to community activities without neglecting his main function—the improvement of instruction. These problems are of far greater importance than the details of opening school, although they are less immediate. It is only possible at this point to mention them. They are treated at length in following sections of the book.

Athletic Schedules

In some high schools it will be necessary to arrange athletic schedules after school opens. Fortunately the necessity for such arrangements is steadily declining; the practice of making athletic schedules well in advance of the playing season is increasing. When it is necessary to arrange such schedules, and the matter cannot be delegated to the coach, the principal should follow the procedure recommended by the state high school athletic association.

Informing Parents of Deficiencies of Prospective Graduates

In secondary schools it will be necessary to keep parents fully informed concerning the progress of students who hope to graduate but whose prospects for doing so are very dim. By sending written notices to parents and by holding personal interviews with the individuals concerned to help make adjustments, the school can fulfill its obligation and prevent false hopes from arising in the minds of these students and their parents. It is only fair that parents should be warned. To allow them to believe their son or daughter will graduate, and then, without warning, to exclude them because of some belatedly discovered condition is certainly poor administration. Notices that students may not graduate should first be sent to the home not later than the middle of the last semester, and preferably much earlier.

Closing the School Year

Students Who Must Leave Before School Closes

A frequent problem for the principal at the end of the term is dealing with students who for some reason may desire to leave before the closing day. The reasons will vary. Some must go to work; others may have an unexpected chance to make a pleasure journey. Whatever policy is adopted must be based on local considerations. The point emphasized here is that some procedure for handling these cases, and some provision either for their completing their work later or for recording it as complete, should be thought out before the end of the year.

The Close of School

It is just as necessary to prepare for the end of the school term as it is to prepare for the opening of school. Probably the best procedure to follow is to include all necessary announcements relative to the closing of school in a bulletin issued to all teachers sufficiently far in advance of the close of school so that teachers will not be unduly rushed in compiling the necessary records. Placing all requirements in a bulletin will insure the principal against neglecting to obtain information which he should have on file in the office. Such a bulletin should be issued at least a month before the end of school, and a check list should be prepared where those items that teachers have completed may be recorded.

As a list of topics for such a final bulletin to teachers, the following is recommended:

1. A résumé of the grading system.
2. Instructions for filing in the office the final reports of student progress.
3. The final examination schedule, if such examinations are held.
4. Lists of students to be filed by subject or grade.
5. Procedures to be followed in collecting textbooks.
6. Collection of fines on misused books.
7. The return of locker keys or locks.
8. The date on which teachers may leave. Unless this is made specific, the principal will be besieged with requests for special consideration.
9. Teachers' requests for supplies and equipment. These may have been collected earlier. When such information is collected will depend on budget procedure.
10. Teachers' requests for repairs or building changes. It is quite possible that the necessity for repairs and alterations has been surveyed earlier in the year.

This list is suggestive rather than inclusive. The items included in any school bulletin for teachers relative to the closing of school will be conditioned by the organization and the policies in force locally.

To insure the orderly collection of the necessary materials it is a good plan to refer to specific items in the daily bulletin, with the date on which each item is due.

The Annual Report

From time to time during the year, the principal will collect information to be included in the annual report to the superintendent. The principal should collect it in written form from the teachers or department heads during the year to insure having the necessary information. He then compiles it. In some cases the central office will indicate what is desired. In other cases the principal will use his best judgment. The compilation and interpretive writing of such a report comprise an excellent opportunity for summarizing the year's work. It will undoubtedly call attention to some phases of the year's work which should be changed or strengthened in the future.

While it has generally been agreed by writers on administration that the principal should make an annual report, the practice is not so common as it should be. The following are suggested for inclusion.

1. Summary of attendance
2. Summary of enrollment
3. Records regarding the faculty
4. Financial report on activities
5. Housing problems
6. Number of graduates
7. Organization and administrative control
8. Recommendations for the next year
9. Record of supervision
10. Results of the testing program
11. Statement of tuition pupils
12. Progressive attitude of faculty

In addition to the usual items listed, other items such as a description of the guidance system, extracurricular activities, awards, a statement about failures, study of graduates in more advanced educational units, assembly programs, and the parent–teacher organization may well be included.

The principal will undoubtedly report many matters in writing to the superintendent at his request or for his consideration. Such reports can probably best be prepared in narrative form. If they are to be read and understood by the board of education as well as by the superintendent, they should be free of technical educational terms which laymen would not understand. There seems to be a trend in the annual report of superintendents of schools to adopt a pictorial form of explaining the work of the schools. Where such policy is in force, the local principal should assist if he is asked to, but the obligation to furnish a narrative report to the superintendent for the principal's local school has not been removed.

Selected References

"Are Principals Represented in Bargaining Units?" *Research Bulletin—NEA,* 46 (October 1968), 84–87.

BAUMAN, W. S., "Four Quarter Plan Uses School All Year Long," *Nation's Schools,* 80 (November 1967), 69–70.

BROWN, R. E., "Humanizing the Role of the Elementary School Principal," *National Elementary Principal,* 49 (April 1970), 24–26.

CHAMBER, G. A., "PPBS: New Challenges and Opportunities for the Principal in Financial Planning and Management," *North Central Association Quarterly,* 42 (Spring 1968), 301–6.

CUNNINGHAM, L. L., "Hey, Man, You Our Principal? Urban Education As I Saw It," *Phi Delta Kappan,* 51 (November 1969), 123–28.

ELLENA, W. J., "Extending the School Year," *Today's Education,* 58 (May 1969), 48–49.

FERREIRA, J. L., "Administrative Internship and Role Change: A Study of the Relationship Between Interaction and Attitudes," *Educational Administration Quarterly,* 6 (Winter 1970), 77–90.

GOLDHAMMER, KEITH, and G. L. BECKER, "What Makes a Good Elementary School Principal?" *American Education,* 6 (April 1970), 11–13.

GORTON, R. A., "Principal's Orientation Toward Participation in School Decision-Making," *Journal of Secondary Education,* 45 (March 1970), 124–29.

HICKS, WILLIAM V., and MARSHALL C. JAMESON, *The Elementary School Principal at Work.* Englewood Cliffs, N.J.: Prentice-Hall, Inc., 1957.

"Instructional System for Training Principals," Project on the administrator's internship in secondary school improvement. *National Association of Secondary School Principals Bulletin,* 53 (January 1969), 11–18.

JAFFE, A., "Principal and Teacher—School Board Negotiations," *National Association of Secondary School Principals Bulletin,* 52 (May 1968), 105–9.

KURZBANO, "Issues Facing the Elementary Principal," *High Points* (Spring 1967), 12–13.

KYTE, G. C., *The Principal at Work.* rev. ed., Boston: Ginn and Company, 1952, pp. 105–19.

LEWIN, D., "Changing Role of the Urban Principal," *Elementary School Journal,* 68 (April 1968), 329–33.

MICHAEL, L. S., "Principal and Trends in Professional Negotiations," *National Association of Secondary School Principals Bulletin,* 52 (May 1968), 105–9.

National Education Association, "Rescheduling the School Year," *Research Division, NEA Research Bulletin,* 46 (October 1968), 67–70.

NAYLOR, D. H., and J. V. TRAUGHBER, "Changing World of the Principal As We See It," *National Elementary Principal,* 47 (April 1968), 8–12.

NORTON, J. K., "How to Solve Seven Major Problems in Administration," *School Management*, XVII (October 1947), 42.

RICE, A. H., "Annual Reports Are Better," *Nation's Schools*, XLIX (March 1952).

RUCHTER, C. O., "Annual School Reports," *Nation's Schools*, XLVII (May 1951), 41–43.

SCHUSTER, H. H., "Principal and Teacher for Non-Graded Schools—Pre-Service and In-Service Education," *National Elementary Principal*, 47 (January 1968), 10–14.

SHANNON, T. A., "Principal's Management Role in Collective Negotiations, Grievances and Strikes," *Journal of Secondary Education*, 45 (February 1970), 51–56.

"Special Kind of Internship for Principals," *National Association of Secondary School Principals Bulletin*, 53 (January 1969), 3–10.

4

Making a School Schedule

Schedule-Making in Elementary Schools

Schedule-making in the conventionally organized elementary school does not present any great difficulties for the principal. The hours for the opening and closing of school and usually for the noon intermission are determined by the central office, as is the time allotment for the different subjects of instruction. The principal is generally, but not always, free to set the time of the daily intermissions. He is also expected to arrange periods for teaching special subjects in the various rooms so that the supervisors from the central office may carry out their duties without conflict or loss of time.

The information regarding fixed periods and time allotments for subjects is transmitted by the principal to teachers, who are held responsible for constructing daily schedules. Copies of the schedules are usually sent to the central office as well as kept on file in the principal's office. Not infrequently copies are placed in pockets on the classroom doors for visitor convenience.

If a division of an elementary school—for example, the fourth, fifth, and sixth grades—is departmentalized, the principal's responsibility for making the schedule is greatly increased. He must then decide whether the classrooms will be used as units for teachers or for students. If the rooms are used for teachers, the classes are transferred from room to room for work with the different teachers; if for students, then the teachers must move from room to room to meet the groups of students to which they are assigned. Schedule-making in such schools presents numerous problems;

the responsibility for solving them belongs to the principal, irrespective of how the schedule is actually prepared. The wise principal will invariably utilize the teachers of the departmental unit concerned in the preparation of the schedule, but he may find it necessary to participate more extenively in schedule construction in schools with departmental organization than in schools organized according to the conventional teacher-to-the-room plan.

Self-Contained Unit

More and more often, elementary schools are being organized with each room as a self-contained unit. In the lower grades each teacher ordinarily teaches all subjects. The problem of schedule-making is thus very simple: it consists of making sure that each teacher conforms in subject time limit to directions from the central office. At the upper grade level, specialists are often provided on a part-time or full-time basis in art, physical education, and music. Here the problem becomes one of arranging each room schedule so that the specialist's time is used to greatest advantage. This is ordinarily a relatively simple problem.

In a multiunit school or a teamteaching situation in an elementary school, the team leader makes out the schedule for a group of students and files it in the office.

Schedule-Making in Secondary Schools

The Importance of Schedule-Making in Secondary Schools

The principal of the school is responsible for making the schedule. Usually he is the person who does it, although he may delegate it to someone else in the organization. If the responsibility is delegated, it normally becomes the responsibility of the assistant principal or chairman of the schedule committee.[1] Schedule-making usually presents greater problems to principals of secondary schools than of elementary schools.

Steps in Schedule-Making: Preliminary Registration

There are two widely used methods of schedule-making: the block, or group, method and the mosaic, or individual, method. Some writers include a third, the combination, which incorporates features of the block and the

---

[1]See B. C. Gustavson, "20th Century Schedule-Making," *National Association of Secondary School Principals Bulletin*, 172 (October 1950), 33–46; and L. G. Feldman, "Programming Classes by Means of a Punch Card System," *National Association of Secondary School Principals Bulletin* 172 (October 1950), 23–28.

mosaic methods. Whatever system is used, certain steps are necessary before a complete schedule can be made. The first step is to collect information about the number of students who will probably enroll and the subjects these students will elect. This step is commonly called *preliminary registration.*

Guidance Needed

If preliminary registration is to be of maximum value, a competent and interested person must be provided to guide students in planning their programs of studies over a period of years. Preliminary registrations must also be obtained from students enrolled in the contributing schools who will enroll in the school during the next term. The guidance functions of schedule-making are treated in Chapter 11, which deals with the problems of personnel administration.

Kinds of Preliminary Registration Cards

The purpose of preliminary registration is to ascertain what subjects are desired by students for the following semester or year. Probably the most satisfactory form for collecting information is a preliminary registration card, illustrated in Fig. 5. Although slips of paper, mimeographed sheets, or booklets may be used for preliminary registration, a printed card is the most common form. A simple card which provides space for the student's present schedule, elections for the next period, student's name, grade classification, sex, telephone number, and a space for parental and school approval are sufficient. No form which could be suggested would be satisfactory to every school; local schools can make such changes as are desirable according to local needs.

Responsibility of Principal for Preliminary Registration

The responsibility for preliminary registration belongs to the principal of the school. In some cases, particularly in large schools, it is delegated to some other person or persons, usually the homeroom teachers. No matter who accepts responsibility for preliminary registration, it is imperative that students be furnished reliable information about required and elective courses, requirements in different curriculums, and college entrance requirements, in order that the students and their parents may make intelligent choices. Accurate information is part of the guidance work which a school must assume.

To obtain parental signatures on all preliminary registration cards is a desirable but time-consuming process which requires a great deal of follow-up work on the part of the principal or teachers to whom the task has been delegated. But those parental signatures are highly desirable, because they

PRELIMINARY REGISTRATION CARD

(Name of School)

Name ———————————— Telephone No. ———— Present Grade ————

Address ———————————— Check: Boy ———— Girl ————

Studies Now Taken	Studies Desired Next Year	Room	Period

I approve of the selections.

Parent ———————————— Date ———— Adviser's Approval ————————

Fig. 5. Preliminary registration card.

insure family consideration of the future educational plans of each child. The adviser's approval insures that the student has been advised in so far as the school has definite knowledge of his needs.

Tabulation and Use of the Preliminary Registration Data

The data which have been collected on the preliminary registration cards must be tabulated prior to use. While the principal often has a share in the work of tabulation, the task is generally assigned to clerks or home-room teachers in schools where such administrative assistants are available. From the tabulated data it is a simple matter to determine the number of

class sections needed for the following term by dividing the number of preliminary registrations by the desired class sizes. It may be necessary at this
point to eliminate certain courses listed in the preliminary registration because the enrollment does not warrant their being offered. And as a result,
changes may have to be made in the preliminary registration of the pupils
who are affected.

From the number of sections necessary to accommodate the students
it is possible to determine the teaching corps needed for the following year.
Since preliminary registration data are used to determine staff needs, it is
desirable that tabulation be completed well before the opening of the new
term, say six or eight weeks ahead.

Table 3 illustrates the procedure for determining both teacher assign-

Table 3

SECTION OF INITIAL TEACHER-
ASSIGNMENT SHEET

Subject	Total Regis- tration	Sections Needed	Teacher Assignment
English 8	225	7	Smith (3); Bork (2); Adams (2)
English 6	250	8	Smith (2); Bork (3); Adams (3)
English 4	315	11	Roberts (4); Allen (4); To be secured (3)
Soc. Prob. 8	221	7	Walters (4); To be secured (3)
Soc. Science 6	268	9	Perry (5); Warren (2); To be secured (2)
Soc. Science 4	198	6	Walters (1); Reid (5)
Physics 1	84	3	Hunt (3)
Chemistry 1	95	3	Hunt (2); Rosecrans (1)
Latin 3	22	1	Rosecrans (1)
Latin 2	46	2	Goss (2)
Latin 1	75	3	Goss (3)
Auto Mechanics	140	5	Torgerson (5)
General Metals	47	2	Kepke (2)
Mechanical Drawing 1	98	3	Kepke (3)
Typewriting 2	40	1	Peterson (1)
Typewriting 1	146	4	Peterson (4)
Bookkeeping 1	102	3	Greening (3)
Stenography 1	68	2	Greening (2)

ments and the need for additional teachers in a senior high school with an enrollment of about 800 students. Extension of this procedure to the other departments will provide the principal with the data essential in the assignment of the entire corps.

It is also valuable to make a supplementary sheet on which the teachers' assignments are listed, so that no teachers are overlooked and no sections are without teachers. Table 4 gives a partial summary of the teacher-assignment sheet in Table 3.

Other Preliminary Steps in Schedule-Making

There are a number of further decisions which have to be made before the schedule is complete. Minimum and maximum class sizes must have been determined and applied to the preliminary registration, and the requisite number of teachers must have been determined or secured based on the policy in the local school system. In some schools the enrollment is so large that it is necessary to resort to double sessions. In others, overlapping sessions are necessary, some pupils beginning the school day at 8:00 A.M., some at 9:00 A.M., and others at 10:00 A.M. The problems pertaining to overlapping or double sessions must be settled before the schedule is built. The decision as to the time of opening and closing school must also be made. Ordinarily, high schools begin about 8:30 and close about 3:30, although considerable variation exists.

A decision must also be made concerning arrangements for the lunch period. Common practice tends to allow about forty-five minutes for lunch

Table 4

SECTION OF REVISED TEACHER-
ASSIGNMENT SHEET

Name	*Assignment*	*Total Load*
Smith	English 8 (3) English 6 (2)	5
Bork	English 8 (2) English 6 (3)	5
Adams	English 8 (2) English 6 (3)	5
Roberts	English 4 (4) Play Coaching	5
Allen	English 4 (4) Publications	5
*To Be Secured[a]	English 4 (3) Study Hall (3)	6
*To Be Secured[a]	Soc. Prob. 8 (3) Social Science 6 (2)	5
Perry	Soc. Science 6 (5)	5
Walters	Soc. Prob. 8 (4) Social Science 4 (1)	5
Reid	Soc. Science 4 (5)	5
Hunt	Physics (3) Chemistry (2)	5

[a]Items that require further attention are more easily spotted by means of asterisks.

in urban schools. The decision concerning the lunch hour is usually based on a number of factors. Small schools usually close for approximately an hour because many students go home for lunch, although this practice is diminishing. In large schools students usually eat lunch at school. The number of lunch periods is determined by the enrollment and the capacity of the lunchroom. Ordinarily, not more than three periods are needed, although in large schools with small lunchrooms six or seven periods are not unheard of. If a continuous program with several lunch periods is necessary, the difficulty of schedule-making is increased because single-period classes cannot ordinarily be assigned to any of the lunch hours lest conflicts arise for some pupils.

Provision for Activities

Another decision that must be made before the schedule is constructed concerns the provision for an activity period. Frequently, schools provide a homeroom period to care for administrative details, and in some cases to provide for part of the school's guidance service. Many schools also provide a period at the close of the school day for club activities, make-up work, study, or athletic squad practice. Provision should be made for activities in the school's program, and decisions concerning them must be made before the schedule is completed.

Length and Number of Periods

If periods are fifty-five or sixty minutes in length, it is customary to have six such periods in the day, devoting part of classroom time to supervised study under the direction of the teacher. In such a case, science and practical arts classes ordinarily meet five times per week. However, when the periods are forty or forty-five minutes in length, classes in laboratory science meet seven hours per week and practical arts classes meet for ten periods each week or double periods every day. The length of the period is an important item to consider in making the schedule. R. C. Puckett showed that, in thirty schedules for ten high schools, if the long period method with no double periods for any classes is used, there are almost 50 percent fewer conflicts than if the shorter period method is used with double periods for some subjects for thirty schedules for the same ten schools and the same students.[2] Since Puckett used the same techniques in each of the sixty schedules, there should remain little doubt that the long period method reduces schedule-making difficulties.

Teachers who have daily lab classes such as home economics are usually opposed to the single period of fifty-five minutes. However, after

---

[2] R. C. Puckett, "The Difficulties of Making a High School Schedule," (Doctoral thesis in education, University of Iowa, 1943), p. 41.

trying longer periods they usually find that they can adjust their procedures so that class period of fifty-five minutes is ample. The time-waste that can so easily creep into the double period is eliminated. And the unit cost per pupil-hour becomes comparable to other subject costs, a condition which cannot be under the double-period plan.

It is also necessary to decide on the length of the intermission between classes. From three to five minutes is usually allowed.

List of Rooms

Before the schedule is made, it is advisable to list the available rooms, their size, and the purposes for which they may be used. Care must be taken in the case of rooms having specialized equipment to see that each class which requires the equipment is scheduled there, and that two classes are not scheduled for a particular special room during the same period. In certain cases, special rooms may be used for regular classes if the equipment is not of such nature as to prevent its use by other classes. A science laboratory may be used by a mathematics class, but a typewriting room is so specialized that it cannot be used for classes other than typewriting.

Training Teachers

Before the schedule is finally made, training teachers for specific assignments should be carefully checked by the principal if he does not already have their qualifications clearly in mind. Teachers are frequently assigned to fields where they have insufficient training. Precautions should be taken when class sections are assigned to teachers; any necessary new appointees should be elected to fill existing combinations. In a small school where there is only one section of each subject, teachers may, of necessity, have to undertake as many different preparations as they teach classes. In larger schools it is often possible to give teachers class assignments requiring only one or two different preparations. Some teachers prefer one preparation, claiming that as a result they give more attention to the needs of individual students. Other teachers lose their enthusiasm before the end of the day if they are assigned five or six sections of the same subject. If conditions warrant, an assignment requiring two teacher preparations is a very satisfactory load. But whatever plan is adopted, teacher assignments must be made before the schedule of classes can be completed.

Ability Grouping

Another step in schedule-making is to decide whether or not pupils are to be grouped according to ability. Grouping by ability greatly increases the difficulty of schedule-making because it reduces the number of sections to which a pupil may be assigned without conflict.

Revising the Preliminary Registration

The list of failures must be checked against the preliminary registration. Pupils who fail in required courses or in a sequence course, such as English 10, must have their program changed so that they meet the requirements of the school or complete the prerequisite courses.

When the foregoing preliminary steps have been completed, the principal or the person designated by him may begin construction of the schedule. It is common practice to conduct the preliminary registration in May, completing the schedule during the summer. In any case, preliminary duties must be finished before school closes in June so that everything may be ready before school opens in September.

Group or Block Method

The group method is useful for platoon elementary schools and junior high schools where very little or no student election is allowed. The *block* system is reported to be used with success in small senior high schools where half or more of the program is required at each grade level.[3] It is sometimes usable in large senior high schools, but here it cannot be used completely or to great advantage in the upper grades because the wide variations in electives make it difficult if not impossible to classify all students into nonconflicting groups. The mosaic method, if used with a conflict sheet, is much easier to employ in four-year or senior high schools where students have a wide choice of electives—no matter what the enrollment. It is in such cases that a more precise method than the group system is probably less time-consuming.

The group system has been claimed by some writers to be so simple that it cares for nearly all of the difficulties of the schedule-maker. This claim may be true for the junior high school, but it is certainly not true for the senior high school. Conflicts in students' programs appear which necessitate changing individuals from one group to another. Differences in class size also necessitate changing students from one group to another.

Briefly, the group method consists of determining the number of groups of pupils taking the same combination of subjects and dividing them into the required number of sections. Pupils in each group are assigned to classes at different periods in the day.

Suppose seventy-eight students have registered for English 2, History 2, Algebra 1, and General Science. This will be enough students to form three blocks of twenty-six students each. The schedule-maker may then

---

[3]D. J. Eveslage, "Scheduling Balanced Classes," *National Association of Secondary School Principals Bulletin*, 172 (October 1950), 47.

select a series of periods for each block. For block 1, he could have English 2 the first period, History 2 the third period, Algebra 1 the fifth period, and General Science the seventh period. For block 2, he could have English 2 the second period, History 2 the fourth period, Algebra 1 the sixth period, and General Science the eighth period. For block 3, he could select English 2 the third period, History 2 the fifth period, Algebra 1 the seventh period, and General Science the first period.

The arrangement of these classes in the schedule is shown in Table 5.

The block method may well be called *group* schedule-making because the principal deals with groups of pupils rather than with individuals. *Group* schedule-making is a more accurate a term than *block*, which came into educational literature more than three decades ago. Both terms are given here to indicate that they are identical, but the authors prefer the term group schedule-making to the less precise term block.

Making a Junior High School Schedule

Suppose 195 boys and girls are enrolled in the seventh grade of a junior high school. It would be possible to assign approximately thirty-three students to each of six classes and arrange six nonconflicting groups of classes. In this way the schedule would be complete. Or a larger number could be assigned to the most able section, a smaller number to the least able section, and the average number to the middle sections. In junior high schools which have few or no electives, group scheduling may be combined with ability grouping without materially increasing the difficulties of schedule-making.

Electives in Group Scheduling

If all pupils are allowed one elective, as is often the case in junior high schools, one period of the day, say, the second hour, may be set aside for electives and the group schedules built around it. All students would then

Table 5

ARRANGEMENT OF THREE NON-
CONFLICTING GROUPS IN NINTH GRADE

Class	Block I	Period for Recitation Block II	Block III
English 2	1	2	3
History 2	3	4	5
Algebra 1	5	6	7
General Science	7	8	1

be assigned to the elective of their choice at the hour set aside for electives. This program allows for physical education classes of approximately fifty students of each sex, double-size music classes, and two sections of practical arts all meeting at the same time to allow a normal-size class for each sex. Classes in English, mathematics, and social science are distributed throughout the day.

The partial group or block program for the ninth grade of a junior high school provides block sections in English and social science. Three sections of physical education are scheduled at the same time to allow large-size classes for both boys and girls. The remainder of the schedule can be filled in by the mosaic method discussed in the next section. Such a partial group schedule has advantages in that it is easy to construct and can be used in connection with ability grouping if desired. It does not necessarily provide against oversize sections, as the individual pupil choices may necessitate moving a pupil from the section to which he was assigned. As an illustration of a combination program, the required sections are arranged by the group method and the elective classes are distributed by the mosaic method.

Criteria of Good Master Schedule

As long ago as 1947 Wilbur De Vilbiss published four criteria for a good master schedule which all high school principals should consider before calling the schedule satisfactory.[4] These criteria are:

1. To make it possible to provide and to administer the kind of learning experiences needed to implement the purposes of the school. This includes a flexible enough schedule to provide for common learnings and free activities.
2. To provide maximum utilization of all the human resources within the school for the benefit of the students. This includes both allowing the principal time for supervision as well as for management, and assigning teachers to subjects consistent with their training.
3. To provide the maximum utilization of all the physical resources of the school.
4. To facilitate an effective program of guidance.

Focusing attention on these criteria is insurance against overlooking them. The individual method of schedule-making described below provides that those factors which can be reduced to paper, such as equitable loads and maximum utilization of the physical plant, are checked at each step in the process.

---

[4]Wilbur De Vilbiss, "Criteria of a Good Master Schedule," *National Association of Secondary School Principals Bulletin*, 149 (November 1947), 31–38.

The Mosaic Method, or Individual Schedule-Making

The mosaic or individual schedule-making method consists of placing class sections on the schedule where the schedule-maker thinks there will be the fewest conflicts for the individual student. In utilizing the individual schedule-making system each of the class sections are placed on the master schedule until all sections have been assigned. The class sections then represent a mosaic or pattern built up by placing individual sections on the master schedule in random fashion. The term *mosaic* serves no useful purpose except that it is understood by many school administrators. The authors feel that *individual schedule-making* is a more accurate description of the process.

Individual schedule-making is a precise and simple method when used with a conflict sheet to prevent or reduce to an acceptable minimum the number of individual conflicts. Using the individual schedule-making method, class sections are placed on the master schedule one at a time, and the classes are so placed that *individual students may be scheduled for elected subjects without conflict,* or so the *conflicts have been reduced to an acceptable minimum.*

Conflicts

The problem of conflicts, or the impossibility of arranging an individual pupil's program to contain the subject combination he wishes, is the most difficult problem facing the schedule-maker. In making six schedules for each of ten schools, Puckett[5] found this to be the only major problem. Such items as difficulties in room or study-hall assignments, full sections, student changes in program, or difficulty in changing individuals from one section to another were almost nonexistent when the mosaic system and a conflict sheet were used. By the use of a conflict sheet, most of the conflict difficulties can be obviated. Puckett found 0.045 conflict per student in making three long-period (fifty-five or sixty minute classes without double periods) schedules for each of ten schools, and 0.08 conflict per student in making three short-period (forty to forty-five minute classes with some double periods) schedules for the same ten schools.[6] He was the first writer to indicate the value of the conflict sheet in making a schedule contain no or the minimum number of conflicts.

---

[5]"The Difficulties of Making a High School Schedule," pp. 38–39.
[6]Puckett, "The Difficulties of Making a High School Schedule," p. 41.

Constructing a Conflict Sheet

A conflict sheet simply lists subjects elected by students which will conflict if placed in the same period. If a student is taking English 2, History 2, Algebra 1, and General Science, placing of any two subjects at the same hour will produce a conflict. Theoretically, there are six possible conflicts:

English 2 with History 2 (1); with Algebra 1 (2); with General Science (3);
History 2 with Algebra 1 (4); with General Science (5);
Algebra 1 with General Science (6)

A simple conflict sheet for these four subjects is shown diagrammatically in Fig. 6. A study of this sample conflict sheet shows that English 2 and History 2 will conflict if placed at the same period (conflict 1); similarly, Algebra 1 and General Science will conflict if placed at the same period (conflict 6). Each single-section subject which will conflict must be placed at a different period of the day.

A complete conflict sheet lists all the subjects to be offered both horizontally along the top of the sheet and diagonally across the sheet. Only half the sheet is used (as is shown in Fig. 7) in order to eliminate a second set of squares and to make the sheet easier to work with.

ENGLISH 2	HISTORY 2	ALGEBRA 1	GENERAL SCIENCE
ENGLISH 2	(1)	(2)	(3)
	HISTORY 2	(4)	(5)
		ALGEBRA 1	(6)
			GENERAL SCIENCE

Fig. 6. A conflict sheet for English 2, History 2, Algebra 1, and General Science.

Time Needed to Prepare a Conflict Sheet

The preparation of a conflict sheet may at first look like a time-consuming process, but it is not necessarily so. A conflict sheet for a senior high school of 1,200 enrollment can be prepared in about four hours. A competent clerk can do it just as satisfactorily as the principal. It is not necessary to chart all the possible conflicts on every student's preliminary registration. Only the conflicts between the single-section classes need be plotted. For example, if a student is registered for English 12 (five sections), physics (three sections), Latin 3 (one section), and History 3 (one section), it is necessary to plot only the one conflict between History 3 and Latin 3. For an individual who wishes to enroll in English 12 (five sections), Chemistry (three sections), Printing (one section), and General Metal (two sections), there will be no conflicts to record, as he has only one single-section class. A few conflicts may be plotted between the classes which have many sections just to show that they do exist. This will also permit placement on the class sheet of the sections (twelfth, eleventh, or tenth grade) with which the subject conflicts most frequently in English. All conflicts are plotted on the conflict sheet reproduced in Fig. 7 by way of illustration, although this need not be done in actual practice. After the conflict sheet has been constructed, class sections can then be placed on the schedule.

In a senior high school of 1,200 enrollment, the construction of the schedule itself should require not more than two hours. With the conflict sheet before him, *the principal knows how he may best arrange the schedule; without the conflict sheet, schedule-making is guesswork.* It is entirely possible to make a schedule for a senior high school of 1,500 enrollment without a single conflict, although this does not ordinarily occur. It should be possible for anyone who exercises care to build a schedule for a high school of 1,000 students without more than six or eight conflicts. If a program cannot be made without conflicts, one constructed with a conflict sheet will contain the minimum number.

I. J. Reiste[7] published a method of schedule-making which he indicated would eliminate the need for a conflict sheet. In this system, tabs are affixed to the edge of students' registration cards to indicate selection of subjects. These tabs have holes punched in them. By placing the cards on edge in a tray, it is possible to insert a needle or pick through the holes of all cards which are tabbed for a given single subject, say, German 3. One can then see by inspection whether or not another single-section class, say, French 4, placed on the tentative schedule at the same period as German

---

[7] I. J. Reiste, "Simplified Schedule-Making," *School Executive*, LVII (June 1943), 22–23.

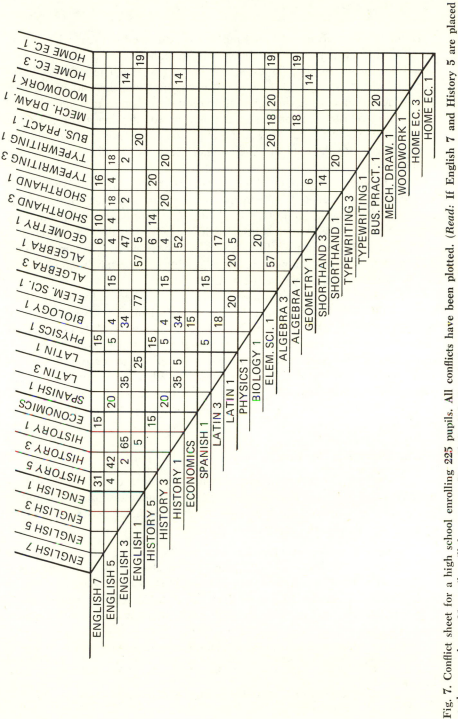

Fig. 7. Conflict sheet for a high school enrolling **225** pupils. All conflicts have been plotted. (*Read:* If English **7** and History **5** are placed at the same hour, **31** pupils will have a conflict; if English **7** and Economics are placed at the same hour, **15** will have a conflict, and so on.)

3, conflicts with it. If no tabs for French 4 are attached to the cards of those enrolled in German 3, no conflict exists. If conflicts exist, one proceeds exactly as was described in using the conflict sheet. The method is ingenious, but in reality it is a mechanical conflict sheet instead of a paper one. Whether or not the time and effort required to place tabs on students' preliminary registrations are less arduous than for making a conflict sheet remains to be determined. This method has one advantage in small schools: it shows *who* has the conflict. The conflict sheet shows only that there is a conflict.

L. G. Feldman developed a variation of the tab system by which the subjects are punched out.[8] When the keysorter is inserted in holes in the cards representing the subjects, those which have not been punched out fall into a tray. If the keysorter is inserted in French, the cards of all the students who desire to enroll in French remain, since that hole is punched out. This system does not show conflict as readily as the tab method, but a conflict sheet could, of course, be constructed.

Leo Ivok once described a way to prepare a schedule for a small high school which eliminates conflicts and prevents misplacing a single student, or class section, and allows control of teacher-assignment.[9] It is a method of posting all selections on a single sheet so that when classes are scheduled, inspection of the sheet indicates a conflict if period one or two or six appears twice following any group of students. While Ivok did not call his Pupil Studies Sheet a conflict sheet, it serves that function and permits the preparation of a schedule without conflicts or at least with a minimum of conflicts.

Factors Affecting Conflicts

There are a number of factors which increase conflicts and consequently make schedule-making more difficult. Puckett studied the matter intensively by analyzing the difficulties involved in making six schedules for each of ten schools. His conclusions regarding conflicts were:

1. Adding a double-period subject to a pupil's schedule will nearly always increase difficulties. Adding a single-period class to an individual's program will not necessarily cause a greater number of conflicts.[10]

2. There were almost 50 percent fewer conflicts in schools using the long period (fifty-five or sixty minutes) with no double periods as against

---

[8]Feldman, "Programming Classes by Means of a Punch Card System," pp. 25–28.

[9]Leo Ivok, "How To Prepare the Schedule for a Secondary School," *Harvard Workshop Series No. 5.* (Cambridge, Mass.: Harvard Graduate School of Education, 1944).

[10]Puckett, "The Difficulties of Making a High School Schedule," p. 47.

schools using short periods (forty or forty-five minutes) with some subjects meeting for double periods.[11]

3. Students who have irregular schedules, that is, who take subjects not ordinarily offered in their grade (probably because of previous failure), have many more conflicts per hundred students than a similar number of pupils whose elections are regular. For regular students scheduled in long periods (without double periods), the average number of conflicts was 0.013; for the irregular students in the same schools under the same conditions, the average number of conflicts was 0.159, or twelve times as many conflicts per student.[12]

If conflicts exist for a few individuals, in spite of all efforts to eliminate difficulties, it is a relatively simple matter to call the students concerned and have them make substitute choices before school opens.

Making the Schedule

It is advisable in making a schedule to list the hours horizontally across the top of the page and the teachers' names vertically along the left edge, as Table 6 shows. The partial schedule of classes is for the twelfth grade. The complete schedule for a school of this size, about 800, would contain many more classes in science, home economics, and other subjects.

It is advisable to work with one class at a time, beginning with the highest grade, since the problem of conflicts is likely to be most serious at the upper level. The single-section classes are first placed in the various periods of the day, spread as widely apart as is possible. If two single-section classes are assigned to a given period (say, French 4 and Printing) the schedule-maker looks at the conflict sheet to determine whether any conflicts will result. None did, in the case of Table 6, so both were placed at 2:30. German 2, Latin 3, and French 4 were all placed at different periods, since placing any two in any one period would result in conflicts, as determined from the conflict sheet.

Scheduling One Grade at a Time

After the senior class schedule has been constructed, the other classes should be scheduled in order. It is easier to use a fresh sheet for each grade, ruled, as was done for the senior class, to allow for marking off those periods where classes have been assigned to teachers. If this is not done, a teacher may be assigned two classes at the same hour.

Before the schedule is made for a second grade, the partial chart might

---

[11]Puckett, "The Difficulties of Making a High School Schedule," p. 53.
[12]Puckett, "The Difficulties of Making a High School Schedule," p. 52.

PARTIAL SCHEDULE FOR TWELFTH-GRADE CLASS

Table 6

Teacher	Room	Period 1	Period 2	Period 3	Period 4	Period 5	Period 6
Adams	201		Eng. 8		Eng. 8		
Bork	202				Eng. 8		Eng. 8
Smith	203	Eng. 8		Eng. 8		Eng. 8	
Walters	212	Soc. Sc. 12	Soc. Sc. 12	Soc. Sc. 12		Soc. Sc. 12	
To be secured	213		Soc. Sc. 12		Soc. Sc. 12	Soc. Sc. 12	
Rosecrans	301			Latin 3[a]			
Emerson	118	Home Econ. 12[a]					
Kramer	312				German 2[a]		
Mallory	300		F. Art 3[a]				
Wright	313						French 4[a]
Torgenson	137	Auto. Mech.	Auto. Mech.	Auto. Mech.		Auto. Mech.	Auto. Mech.
Jordahl	138						Printing[a]

[a]Single-section classes which are scheduled first.

look something like Table 7, showing that some teacher is occupied each hour. It should be emphasized that this is a partial chart. A completed chart would show a greater number of check marks—approximately the same number each period.

When a schedule for each grade has been made, all may be combined into a master schedule and schedule-making is completed.

It is now desirable to make a room assignment sheet to prevent the assignment of two or more classes to the same room at the same hour. A partial room assignment sheet is given in Table 8. In this school it is necessary to assign certain classes to certain rooms because of the classroom libraries employed in instruction. Consequently teachers in some cases use several rooms, depending on their individual assignments. If a room is needed at any hour, it is possible to refer to the room assignment sheet to determine if it is available. When rooms are used all day, so that teachers cannot use them when they are not teaching, working space may be provided by fitting up a classroom with desks or tables so that teachers may work there during their nonteaching hours.

Assigning Students to Class Sections

Some schools allow students to choose their recitation sections and teachers until certain sections are full. Those who are late in arranging for

Table 7

PARTIAL SCHEDULE FOR AN ELEVENTH-
GRADE CLASS, SHOWING SOME
PERIODS ASSIGNED

				Period			
Teacher	*Room*	*1*	*2*	*3*	*4*	*5*	*6*
Adams	201		X		X		
Bork	202				X		X
Smith	203	X		X		X	
To be secured	213		X		X	X	
Walters	212	X	X	X		X	
Rosecrans	301		X				
Kramer	312				X		
Mallory	300		X				
Wright	313						X
Torgenson	137	X	X	X		X	X
Emerson	118	X					
Jordahl	138						X

their final assignment are assigned to classes where they can be accommodated. Such a procedure may be necessary if no clerical help is available for making out individual programs during the summer. The common procedure, however, is to have the student's program arranged for him without consultation. This method becomes more common as the size of the school increases.

In assigning students to classes, it is desirable to alternate study and class periods so that an individual's class schedule may be spread throughout the day. Some schools allow the student to make out his own schedules until certain sections are filled. Late-comers take what is left. In such a registration procedure, it is necessary to have clerks or teachers keep tabulations of class size and, if enough help is available, make class lists for teachers for the opening day of the new semester.

Ordinarily the schedule is arranged by clerks under the direction of a teacher or the assistant principal. B. C. Gustavson reported a system in use in Erie, Pennsylvania, where much of the clerical work is done by the students in the office practice class under direction of the teacher.[13] When

Table 8

ROOM ASSIGNMENT SHEET

	Period					
Room	1	2	3	4	5	6
137	Torgenson	Torgenson	Torgenson		Torgenson	Torgenson
118	Emerson	White	White	White	Emerson	White
138	Jordahl	Jordahl	Jordahl		Jordahl	Jordahl
201	Adams	Adams	Adams	Adams		Adams
202		Bork	Bork	Bork	Bork	Bork
203	Smith	Wrenn	Smith	Wrenn	Smith	Wrenn
212	Walters	Walters		Walters	Walters	Walters
213	Link	Link	Link		Link	Link
300	Mallory	Mallory	Duncan	Mallory	Mallory	Mallory
301	Rosecrans	Hunt	Hunt	Hunt	Hunt	Hunt
312	Goss	Goss	Goss	Kramer	Goss	Goss
313	Wright		Wright	Wright	Wright	Wright

NOTE: This table is a partial assignment sheet for a high school which has 35 teachers.

---

[13]Gustavson, "20th Century Schedule Making," pp. 43–44.

students are assigned to classes, some provision must be made to assign them to library or study halls for vacant periods.

In order to equalize class sections, it is advisable to keep a tabulation of students assigned to class sections. When it is apparent that some sections are being rapidly filled and others are nearly empty, the person in charge of scheduling must assign more students to the small sections so that the loads are balanced. If the assignments are not approximately equal, enough students must be rescheduled to balance class sizes.

There are many ways of keeping tabulations and making up class lists. Probably the most common is a single tally sheet for tabulations and a series of class lists arranged by departments. Gustavson reported good success in having the girls in the office practice class prepare the individual students' programs and the class lists under supervision of the assistant principal.[14]

Notifying Students

Shortly before the opening of school, students should either receive their programs by mail or be notified where to appear on the first day to receive their schedules. New students should be requested to appear for classification and assignment before the opening day of school. There will, of course, be stragglers who appear each day during the first week, but if the procedure described in this chapter is followed, it is possible to open school on the first day with a real feeling of continuity.

One of the trying problems for the schedule-maker is the influx of a large number of unexpected students. This should not happen in a city if the secondary school head, or his representative, regularly visits the contributing elementary schools and junior high schools to secure preliminary registration from the students enrolled there. If there is an unexpected influx, the extra students are usually distributed evenly to existing classes, although at times extra teachers must be hired to care for the unexpected increases. Careful preliminary registration is the best preventive for such difficulties at the opening of the new term; however, in city schools which draw from rural areas adjacent to them, it is all but impossible to forecast the rural enrollment accurately.

In schools which have transient student populations, the process is the same but less orderly. If 25 percent of the students who register in May do not return in September, or if a third of the student body which appears in September was not resident in May, the opening of school will present many problems. Quite probably the new students will not select the same subjects chosen by those who did not return, although there will be major similari-

---

[14]Gustavson, "20th Century Schedule Making," pp. 43–44.

ties, due to the requirements for graduation. Thus, it may be that new sections will need to be formed, or that single sections previously scheduled must be cancelled because the enrollment does not justify offering the class. The processes described are all pertinent, but the opening days will be less orderly than in a settled community.

Making a Schedule by Machine

In the Bloomington, Indiana High School, F. L. Templeton[15] made a schedule by punching the information regarding each student's schedule on Hollerith cards (see Figs. 8 and 9) and using IBM machines available through the University of Indiana. Many other schools now use this method.

After the punching was done, the cards were sorted by machine; the required number of sections in history, shop, drawing, and so on were formed; and the numbers of the individuals assigned to each section were printed by the machine.

A conflict sheet may be profitably prepared for machine schedule-making. When the choices of each student have been punched on cards, it is possible to run the cards through a sorting machine to secure the basic data for compiling a conflict sheet. The advantage of machine tabulation is that, after the information has been punched, the number of times that any two subjects would conflict may be counted by the machine and entered as a total on the conflict sheet. The possibility of human error in tabulating the conflicts is eliminated, an advantage that cannot be guaranteed manu-

---

[15]F. L. Templeton, "The Use of IBM Techniques in Program-Making and Class Scheduling," *National Association of Secondary School Principals Bulletin*, 172 (October 1950), 15–22.

Fig. 8. Card for machine schedule-making. (Courtesy of International Business Machines Corporation.)

REPRESENTATIVE HIGH SCHOOL
PUPIL'S STUDY PROGRAM

PUPIL'S NAME	OFFICIAL CLASS	HOME ROOM
BAER SAMUEL	7 2	276

CLASS	PERIOD	SECT'N	NO. HRS.	SUBJECT	TEACHER	ROOM	DAYS OF THE WEEK				
							MON	TUE	WED	THU	FRI
4	1	3	2	S H O P	W A L K E R	1 0 1	*		*		*
4	1	2	2	D R A W I N G	C O L L I N S	1 1 3		*		*	
7	3		1	M A T H	F R E E M A N	3 1 1					
4	4		1	T H E O R Y	L I T T L E	2 0 4					
6	5		1	E N G L I S H	S M I T H	3 0 2					
	6			L U N C H							
6	7		1	H I S T O R Y	W H I T T I E R	2 0 2			*		*
6	8	3	1	H E A L T H E D	B L A C K	2 1 3	*	*		*	
	8		1	S T U D Y	C L E W I S	A 1					

Fig. 9. Pupil's study program. (Courtesy of International Business Machines Corporation.)

ally. The time required for the machine to compute the totals for the conflict sheet is probably less than that required to prepare the conflict sheet manually.

Templeton avoids conflicts in single-period classes by checking the number of elections of other subjects on the class list.[16] This is possible because the machine prints the designation of all other students in a selected class on each list. If there are conflicts, one single-section class or the other is moved to another period. If there are not enough periods to avoid all conflicts, the schedule-maker reduces the number to a minimum and has the few students involved make other choices. In this way he has a tabular conflict sheet instead of a chart.

When either a tabular or chart (Fig. 7, page 91) conflict sheet has been constructed, the principal may make the master schedule exactly as described earlier in this chapter. A master schedule may be made which contains no conflicts or in which conflicts have been reduced to the absolute minimum. From that point on, the Hollerith machine takes over. Each individual student's program may be printed and the class lists prepared with duplicates for the office. Not only will time be saved, but the possibility of clerical error will be eliminated, since the machine is not subject to distractions or forgetfulness as human beings always are. If there are a few conflicts which cannot be cared for, the cards of those individual students will

---

[16]Templeton, "The Use of IBM Techniques," p. 21.

be sorted by the machine. These individuals must be reregistered exactly as described earlier in the chapter. The conflict sheet cannot prevent conflicts; it merely reduces them to the minimum number, whether the schedule is made by machine or by hand. The advantage of a machine-made conflict table is that it shows who has the conflict. The handmade conflict chart only shows that conflict exists.

Schedule-making by machine is still subject to refinement and has great possibilities for development in cities where Hollerith machines are available in the central office for other purposes or in the service bureaus of the International Business Machines Corporation which are located in over 100 cities. By arranging the time needed to perform the other tasks expected of the machines, it should be possible to make all the high school schedules in the city with a considerable saving in the amount of clerical time spent in the details of schedule-making. One great benefit of machine scheduling is that errors cannot creep into mechanical tabulation and printing as they almost always do when human beings make hundreds or thousands of entries. If card punching is done accurately—and the punching must be checked carefully for accuracy—the possibility of human error ceases with the beginning of the machine's work. Unfortunately, the possibility of use is at present restricted to schools which have access to these service bureaus. For most of the 29,000 high schools in the United States, the mosaic or individual method with the use of the conflict sheet still provides the most practicable means today.

Variable Modular Scheduling*

More than a dozen years ago, J. Lloyd Trump, Robert Bush, and Dwight Allen first suggested that educational objectives might be better met if schools were organized to allow variations in the size of classes, as well as in the length of time these classes met. Trump first suggested that some phases of instruction might best happen in small groups of ten to fifteen, some in larger groups of one hundred or more and that some part of the students' time should be devoted to independent study. He further suggested that the amount of time allotted to these different instructional modes should vary. Trump and Bush and Allen further suggested that the instructional pattern should vary with the subject matter, and that teachers should have the responsibility for deciding how to best design a specific course.

Because the notion allowed teachers flexibility, the term *flexible scheduling* became attached to these new organizational patterns and has

---

*This section was prepared by Ray Talbert, Educational Coordinates Northwest, Salem, Oregon, for the authors, who accept full responsibility for it.

since come to represent almost any kind of schedule where there is some deviation from the standard schedule. Actually flexible scheduling is a contradiction in itself, since flexible means not set or capable of being changed, and schedule connotes a fixed pattern. This contradiction makes this term inappropriate as a descriptive phrase. A second term which has often been used in connection with an organizational pattern which allows variations in class size and length is *modular schedule.* The term module applies to a unit of time shorter than the standard fifty to fifty-five minute period, and may be used, then, much like a building block in order to vary the length of class meetings.

Rather than divide a six-hour school day into six periods of time, a school on a modular schedule might divide the school day into 18 twenty-minute periods or modules. (This term also lacks precision, since a school on a standard or traditional schedule could be said to operate on a modular schedule, each module being one hour in length.) Schedules which are designed to support the variable course structures being designed by teachers are more appropriately called variable modular schedules. The term VMS will be used to refer to the type of scheduling which supports variable course structuring by teachers.

The number of schools adopting this type of scheduling is steadily increasing, but is still relatively small; approximately 250 schools used it at the time this chapter was written.

The notion that different lengths of time and different sizes of groups might be more effective and efficient is by no means a new idea in education. The double-period for laboratory courses has been used in school schedules for decades. The development of the traditional schedule of classes one hour in length, group size of approximately thirty meeting five days a week has developed largely because of its "schedulability" rather than its appropriateness for instruction. Any school schedule-maker who has attempted to deviate from this standard way of scheduling quickly becomes aware of the number of variables which make schedule building extremely complex.

Computerized Master Schedule Construction

In the early 1960s a few schools in the country attempted to build schedules manually in order to implement the educational designs being advocated by Trump and Bush and Allen. Also at this time professors Robert Oakford of Stanford University and Robert Holz of MIT, acting independently, decided to see if a computer program could be developed which would not only assign students to a manually constructed schedule, but would also generate or build the master schedule as well. The result was the development of two successful computer programs, the Stanford School

Scheduling System (SSSS) and Generalized Academic Simulation Program (GASP). The large majority of schools operating on a VMS have their schedules developed by one of these programs.

A complete description of a computerized scheduling system would be too lengthy to include here, but a brief description of the basic components of the Stanford School Scheduling System will clarify how these systems operate.

1. *Input Data.* The system provides forms for recording the information needed for schedule construction. This information is the same as needed for manual construction. The structure of the courses is determined together with teacher and room assignments. Students' course requests are recorded and all data, properly coded, are punched on data processing cards.

2. *Card Audit.* The punched cards are read and checked for detectable errors and inconsistencies. When all errors have been eliminated, the audit program prepares a data set for input to the scheduling program.

3. *Scheduling Program.* This program computes the schedule of class meetings by processing the data. Each course in the school has, at this point in the program, been ordered in terms of its schedulability. The scheduling program proceeds down this list, course by course, determining where it can best meet during the cycle. First the program determines the time during the cycle the teacher assigned to the course is available. All possible times are established and compared to the times the room assigned to the course is available. These times, then, are those the teacher and room are jointly available; they are possible times for the course to be scheduled. Next the program considers the availability of students enrolled in the courses, and places the section or sections of the course into the schedule in order to maximize the probability of students being scheduled.

   At this point, because various changes may be necessary in order to improve the original schedule developed, changes may be made in course structure, teacher assignments, and so forth, and a second schedule may be generated.

4. *Student Assignment Program.* Students who were not completely assigned to courses in the scheduling production run are assigned to courses by this program.

5. *Translate.* This program produces the completed schedule on forms, including the master schedule, a complete set of class lists, and sets of teacher, room, and student schedules.

Both **SSSS** and **GASP** are available for use through educational consulting firms who have obtained the original programs and have improved or refined them.

Special Considerations

The biggest departure from a standard school schedule is the inclusion of unscheduled time in the school day. Actually this unscheduled time should be thought of as time which hasn't been scheduled—yet. This is the flexible part of the schedule—the time available for varied use. According to what is most appropriate for the individual student, unscheduled or unstructured time may be used for student-teacher conferences, student tutoring, independent study projects, extended time in labs and shop projects, mini-courses, student socialization, remedial work, work experience, and so on. In the broadest sense, this time is to be used to meet the specific needs of individuals.

It is of considerable importance that a school planning to implement VMS give particular attention to the promises and pitfalls of unscheduled time. The promise of VMS is that flexible time should assist in the realization of the goal of individualizing instruction. The pitfall is that for many it can become free time—perceived to be unrelated to instruction and learning. This pitfall is less likely to occur where the attitude is developed that the time is available to be scheduled by teachers and by students, time that is flexible, and will be used in different ways by students. The staff needs to learn to see unstructured time as an integral part of each student's instructional program, time in which they have a better opportunity to work on an individual basis with students.

There will be some students in any school who have a psychological need for structure and cannot, at least initially, function in the VMS environment. Teachers and counselors need to identify quickly those students who, by their behavior or achievement, indicate the need to have regularly scheduled time built back into their schedules.

Implementing a Variable Modular Schedule

A school's educational program contains three basic components: the curriculum, the people, and the organization of the resources involved in teaching and learning the curriculum. The various factors included in these each of three components are highly related. The success of changes brought about in any component depends largely on the extent to which appropriate changes are initiated in the other two.

It is most important to recognize that VMS gives a school the opportunity to use its resources to support its educational rationale. This implies the use of new roles for teachers and students, and opportunity for a wider choice of curricula. Obviously course content which does not meet the needs of students will not automatically become relevant with a change in course structure. A class composed of twelve students does not become a small group with a high level of student involvement unless the teacher utilizes small group discussion techniques. Students will not necessarily utilize effectively time provided for independent study just because the time is available. But VMS at least provides a vehicle for effective change to occur.

As suggested above, the implementation of a VMS requires substantial changes in teacher and student behavior and in curriculum organization. Of particular importance is the implication this holds for the principal as the manager of school. It may be helpful to the principal to look for a moment at the experience of management in industry and at the writings of management theorists.

Industry has long recognized that in a dynamic and changing society there must be an organization (or system) which has both the stability to carry out its day-to-day functions effectively and the ability to modify the system to meet new demands. There is inherently a conflict between status-quo-oriented factors and change-oriented factors, but a company needs both orientations if it is to survive.

School systems have tended to be very stable systems, perpetuating structures and management systems which are status quo, rather than change, oriented. But a school operating on VMS has opted for a change-oriented system. The principal is faced with the need for management skills valuable in any type of system, but which are now of paramount importance. Four of the most essential organizational components which need to be developed are (1) clarification of goals and objectives, (2) problem-solving and decision-making skills, (3) effective communications, and (4) evaluation designs. Mathew Miles[17] has suggested that the first innovation undertaken by a school system might well be to become healthy in these and other factors he describes as important components of a healthy organization.

These points have been presented before continuing the discussion of the VMS and its implementation and operation because we are aware of schools which have initiated VMS and were apparently unaware of these issues. Under such circumstances the outcome was that at best the program fell far short of its potential.

Goal Identification

The first step to be taken in a VMS is to engage the staff in a rigorous examination of their beliefs about the purposes of education in a democratic society, the nature of learning, the nature of students and the community. Then collectively the staff must determine their beliefs and goals. When the

---

[17]Mathew Miles, *Change Processes in the Public Schools*, CASEA (Eugene Ore.: University of Oregon, 1965), pp. 11–34.

staff takes the time to analyze their educational goals carefully and determine how best they can be accomplished, the prospects for significantly improved education is greatly increased. Abraham H. Maslow makes this emphatic statement about goal clarification:

> It seems absolutely clear to me that in an enterprise, if everybody concerned is absolutely clear about the goals and directives and far purposes of the organization, practically all other questions become simple technical questions of fitting means to the ends. But it is also true to the extent that these far goals are confused or conflicting or ambivalent or only partially understood, then all the discussion of techniques and methods and means in the world will have little value.[18]

When a school decides on a VMS the school personnel must be able to say that they are organizing the school in this way because they believe this is the best way to accomplish their stated goals.

With the examination of educational beliefs, the clarification of learning strategies, and so on, it is desirable for the staff to be engaged in skill development in decision-making and problem-solving strategies. A number of educational agencies have developed training packages and have competent and skilled consultants available to work with school personnel to develop these skills.

Deciding on Course Structure

The concept of VMS expands many of the components of a standard schedule. Generally accepted terms have developed which apply to these components.

Cycle. A standard school schedule is generally constructed with a one-day instructional cycle. All subjects in the curriculum are taught each day. Usually the instructional cycle coincides with the days of the week. Most schools using a VMS operate on a five-day instructional cycle. Class meetings occur during this week, not necessarily on succeeding days. Week two in the schedule is a repeat of week one. Many schools have adopted a six-day (or more) instructional cycle. An instructional cycle which does not coincide with the days of the week may present some organizational problems, but has other advantages.

Course phase. Courses in a standard schedule are one-phase courses. In one-phase schedules, courses meet each day for the same length of time with the same number of students in the group. Course phasing is the essence of the VMS. Groups can vary in size and composition; class meetings

---

[18]Abraham H. Maslow, *Eupsychian Management: A Journal* (Homewood, Illinois: Richard D. Irwin, Inc. and The Dorsey Press, 1965), p. 41.

can vary in length and purpose. A science teacher may decide, for example, that the four modes of instruction he would like to utilize are:

1. All students enrolled in the course meet together once a cycle for forty minutes for some type of presentation.
2. Each student has one eighty minute laboratory period per cycle.
3. Each student meets once a cycle in a seminar or discussion group of ten to twelve students. Discussion groups are sixty minutes in length.
4. Each student has 120 minutes a week available for independent study, teacher conferences, additional laboratory time, and so forth.

This course is now for scheduling purposes a three-phase course; that is, it consists of a large group phase, a laboratory phase, and a discussion group phase. The total amount of time the student is assigned to classes during the cycle is three hours. Each student has two hours during the cycle of unscheduled or unstructured available time. These two hours are to be used in whatever way meets the particular needs of each student best.

Unscheduled Time

Experience with the development of VMS has established that successful schedules cannot be built unless both teachers and students have time during the cycle when they are not scheduled to meet in classes. The degree to which unscheduled time is necessary depends on the complexity of the schedule and other variables which tend to make schedule construction difficult. Successful schedules can normally be built if students and teachers have an average of between 30 and 40 percent of their instructional time unscheduled.

The introduction of unscheduled time into VMS is undoubtedly its most controversial aspect. Schools operating on VMS maintain that such available time in the instructional cycle gives a school real potential for individualizing instruction and allowing students a variety of alternatives they would not have otherwise. The basic idea is to allow students the option of doing whatever is most appropriate during their unscheduled time.

Although schools operating on VMS vary considerably, the following list of alternatives is available to students, and is probably typical of any school with VMS. A student may:

1. Study in any of the subject matter resource centers.
2. Work in any of the science open labs.
3. Work out in the gym.
4. Confer with an available teacher.
5. See a counselor.
6. Work in typing, business machines, shorthand, any of the industrial arts shops, the language lab, or the home economics lab.

7. Take a break in the student union.
8. Enroll in a special interest (mini-) course.
9. Engage in off-campus work experience.
10. View audio-visual material in the audio-visual center.
11. Receive special help in the reading clinic.
12. Work as a teacher aide.
13. Engage in tutoring programs.
14. Audit a class.
15. Attend a special lecture by staff, students, or members of the community.
16. Engage in any of the in-depth individual projects in any area of interest.
17. Receive remedial instruction in small groups or on a one-to-one basis.

In the strictest sense, then, VMS does not contain unscheduled time. It is, rather, an issue of *when* a student's time is scheduled and by or with whom. The intent of VMS is that each day both students and teachers have time available which can be used to the best instructional advantage.

It is also important to mention that the constructive use of unscheduled time takes commitment on the part of the school staff. Teachers must see this time as an integral part of their instructional strategy and plan for it to be used advantageously—by teachers and students.

Schools operating on VMS state that in addition to providing a wide choice of instructional alternatives to students, unscheduled time gives students the opportunity to develop skills in self-discipline and self-direction.

Accountability

A variable modular schedule places unique demands upon the staff and the students. The staff must exhibit the highest level of professional responsibility, including the ability to function as an integrated team. Students must play an increasingly larger part in planning and carrying out their learning responsibilities. Attendance accountability is one area where this becomes immediately evident.

The standard or traditional schedule design makes it possible to implement an attendance-checking procedure which allows the school to determine effectively whether or not students are in their assigned places each hour. A VMS with its emphasis on student choice and flexibility in the use of time has in effect placed a higher priority on a learning design than on attendance. Generally, schools using VMS continue to utilize standard attendance-checking procedures. Such procedures are harder to use and, therefore, tend to be less efficient.

In any school, regardless of the type of schedule, consistent attendance problems are a problem only for a small percentage of the total student body, but these attendance problems become very apparent in a school with VMS. The only effective solution is to devote considerable attention to each student to determine the cause for his lack of attendance.

Attendance problems cannot be solved alone by those normally responsible for such troubles, that is, by counselors and others assigned to the area of difficulty. Schools have found it effective practice to have individual staff members assume special responsibility for a few students to whom they relate particularly well. Each teacher also assumes increased responsibility for students who have a poor attendance record in his courses. Teachers seek absentees out as soon as possible after the absence has occurred to discuss the reasons for it. The issue becomes one of the teacher showing concern and caring about the student's academic progress. Punitive action is rarely successful; honest concern and interest in the student's welfare is more likely to get positive results.

It has become apparent that the degree of success realized in implementing a variable modular schedule is dependent largely upon two factors. One is the extent to which each staff member understands and accepts the educational rationale supporting the schedule, and the other is the extent to which he carries out his professional responsibilities. It is important that each staff member recognize the degree to which others depend on him, and realize that the success of the entire program depends on his accountability to some degree.

Schools using VMS are generally change-oriented schools. Schools using this system need a principal who is recognized as a risk-taker. He must be a principal who supports the change efforts of his staff and furthermore, who supports their failures. VMS requires a principal who has learned to use the staff, the students, and the public in the ongoing process of making decisions and finding solutions to problems which cannot be identified until the system is in operation. He must be a principal who has thought through VMS with the faculty, has stated their beliefs about education and learning, has learned how to exert influence to provide leadership to assist the staff, students, and public to work together to achieve their common goal—the most effective educational program possible for each student.

Selected References

ALLINGTON, B., "Noon-Activities: Effective Scheduling of Lunch and Recreation," *Clearing House*, XXV (January 1951), 295–97.

BEGGS, DAVID W., *Decatur-Lakeview High School: A Practical Application of the Trump Plan.* Englewood Cliffs, N.J.: Prentice-Hall, Inc., 1968.

BUSHNELL, DON D., and DWIGHT W. ALLEN, *The Computer in American Education.* New York: John Wiley and Sons, Inc., 1967.

COOMBS, ARTHUR M., ROBERT F. MADGIC, ROBERT V. OAKFORD, TOSHIO SATO and RAY L. TALBERT, *Variable Modular Scheduling, Effective Use of School Time, Plant, and Personnel.* New York: Benziger Brothers, Inc., 1971.

DAVIS, J. C., and D. L. SIMON, "Class Schedules of Large High Schools in Indiana," *National Association of Secondary School Principals Bulletin,* 149 (November 1947), 22–24.

FELDMAN, L. G., "Programming Classes by Means of a Punch Card System," *National Association of Secondary School Principals Bulletin,* 172 (October 1950), 23–28.

GRUENLER, A. M., "Schedule Making for an Overcrowded Junior High School," *National Association of Secondary School Principals Bulletin,* 172 (October 1950), 29–32.

GUSTAVSON, B. C., "20th Century Schedule-Making," *National Association of Secondary School Principals Bulletin,* 172 (October 1950), 33–46.

IVOK, LEO, "How to Prepare the Schedule for a Secondary School," *Harvard Workshop Series No. 5.* Cambridge: Harvard Graduate School of Education, 1944.

JOHNSTON, R. L., "What Scheduling Practices Have Become Most Effective in Today's School?" *National Association of Secondary School Principals Bulletin,* 186 (April 1952), 189–91.

MANLEY, C. BENTON, and CHARLES C. HOLT, "What Is the Case for and Against Machine Techniques for School Scheduling?" *National Association of Secondary School Principals Bulletin,* 43 (April 1959), 195–98.

OTTO, HENRY J., *Elementary School Organization and Administration.* New York: Appleton-Century-Crofts, 1954.

PETREQUIN, GAYNOR, *Individualizing Learning Through Modular-Flexible Programming.* New York: McGraw-Hill Book Company, 1968.

Progressing Toward Better Schools, 3rd Report on Staff Utilization Studies, *National Association of Secondary School Principals Bulletin,* 253 (January 1960), 9–346.

PUCKETT, R. C., "The Difficulties of Making a High School Schedule," Unpublished Doctoral theses in Education (II), *University of Iowa Studies in Education,* IX, No. 3 (April 1934), 33–59.

SILBERMAN, CHARLES, *Crisis in the Classroom.* New York: Random House, Inc., 1970.

SMITH, W. S., "The Conflict Sheet Aids Scheduling," *Nation's Schools,* XXXVII (June 1946), 46.

TRUMP, J. LLOYD, *Images of the Future.* Urbana, Ill.: Commission on Experimental Study of the Utilization of Staff in Secondary Schools, 1959.

WALDMANN, A. JOHN, "Promising Practices in Senior High School Class-Scheduling," *National Association of Secondary School Principals Bulletin,* 178 (April 1951), 26–28.

WILEY, W. DEANE, and LLOYD K. BISHOP, *The Flexibly Scheduled High School.* West Nyack: Parker Publishing Company, Inc., 1968.

5

PPBS and
The Public School Principal*

Public school educators have been thoroughly challenged during the post-World War II era. Immediately following the war, they were forced to meet the occupational demands of a rapidly expanding and increasingly technological economy. In the early 1950s, they were required to develop crash programs that would build sufficient classrooms to hold an exploding school-age population. Later in the decade, Sputnik and the resulting race to space placed America's public school system clearly on the defensive and stimulated a vigorous reassessment of its goals and priorities. And throughout the sixties, both administrators and teachers faced unprecedented demands for curricular and instructional change, both in the public school and on the university campus. Educational television, the new math and new science, teamteaching, computer-assisted instruction, and the development of the middle school were just highlights in the efforts made by public school personnel to meet postwar demands for innovation.

Undergirding all these efforts to innovate was a highly unrealistic view of educational research, for both the popular mass media and professional literature touted research as the key to educational reform, and created an expectation of revolutionary change in the nation's public schools. Naturally, when the expected change did not materialize, as the early 1970s have made all too clear, public disenchantment set in, research suffered, and school administrators and teachers became caught in a debilitating crossfire of continuing demands for change, growing charges of apathy, and mounting pressures for accountability.

---

*This chapter was written by Terry L. Eidell and John M. Nagle and is based in part on the authors' work as research associates in the Center for the Advanced Study of Educational Administration, University of Oregon. It has been edited by the authors, who endorse it wholeheartedly.

The fact is that research in any field produces only small increments of knowledge about an infinitely complex world; this is particularly true when that research deals with human behavior and learning. Given enough time, these incremental gains in knowledge may have some salutary effect upon practical situations, but school personnel generally agree that research in the behavioral sciences typically has little immediate bearing on the actual day-to-day operation of schools. Moreover, as a result of the disillusioning experiences of the last two decades, schoolmen have learned a number of things about stimulating change in the schools. They have learned, for instance, that neither instructional, curricular, nor organizational change can occur in isolation from one another, and that a systemic view of educational organizations is not only advisable, but mandatory. They have learned that change takes time, energy, and money—much more than ever expected. They have discovered that change cannot be successfully brought about through mandate and imposition, particularly in educational organizations where curricular and instructional innovations are almost totally dependent upon the attitudes and behaviors of individual teachers and administrators. And they have learned that the problems associated with change in schools are not radically different from those encountered in many other kinds of formal organizations. As a result, the possibility of borrowing innovations which have proven successful in other organizational settings is more and more recognized as a useful strategy for at least initiating needed educational reforms.

The developing influence of systems theory and its related technologies illustrate well this new stance of public school personnel toward the problems of public education. By definition, a systems approach requires simultaneous attention to all the intricately interrelated elements which comprise the system. It highlights the constraints of time, people, and things. It demands attention to both the human and technical dimensions of an organization. And it is applicable to all organizations, regardless of their particular goals and objectives. It is, therefore, not at all surprising that one of the most highly touted of the systems-related technologies currently attracting the attention of public school administrators is Planning-Programming-Budgeting Systems PPBS). As the remainder of this section suggests, the potential impact which PPBS is likely to have upon the roles and responsibilities of public secondary school principals is indeed considerable.

PPBS—What Is It?

PPBS can be most simply identified as a technological approach to educational planning. As such, it is not a thing which, like a book or a building or an administrative staff, can be pointed to, observed, and measured. Nor is it an end in itself, a product which has value and worth of its own. Rather, PPBS as an acronym stands for a complex set of interrelated processes or activities that, taken together, can result in improved decision making and resource allocation in complex organizations. It represents, at least in theory, a strategy for improved organizational planning in much the same way that the scientific method represents a strategy for improved scientific investigation.

When applied to schools in particular, PPBS is considered to be a tool for increasing the probability that educational objectives for youngsters can and will be achieved most effectively and efficiently. The crux of PPBS is that it can provide educational decision-makers—both teachers and administrators—with a rational, output-oriented, data-based framework or process for systematically relating educational activities to organizational goals and objectives. Moreover, it can provide public school administrators with an explicit process for making more effective and efficient decisions about the allocation of limited resources among alternative activities designed to achieve particular educational objectives. The essence of that process is the development and presentation of relevant information about the full implications—the costs, benefits, and constraints—associated with each alternative course of action.

Interest in the application of PPBS to schools and to other public agencies has led to the development of a sizeable body of literature regarding those applications. Naturally, because PPBS is still highly developmental and limited in its operational models, definitions and conceptualizations of it are both multiple and typically incomplete. Nonetheless, it is possible to infer from the literature some common characterizations of what it is and even a standard conceptualization of PPBS which seems to underlie, either implicitly or explicitly, nearly every application or proposed application of it in the nation's public school systems.

One of the clearest and most comprehensive descriptions of the three major processes incorporated in PPBS—planning, programming, and budgeting—is that which follows, drawn from the literature devoted to public administration. As the author suggests, ". . . planning, programming, budgeting is a combination of three related, mutually supporting, but quite distinct phases."

> Planning is the initial step. It involves the formulation and projection of goals and objectives towards which the organization must direct all its activities, and the development of strategies to achieve these goals and objectives. Specifically, it involves through a systematic consideration of alternatives, using various techniques including that which is known as systems analysis.
>
> Programming, the second stage, is the devising of the means that are to be utilized to achieve the objectives. It is the more specific determination of the manpower, materials, facilities, and funds necessary for carry-

ing out agreed programs—the process of producing a long-range plan that is organized by identifiable programs and activities rather than by objects of expenditure as traditional budgets are. In other words, it is a plan classified by the outputs of the organization rather than by the inputs in which the resource requirements are identified with or related to these program outputs. It is also a process that extends far enough into the future to show to the extent practical and necessary the full resource requirements for the program outputs. It, too, to be well done, is dependent on systems analysis.

The third phase, budgeting, which in its traditional form has been described unflatteringly as a means of ensuring the uniform distribution of dissatisfaction, is the process of transforming long-range programs into the terms of a periodic fiscal budget, the process of laying down in the form of a detailed budget the financial implications of the programs and activities to achieve the agreed objectives.[1]

Broadly described, therefore, a PPBS provides the framework, structure, or process for systematically relating organizational activities or programs in such a way that organizational personnel can clarify the objectives of those programs and can make more effective and efficient decisions regarding the future allocation of organizational resources among alternative means for achieving those program objectives.

But broad descriptions of characterizations have only limited usefulness to public school personnel who are responsible for the day-to-day operation of a complex school organization. In response to this need, a number of efforts have been made during the last decade to develop a conceptualization of PPBS that would be more specific and more applicable to schools. Examples are PPBS projects mounted by the Research Corporation of the Association of School Business Officials; the Center for the Advanced Study of Educational Administration, one of the nation's eight federally supported research and development centers in education; Fels Institute at the University of Pennsylvania; the state of California which mandated PPBS for schools in the late 1960s; and the host of independent and piecemeal efforts made by local school districts to implement program budgeting and accounting procedures.

Naturally, the diversity of these projects has resulted in a number of conceptualizations of PPBS for schools. But only in the first two of the above projects, however, has there been a concerted attempt to fully explicate a conceptual model of PPBS which adequately addresses itself to the dynamics of organizations, decision making and the planning process itself. Most other projects have produced less conceptualization and more lists of procedures or sets of steps for implementing PPBS. As a result, the

---

[1]Herbert R. Balls, "Planning, Programming and Budgeting in Canada," *Public Administration*, 48 (Autumn 1970), 292–93.

standard conceptualization of PPBS—how it is typically conceived—tends to resemble a carefully sequenced summary of things to be done by school district personnel. The flowchart presented in Fig. 10 depicts in schematic form the cyclical process described below as the standard conceptualization of PPBS for public schools.[2]

1. District personnel identify and refine the complete set of educational philosophies, goals, and objectives which either do or should guide school district activities. This set is expected to be educationally sound, relevant to the needs of students, and supported by citizens in the community and professional personnel in the schools.

2. District personnel translate defined philosophies, goals, and objectives into organizational "programs" and "sub-programs." In common PPBS parlance, a "program" is considered to be "a set of activities organized or grouped to achieve a particular objective or set of objectives." The major intent here is that district personnel identify and structure as programs all the activities or sets of activities that are necessary to the achievement of the district's defined set of philosophies, goals, and objectives. As a result, all school district activities—including both instructional and instructional-support activities—become organized, at least theoretically, in terms of desired school outputs rather than in terms of traditional organizational units or functions.

3. District personnel examine in detail the ongoing activities within each program defined, and they identify the actual and the desired inputs, processes, and outputs associated with each program.

4. Where it is possible to identify significant differences between the actual and desired characteristics of the various programs defined—their inputs, processes, and outputs—district personnel generate alternative programs or alternative activities within programs, which, if implemented, might achieve the desired outcomes with increased efficiency and effectiveness.

5. Employing techniques associated with benefit-cost analysis and cost-effectiveness analysis, district personnel analyze and evaluate each of the generated alternatives in terms of their anticipated or predicted inputs, processes, and outputs. To the extent possible, analyses are expected to be quantitative and comparably-based, for district personnel must ultimately select from the alternatives those particular programs and activities which can be implemented with the greatest probability of success.

6. District personnel implement the alternatives selected, monitor their performance—inputs, processes, and outputs—and periodically evaluate

---

[2]Both Fig. 10 and the summary statement have been adapted with permission of the authors from Terry L. Eidell and John M. Nagle, *Conceptualization of PPBS and Data-Based Educational Planning*, CASEA Technical Report Number 6 (Eugene, Oregon: University of Oregon, 1970) pp. 4–5.

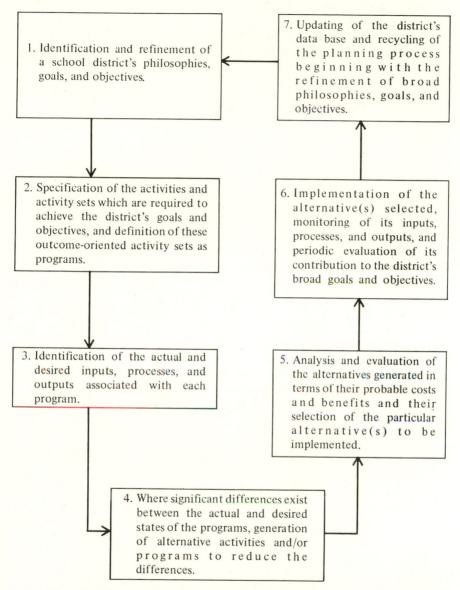

Fig. 10. The standard conceptualization of PPBS for public schools.

their outcomes in terms of the originally defined school district philosophies, goals, and objectives.

7. Finally, through carefully structured cybernetic channels, district personnel carefully analyze the evaluative data obtained, update their data base of information related to inputs, processes, and outputs, and then recycle the entire sequence, starting with the further refinement of philosophies, goals, and objectives and proceeding through all steps outlined to the final evaluation of implemented program alternatives.

The Pressure to Adopt PPBS in Public Education

There are a number of reasons why public school administrators and local boards of education are currently so interested in PPBS. The most obvious reason is, of course, the fact that by 1970 nearly three-fourths of all state legislatures in the United States had either already mandated or were in the process of mandating that public school districts develop statewide planning-programming-budgeting systems. In most states, these mandates meant that school districts should be able to budget and report their annual expenditures in a program budget format. But being able to cost out ongoing activities in a school district is merely the first step toward being able to justify those activities and their costs in terms of educational outcomes for youngsters. If, therefore, innovation was the rallying cry in education during the sixties, accountability will most assuredly be the rallying cry during this next decade, and PPBS is viewed by many state legislators at the most promising vehicle for achieving that accountability.

A number of recent developments both in and out of education serve to stimulate and reinforce this growing press for accountability and interest in PPBS. First, on a primarily theoretical level, recent writings on the economics of education suggest that it is now possible to develop a variety of mathematically-based techniques for increasing the rationality of economic decision making. The developing science of operations research, the use of complex linear programming models to solve equally complex organizational problems, and the continuing attempt to evaluate educational activities quantitatively in terms of their benefits and costs all exemplify these developing technologies. Second, to an increasing degree each year, the demand for publicly supported activities far outstrips the availability of public resources. As a result, public schools face increasing competition in their perenial battle for an adequate piece of the rapidly shrinking public tax dollar. Third, and closely related to the growing disparity between economic supply and the demand for more resources, is the increasing need for better evaluation of the use of public monies. Because of the recent expansion of public service programs around the nation—in such areas as education, welfare, housing, health services, and so forth—and the resulting competition among these programs for the public's financial support, it is more and more essential that each program be able to produce credible evidence that it can and has achieved worthwhile objectives.

Fourth, as suggested earlier, public educators were generally allowed the luxury of experimenting with a wide variety of new instructional, curricular, and administrative techniques throughout the last decade. In all likelihood, the experimental honeymoon is now over, and, if any of the developed innovations are to have continued legitimacy, their comparative educational costs and benefits must now be carefully evaluated. Fifth, the developing technologies of data processing now make it possible for us to collect, store, synthesize, analyze, and retrieve vast quantities of information relevant to the inputs, processes, and outputs of education. The mere availability of such data processing power makes the adoption of a planning system like PPBS an attractive alternative to the kind of information-free, seat-of-the-pants planning which has for so long characterized the teaching–learning process. And sixth, the role of the budgeting process itself as it relates to publicly supported activities has changed radically during the last half century, moving gradually from a focus upon *control* of expenditures to a focus upon *management* of activities and finally to its current emphasis upon the *planning* of programs.

In summary, the mounting pressures to adopt PPBS in schools and the resulting interest it holds for school administrators can ultimately be traced to the need for better and more information about the nation's public school systems, to the growing demand for accountability when public dollars are involved, and to the poverty of planning which has typically characterized an educational organization.

PPBS: Its Tendency to Bureaucratize

As intimated earlier, PPBS is certainly not unique to public education. Rather, it was first developed as a management tool for use in the Ford Motor Company and the U.S. Department of Defense, two different kinds of noneducation organizations, both of which have long been characterized by their extreme size and high degree of bureaucracy. By the mid-1920s, a number of the nation's largest private corporations had already begun to experiment with a kind of program budgeting and accounting, with an initial version of systems analysis, and with a variety of techniques which were then described as scientific management and later identified as operations research. David Novick points out, for instance, that General Motor's Budget and Finance Procedures for 1924 incorporated many of the basic features of PPBS, and that "probably the greatest innovations in systems analysis were initiated in the 1920s in the Bell Laboratories."[3] The other source of PPBS has been the federal government, particularly in its activities related to national defense. Novick cites the Controlled Materials Plan developed in 1942 as "the first program budget used in the federal government"; the plan was a comprehensive system for controlling wartime production in the United States as well as for distributing both military and nonmilitary products.[4] In addition, techniques relevant to operations research, an integral part of PPBS, were widely developed and used by the branches of the military in both this country and Britain to detect and track unseen enemy aircraft, control anti-aircraft gunnery, and design more effective submarine warfare.

It was undoubtedly Secretary of Defense Robert S. McNamara, however, who contributed most to publicizing PPBS and its widespread acceptance as a revolutionary management technique for both private enterprise and governmental units—in theory at least, if not in practice. McNamara's successful application of PPBS, first when he was at Ford Motor Company and later as Secretary of Defense, has become almost legendary. When President Johnson issued his now famous (or infamous) Executive Order in 1965 mandating that PPBS be adopted by all federal departments, offices, agencies, and bureaus, the ultimate seal of approval was placed upon PPBS as the primary model for planning and management throughout the nation's massive federal bureaucracy.

With its origins so deeply entrenched in both private and public bureaucracies, it is little wonder that PPBS as it is typically conceptualized and implemented tends to bureaucratize rather than open up an organization. And this bureaucratizing tendency is particularly characteristic of the standard conceptualization of PPBS which was presented earlier—an observation that ought to raise serious concerns for a public school administrator. In fact, it can be seriously questioned whether the model of PPBS developed for private enterprise and for the federal bureaucracy can ever be legitimately applied to an educational organization.

Public schools certainly do not have relatively simple, unitary purposes, nor are they characterized by the kind of uniformity and interchangeability of parts that typify any assembly line and most governmental units. Rather, public schools are complex social organizations which must emphasize both the uniqueness of each product acted upon and the individual characteristics of each student–teacher relationship. Many would, in fact, argue that highly standardized processes and unitary goals would be

---

[3]David Novick, ed., "The Origin and History of Program Budgeting," in *Program Budgeting*, (Cambridge, Mass.: Harvard University Press, 1965), p. XXIII.
[4]Novick, "Origin and History of Program Budgeting," p. XVIII.

not only dysfunctional, but almost immoral if they became essential to a school's continued operation. Nevertheless, as a brief exploration of how it is usually implemented in schools will suggest, the standard conceptualization of PPBS clearly tends to bureaucratize—centralizing decision making, controlling communication, standardizing both goals and activities, strengthening the administrative hierarchy, and guaranteeing that the flow of nearly all authority and decisions in the organization is from the top down.

The initial activities defined in the standard conceptualization of PPBS are the identification of a school district's philosophies, goals, and objectives and the definition of its programs or sets of activities organized to achieve those goals and objectives. Since schools are publicly supported, and since they employ personnel who are relatively well-educated, it would be foolhardy to suggest that these initial PPBS activities ought to be carried out exclusively by a district's central office staff. Consequently, recognizing the legitimate demands of both taxpayers and teachers for a voice in decisions affecting the purposes and operations of public schools, most efforts to implement the standard conceptualization of PPBS include elaborate schemes for involving large numbers of both lay and teacher personnel in those initial phases of implementation. Most often, these schemes include an extensive network of committees organized to provide not only teachers and taxpayers, but also students, administrators, and board members with ample opportunity to influence the definition of broad goals, specification of district programs, and selection of specific program objectives.

For the average taxpayer, this type of involvement in goal definition and program specification is probably sufficient, since, if the committee structure is comprehensive and interrelated, it can provide him with considerably more opportunity than he typically has to influence the purposes that guide and the activities that characterize those public schools supported by his personal tax dollars. For the average teacher in the district, however, this type of involvement will just as probably not be sufficient. While it may permit him to have some influence during the initial phases of implementing PPBS, the ultimate outcome of these activities will be to increase more than ever the unitary, bureaucratic, organizational structure of his school district. Regardless of how involved he may be in defining broad educational goals, specifying district programs, and identifying specific program objectives, a teacher may realize that, once the total system is set in motion, he will be entrapped in a monolithic structure that demands identical performance or output achievement from all teachers of the same grade and subject. If, for instance, he teaches ninth grade social studies, his general objectives and specific performance criteria for youngsters will be little different from those of any other ninth grade social studies teacher in the district. The process of moving deductively in the standard conceptualization of PPBS from goals and objectives to programs and activities creates an organizational structure which is as operationally rigid as it is logically consistent. As a result, once a teacher's involvement in the initial phases of implementing PPBS has been consummated, he will find himself irrevocably locked into a system which permits little individuality and actually inhibits personal creativity. Further evidence of this bureaucratizing tendency of the standard conceptualization of PPBS can be seen when we examine its implications for the role of a secondary school principal.

The Standard Conceptualization of PPBS and the Role of a Public School Principal

Given the current impetus for adopting technological systems like PPBS to assist in the management and operation of public schools, it appears inevitable that the role and tasks of public school administrators will change significantly during the next decade. In 1969, the Commission on Administrative Technology of the American Association of School Administrators published the results of its extensive, three-year study of the developing management technologies that are particularly relevant to the administration of schools. Speaking specifically about the implications of these technologies for the role of a public school administrator, the Commission's members concluded that

> A basic assumption is that technology will redefine the role of the school administrator. In so doing, it will enable him to reorder priorities and reallocate energies in his usually overcommitted schedule. It exacts a price, for those who seek to take advantage of any new technology must acquire new skills and insights.[5]

Thus, the question is not so much *whether* a public school principal's role will change as his district attempts to implement the standard conceptualization of PPBS, but rather *how* that role will change vis a vis the curriculum, a teaching staff, and the budget-making process itself.

As indicated above, implementation of the standard conceptualization of PPBS begins with a district-wide effort to define broad goals and philosophies, identify programs that will achieve those goals, and then specify each program's particular performance objectives. This is typically accomplished by means of an extensive network of committees composed of teachers, administrators, students, parents, board members, and other taxpayers. A secondary school principal will naturally want to encourage maximum participation of his staff members in these initial phases of implemen-

---

[5]Stephen J. Knezevich, ed., *Administrative Technology and the School Executive,* A Report submitted by the AASA Commission on Administrative Technology (Washington: The Association, 1969), pp. 13–14.

tation, both because the impact of these activities on the future shape of a school district and its individual schools may be considerable, and because staff involvement from the beginning will help build staff commitment to the structure of programs and objectives which result.

To illustrate the potential impact of these initial phases of implementation upon the future shape of a school district, it is entirely likely that implementing the standard conceptualization of PPBS will produce a completely new structure of courses within schools and school districts. The current course structure in most public schools—especially in secondary schools—is based upon traditional classifications of knowledge into such disciplines as mathematics, history, chemistry, English, foreign languages, and so forth. It seems highly unlikely that the broad goals defined for an entire school district will yield, through deductive unpacking, a structure of operational programs and program objectives that matches neatly with such a traditional, but pervasive curriculum and course structure. Rather, it seems reasonable to expect that implementing the standard conceptualization of PPBS will inevitably lead to an almost complete restructuring of curriculum, course titles, and instructional activities. One might guess, for instance, that the eventual curriculum structure might be a set of problem-centered, interdisciplinary programs, each one related to a particular aspect of a youngster's intellectual, physical, social, and psychological development. Or the curriculum structure might consist of programs addressed to each of American Association of School Administrator's Twelve Imperatives for Education or of programs addressed to the venerable Seven Cardinal Principles. The point is that existing course distinctions will probably disappear completely if the standard conceptualization of PPBS is ever fully implemented. While such a radical restructuring of a school district's instructional activities might well have salutary effects upon student learning, it would obviously pose serious problems for a public school staff accustomed to working in a more traditional, discipline-oriented structure—particularly if staff involvement in the restructuring were only minimal. Thus, at the very least, a principal must be aware of the potential for curriculum revision and of the possible interpersonal difficulties which can occur when radical changes are made in an organization's operating structure.

Once the tasks of district-wide goal setting have been completed and operating programs—each with its own set of prescribed objectives—have been assigned to particular schools, each principal in a district will be faced with primary responsibility for actually implementing PPBS in his building. In doing so, he will have to perform at least five major roles. First, he will have to assist his staff in accommodating to a host of new demands placed upon them—adjustment to new curricular structures, functioning in new and unfamiliar workgroups, making more explicit expected behaviors to youngsters, and being held accountable for the instructional objectives defined. Second, a principal will have to monitor continually the output information relevant to each program in order to determine who is and who is not achieving each program's prescribed objectives. If he discovers that certain teachers or perhaps even whole programs have failed to meet their prescribed objectives, it will be the building principal who will have primary responsibility for seeing that teachers' work is upgraded and objectives met. Third, as a consequence, a principal will have to work with his staff more often than he customarily does in an effort to help them perfect instructional methods for achieving prescribed objectives. In some instances, his instructional leadership will be directed toward meeting objectives not already being achieved; in other instances his efforts will be aimed at perfecting less costly methods for achieving objectives currently being met.

Fourth, a building principal will have to monitor carefully the costs of each program operating in his school; one of his major responsibilities will be the manipulation of resources between and among programs in order to discover the best possible mix of personnel, materials, and facilities for achieving the total array of program objectives assigned to his school. Finding a workable balance between program effectiveness and program efficiency will be a continuing dilemma for him. And fifth, in most school districts which implement the standard conceptualization of PPBS, principals will have to confront two realities. On the one hand, it will be a rare program indeed that consistently achieves all its prescribed objectives; on the other hand, it will be a rare school which has been allocated sufficient resources to implement fully all of its prescribed programs. Thus, to the extent that a principal finds it impossible for his school either to mount the desired programs or to achieve the desired objectives, he will have to engage with other building principals in a continual round of negotiations with central office personnel—negotiations characterized by each principal arguing for increased resources, reduced programs, and lower expectations for the youngsters who attend his school. Clearly, the proclivity of the district will be to standardize; protection of individual differences within each school will be a primary responsibility of each building principal.

In summary then, the standard conceptualization of PPBS for schools is derived from and designed for use in highly bureaucratic organizations. Operating programs within individual schools can be legitimated only if they can be deductively derived from the district's broad philosophies and goals. Specific objectives for each program are prescribed through the same deductive process. Authority and communication flow almost exclusively from school board to central office to building principal to teacher to students. Standardization and uniformity are natural outcomes, for the centralized decision-making structure implicit in the standard conceptualization of PPBS produces a highly unitary organization in which the objectives to be achieved by workers are centrally determined, and the role of each worker is heavily prescribed. The strength of any bureaucracy lies, of course, in its ability to specify very precisely the organizational tasks to be performed by each member. Moreover, the role of middle management personnel—like secondary school building principals—is also clearly prescribed; their primary responsibility is to monitor the workers and see that they carry out their assigned tasks and meet their assigned objectives. Ultimately while the standard conceptualization of PPBS incorporates involvement of both a school district's patrons and its teachers and administrators in the definition of broad goals, identification of programs, and specification of objectives, the essential thrust of the standard conceptualization is to increase bureaucratization in a school district and severely limit the kind of flexibility desirable in these organizations which employ predominantly well-educated and relatively independent professional personnel. The cherished perception of teachers that they are professionals is clearly threatened by this standard conceptualization of PPBS for schools.

An Alternative to the Standard Conceptualization

Since the standard conceptualization of PPBS underlies nearly all of the early attempts to implement educational planning-programming-budgeting systems, public school district personnel have found themselves in an increasingly serious dilemma: Should they ignore societal demands for accountability and risk the loss of public support for their schools? Or should they adopt the predominant model of PPBS, even though it seriously circumscribes the freedom and individuality of their teachers? Because neither of these courses of action is very desirable, many public school administrators have sought some other alternative which could provide a viable answer to their dilemma. One example of such an alternative is Data-Based Educational Planning Systems (DEPS), a version of a planning-programming-budgeting system which has recently been developed and tested at the Center for the Advanced Study of Educational Administration (CASEA).[6]

In order to reduce the bureaucratizing effects which result when a unitary set of goals, programs, and program objectives are deductively imposed upon an ongoing school district, DEPS incorporates a unique mechanism which permits the school district to attain its broad goals and at the same time both facilitates organizational flexibility and encourages respon-

---

[6]CASEA, based at the University of Oregon, is one of eight publicly supported research and development centers in education. Project 5001, begun in June 1969, has had as its primary objectives the development of a data-based planning system for public schools, the creation of instructional materials relevant to that system, and the testing of the system in South Lane School District, Cottage Grove, Oregon. The specific descriptions of DEPS are derived with permission from working documents developed by Project 5001 staff members.

sible creativity from each staff member in the district. Based upon the assumption that teachers are employed professionals—rather than simply workers in large, impersonal bureaucracies—DEPS helps a school district achieve both organizational *accountability* and organizational *flexibility* by identifying for planning purposes two kinds of separate, but highly interrelated programs: *operating* and *intellectual* programs.

An operating program is defined in DEPS as a group of activities (1) which are organized to achieve a particular set of objectives, and (2) for which data are available regarding both the *desired* and *actual* outcomes, procedures, and costs of the included activities. Operating programs in DEPS are typically planned and carried out by individuals or by small groups of individuals; they usually represent highly discrete activities within a school district. For instance, each of the subject areas taught in second grade in a particular elementary school might well be separate operating programs; so too might each course taught in a junior or senior high school as well as each of the district's many instructional-support activities, like providing food services, maintaining buildings, operating buses, supervising instruction, preparing budgets, and so forth. Clearly, operating programs in DEPS are based upon a school district's current curricular and organizational structures. They are not defined by logical deduction from the district's broad goals and philosophies, as they are in the standard conceptualization of PPBS.

Moreover, DEPS requires that the personnel responsible for each operating program be able to explicate a detailed plan for the program's activities, collect specific information regarding the implementation of that plan, and then employ this information to make decisions about the program's future. In other words, DEPS requires that school district personnel engage in a particular kind of rational, data-based planning of the district's operating programs. Fig. 11 presents a schematic diagram of the steps involved in this particular kind of program planning. Note that the entire planning process is cyclical, involving program personnel in development of an initial plan, implementation of that plan, collection of outcome information, analysis of expected and actual outcomes, generation of alternatives, selection of a new plan, implementation of it, and so forth. Note also that six specific kinds of information about a program are critical to the process of planning in DEPS—three kinds of *desired* information and three comparable kinds of *actual* information:

1. The program's *desired outputs* expressed in terms of behavioral or performance objectives
2. Its *desired processes*, that is, the specific instructional, evaluative, and/or administrative arrangements and procedures that will be employed to achieve the desired outputs

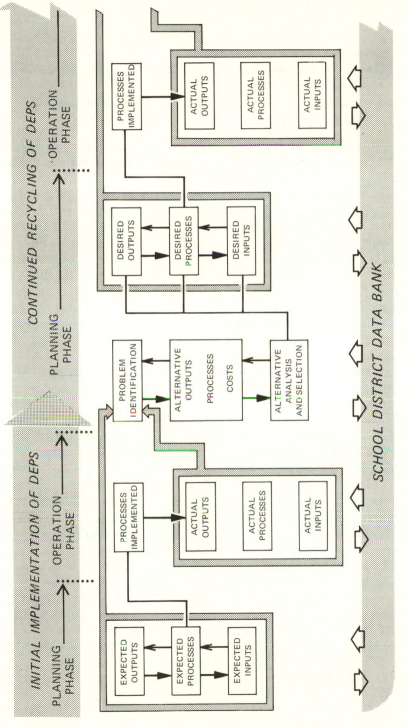

Fig. 11. The process of planning in DEPS. (*Presented here with permission of CASEA, University of Oregon, Eugene, Oregon.)

125

3. Its *desired inputs* or the resources required to mount those desired processes
4. Its *actual outputs* expressed in terms of its original behavioral or performance objectives
5. Its *actual processes* expressed in terms of its desired processes; and
6. Its *actual inputs* expressed in terms of its desired inputs

These six kinds of information become, then, the critical data files for planning, implementing, and evaluating each operating program in a school district.

The second kind of program in DEPS is an intellectual program. The intellectual program is so named because it can never be observed and measured in both time and space as an operating program can. Rather, an intellectual program in DEPS consists of a broad goal which has been unpacked deductively to at least two, and perhaps more, levels of general and specific objectives. A district will therefore have as many intellectual programs as it has broad goals, and the format of each will resemble the schematic presented in Fig. 12. Development of these intellectual programs —the broad goal statements and their related objectives—requires the involvement not only of a district's professional personnel, but that of its students and taxpayers as well.

To some extent, the development of intellectual programs in DEPS resembles the identification of goals and objectives in the standard conceptualization of PPBS. Both processes consider an entire school district. Both encourage maximum involvement of diverse groups, and both processes require deductive expansion of broad goals to related sets of objectives. Where the processes differ is in the use they make of the goals and objectives defined. In the standard conceptualization, the goal statements are actually used to define a district's operating programs; in DEPS the intellectual programs have an integrity of their own, and they remain separate from the operating programs which are defined by this district's already established, ongoing activities. Therefore in DEPS an operating program is considered to be the mechanism or vehicle for achieving the desired outcomes explicated in an intellectual program; while it is inexorably linked to that intellectual program, it is not derived from it. The strength of this distinction drawn in DEPS is that while intellectual programs set the requirements to be met by operating programs, thus insuring accountability of a school district to its patrons, professional staff members of the district are both free and encouraged to organize themselves into whatever configuration of operating programs they feel will most effectively meet the district's broad goals. In DEPS, both accountability to patrons and flexibility within the organization are preserved.

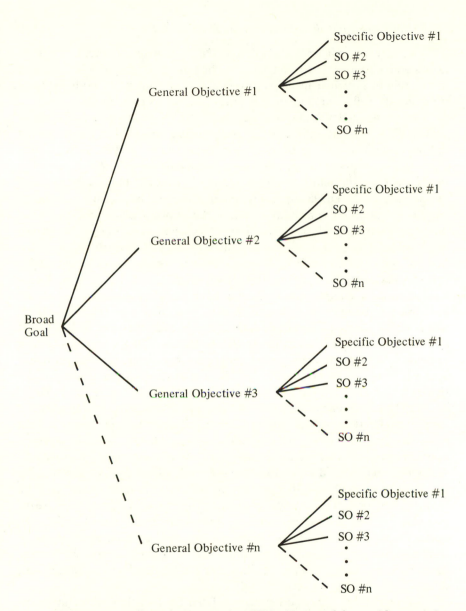

Fig. 12. An intellectual program in DEPS. (Presented here with permission of CASEA, University of Oregon, Eugene, Oregon.)

DEPS and the Role of a Public School Principal

As already indicated, the crux of DEPS is a set of intellectual programs and a set of related, but separate operating programs. The role of a public school principal in helping to develop and maintain both kinds of programs as well as in mediating between the two is considerable.

In terms of developing the necessary DEPS intellectual programs, a principal's role is not unlike that of the principal involved in implementing the initial activities in the standard conceptualization of PPBS. Both principals will want to encourage maximum participation by their staff members in the district-wide effort to define broad educational philosophies, goals, and objectives. In DEPS especially teachers will be in a position to make extremely important contributions when the effort is made to expand deductively each of the broad goals into its component objectives at greater and greater levels of specificity. Achieving logical consistency and coherence within each intellectual program will require considerable input from individuals who have had direct experience with public school curriculum and the complexities of writing educational objectives.

As for the operating programs in his building, a principal in DEPS will have to play a considerably different role than the principal involved in the standard conceptualization of PPBS. Because DEPS provides for the spawning of intellectual programs and operating programs from different sources, there will be no need in DEPS to restructure dramatically the activities which already exist in a school. While this will obviate the necessity of entirely reorganizing his school's structure of courses, it will create a somewhat different problem for a building principal; he will have to take a leadership role in encouraging his staff to submit each of the many ongoing operating programs in which they are involved to much more extensive and systematic planning, data collection, and evaluation. This means that he will have to assist them either directly or indirectly in their efforts to write performance objectives, design evaluation instruments, create alternative processes, obtain necessary resources, and so forth. In a very real sense, because operating programs in DEPS are identified as close to the point of student–teacher interaction as possible, the building principal is the administrator most able to either facilitate or inhibit development of a school district's operating programs.

A good deal of this power derives from the fact that a building principal in DEPS will find that one of his major responsibilities is that of matching the objectives attained by his school's operating programs with objectives incorporated in the district's intellectual programs. That is, a building principal will be expected to take a leadership role in assessing what the operating programs in his school are achieving, in comparing these achievements with the desired outcomes explicated in the district's intellectual programs, and in informing his instructional staff of the discrepancies which exist between what is being achieved and the desired achievements. Given this information regarding discrepancies, the principal will have to work with teachers to refine and redesign current programs as well as to initiate new operating programs that may be needed in order to achieve the district's broad goals within the framework of its available resources.

One final observation regarding the role of a building principal in DEPS should be made. To insure that the system is properly implemented, it is critical that a principal view himself as a colleague of his professional teaching staff. Behaving as a bureaucrat who simply assigns objectives to each of his school's operating programs, he will be implementing not DEPS, but the standard conceptualization of PPBS. To preserve the nonbureaucratic character of DEPS, a principal must view his role as that of helping his colleagues to understand the requirements placed upon their own relevant operating programs. If he can behave accordingly, he will markedly enhance his staff's initiative and their creative response to the commonly shared problem of meeting the district's broad goals and objectives. While a principal will obviously need to monitor each operating program to see that agreed-upon plans are fully carried out and evaluated, DEPS will not place him in the position of having to coerce teachers to meet the demands of programs and objectives over which they have little or no control. Rather, his monitoring of operating programs in DEPS will take the form of assisting his teachers to follow a course of action which they have planned and to which they are presumably committed. DEPS would seem to enhance considerably a building principal's opportunity to be much less a bureaucratic leader and more a leader of colleagues.

PPBS: Its Costs and the Rate of its Implementation

During any discussion of PPBS—whether related to its standard conceptualization or to DEPS—two additional questions inevitably arise: How will PPBS affect a school district's overall operating costs? and How long will it take to implement it in an ongoing school district? While these are certainly reasonable questions, it is not yet possible to answer either of them in any definitive way. As of this writing, the development of comprehensive planning systems for public schools is still very recent; there is, in fact, no single school district in the country which has *fully* operationalized a PPBS. Answers to the two questions must be both tentative and inferential.

One conclusion seems certain though. Despite the fact that many advocates of PPBS argue that its adoption will help schools reduce their overall expenditures, a significant reduction in operating expenditures is neither the intended purpose nor the probable outcome of implementing PPBS. Since any PPB system requires teachers and administrators to engage in much more rigorous and formalized planning processes than they customarily have time for, it is difficult to envision any dramatic reduction in a school's operating cost. In fact, the additional time required for planning may actually increase costs.

On the other hand, of course, careful planning, explication of measurable objectives, and generation of alternatives ought to enable school districts to reduce unwarranted expenditures and redistribute current costs, while at the same time increasing student learning. Moreover, because a PPB system will provide decision-makers with detailed information on the actual costs of achieving particular educational objectives, they will be able, perhaps for the first time, to relate operating costs to the district's broad, community-based educational goals. They will be able to ask their citizenry, "Is this particular educational goal worth these dollars?"

Estimates of how long it will take to implement PPBS in a school district typically range anywhere from one to ten years. This relatively wide range of estimates undoubtedly reflects a general misunderstanding about the nature of PPBS and its complexity as an innovation. If, for instance, one assumes that PPBS is nothing more than the development of procedures for program budgeting and accounting, one year may well be adequate for implementation. But, as described in the preceding pages, PPBS is clearly more than a sophisticated cost accounting system. Rather, it is a highly complex and reactive innovation that requires all professional personnel in a school district to learn new patterns of behavior and to adopt new attitudes toward educational planning. Learning new behaviors and adopting new attitudes do not occur overnight in a multifaceted organization like a school.

Thus, school districts which decide to implement some form of comprehensive PPB system would be well advised to seek the assistance of competent external consultants and to allow from five to ten years for gradual implementation of the total system. While this may seem to be an extremely long period of time, an evolutionary strategy for implementation, characterized by approximation and incrementation, seems to have much greater promise of success than a strategy which is revolutionary, demands instantaneous change, and ultimately creates dissension and chaos.

Conclusion

In this chapter we have attempted to sketch briefly the genesis of PPBS, to describe some of the societal and technological forces which seem to be propelling schools into PPBS, and to explicate two rather different forms of PPBS—the standard form and DEPS. This information has been provided as a medium through which the role of the public school principal involved in PPBS may be considered. The standard PPBS model was characterized as bureaucratic while the DEPS model was said to be collegial, and these basic characterizations led to some important distinctions vis a vis the role of a public school principal involved with PPBS in his school. While the information presented on PPBS provides only an overview, and the analyses presented of the principal's role as bureaucrat or as colleague are necessarily sketchy, we believe that principals and prospective principals can employ these characterizations usefully both in evaluating alternative PPB systems and in developing more complete role descriptions for themselves.

Selected References

EIDELL, TERRY L., and JOHN M. NAGLE, *Data-Based Educational Planning Systems (DEPS): Achieving Accountability in Schools*. Forthcoming.

HAGGART, SUE A., and others, *Program Budgeting for School District Planning: Concepts and Applications—Memorandum RM–6116–RC*. Santa Monica: RAND Corporation, 1969.

HARTLEY, HARRY J., *Educational Planning-Programming-Budgeting: A Systems Approach*. Englewood Cliffs, N.J.: Prentice-Hall, Inc., 1968.

LYDEN, FREMONT J., and ERNEST G. MILLER, eds. *Planning-Programming-Budgeting: A Systems Approach to Management*. Chicago: Markham Publishing Company, 1968.

6

Instructional Leadership

Throughout this book, the authors' contention is that the effectiveness of a school is largely dependent upon the type of leadership the school principal provides. To give an exact description of what leadership is, how it is developed, and how it is exercised is a difficult task. Much has been written in recent years concerning the concept, and there appears to be no definite research that can be used to prepare a definite prescription.

Misconceptions

One of the common misconceptions concerning leadership is that a status position such as the principalship automatically insures its existence. It is true that a certain amount of prestige attaches to the principal by virtue of his office. Persons employed in a school system are inclined to accept leadership from the principal. But in the climate of today's society, teachers are not required to follow unless the leadership is present. Thus principals may not expect loyalty and strict followership unless they involve teachers in planning instructional improvement and earn the position of leadership which the office tentatively allows them.

Another common fallacy is that leadership in one situation guarantees it in a different situation. Many examples could be cited to show that someone who is a good leader in one situation may prove to be ineffective in another. Mistakes in judgment, made too often, result in a loss of confidence in a leader. A wise leader may find it advantageous to give the leadership function to another in the interest of the total situation.

Another misconception is that leadership is an inherited trait, one that cannot be developed. In other words, leaders are born, not made. There have been attempts to identify traits inherent in leadership; these have often been physical traits. But it would be a mistake to assume that the possession of specific traits guarantees a situation in which the individual gains acceptance as a leader.

It has also been fairly common to assume that administration and leadership are synonymous. That is not the case. It is possible to administer a situation without exercising good leadership. Administration is often done by following rules and regulations; leadership cannot be exercised in quite the same manner. The principal interested in improving his leadership skills would be well-advised to study the various theories of leadership and to become acquainted with studies dealing with the subject. One significant study conducted some years ago is useful for reference as an example of the kind of research needed. R. M. Stogdill reviewed 124 studies of the characteristics of leaders.[1] His review is as follows:

1. Supported by uniformly positive evidence from ten or more of the studies surveyed is the conclusion that the average person who occupies a position of leadership exceeds the average member of his group to some degree in the following respects: (1) sociability; (2) initiative; (3) persistence; (4) knowing how to get things done; (5) self-confidence; (6) alertness to, and insight into, situations; (7) cooperativeness; (8) popularity; (9) adaptability; and (10) verbal facility.

2. Supported by uniformly positive evidence from fifteen or more of the studies surveyed is the conclusion that the average person who occupies a position of leadership exceeds the average member of his group in the following respects: (1) intelligence, (2) scholarship, (3) dependability in exercising responsibilities, (4) activity and social participation, and (5) socioeconomic status.

   The qualities, characteristics, and skills required in a leader are determined to a large extent by the demands of the situation in which he is to function as a leader.

Intellectual fortitude and personal integrity are positively related to leadership in adult groups. Such personal characteristics as originality, popularity, sociability, good judgment, good humor, and cooperativeness tend to be related to successful leadership. There appears to be very little relationship between age, height, or appearance so long as appearance is not too deviant from that of the other members of the group. It seems clear, too, that leadership cannot be discussed adequately apart from the situation in which it operates.

---

[1] R. M. Stogdill, "Personal Factors Associated with Leadership: A Survey of the Literature," *Journal of Psychology*, XXV (January 1948), 35–71.

Leadership Patterns

While leadership does not operate except in specific situations, it is not passive, nor is it just the possession of certain traits. It appears to be a working relationship among members of a group in which the leader acquires status through active participation and demonstration of his capacity for carrying cooperative tasks through to completion. There is a feeling, too, that leaders have opinions on many subjects and are willing to discuss them without attempting to force their opinions on other members of the group.

The patterns of principal leadership and characteristic reactions of staff have been discussed by George B. Redfern.[2] First, he described directive behavior as that which is aggressive and domineering. The reaction that follows it is either resistive or acquiescent. The staff resents high-handed action, and they either resist or go along to avoid unpleasantness. Second, guiding behavior is listed. Such behavior leads to the release of staff potential and facilitates work. Staff reaction is favorable and accepting, since their work as individuals is recognized. Third listed is the pattern of leadership expressed as vacillating behavior. This type of action is characterized as inconsistent and allows the staff to take the initiative, while the principal withdraws. The result is that the staff becomes uncertain and uncomfortable. The fourth type described is appeasing behavior. A principal who operates in this manner is characterized by timidity and insecurity. He may be striving for personal popularity, or be unable to stand criticism by the staff or his superiors. The natural reaction to this type of leadership is resentment. The tendency is for the staff to take over the leadership role and replace the existing leaders.

As a result of his observations, Redfern listed the following ingredients of good personnel management in leadership.[3] They are insight, personal security, sensitivity, mature behavior, flexibility, and personal fulfillment. It would seem that any principal having these qualities would be equipped to be an effective leader. The result of his leadership should be an understanding of his task and the ability to serve as a change agent in accomplishing the objectives of the educational enterprise.

Group Dynamics

Working with a group is one of the routes to earned leadership; this obviously entails the ability to work with people. To establish proper relationships, the leader needs to have the ability to make people feel com-

---

[2]George B. Redfern, *Improving Principal-Faculty Relationships* (Englewood Cliffs, New Jersey: Prentice-Hall, Inc., 1966), pp. 14, 15–16.

[3]Redfern, *Improving Principal-Faculty Relationships*, pp. 15–16.

fortable in his presence. School administrators consistently report that their training in human relationships has been one of the weakest areas of their training programs. A characteristic of the most successful leaders is their adeptness at getting committees and groups to function, or getting groups to think through and to attack their problems. Not infrequently the wise administrator is the one who knows what individuals should be included in a particular group. Skill in group work, sometimes called *group dynamics*, is an ability for a leader to develop if he is to earn the title. Time must be provided for teachers to think and work together. This may take the form of lighter teaching loads, freedom from time-consuming or onerous custodial tasks or clerical routines, or regularly dismissing children early for an hour or two to provide time for group work. In discussing the supervisory functions that follow, it is assumed that both the principal and the teachers will be provided sufficient time to think and act creatively in improving instruction.

Improving Instruction

The principal is confronted with a variety of tasks. Managing a school is time-consuming and demanding. Many of the tasks are routine, while others require planning and expertise. Changed societal conditions have resulted in conditions that make the task more difficult. In spite of all this, still and always, the principal's most important task is the improvement of instruction. It is for this reason that the principal must develop a strategy which will enable him to accomplish that objective.

Planning for Instructional Activities

The National Association of Secondary School Principals has conducted in-depth studies of both the senior and junior high school principalship. The study of the junior high school principalship revealed that the average principal spends from fifty to fifty-four hours each week pursuing his duties.[4] The activities that seemed to make considerable time demands are as follows: (1) administrative planning alone or with subordinates, (2) meeting with groups of teachers on curriculum or instructional matters, (3) working with individual teachers in relation to their teaching proficiency, and (4) meetings with students on disciplinary matters. The principals were asked to list the percentage of time devoted to the listed activities.[5] Only three of the activities will be listed here: (1) meetings with

---

[4]National Association of Secondary School Principals, *The Junior High School Principalship* (Washington, D.C.: The Association, 1966), p. 54.

[5]National Association of Secondary School Principals, *The Senior High School Principalship* (Washington, D.C.: The Association, 1965), p. 81.

groups of teachers regarding curriculum and other matters, (2) meetings with *groups* of teachers on matters other than curriculum and instruction, and (3) work with teachers in relation to their teaching proficiency.

An examination of the responses to the questionnaires to principals of junior and senior high schools reveals that principals spent about the same amount of time in these activities. Few principals completely neglected the matter of curriculum, but more than half of those responding spent no more than 6 percent of their time in dealing with curriculum problems.

Less than 10 percent of the principals did not have meetings with teachers on matters other than curriculum and instruction. More than 75 percent of the principals spent from 1 to 6 percent of their time in such meetings. Comparatively few spend more than 10 percent of their time working with teachers on matters other than instructional issues.

With respect to working with individual teachers to improve their efficiency, about 6 percent reported that this is not one of their functions. More than 50 percent of the principals reported that they spend from 1 to 6 percent of their time on this activity. Few principals, at either level, spend more than 15 percent of their time in supervising individual teachers.

The study also provided a summary of the relative time spent on various activities by the senior high school principal. Administrative planning alone or with subordinates was listed as the most time-consuming activity. This was followed in order by meetings with students on matters other than discipline, work with individual teachers regarding their teaching proficiency, meetings with teachers on matters of curriculum or instruction, and correspondence.

While it would be unwise to make sweeping generalizations from the facts presented, it does seem that the principal is unable to devote enough time to matters that concern instruction. The principal should not be indicted for this omission. He is very often hampered in his duties by the nature of the organization, by an excess of clerical duties, and by the lack of assistants. It is the responsibility of the principal to request changes that will give him more time for consideration of instructional needs.

Teacher Evaluation

The evaluation of teachers is often looked upon as a necessary evil, yet it has been carried on since schools were started. The earliest evaluation was done by school boards; it is now the duty of the school administrator. Many teachers have been uncomfortable with the evaluative process because the purposes of evaluation have not been made clear; they have had little part in developing evaluative instruments in the past. The solution to the problem is to be found in securing the acceptance by teachers of the true purposes of evaluation, and in enlisting their cooperation in finding methods of evaluation which will prove to be mutually helpful to teachers and administrative officers.

The following are some principles that may constitute the basis for solving the problem. First, the primary purpose of evaluation is the improvement of teaching. To this end evaluations should be made periodically by those charged with the responsibility of supervision. These evaluations should be considered with teachers as a means of helping them discover needs for improvement and appraise the nature of the progress being made. Second, the plan of evaluation used in any school system should be developed through the cooperative efforts of teachers, administrative officers, and supervisory officers. The purpose of the plan should be to facilitate both self-analysis by teachers and supervisor analysis by supervisory officers. Third, the evaluation of teacher efficiency should be reviewed for administrative purposes (a) when teachers are being counseled with respect to their future professional growth and development, (b) when probationary teachers are reappointed or given permanent appointments, (c) when annual salary increases are given, (d) when teachers are advanced from a lower to a higher classification on the salary schedule, and (e) when promotions are made within a school system. Administrative evaluation necessitates keeping records of teacher improvement. In this connection it is suggested that a cumulative folder for each teacher be kept in which are filed the credentials of the teacher, evidence of his growth, and improvement after initial appointment. Fourth, those who are subject to evaluation should be given the opportunity to review the evaluation and make comments concerning their perception of the validity of the findings. In some cases, teachers are asked to sign the evaluation as evidence of having seen it.

If it is reasonable that the principal rate the teachers, then it is also reasonable that the teachers rate the principal. The scale need not be the same; it should be based on those items which make for success in administration and supervision rather than on specific classroom techniques. Among the items on which a principal might be rated are supervision, attitude toward teachers and students, balance between administration and supervision, organization, assignment of extracurricular duties, and relations with parents. The use of such a rating can hardly fail to result in the improvement of a professional and conscientious principal.

No one is so nearly perfect that improvement is impossible, although few are aware of their specific handicaps. The most common reasons for the failure of principals are: (1) lack of professional training; (2) failure to exercise personal qualities of tact, sympathy, friendliness, and respect for others; and (3) neglecting to participate in the social and civic life of the community. On the first two of these reasons, the teachers' judgments of the principal's worth should prove valuable. The principal can independently evaluate his participation in the social and civic life of the community.

Supervisory Techniques

There is need for some type of supervision in all schools. While the training of teachers has been considerably improved and state requirements for certification have been up-graded, most school systems face problems in keeping instructional techniques in line with modern research. There is further need for coordination of effort and orientation of faculty members in the use of new techniques.

Prior to 1920, supervision in both elementary and secondary schools consisted of inspection. The visit was unannounced, and in the ensuing conference, the "expert" principal told the teacher what to do. For another ten or fifteen years, supervision was thought of as direction. The supervisor knew what should be taught and when and how it should be taught. Since 1935 the concept of supervision has changed to one of coordination and service—the principal should perform this role. In some cases, central office supervisors are highly qualified professionals who assist principals. The principal who fails to utilize their services is failing his responsibilities, because the principal's authority is not undermined through their assistance. Supervisors work with the principal; their suggestions go through his hands.

Types of Teachers in Need of Supervision

All teachers need assistance and encouragement in reaching the highest level of professional development possible. Certainly no one questions the advisability of wise and competent supervisory help for beginning teachers. Because many teachers fail and leave the profession because of the frustrations they meet in the first year of teaching, every principal should have a definite plan for helping new teachers.

In addition to new teachers who need to be oriented to a school situation, at least two kinds of experienced teachers need supervisory help. These are the experienced competent teacher who wishes to increase the scope of his professional activity and the mature teacher who insists upon teaching in the way he or she has been taught in bygone years. The former may wish to try a teaching method which is entirely new. Innovation should be encouraged, and it can be made possible through a variety of supervisory procedures discussed later in the chapter.

Planning a Supervisory Program

In order to plan wisely, it is necessary to survey carefully the instructional situation as it is. The principal may feel that fundamental changes are needed in school organization, staff utilization, evaluative procedures, and similar areas. He may wish to involve the faculty in better methods of instruction through writing performance-based objectives. The number of possibilities for improving instruction is almost endless, but the important thing is to survey the situation carefully.

It is not enough to have the principal's interest; unless the staff is involved in appraising needs and planning the strategies, no plan will be very successful. Ample time should be provided to discuss needs, data needed, procedures to be followed, and plans to be developed for evaluating the effectiveness of the effort.

In planning a supervisory program, the principal needs to make a realistic appraisal of the amount of time and energy he can devote to this part of his responsibilities. Most writers in education would probably agree that at least half or more of the principal's time should be devoted to problems that relate to the improvement of instruction.

The Classroom Visit

In the minds of many teachers and principals classroom visitation has been so closely associated with supervision that the terms are virtually synonymous. In all too many cases, the classroom visit only results in inspection and rating rather than in analysis of the learning situation or diagnosis of pupil difficulties and follow-up remedial instruction.

Teachers have not been entirely satisfied with the results of classroom visitation chiefly because such visits are unplanned and very often nothing happens after visitation. The teacher may not even be provided the courtesy of an interview for the purpose of discussing what the principal saw. Both elementary and high school teachers have generally agreed that the classroom visit is desirable if it helps improve teaching.

Classroom visitation can be of benefit to both the principal and the teacher when properly employed. In a planned program of supervision, particularly when teachers have helped to formulate the plan, the classroom visit fits logically into the picture. If a remedial program in reading following a survey of local conditions and teacher concern is being conducted, classroom visitation logically must follow to ascertain how the remedial work is proceeding—for the purpose of improving instruction. It is in no way a means of rating the teacher for purposes of determining salary for the ensuing year or of reaching a decision regarding re-employment. In some cases, the visit may be to become acquainted with a teacher's efficiency in classroom management and relationships. In such instances, the principal would observe such things as: (1) organization skills (how he plans and organizes work); (2) management skills (how he disciplines and manages the group); (3) atmosphere for learning (how he maintains a healthy classroom environment); (4) relationships with students (how he recognizes individual differences and shows interest in students); (5) reports and records (how he prepares adequate reports and keeps accurate records). Having a definite purpose to the visitation is essential.

Extensive classroom visitation makes heavy demands on the time of the principal. In a planned program teachers are likely to ask the principal to come to the classroom to observe specific practices. Such invitations should not be refused unless the principal has other appointments which cannot be broken, since such visits afford opportunities for developing the best types of professional relations. Common practice indicates that most classroom visits are too short except for purposes of inspection—a questionable practice. The length of time the principal should remain in a classroom depends upon the purpose of his visit.

Observation Techniques

Some principals have attempted to make visitation and observation more objective by planning specific procedures to record what has taken place. One system that has created considerable interest is the Flanders system.[6] The observer needs some practice to use the system properly. In this system, over a specified time period, verbal behavior is recorded. Ten categories are listed for observation, including: (1) accepts feeling, (2) praises or encourages, (3) accepts or uses ideas of student, (4) asks questions, (5) lectures, (6) gives directions, and (7) criticizes or justifies authority. Student reaction is categorized as: (8) student-talk response and (9) student-talk initiation. The tenth category provides for indicating periods of silence or confusion.

The system described provides a technique for determining the degree to which the teacher dominates the discussion and whether the students are playing a major role in the experience. It is possible to have a lesson taped and used in group meetings for discussion concerning teaching techniques.

Individual Conferences

Most principals take time to hold individual conferences with teachers. This practice should certainly be used in assisting new teachers. It can be used effectively with most teachers, even though many teachers feel they are a waste of time because of the manner in which the conference is conducted. Conferences must have a purpose and should be planned in advance.

If a conference is to be helpful, the relationship between the teacher

---

[6] J. Edmund Amidon and John B. Hough, *Interaction Analysis: Theory, Research and Application* (Reading, Massachusetts: Addison-Wesley Publishing Company, Inc., 1967), p. 389.

and the principal must be cordial yet somewhat impersonal. The conference allows opportunity for the principal to become acquainted with the teacher's professional ambitions and to encourage them. It also provides the opportunity to clear up misunderstandings and misconceptions.

The conference should be held at a time convenient to both teacher and principal. The best time is usually an unassigned period in the teacher's schedule or after school; the conference is generally held in the principal's office. If the conference is to be of value, the teacher should be encouraged to do most of the talking. If the teacher can be induced to analyze strengths and weaknesses in procedures, change is likely to be received better. The principal ordinarily should ask questions or make suggestions without being too direct in his approach.

The conference also provides a chance for commendation. Honest praise is a far greater incentive to future development than sharp reproof, no matter how deserved the latter may be. Human beings neglect the decency of honest commendation and speak only of the unsatisfactory in all too many cases. This statement is true for the relations between principal and teacher as well as between teacher and student. However, to praise in an effort to appear to be a good fellow results in distrust on the part of teachers.

Group Conferences

Through the development of departments, teamteaching, and open classrooms, the principal has an opportunity to meet with teachers in groups. He may be requested to serve such groups as an advisor or consultant. Only those topics appropriate to the group should be considered in such meetings. Otherwise, the results of the effort can be disappointing to both principal and group members.

General Faculty Meetings

General teachers' meetings have long been mentioned as a main supervisory technique. Such meetings are often considered a complete waste of time by teachers; one reason why general meetings are held in such low esteem by teachers is that the principal tends to use the time for dealing with administrative routine which could have been more satisfactorily placed in a bulletin rather than read or explained to the faculty. It is sometimes necessary to have administrative meetings, but they should be held only when necessary and properly identified as administrative in nature.

General faculty meetings can be worthwhile experiences for all, and there are some general principles to be followed in developing guidelines to be considered. First, they should be planned in advance; teachers should know the time and place well in advance of the meeting. Second, it is desirable to hold faculty meetings during the school day, if possible. In the event that they must be held after school, some form of refreshments should be provided prior to the meeting. If funds are not available for such expenditures, the expenses should be borne by the principal. Third, a faculty committee should be formed to assist in preparing the topics for the meeting. No one is in a better position to assess the interests and needs of the faculty than the classroom teacher; their participation should be solicited.

Fourth, the meeting should be attended by all members of the professional staff. Coaches and directors of activities should plan their schedules so that they can attend faculty meetings. Excusing certain staff members is a practice to be avoided. To do otherwise is admitting that the meetings are unimportant. Special teachers, nurses, media specialists, and the like are all valuable members of the staff who are able to make significant contributions to the meeting. They should be allowed the privilege of participating. Fifth, better participation will be secured if the staff receives a meeting agenda the day before it is scheduled. This permits an opportunity to raise questions and provide information. Finally, the meeting should not be too long and should close on time. There is nothing more exasperating than a meeting so long that teachers suffer personal inconvenience. There will be less unhappiness among the teachers if they are sure that the meeting will close on time.

Demonstration Teaching

Demonstration lessons have been used over the years to provide examples of good teaching. While it is probably used less now than formerly, there are still advantages to it. Skillful teachers have the opportunity to demonstrate new methods in providing learning experiences. Demonstrations also provide an opportunity for members of one department to become acquainted with methods that are effective in other disciplines. At one time principals did the demonstration teaching, but it is questionable whether many principals would be as well qualified as their staff members to do the demonstrating today.

To be maximally effective, the demonstration should obviously be planned. In preparation the teacher or group of teachers who are to observe should know and discuss with the principal the purpose of the demonstration they are to see. An outline of the demonstration may be made available so that no one is in doubt as to the purpose and proposed procedure. When the demonstration is completed, it will prove of value to have the visitors participate in a conference with the demonstration teachers so that questions which have arisen may be answered. At times it may be advisable to hold a series of demonstrations so that the whole teaching cycle may be observed.

Demonstrations are particularly effective when the purpose is to show the use of new equipment to be used in learning experiences. Commercial companies now employ people trained in educational procedures to demonstrate new materials and machines. It is a mistake to overlook the opportunity for expert assistance in orienting staff members to make maximum use of materials and equipment.

Intervisitation

Teachers and principals show moderate enthusiasm for intervisitation. In practice, intervisitation is not widely practiced. This is to be expected, since demonstration teaching is practiced so infrequently. The values which may accrue from intervisitation are the same as those expected from demonstration—if the visitation is planned as carefully as a demonstration and is discussed afterward. The practice of setting a visiting day for which a local school is closed is likely to be ineffective, since it is rare that all teachers in a school can use such a day to see a specific teaching act from which they hope to benefit. Visitation should be preceded by correspondence, and should occur when the best results may be expected. It is extremely unlikely that arrangements for an entire school faculty could be made at once. Benefits may also be expected from intervisitation within a building when there is planning beforehand and conference afterward.

Microteaching

Through a grant obtained from the Office of Education, a team from the Stanford University School of Education investigated the use of videotape in the development of technical skills of teaching.[7] As a result, microteaching is used in many teacher training institutions, and as a supervisory technique for improving the skills of experienced teachers. If the technique is to be used properly, definite skills need to be defined and analyzed. Through the medium of a videotape recorder, the methods of the teacher become subject to the evaluation of the observers. The lesson lasts for a very short period of time and the number of students used is limited. Time is alloted for discussion and the teaching act may be repeated.

Five essential propositions form the core of the microteaching idea.[8] First, real teaching takes place. Second, class size, time, and scope of con-

---

[7]Dwight Allen and Kevin Ryan, *Microteaching* (Reading, Massachusetts: Addison-Wesley Publishing Company, Inc., 1969), p. v.

[8]Allen and Ryan, *Microteaching*, pp. 2–3.

tent is reduced to lessen the complexities of classroom teaching. Third, specific tasks are set for mastery. Fourth, the training program offers a high degree of control. Fifth, there is an opportunity for immediate feedback, and the trainee engages in a critique of his performance.

The use of microteaching appears to have many advantages as a supervisory tool. While it is highly desirable to have a videotape recorder for using the technique, it is not absolutely essential. The plan has all of the advantages of demonstration teaching and provides additional dimensions as well.

Supervisory Bulletins

Bulletins are commonly used to reduce administrative matters to written form, in order to handle such matters in a form more economical than teachers' meetings. Such bulletins may also be used to improve the instructional program. Bulletins may be duplicated and a copy sent to each teacher, or they may be typewritten and posted on the teachers' bulletin board. For large faculties the duplicated bulletin will undoubtedly prove more effective. Supervisory bulletins may summarize the results of the last teachers' meeting or they may carry suggestions for study for the next one. They may consist of brief annotated bibliographies or citation of a professional article of special interest to a group of teachers. Such material would, of course, be issued only to the interested group. Reports of outstanding work in the school, citations of the name and class of the teacher, may also be included. The results of a testing program, with adequate interpretive comment, may be profitably placed in a bulletin so that teachers can study the results before discussion by the group or with individuals. Although the bulletin cannot be the major supervisory technique, it is one which should not be overlooked by a principal who desires to make his services maximally effective.

Professional Reading and Study

To facilitate professional study while in service, the board of education should make a small sum of money available so that the principal and the teacher committee may purchase a carefully selected list of professional books and magazines for use as the basis of individual reading or group study during the year. The bulletin may be used to draw attention to pertinent material. While the practice of furnishing professional books and magazines is not widespread, it is increasing.

But professional reading during the school year is not enough. The academic and professional training of teachers has been shown to be frequently inadequate. The best and easiest source of additional training is a good university, although a satisfactory result may be secured through independent work by teachers who have the necessary persistence. There is an opportunity for the principal to foster a desire for additional training on the part of the faculty through late afternoon and Saturday classes, extension courses, summer session attendance, or advanced study during a leave of absence.

What is more needed than new research in the public schools is an interpretation of the already existing research and application of it to classroom practice. It is no less desirable or worthy of commendation to apply research to a classroom situation than it is to compile new research. The principal, by virtue of his position and because of the training which he should possess, is the logical person to bring the results of research into local school planning. The discoveries of research workers in the universities or bureaus of research in city school systems is not productive until it is translated into practice. The basic difference between oral and silent reading was discovered by scientific study; research influenced practice when school administrators appreciated the difference and the findings were introduced into the schools.

This statement must not be construed as an implication that research should not be carried out in public school systems—it certainly should be when there is need for it. In any school in which planned supervision is practiced, there will be ample opportunity for research. Surveys, the development of techniques, and classroom experimentation are particularly necessary in school systems. They do not require elaborate equipment, as is often the case in basic scientific research. They are valuable nontheless, for they offer opportunities to enlist teachers as active participants in the study of educational problems. While the interpretation of existing research is more important than is the production of new research, any public school system which has an adequate supervisory plan is sure to include research at some point.

Other very valuable supervisory techniques are educational diagnosis and remedial treatment, the use of tests, and curriculum reconstruction. Because of their importance, these topics are treated separately in subsequent chapters.

Educational Workshops

Frequently the inservice training program, sometimes referred to as professional career development, centers around a workshop. Workshops may be informal organizations in a local school system with a member of the staff serving as resource person. In some cases, it is possible to establish a relationship with a neighboring university to approve the program and offer credit for participation.

Another type of workshop—the original type—usually conducted on a university campus, is the gathering of a group of mature persons interested in a specific problem. A group of resource persons is formed to assist members of the workshop in defining their individual problems and to assist the individuals in finding solutions to these problems. The cooperating school districts usually participate by furnishing part of the cost, tuition and transportation, for example. The teachers may contribute their time and living expenses.

Ordinarily this type of workshop provides for both study and recreation. In many cases, participants work and live in the area set aside for the workshop. They spend time in the intensive study of teaching methods, growth and development, curriculum, school organization, and personnel concerns. Since the school district receives the benefit of the teacher's effort in the workshop, teachers should be paid at their regular rate for participation. This makes it possible for participants to be chosen for their probable contribution rather than on the basis of those who can afford to participate. Furthermore, it is only fair that teachers who work eleven months instead of nine should receive extra remuneration.

Advantages claimed for the workshop. The workshop is based upon well-known principles of learning, such as interest, a felt need, and group procedures. It employs new methods of dealing with and learning through individual problems, resource groups, expert leadership, round table discussions, and writing. Among the advantages claimed for the workshop are:

1. It is concerned with specific needs and problems in a specific location.
2. The participant develops individually, socially, and emotionally as well as professionally.
3. It provides an opportunity for participants to make a contribution to the solution of relevant problems.
4. It provides a means of supplying practical assistance to people in specific positions.
5. It provides easy access to competent assistance.
6. It provides an open climate for both individual and group consideration of educational problems.
7. It furnishes a stimulus to continued professional development.
8. The materials and ideas developed in workshops are useful in school situations.

Workshops and professional development programs are not panaceas for the ills which may plague any particular school system. They do provide a technique by which the principal and his teachers may improve the learning experience for students.

Changes in Education

The literature in the field of education today is filled with such terms as open classrooms, ungraded schools, modular schedules, differentiated staffing, microteaching, closed circuit television, flexible scheduling, individualized learning, and so forth. Significant changes have taken place in school organization, teaching methods, and instructional materials, and the underlying reason for these changes is the adaptation of the learning experience to the needs of the individual. The rapidity and complexity of the changes have placed new demands upon the principal as he seeks to involve his faculty in adapting to the use of new techniques. It is impossible in a chapter such as this to deal adequately with all the changes that are occurring, but some will be discussed briefly. If the principal is to assume the leadership role in the improvement of educational experiences for students in his school, he needs professional study to become the change agent.

The Open Space Concept

For many years, a school meant a number of classrooms all approximately the same size, accommodating the same number of pupils, together with some usual auxiliary facilities. An elementary pupil advanced from one grade to the next usually upon an annual schedule. Today, however, many schools use the nongraded concept. A pupil attains the objectives that are determined for a given level and then proceeds to the next level where he deals with a different and appropriate set of objectives. He thus proceeds at his own rate.

Traditionally one teacher presided over the class at a given grade level. All subjects were taught and all evaluations made by one teacher. Schools using the open space idea and utilizing the nongraded concept usually organize the teachers into teams appropriate to the work of a given level. Thus, even at the primary level, the pupils have the opportunity for personal relationships with not one but several teachers. The team works cooperatively in determining performance-based objectives, preparing instructional materials, and determining the criteria for evaluating progress. Both teaching methods and progress evaluation are directed to the individual pupil. His strengths are encouraged and his weaknesses are made a matter of record, with methods and materials being designed to remove those weaknesses.

From what has been said, it is evident that the nongraded school is different from the school that has existed for a good many years. But before the concept can be used to its greatest extent, many changes are needed: the faculty must believe that it is a worthwhile concept; facilities must be adequate to accomplish the change; space must be adequate and instructional materials centers must be a part of the operation; and new curriculum materials are required. It is also necessary to keep the parents informed concerning its development; a favorable attitude upon their part is basic to its success. Experience in schools that have tried the idea seems to indicate that the results to be obtained are worth the efforts.

Teamteaching

For a good many years, most secondary schools operated under a fixed schedule that would permit students to offer their credentials to higher institutions and to employment agencies with accomplishments measured in terms of the Carnegie Unit. Specific time allotments for the various academic disciplines were standard, and other subjects, by virtue of the limitations of scheduling, tended toward the same pattern. This arrangement is no longer true in many school systems; schedules are now described in many terms such as flexible and modular.

One of the outcomes of having more flexibility in the schedule has been the development of teamteaching. Teamteaching is an arrangement of the staff into teams which are jointly responsible for working together to provide for a significant part of the students' learning experiences. Two or more members of the teaching staff form the team and in many cases they are assisted by aides or paraprofessional help.

The matter of team organization is a subject for local determination. A team may be made up of teachers who teach the same subject at the same level. For example, in a school offering twenty classes of American History, all the teachers of this subject might form a team. A decision would be made as to the responsibilities of each team member after group consideration of each member's special interests. Teamteaching techniques are appropriate for many areas of instruction—even in physical education.[9]

Another approach would provide for forming a team of teachers who would teach different disciplines. A team such as this would use a large block of time and determine for themselves the amount of time spent on any of the disciplines within a given day or week. The interdisciplinary approach serves to break down the usual compartmentalization that has characterized most teaching. A project developed in East Ladue Junior High School of St. Louis, Missouri, included four academic solids (mathematics,

---

[9]David Reams and T. J. Bleier, "Developing Teamteaching in Physical Education," *National Association of Secondary School Principals Bulletin*, 53, No. 340 (November 1969), 9–18.

science, social studies, and language arts at the seventh grade level.[10] In the light of the success of the project, the future objectives of the program were described as follows:

1. To provide flexibility in the grouping of students for instruction
2. To provide flexibility and variety in the time allocations of the four academic subjects involved (math, science, social studies, language arts)
3. To define and develop learning experiences which cultivate greater efficiency in independent study
4. To provide more opportunity for students to exercise self-direction, responsibility, and self-reliance in the pursuit of their education
5. To transfer to teachers the power to make managerial and substantive decisions without creating greater problems than they solve
6. To provide a climate which encourages sharing among teachers of the same grade level as they respond to problems common to all or some of the team disciplines
7. To encourage cooperative planning, teaching, and evaluating on the part of teachers for engendering increased understanding of each child's growth and development reflected in the classroom pursuits

Most teamteaching arrangements utilize methods of independent study, large and small group discussion, and flexibility in time allotments. It is clear that the teamteaching concept involves changes in the traditional system. Its success is possible only when it is well planned and has the support of the professional staff.

Differentiated Staffing

The rationale behind the concept of differentiated staffing is that different levels of competency may be used in the instructional process. Some of the activities require a high degree of expertise, while other tasks may be fairly routine in nature. J. Lloyd Trump, an early advocate of differentiated staffing, suggested that future schools would differentiate the kinds of competencies needed in instruction and would organize the staff to secure better utilization.[11]

A review of the literature reveals the general tendency to establish four levels. One level would involve a teacher with considerable expertise, competence, and leadership potential; a second level would be made up of

---

[10]George Beltz and John Shaughnessy, "Interdisciplinary Team Teaching," *National Association of Secondary School Principals Bulletin*, 54, No. 347 (September 1970), 47–60.

[11]J. Lloyd Trump, *Images of the Future* (Urbana, Illinois: Commission on Experimental Study of the Utilization of Staff in Secondary Schools, 1959), p. 15.

teachers who would spend their entire time instructing students. The work of the traditional teacher would be accomplished at this level. A third level might include teachers who would have not attained tenure status; they could be beginning teachers. The fourth level would be made up of paraprofessionals or teacher aides. Their chief responsibility could be the preparation of materials, clerical work, and other duties of supportive nature.

Another arrangement suggested by Lloyd K. Bishop contains five levels:[12] (1) intern teacher: one with no previous experience; (2) associate teacher: a certified teacher but not of tenure status; (3) staff teacher: a teacher on tenure, or in other words, a general classroom teacher; (4) master teacher: one with a master's degree and qualifications to assume leadership; and (5) instructional specialist: the highest category, one who would be expected to have ability in curriculum building, research, and so forth. Bishop further suggests that supporting personnel in the form of instructional associate, instructional assistant, and instructional aide or clerical aide should be provided. The instructional associate would have two years of college training, and the instructional assistants and aides would be high school graduates.

It is evident that staff utilization developments create situations where different levels and different kinds of competencies can be utilized. Furthermore, compensation may be determined accordingly. Greater responsibilities and higher competencies may be rewarded through payment of higher salaries. Possibilities for research and experimentation are increased. The end result should be a better learning experience for pupils with a high priority on individualized learning.

Innovations such as those described here cannot be satisfactorily achieved unless those who are involved share in planning the changes. The community, faculty, and students should be made aware of the changes and be kept fully informed concerning them; the responsibility rests largely with the school principal for coordinating the efforts. Such activities should have high priority as the principal plans his program of professional career development.

Selected References

ACKERLEY, ROBERT L., *The Reasonable Exercise of Authority*. Washington: National Association of Secondary School Principals, 1969.

ALEXANDER, WILLIAM M., *The Changing Secondary Curriculum: Readings*. New York: Holt, Rinehart and Winston, Inc., 1969.

ANRIG, GREGORY R., "Student Unrest: High Schools Brace," *The American School Board Journal*, 157 (October 1969), 20–24.

12Lloyd K. Bishop, "Comprehensive Staff Differentiation," *New York University Education Quarterly* (Spring 1971), pp. 22–23.

BAILEY, STEPHEN R., *Disruption in Urban Public Secondary Schools*. Washington: National Association of Secondary School Principals, 1970.

BARBER, WILLIAM R., "The Principal and Morale," *School and Community,* LVI (March 1970), 23.

BENT, RUDYARD K., and HENRY H. KRONENBERG, *Principles of Secondary Education* (5th ed.). New York: McGraw-Hill Book Company, 1966.

CHESLER, MARK, CARL JORGENSEN, and PHYLLIS ERENBERG, *Planning Educational Change: Integrating the Desegregated School*. Washington, D.C.: Government Printing Office, 1970.

CULBERTSON, JACK, and STEPHEN HENCLEY, *Preparing New Administrators: New Perspectives*. Columbus, Ohio: University Council for Educational Administration, 1962.

EIDELL, TERRY L., and JOANNE M. KITCHEL, eds., *Knowledge Production and Utilization in Educational Administration*. Columbus, Ohio: University Council for Educational Administration, 1968.

FREY, SHERMAN H., and KEITH R. GETSCHMAN, eds., *School Administration: Selected Readings*. New York: Thomas Y. Crowell Company, 1968.

GOLDMAN, SAMUEL, *The School Principal*. New York: Center for Applied Research in Education, 1966.

HUGHES, LARRY W., and GERALD C. UBBEN, "New Leadership for the Secondary School," *National Association of Secondary School Principals Bulletin*, 54 (September 1970), 61–79.

IRWIN, P. H., and F. W. LANGHAM, JR., "Change Seekers: Management of Change," *Harvard Business Review*, 44 (January 1966), 81–92.

MARJORIBANKS, KEVIN, "Bureaucratic Structure in Schools and Its Relationship to Dogmatic Leadership," *The Journal of Educational Research*, 63 (April 1970), 355–58.

MILLER, VAN, *The Public Administration of American School Systems*. New York: The Macmillan Company, 1965.

OTTO, HENRY J., and DAVID C. SANDERS, *Elementary School Organization and Administration* (4th ed.). New York: Appleton-Century-Crofts, 1964.

PUNKE, H. H., "Education for Leadership," *Adult Leadership*, 14 (March 1966), 297–98.

RUBIN, LOUIS J., *Frontiers in School Leadership*. Chicago: Rand McNally and Company, 1970.

STEWART, BOB R., "Supervisory Behavior," *Educational Leadership*, 27 (February 1970), 521–27.

VACCA, RICHARD S., "The Principal's Responsibility in Relation to Court Decisions Involving Public Education," *The High School Journal*, 53 (February 1970), 323–32.

WHITE, BEVERLY L., "The Package and the Supervisor," *Educational Leadership*, 27 (May 1970), 788–91.

WILSON, ROBERT E., *Educational Administration*. Columbus, Ohio: Charles E. Merril Publishing Company, 1966.

7

Educational Diagnosis
and Compensatory Programs

The Need for Educational Diagnosis

Children do not all learn the same bit of knowledge equally well at the same rate, nor do they all adapt well to the school environment in the same length of time. Because of this, facts relating to predictability of grade overlapping in language skills indicate that approximately two-thirds of any class will deviate from the grade norm by one or more grade levels. The variations in grade overlapping in arithmetic are substantial; it is estimated that approximately three-tenths of the pupils in an intermediate grade class deviate from the class norm by one or more grade equivalence in arithmetic.

Experienced administrators and teachers recognize that these differences in achievement exist, extending upward as well as downward. Provisions for those pupils achieving at a higher level than their peers cannot be neglected, but the emphasis of this chapter is on identifying and providing for those pupils whose achievement is on a lower level.

A number of questions face the administrator and teacher as they plan for slower and less accurate learners. Which of them are "pseudolaggards" who possess ability, but cannot or will not demonstrate it in class or on standardized tests? Which of these backward pupils cannot be considered as underachievers because they are learning at a rate appropriate to their mental ability, physical condition, and experience background? Which of these students are best helped by low-pressure developmental instruction? For which of them can corrective provisions be made in the regular classroom? Which of them require individual help from a specialist? What

152

should the nature of the corrective program be? When should referral be made to nonschool specialists for diagnosis or therapy?

Educational Diagnosis

It is as unreasonable to expect a principal to be a skilled diagnostician as it is to expect a classroom teacher to have skills in that area. But both the administrator and the teacher should be familiar with some of the studies that have been conducted on the subject of diagnosis; they should also have some knowledge about instruments used to identify students with learning disabilities; and they should understand the approaches in teaching that might be used in the school to maximize learning opportunities for all children. If the learning difficulties of young people are not identified and if opportunities are not provided for them to develop, they will in all probability develop negative attitudes toward learning, toward the school which has denied them an opportunity to learn, and even toward life. It is unrealistic to expect every school within a system to provide its own means of advanced educational diagnosis, and it is just as unreasonable to expect that thorough diagnosis must or can be provided for all pupils. However it is not unreasonable to expect every school to play a vital and basic role in the identification of those youngsters with unusual learning problems. It is essential then that the learning disabilities of children be identified at the earliest possible stage.

Studies of Educational Diagnosis

William E. Ferinden and Sherman Jacobson reported a study they conducted which had the objective of developing a test battery which would be valid for diagnosing potential learning disabilities at the kindergarten level.[1] The first step in the investigation was to identify children who would experience the greatest difficulty in learning to read. Sixty-seven children were involved in the study from ten kindergarten classes. Eight of the classes included primarily culturally deprived students, and two classes were comprised mainly of middle-class students. Teachers selected pupils whom they believed would develop learning problems and pupils whom they believed to be most capable of performing at first grade level. A school psychologist and two learning disability specialists used four diagnostic tests: the Wide Range Achievement Test (WRAT); the EEIS; the Bender Visual-Motor Gestalt Test; and the Metropolitan Reading Readiness Test (MRRT), Form R. They reported that for this age group the Bender Gestalt

---

[1]William E. Ferinden, Jr., and Sherman Jacobson, "Early Identification of Learning Disabilities," *Journal of Learning Disabilities*, 3, No. 11 (November 1970), 48–54.

was not reliable, and that the MRRT was an effective predictor only if the total test scores fell below 30 percent. The WRAT and the EEIS, however, were reliable for predicting which children would not experience reading success in the first grade.

The authors indicated that teachers' observations concerning reading success were 80 percent accurate; they added that if teachers used the validated abbreviated WRAT and EEIS instruments, they would be 90 percent accurate in discovering potential learning disabilities. The teacher's importance is indicated by the authors' statement: "The teacher has a key role in the early identification of children with learning disabilities."[2] They also concluded that if teachers were taught to administer diagnostic tests, the clinical team could spend more time in consultation and remediation.

Banas and Wills[3] report that the child vulnerable to learning problems has a normal or above normal I.Q. but is not achieving his full academic potential because of any one of a number of dysfunctions. According to them, a child may be labeled dyslexic, educationally handicapped, learning disabled, or just plain lazy. They stress that the child's perceptual disability is not readily apparent, and that pediatricians and educators do not always recognize the signs of learning disability. Because the child is often bright, expectations are high—sometimes leading to emotional problems and frustration.

The authors stress that the nature of the factors interfering with learning progress must be defined. An analysis of the patterns of strengths and weaknesses is the key, and the types of errors, the strengths and compensations, rather than test scores are significant factors in understanding this child.

The question is often asked, "Are such diagnostic and remedial attempts, provisions, and materials worth the effort?" No one who has participated in the analysis and successful remediation of an underachiever, or observed the impact of this restructuring upon the lives of the pupil, his parents, and his teachers has the slightest doubt of the value of such a program. Relatively few disability cases fail to improve after receiving good diagnostic and remedial aid. Even in such cases, no educator can seriously argue that human happiness is not worth every effort in its behalf.

The remaining sections of this chapter will be addressed to those aspects of educational diagnosis and remediation with which every administrator should be familiar. Specific attention will be given to an overview of those factors associated with instances of educational disability, consideration of some basic principles of remedial instruction, and a more detailed

---

[2]Ferinden and Jacobson, "Early Identification of Learning Disabilities," p. 52.
[3]Norma Banas and I. H. Wills, "The Vulnerable Child and Prescriptive Teaching," *Academic Therapy*, IV, No. 3 (Spring 1969), 215–19.

examination of the identification of reading difficulties and materials useful in helping students who have reading problems.

Factors Associated With Learning Difficulties

For some time, research efforts were concentrated on identifying a single factor which would account for pupils' learning problems. Today, it is generally conceded that a complex of factors is usually involved, and the diagnostic task is now concerned with determining the relative influence of the various factors associated with the disability.

The following are factors which should be of prime consideration to principals and teachers.

Intellectual Factors

Intelligence as a measure of school learning capacity is a major factor to be considered in the diagnosis of learning difficulty. As a result of a number of research studies, most authorities in the area of remedial education suggest that underachievement should be defined as the discrepancy between the present achievement age and the present mental age of the pupil. Some school systems and remedial clinics will not provide special remedial services unless the difference between mental age and achievement age is more than one year for primary-grade pupils and two years or more for intermediate- and upper-grade pupils. In order to initiate a successful remedial program it is best to select those pupils with a good language background, a fair attitude toward learning, and the greatest discrepancy between mental age and achievement age.

Mental ability plays yet another role in educational diagnosis. While the intelligence quotient is an index of brightness—a ratio of learning rate $(IQ = \dfrac{\text{Mental Age}}{\text{Chronological Age}} \times 100)$—mental age itself is an index of the present mental maturity or power of the pupil. Numerous studies have pointed out that mental maturity involves a readiness to profit from initial skills instruction. While it is held that the specific mental age necessary for initial school success is dependent upon a number of pupil attributes as well as upon the nature of initial instruction, most authorities agree that mental maturity is a readiness factor of considerable importance. Every investigation shows that serious learning disability begins with the inappropriate adjustment of initial instruction to the mental maturity of the youngster.

Not all measures of intelligence are equally appropriate for the purposes of educational diagnosis. Group verbal intelligence tests tend to underestimate the aptitude of those children with reading and language disabilities, those with sensory and motor defects, those who are generally in-secure, and those children who react negatively to time pressure. The validity of group nonverbal tests is still a matter of conjecture among some authorities in educational measurement. The current acceptable practice in case investigation is to administer a standardized individual intelligence test such as the Revised Stanford-Binet Scales or one of the Wechsler intelligence tests to obtain a reasonable estimate of skills capacity. A few investigators have produced evidence that even these individual measuring processes have a tendency to underestimate the language-disabled child.

Intellectual power, while seldom considered to be the single most significant factor in educational disability, plays a key role in most school learning. Children with I.Q.'s of less than 70 can develop adequate basic skills, but more frequently they do not. On the other hand, few children with I.Q.'s of 130 and above fail to master the basic academic skills, regardless of the quality of education provided.

Physical Status Factors

School learning calls for an active interaction between sensory acuity and cognitive-motor response. It draws upon the experience background of the pupil which in turn is dependent upon his sensory-cognitive response interaction. Physical factors have long been known to exert an influence on learning. The child who cannot hear well, or whose eyesight is so defective that he cannot see what is being done in the classroom, cannot be expected to learn. The educational results which have followed the correction of faulty eyesight or hearing of children are too well known to require repetition here.

Malnutrition, which obviously interferes with normal learning, is unfortunately found more frequently than it is pleasant to contemplate—especially in schools in underprivileged areas. Not only can vitamin deficiencies or toxins in the blood cause physical conditions in children which handicap them in their educational work, but the glands of internal secretion also may at times fail to function properly, thus producing conditions in children which hinder school progress. Physical defects, such as those resulting from birth injuries, inherited disease, and accidents are also great handicaps for pupils in their school work.

Such physical deterrents cannot be diagnosed by teachers, but their presence may be suspected, particularly those which relate to malnutrition, sight, and hearing. The proper diagnosis of such defects should be made by medical practitioners who can prescribe proper treatment. The local school staff should have access to competent medical officers who can diagnose the needs of the physically handicapped. All children with low achievement records should be given a thorough physical examination; many may require careful and expert psychological diagnosis as well. Fortunately, medical service is becoming available to more school systems each year, and it may hopefully be expected to be even more prevalent in the future.

Social and Emotional Adjustment Factors

Within the last two decades, a substantial amount of the literature pertaining to underachievement has been concerned with the adjustment patterns of poor learners. To date there appears to be no consensus on the issues involved other than that an unusually large percentage of underachievers do exhibit abnormal adjustment patterns. Some writers have interpreted this to be the natural by-product of skill disability—the result of years of classroom frustration and parental pressure. Other investigators are of the opinion that poor adjustment factors precipitate learning disability, although they are not in agreement as to how this occurs. Some maintain that difficulty is to be expected as a result of the maladjusted child's inability to concentrate or to cooperate in closely structured skills instruction. It has also been suggested by other psychologists that the maladjusted child resists learning skills as a means of controlling or punishing the adults in his life.

But whether cause, effect, or concomitance, those who have worked with severe skills disability cases quickly become aware of the anxiety manifested by such children about their skill deficiency, the learning situation, and the attitudes of others concerning their adequacy. The necessity of establishing good learning rapport with these youngsters is a prime concern of remedial education.

There are implications here for school personnel that early identification, minor correction, and prevention can go a long way. Standardized personality tests are useful as rough screening measures, but they are far from exact. Projective techniques demand special training and experience on the part of teachers. Nevertheless, the qualifications for a good teacher should include an understanding of child development and keen powers of human observation. Some authorities are convinced that teachers, particularly at the early primary levels, can prevent much learning difficulty by identifying those youngsters having difficulty adjusting to peers, school rules, and adults. Studies have pointed out the need for greater teacher sensitivity to unusual patterns of aggression and nonmoral behavior.

Many pupil adjustment problems have been solved early by a wise and sympathetic teacher. Other problems are severe enough to require special attention from a counselor, case worker, school psychologist, or psychiatrist. Every school should have access to such counseling resources, as well as medical specialists. Procedures for referral of emotional health problems are quite similar to those for referral of physical health problems. Professional educators can fulfill a responsibility to public education in overcoming the stigmatization of emotional difficulties by acting in a calm, direct, accepting manner in identification, referral, and support of such children.

In every school personality clashes between pupils and teachers will prevent learning at times. Teachers who are suspicious of children's honesty or who resort to sarcasm are likely to have many cases of ineffective learning on the part of individual children. And even with the best of teachers, occasional strained relations which prevent effective learning will occur. At times the transfer of a student to another teacher will solve the difficulty, but such transfers should not be made to satisfy the whims of either teacher or student. At other times, wise counsel by the principal can resolve difficulties and restore harmony.

Experiential Background Factors

Investigation of the relationship between the nature and amount of experience background and underachievement is relatively recent. An increasing body of evidence pertaining to this relationship should be forthcoming, but broadly speaking, this area of concern includes all factors not innate to the individual child. It has been the practice to narrow experiential background concerns to those issues pertinent to the negative influence of abnormal home and nonschool environment upon school achievement. Studies have concerned themselves with relating underachievement in skills to such factors as low socioeconomic status; non-English-speaking homes; isolation from other children; limited general cultural contact; frequent shift of home and school; negative attitude climate at home toward school and education; inadequate preschool experiences with books, language, and number concepts; and absence of educated models within the home and neighborhood.

The problem of lower class youth attending American middle-class schools has made clear the fact that it is unreasonable to expect the same standards of achievement for these children that we expect for middle-class youth of comparable intelligence. The lower class child appears to be limited in his experience and language background, in identification with educated models, and in reward for that school success which he does obtain. At upper grade levels, he may find that he follows a curriculum rather unrelated to his life needs, that he has classes with teachers who cannot or will not extend themselves in his behalf, and, due to lack of encouragement, he is likely to find himself frozen out of the nonacademic aspects of school life.

Basic Principles of Remedial Instruction

1. Remedial instruction should be based upon thorough diagnosis. No program to overcome deficiencies should be undertaken until the specific problem or problems of the individual are identified. Too often, we treat symptoms and are then dismayed at the meager results achieved.

2. The materials used should be at the student's level. It is highly desirable that all students experience success; this is particularly true of those who, because of their learning disabilities, have experienced only failure. With imagination and a good working knowledge of where the student is in his development, the teacher can select materials that the student can handle. He will therefore be encouraged to take the next step because he knows that he can manage it. One promising approach in this area, peer-produced materials, will be discussed in a later chapter.

3. The materials should be interesting in content and in style. History, biographies, novels, and stories have been rewritten which employ a simplified vocabulary while retaining the beauty and flow of the original passages. These have also been adapted to the various audio-visual media.

4. The student should be aware of the nature of his disability. Remedial work is probably most effective when done individually, but it can also be done with groups of students with similar difficulties. The basic principle is to let the student know that the disability exists, and that steps will be taken to overcome it (small steps with built-in success).

Remedial work must be done regularly and systematically. Plateaus of learning will be encountered which neither teacher nor student can permit to discourage them. If an approach fails, don't give up the student— give up the method!

Identification of Reading Difficulties

It has already been pointed out in this chapter that it is the responsibility of the classroom teacher and principal to care for minor diagnosis and corrective provisions. A working knowledge of specific diagnostic procedures should be a part of the principal's personal data bank so that he can allocate more intelligently the needed resources, and offer effective leadership for this important segment of the school's program.

In some schools today, much of this responsibility is being delegated by the principal to a curriculum coordinator who is expected to work with the teacher and the child while the administrator keeps himself somewhat removed from the problem. The work of this curriculum specialist often covers a very broad area. He or she often functions as record keeper, truant officer, crying-towel distributor, liaison between teacher and principal, tester, substitute teacher, book and supply carrier, curriculum innovator, and specialist in every subject field.

If the school is fortunate enough to have a remedial reading teacher or any kind of clinical facility, the curriculum coordinator can and will work closely with those specialists. This does not, however, preclude the necessity for the principal to have firsthand knowledge and a good understanding of the specific diagnostic procedures used in his school.

It has been said that all good teaching of reading is diagnostic. As teaching and learning are occurring, the teacher should be observing and recording individual strengths and weaknesses for the purpose of adjusting instruction to those needs.

Among teachers and parents there is a growing recognition of the importance of vision as a factor in the reading progress and general well-being of children. No screening test is as reliable in detecting vision problems as the observant teacher with the school records of a child's performance. The American Optometric Association's Committee on Visual Problems of Children and Youth has compiled a list of symptoms—*Teacher's Guide to Vision Problems*[4]—which is helpful to the teacher as she compiles information on each pupil.

The limitations of the Snellen letter test at twenty feet are now well-known. The ability to fuse at near point is of far greater significance to the child's ability to read than whether or not he can see across a playground or hit a target twenty feet away.

Once the alert teacher observes signs of possible vision dysfunction, the principal should know that the *Keystone Visual Survey*,[5] which can be quickly and easily given on a telebinocular machine, will give a very accurate screening which in turn will indicate whether or not a child should be referred to an eye specialist. The telebinocular uses stereograms which provide information on vision at both near and far points. It measures such things as fusion, stereopsis, color perception, acuity, and vertical and lateral posture. Special stereograms are available at the readiness and pre-reading levels.

Whether or not a child is fitted with glasses, it is often necessary to expose him to visual training where a normal sequence of visual skills will be developed and proper visual habits acquired. Limited visual training may be carried out in the classroom through various visual tracking materials, but for the most part this is best left to the professional optometrist. More and more local optometrists are working cooperatively with the reading specialists, and fortunately so.

The ability to distinguish between sounds is essential to the reading process. Hearing losses or poor auditory discrimination may interfere with the use of sounds as aids to word recognition. If through teacher observation a child is thought to have a hearing loss, the principal needs to know that either a detailed pure tone test or a quick sweep test on a Maico Audiometer will give an indication of the amount of loss at various frequencies. Before this referral is made, a check for wax stoppage in the ear should be made.

---

[4]*Teacher's Guide to Vision Problems* (St. Louis: American Optometric Association, 1967).

[5]*Keystone Visual Survey* (Meadville, Pennsylvania: Keystone View Company, 1961).

If a principal is fortunate enough to have an Audiometer as part of his permanent inventory, a small room with burlap or monks cloth on two walls and carpeting on the floor will acoustically deaden the room and make accurate screening much more possible. Some machines (Audio-Rater-Bausch Lomb) now come equipped with earphones which encase liquid which deadens extraneous noises.

In this chapter, reference is made to the use of the Standard-Binet scales or the Wechsler Intelligence Scale for Children for measurement of intelligence.

The scores from such tests provide an indication of the student's potential and, along with teacher observations, will help clarify the possible need for remediation. In most school systems these tests are given and interpreted only by psychologists. This means that depending upon the availability of school psychologists, a great many, or more realistically very few, WISCs are given during a school year. The principal should know about the *Slosson Intelligence Test for Children and Adults.*[6] This test can be given and scored within ten to twenty minutes and can be administered by professional personnel who have not had specialized training in testing. It correlates very favorably with the WISC.

The *Peabody Picture Vocabulary Test*[7] requires no special educational preparation to administer other than familiarity with the test materials and some practice in giving it. This test is untimed and usually takes about ten minutes. Tables supplied by the publisher convert raw scores to I.Q. figures, age equivalencies, and percentile equivalencies. As is so often the case, neither the Slosson nor the Peabody test is geared to the disadvantaged child with a poor language background, and so cannot be considered valid in such cases.

Sooner or later a principal is going to have an "enlightened" and slightly desperate mother tell him that her child is a "dyslexic" or has a "specific learning disability." Whether or not the principal subscribes to the theories concerning brain dominance in relation to reading achievement, he should be familiar with terms and general concepts of those theories. Since the medical and educational professions are at odds within themselves over the claims of such theorists as Dolman and Delacato, the school administrator is not expected to have taken a stand one way or another, but he should be knowledgeable and willing to listen to the distraught parent whose last hope may be lumping all her child's failures into the dyslexia category.

Usually children who are placed in this category are of average or

---

[6]*Slosson Intelligence Test for Children and Adults* (East Aurora, N.Y.: Slosson Educational Publishers, 1963).

[7]*Peabody Picture Vocabulary Test* (Circle Pines, Minn.: American Guidance Service, Inc., 1965).

above average intelligence, but they fail to become good readers. There are usually more boys than girls in this group. They tend to be hyperactive and poorly coordinated. They have short attention spans and find concentration difficult. They may write backward, reverse letters such as "b" and "d" or "p" and "q." They reverse words, say "no" for "on" and "was" for "saw." They may be found to be right-handed and footed but left-eyed, thus indicating that crossed or mixed dominance may be present. The theory explaining such children's failure to read is that it is often due to a lack of complete development of the dominant half of the brain. No remediation should be attempted until development of complete dominance has been established.

The principal should know the simple diagnostic procedures which can be followed to identify dominance and laterality-directionality. The child may be asked to walk a chalk line or a walking beam forward and backward. He may be asked to throw and catch a ball; use scissors; write his name; kick a ball; hop on one foot; look through a tube, a cone, or a small hole in a card. All these procedures will give quick indication of dominance and laterality-directionality. Laterality and body image must be established before directionality can be obtained.

If more refined and comprehensive screening is desired, the Frostig Developmental Test of Visual Perception,[8] or the *Developmental Test of Visual-Motor Integration* (VMI)[9] may be administered. Many adaptations of the Bender Gestalt forms test are used to detect visual perceptual and visual motor deficiencies. These tests can also give some indication of possible minimal brain damage.

Once possible physical reasons for the child's inability to read have been eliminated, diagnostic tests for specific skills may be given. To identify difficulties in phonics, sight word identification, oral reading, and comprehension, various batteries are available. Popular among these are:

Spache Diagnostic Reading Scales, by George D. Spache, 1963. California Test Bureau, Del Monte Research, 2165 Park Blvd., Monterey, California 93940.

Standardized Oral Reading Paragraphs, by Gray, 1963. Test Division of Bobbs-Merrill Company, Inc., 4300 West 62nd Street, Indianapolis, Indiana 46268.

Durrell Analysis of Reading Difficulty, by Donald Durrell, 1955. Harcourt Brace Jovanovich, Inc., 757 Third Avenue, New York, N.Y. 10017.

Primary Reading Tests, by Gates-MacGinitie, 1965. Teachers College Press, Teachers College, Columbia University, New York, N.Y. 10027.

---

[8]Marianne Frostig and David Horne, *The Frostig Program for the Development of Visual Perception* (Chicago: Follett Publishing Company, 1964).

[9]*Developmental Test of Visual-Motor Integration* (Chicago: Follett Educational Corp., 1967).

Phonics Knowledge Survey, by Dolores Durkin and Leonard Meshover, 1964. Teachers College Press, Teachers College, Columbia University, New York, N.Y. 10027.

Reading Readiness Analysis, by Murphy and Durrell, 1964. Harcourt Brace Jovanovich, Inc., 757 Third Avenue, New York, N.Y. 10017.

Developmental Reading Tests, by Bond, Clymer and Hoyt, 1955. Lyons & Carnahan, 407 East 25th Street, Chicago, Ill. 60616.

Reading Aptitude Tests, by Marion Monroe. Houghton Mifflin Company, 110 Tremont Street, Boston, Mass. 02107.

In addition, a complete diagnostic battery may include tests of auditory discrimination, speech analysis, word analysis, spelling, and handwriting. All of these combine to give a reading behavior record which may be sent to the classroom teacher for help in her individualized planning, and for inclusion in the student's cumulative folder.

Many publishers of basal readers are now including very good short, but comprehensive, diagnostic tests which should be administered by the classroom teacher. Along with these tests, an inventory of reading attitudes may also prove helpful in the selection of materials to be used by an individual student.

Materials for Use in Working With Reading Disabilities

In the event that clinical facilities are not available to a school, a principal may secure a number of materials for use in a visual-perceptual training program which can be carried out by classroom teachers. These materials are for the most part available on ditto masters which may be inexpensively duplicated. Widely used among materials of this type are visual discrimination and visual motor practice exercises put out by Continental Press (127 Cain St., N.W. Atlanta, Ga. 30303). *The Frostig Program for the Development of Visual Perception*[10] includes exercises, worksheets, and workbooks for use in a training program. Many schools are making use of volunteer mothers who offer a visual-perceptual program based on Frostig materials.

Ann Arbor Publishers puts out a self-instruction workbook for perceptual skills in reading called *Visual Tracking* by the Ann Arbor Press, P.O. Box 1446, Ann Arbor, Mich. 48104. The exercises provide practice in the improvement of visual discrimination through a left-to-right progression, and provide for improving skill in following a line of print. Errors which result because of reversals, omissions, substitutions, and/or additions may be corrected. The test also serves to reinforce alphabet skills.

---

[10]Marianne Frostig and David Horne, 1964.

Nearly all schools have filmstrip machines available. A fine set of visual-perception skill filmstrips is available at small cost from Educational Activities, Inc. (Box 392, Freeport, N.Y. 11520).

The G. N. Getman *Developing Learning Readiness Program*[11] is a visual motor tactile skills program. It includes templates; filmstrips; worksheets on ditto masters; space masks; eye movement charts; space sighters; pressure sensitive targets; and movable Melvin, a manipulative puppet designed to help establish body image. Also, simple materials such as peg boards, beads for stringing, parquetry blocks and the commercial "Etch-a-Sketch" are all useful tools in developing eye-hand coordination, visual discrimination, and left-to-right progression.

The *Remediation of Learning Disabilities*[12] by Robert E. Vallett is a program designed to aid persons working with pupils with learning disabilities. It contains concrete activities and exercises to help develop the skills required by the individual needs of a given pupil. Other materials are:

Good Reading for Poor Readers, by George D. Spache, 1970. The Garrard Press, 1607 N. Market Street, Champaign, Ill. 61820.

The Slow Learner in the Classroom, by Newell C. Kephart, 1960. Charles E. Merrill Publishing Company, 1300 Alum Creek Drive, Columbus, Ohio 43216.

Common Sense in Teacher Reading, by Roma Gans, 1963. The Bobbs-Merrill Company, Inc., 4300 West 62nd Street, Indianapolis, Indiana 46268.

Remedial Training for Children with Specific Disability in Reading, Spelling and Penmanship, by Anne Gillingham and Bessie Stillman, 1965. Educators Publishing Service, 75 Moulton Street, Cambridge, Mass. 02138

Phonics in Listening, In Speaking, In Reading, In Writing, by Scott and Thompson, 1962. McGraw Hill Book Company, Webster Division, Manchester Rd., Manchester, Mo. 63011.

Talking Time, by Scott and Thompson, 1951. McGraw Hill Book Company, Webster Division, Manchester Rd., Manchester, Mo. 63011.

Every major publisher of basal readers is now offering complete programs with catchy titles in remedial, individualized, slow learner, and advanced or challenge reading. All have their good points. Kits also abound to provide for every conceivable reading need. Machines with complete programs flood the market. A principal should keep current and provide himself with every opportunity to review and evaluate some of these in-

---

[11]G. N. Getman, *Developing Learning Readiness Program* (Manchester, Mo.: Webster Division, McGraw Hill Book Company).

[12]Robert E. Vallett, *The Remediation of Learning Difficulties* (Palo Alto, Ca.: Fearon Publishers, Inc., 1967).

novations for possible use in his school. Major book companies are willing and eager to provide sample materials or to set up demonstrations and/or teacher workshops at no charge to the school. An hour or two spent with their representatives would be a good investment.

Selected References

BANAS, NORMA, and I. H. WILLS, "The Vulnerable Child and Prescriptive Teaching," *Academic Therapy*, IV, No. 3 (Spring 1969).

BOND, CLYMER, and J. HOYT, *Developmental Reading Tests (Silent Diagnostic)*. Chicago: Lyons & Carnahan, 1955.

Development Test of Visual-Motor Integration, Follet Educational Corp., Chicago, Ill., 1967.

DURKIN, DOLORES, and LEONARD MESHOVER, *Phonics Knowledge Survey*. New York: Teachers College, Columbia University, 1964.

DURRELL, DONALD, *Durrell Analysis of Reading Difficulty*. Yonkers-on-Hudson, New York: World Book Co., 1955.

FERINDEN, WILLIAM E. JR., and SHERMAN JACOBSON, "Early Identification of Learning Disabilities," *Journal of Learning Disabilities*, 3, No. 11 (November 11, 1970).

FROSTIG, MARIANNE, and DAVID HORNE, *The Frostig Program for the Development of Visual Perception*. Chicago: Follett Publishing Company, 1964.

GANS, ROMA, *Common Sense in Teaching Reading*. Indianapolis: The Bobbs Merrill Company, Inc., 1963.

GATES-MACGINITIE, *Reading Tests*. Teachers College, Columbia University, New York, 1965.

GETMAN, G. N., *Developing Learning Readiness Program*. New York: McGraw Hill Book Company, 1968.

GETMAN, G. N., and E. R. KANE, *The Physiology of Readiness*. Minneapolis, Minn.: Programs to Accelerate School Success, 1964.

GILLINGHAM, ANNE, and BESSIE W. STILLMAN, *Remedial Training for Children with Specific Disability in Reading, Spelling and Penmanship*. Cambridge, Mass.: Educators Publishing Service, Inc., 1965.

GRAY, WILLIAM S., *Standardized Oral Reading Paragraphs*. New York: Test Division of Bobbs Merrill Company, Inc., 1963.

KEPHART, NEWELL C., *The Slow Learner in the Classroom*. Columbus, Ohio: Charles E. Merrill Books, Inc., 1960.

Keystone Visual Survey, Keystone View Company, Meadville, Pa., 1961.

KIRK, S. A., *Diagnosis and Remediation of Psycholinguistic Disabilities*. Urbana, Ill.: University of Illinois Press, 1966.

MONROE, MARION, *Reading Aptitude Tests*. Cambridge, Mass.: The Riverside Press, 1963.

MURPHY, HELEN A., and DONALD D. DURRELL, *Reading Readiness Analysis.* New York: Harcourt, Brace and World, Inc., 1964.

Peabody Picture Vocabulary Test, American Guidance Service, Inc., Circle Pines, Minn., 1965.

SCOTT, LOUISE BINDER, and J. J. THOMPSON, *Phonics in Listening, In Speaking, In Reading, In Writing.* Manchester, Mo.: Webster Division, McGraw Hill Book Company, 1962.

————, *Talking Time.* New York: McGraw Hill Book Company, 1951.

Slosson Intelligence Test for Children and Adults. Slosson Educational Publishers, East Aurora, New York, 1963.

SPACHE, GEORGE D., *Diagnostic Reading Scales.* Monterey, Calif.: California Test Bureau, 1963.

————, *Good Reading for Poor Readers.* Champaign, Ill.: The Garrard Press, 1968.

Teacher's Guide to Vision Problems, American Optometric Association, St. Louis, Mo., 1963.

VALLETT, ROBERT E., *The Remediation of Learning Difficulties.* Palo Alto, Calif.: Fearon Publishers, Inc., 1967.

Visual Tracking, Ann Arbor Press, Ann Arbor, Michigan, 1962.

8

Some Approaches to Teaching

An old refrain heard in faculty lounges throughout the land is, "I love teaching, but I wish I had a principal who would let me try things. He's a nice guy, but all he's interested in is that I arrive on time and leave on time, that the kids are quiet, the parents happy, and that I don't rock the boat."

At the same time in administrative offices throughout the land, the principal is musing, "I wish my teachers would try something new in teaching. What can I do to help them?" A principal has taken the first step forward in helping his teachers when he has honestly asked himself the question, "What can I do to help them?" This question, in itself, indicates that he views his role as primarily that of a facilitator in the teaching-learning process. His efforts and yours as principal and educator must be focused upon the teaching and learning that occurs in the classroom, in the hallway, in the gymnasium, on the playground, on the athletic field, on the buses—in short, wherever students come together under the jurisdiction of the school.

The primary purpose of this chapter is to describe briefly some approaches to teaching which have been tried with rather good results. One or two of the approaches might be profitably undertaken in any school if the principal discusses them with his teachers, encourages them to modify the approaches so that they fit their style of teaching, and provides the necessary resources and personal support necessary to ensure a reasonable amount of success.

167

Individualized Instruction

There is general agreement today that all students do not learn at the same rate. Indeed, an individual student does not learn at the same rate in any given subject on any one day. It is important that the teacher recognize this fact and keep in mind that the ultimate goal is the student's mastery of a subject. The materials and the assistance given by the teacher should permit the learner to set a rate that fits his learning style, but that also prompts regular progress toward achieving the teacher's and the student's learning goals.

Wayne E. Williamson, in reporting on an experimental program at John Dewey High School in New York City, writes:

> It is conceded that (1) most students can achieve mastery if given time for learning rate; thus, (2) it is essential that school programs are altered to the time students need for learning. Furthermore, (3) it is profitable to provide optional or alternate opportunities for learning. A precondition to mastery (4) is the formulation of specific objectives for the learning sequence, and that the learner (5) must be aware of the nature of the task he is to learn and the procedures involved in learning it. It (6) is desirable to segment a course or subject into small units of learning, and to evaluate at the termination of each unit. And, lastly, (7) it is conducive to increased effort toward learning if students are handled as individuals in small groups to go over their difficulties as related to subject matter and tests and given continuous feedback by their teachers concerning specific strengths and weaknesses.[1]

Individualized instruction does not just happen because a principal or teacher thinks that it is a good idea. One basic element necessary to a good individualized instructional program is clearly defined objectives for each unit and each course, developed and understood by both teacher and student. For years objectives have been phrased in lofty terms which were beautiful but so general that no one could possibly determine the extent to which the objectives were reached. Today greater specificity is needed in writing objectives so that the pupil's progress toward achieving the objective can be more adequately measured. A popular term for such specific measurable objectives is *performance based objectives*. Thorwald Esbensen has

---

[1]Wayne E. Williamson, "A New Learning Center Thrives in New York," *The Clearing House*, 45, No. 1 (September 1970), 26. Reprinted by permission from the 1970 issue of *The Clearing House*.

written, "A performance objective is a description of an observable task to be performed by a learner to demonstrate that he has learned something."[2] He went on to say that, "The basic reason for using performance objectives is that no matter what it is that teachers and students are trying to do within the framework of formal schooling, they need to be able to tell, as they go along, how well they are doing it."[3]

Writing objectives in a specific manner so that the student, teacher, administrator, and parent can readily tell student progress or lack of it seems reasonable, but many teachers resist writing performance based objectives rather vigorously. They contend that objectives constructed in this way are too small, too narrow, and that they are teaching far more than can be expressed in written terms. They point out that performance based objectives can be written in the cognitive area (that which can be observed and measured), but it is difficult or impossible to write them for the affective domain (attitudes, values, commitments, and so forth). And to many teachers performance based objectives seem sterile, cold, and impersonal. Such arguments have a certain amount of validity, but the pressure is great and growing for schools to be held more accountable for what is happening in the classroom. It seems quite evident that the emphasis will be placed more and more upon the product turned out—the student and what he knows and is capable of doing when he finishes this part of his education. Although the prime goal of performance based objectives is *student achievement*, it seems very apparent that teachers will be judged more and more on the extent to which their students learn to do those measurable and observable things they are supposed to learn. Less and less credence will be given to those things which the teacher does in the hope that something will result.

Writing performance based objectives is a difficult and time-consuming task. For this reason, teachers should be given released time from classroom duties to write such objectives. They should also be encouraged to attend workshops and conferences sponsored by universities and state departments of education designed to assist them in understanding the value of performance based objectives, how they are written, field-tested, and then revised on the basis of experience gained. Committees composed of grade level or subject area teachers might be set up to write the objectives together. And because many school districts and states have written performance based objectives for most grade levels and subject areas, these objectives could be obtained, adapted, and improved for the local school. It is really not necessary to "rediscover the wheel" in writing performance

---

[2]Thorwald Esbensen, *Using Performance Objectives* (Tallahassee, Fla.: Office of Publications and Textbook Services, 1970), p. 11.

[3]Esbensen, *Using Performance Objectives*, p. 18.

based objectives, but it is essential that administrators and teachers know what has been done in other parts of the country in order to save themselves the time and labor of doing something that has already been done.

James E. Hagerty has suggested an approach for teaching a class where a few of the students are ahead of the rest, some are performing at grade level, several are performing at lower levels, a couple of discipline problems, and a new arrival. He suggests that one way to take care of the individual differences in such a group is to arrange the students into "Ad Hoc" groups according to levels of performance, and follow these basic steps:

1. State the idea or skill to be learned in terms of behavioral objectives that each individual in the class can readily understand.
2. Let each student evaluate himself according to these objectives to determine what he needs to learn further to attain them.
3. Diagnose the different learning requirements among the students and group them according to the similarities of their needs.
4. Make available diversified materials and learning activities that best suit each group's needs.
5. Let each student evaluate his progress in terms of his own group's progress.[4]

Hagerty also suggests:

Students can learn more effectively in a classroom situation if they are performing in groups that are contrived to meet their specific needs for a specific learning objective. As the objectives change during the year, so will the needs of each member of the class. Each new learning objective will require new "Ad Hoc" groupings.[5]

Approaches to Teaching the "Tuned Out"

A country as rich and as great as the United States, possessing such great resources, both natural and human, cannot permit any young person to believe that there is no place for him in its society. Each person at some time believes that he has value—as a fighter, as a person attractive to the opposite sex, or one who is able to run farther, swim faster, hold his breath longer, read signs at a greater distance than his peers. But along the way something may happen to him in the home, community, or school, and he may lose his pride in himself, and in his ability to perform. The school has

---

[4]James E. Hagerty, "Individualized Instruction Through 'Ad Hoc' Grouping," *The Clearing House*, 45, No. 2 (October 1970), 71.

[5]Hagerty, "Individualizing Instruction," p. 71.

the responsibility of seeing that each pupil has a successful school experience. If the schools genuinely believe that each person should have the opportunity to develop, then school administrators will deliberately plan programs to maximize the opportunity for such development to occur. Some approaches which have proved successful in creating an atmosphere in which growth can occur will be briefly considered in this section.

Peer-Produced Materials

Dr. Ward Brunson of Florida Atlantic University contends that it is difficult for most adults to think on a third grade level, but a third grader has no trouble at all interesting other third graders.[6] Putting this idea into practice, he has worked with teachers and helped them to accept the basic idea that every experience—field trips, conversation, music and art classes —can be a very reasonable basis for a student research project. Students do their own photography, research, script writing, titling, and even choose the background music for slide and tape shows. The procedure for writing a story is simple. A pupil tells his story to a tape recorder; it is then typed just as the pupil tells it. When played back, the teacher listens with the pupil to the recording; to avoid the possibility of reinforcing poor grammar and expression, the teacher may suggest other ways of telling certain sections of the story. After the pupil makes the revisions, either he or another pupil draws the illustrations. The material is then laminated and bound and placed in the library. It might be a humbling experience for writers of children's books to compare the circulation figures of their creative efforts to those of peer-produced materials! This approach is appropriate in any subject or at any grade level.

Student Tutors

There is nothing new in students helping other students to learn. Students have probably always crammed for examinations together, performed laboratory experiments together, and studied together. More advanced students have often been used to assist other students experiencing learning difficulties. Under the Lancastrian Monitorial System, teachers instruct older students who in turn drill younger students on their lessons.

The primary purpose of such practice was to instruct the learners, but the value to the tutor is also now recognized. In order to help another person learn, the instructor must know a great deal more about the subject than he will ever be able to share. Usually, his own interest in the subject becomes more intense as he attempts to stimulate the student's desire to

---

[6]Based on personal correspondence and discussion with Dr. Brunson.

learn. The act of explaining so that another person understands clarifies the points in the tutor's mind.

Youth want to serve, and using them as tutors will provide a constructive outlet for their energies. The experience may both help them to make occupational choices and enables the classroom teacher to spend more time with students who are making normal progress.

Games as a Teaching-Learning Approach

Education is designed to short cut experience, to reduce the number of times an individual must retrace the steps taken by others, and to avoid the failures which others have encountered as they developed their personal lifestyles and learned to survive in a complex society. Simulated materials have long been used in colleges of education, particularly in preparing administrators. A school and the community it serves is set up and described in detail, including the physical plant, budget, staff, enrollment, pressure groups, individuals in the community, and so forth. The administrator then deals with this simulated reality. A set of in-basket materials is provided with information on curriculum, staff, community, student, political, and social problems which the administrator-in-training attempts to resolve.

The military has also used the games approach in setting up field problems. Colleges of business administration together with many other disciplines have used the simulation approach. Basic to all simulation situations is the attempt to make them represent as nearly as possible the decision-making processes which go on outside the classroom. There is no reason why this same approach could not be adapted to any grade level or subject in the public schools.

James S. Coleman describes one of the games developed at Johns Hopkins. It was a legislative game designed to teach the basic structure of representative government.

> Six to eleven players sit around a table or circle of desks. The chairman deals a set of fifty-two cards each representing a segment of a constituency and giving the positions of the constituents on one of eight issues. The cards the player holds represent the positions of his constituents on some or all of the eight issues—civil rights, aid to education, medical care, defense appropriation, national seashore park in constituency A, offshore oil, federal dam in constituency B, and retaining a military base in constituency C.
>
> The player, as legislator, is attempting to gain reelection, and he can do so only through satisfying the wishes as indicated on his card, of the majority of his constituents. For example, if he has eighty constituents in favor of an aid to education bill and twenty against it, he has a net

gain of sixty votes toward reelection if the bill passes or a net loss of sixty if it fails.[7]

Coleman describes the process by which a player brings up an issue on the floor, followed by a two-minute negotiation session. During this session, each player attempts to exchange his support for an issue in which his fellow player is interested in return for that player's support of an issue in which he is interested. At the end of this period, a vote is taken where each player-legislator has one vote; the session proceeds to an issue raised by the next player. When all the bills have been acted on, each legislator determines his reelection or defeat by adding up the votes of satisfied or dissatisfied constituents. The overall winner is the player who is reelected by the largest majority. He reports that this process is the first level of the game which consists of eight levels, each becoming more complex.

A number of advantages in the games approach according to Coleman are: (1) Pupils learn best by experiencing the consequences of their actions; (2) schools often find it so difficult to teach about the complexity of modern society that many students leave school with no real experiences which prepare them to face the multitude of decisions and problems of adult life; (3) learning through games is attention-focusing; (4) games tend to diminish the teacher's role as judge and jury while maximizing student opportunities to see the consequences of personal actions as he wins or loses; (5) games develop in the student a sense of being able to affect his future through his efforts; (6) by seeing the consequences of his actions in games the student is impressed rather forcibly with the idea that his future depends upon his present actions; and (7) young people come to realize that there are rules by which games are played, and if the rules are not followed, chaos results.[8]

Two sources of information about games are:

Project Simile, Western Behavioral Sciences Institute, 1121 Torrey Pines Road, LaJolla, California, 92037.
Charles E. Merrill Publishing Co., 1300 Alum Creek Dr., Columbus, Ohio 43216.

Teamteaching

Combining the talents of several teachers in planning instructional objectives, collecting or writing course material, selecting appropriate audio-visual materials, developing various teaching strategies, and agreeing upon

---

[7]James S. Coleman, "Learning Through Games," *NEA Journal* (January 1967), 69–70.

[8]Coleman, "Learning Through Games," pp. 69–70.

evaluation instruments and procedures is a promising educational development. Teamteaching utilizes the unique abilities of each teacher, employing strengths in one teacher to counterbalance any weaknesses in another. Differentiated staffing with salary differentials for team leaders, curriculum theory specialists, or media specialists is often advocated, but there is much in favor of a situation where each teacher contributes his own special and unique talents without any difference in salary. Peer relationships are important and satisfying. Furthermore, it is more democratic, recognizing that teacher contributions vary from day to day. In one situation, a teacher may make a major teaching contribution; in the next instance another teacher in the group may be the main contributor. The important thing with teamteaching is to establish a relationship where each member's contributions will be encouraged and rewarded. The *team* is the objective to be achieved rather than the promoting of an individual teacher.

Effective teamteaching can result only when certain elements are present.

1. Released time for teachers to plan together.
2. Duplicating facilities readily available.
3. Audio-visual equipment, and software, available.
4. Paraprofessionals to assume responsibility for many routine details, including supervising independent study, assembling materials, operating equipment, drafting reports, and assisting in evaluation.
5. Interest and enthusiastic support from the administrator. The principal must be aware of what is being attempted with what results.
6. Complete information available on each pupil. True teamteaching focuses on the individual—his rate of learning, interests, deficiencies, anxieties, aspirations, and approaches used in the past which have made him productive or have failed to motivate him.
7. Opportunity for inservice teachers to participate in workshops, visit other schools to observe approaches in teamteaching, and consultants and advisors should be brought in from universities, state departments of education, and other school districts.
8. Materials on teamteaching available to the faculty for self-study.
9. Faculty meetings including discussion of the advantages and disadvantages of teamteaching.
10. The traditional school day, broken into classes of equal length, is not appropriate for teamteaching, which calls for longer periods of time with larger groups of students for more formal presentations. Opportunity is needed to break down into small groups for discussion, individual study, data gathering, and reflection.

Teamteaching, as is true of any single approach, is not the final answer in the teaching-learning process. But it is one approach which might be explored by a school interested in finding new ways to maximize growth opportunities for each pupil, each teacher, and each administrator.

Reinforcement, Punishment, and Behavior Change

In the general research literature, several terms used more or less synonymously are "contingency management," "operant conditioning," "behavior modification," and "behavioral engineering." A working definition of *contingency management* is the conditions under which a response is followed by a positive, negative, or punishing stimulus or the removal of any of these.[9] One definition of *operant conditioning* is that type of conditioning of behavior which occurs through making reinforcement contingent upon the behavior.[10] *Behavior modification* and *behavioral engineering* could be considered to have the same meaning as operant conditioning or contingency management. The term *operant* is used to describe the act of the child or teacher or anyone else operating on the environment.

Positive Reinforcement

A *positive reinforcer* is one which brings about an increase in the rate or kind of a behavior. Numerous stimuli have been used as positive reinforcers for various kinds of behavior in the classroom with various kinds of children both on an individual basis and on a group basis. Tokens, for example, have been used with groups of retarded children to increase attention and at the same time decrease disruptive behavior in the classroom. Clark, Lachowicz, and Wolf[11] used tokens which could later be exchanged for money to increase completion of remedial workbook assignments of five female school dropouts. Tokens alone or in conjunction with other generalized reinforcers such as praise and social approval have been used to a large extent to decrease disruptive behavior in the classroom.[12]

---

[9]C. B. Ferster and B. F. Skinner, *Schedules of Reinforcement* (New York: Appleton-Century-Crofts, Inc., 1957), p. 725. Copyright 1957 by Appleton-Century-Crofts.

[10]M. L. Meacham and A. E. Wiesen, *Changing Classroom Behavior: A Manual for Precision Teaching* (Scranton, Pa.: International Textbook Company, 1971), p. 203.

[11]M. Clark, J. Lachowicz, and M. Wolf, "A Pilot Basic Education Program for School Dropouts Incorporating a Token Reinforcement System," *Behavior Research and Therapy*, 6 (1968), 183–88.

[12]K. D. O'Leary and W. C. Becker, "Behavior Modification of an Adjustment Class: A Token Reinforcement Program," *Exceptional Children*, 33 (1967), 637–42; K. D. O'Leary, W. C. Becker, M. B. Evans, and R. A. Saudargas, "A Token Reinforcement Program in a Public School: A Replication and Systematic Analysis," *Journal of Applied Behavior Analysis*, 2 (1969), 3–13; P. L. Knowles, T. D. Prutsman, and E. Smith, "An Evaluation of the Operant Method of Teaching Disruptive and Nonlearning Students in the Classroom," *NDEA Special Project Report*, (1969), pp. 1–101.

Praise, usually in the form of some type of verbal approval and teacher attention, has also been used extensively in the classroom both to increase appropriate behavior and to extinguish inappropriate behavior by withholding praise. In studies, these appropriate and inappropriate behaviors have been modified in academic as well as discipline areas.[13]

In one in-house research study it was found that a particular group of first graders would work very hard in the classroom simply to be allowed to turn their teacher around and around in the swivel chair at the end of the period; since the rate of work output increased, the reward of turning the teacher in the swivel chair became a positive reinforcer for working behavior. A compliment on a drawing, an essay, a lab experiment completed, a mathematical problem solved, a piece of wood planed true, a solo, a speech—a thousand and one opportunities exist in classrooms that teachers can use to reinforce a student's efforts positively.

Traditionally, teachers are assumed to have eyes in the back of their heads to catch students in infractions, as well as to recognize a hand raised by a student who has a question. Both recognitions may be positive reinforcers. A nod of the head as a student is making a comment indicates that the teacher is listening to what the student is saying, perhaps further motivating that student to express himself. A smile or greeting when students come into the classroom, or when the teacher meets them in the hallway, on the campus, in the store is evidence that the teacher recognizes the student as a person; this may encourage him to remain or become the kind of person who is worthy of such extra attention. A teacher cannot remain immobile in a classroom and reinforce students. Some authors have suggested that each student should be positively reinforced at least twice within the forty-five minute classroom period.

One of the most powerful—and perhaps most ignored—positive reinforcer is that of *listening*. The major form of communication is talking, but the emphasis in the classroom is too often upon improving writing techniques, with little or no emphasis upon improving oral expression. Children who have difficulty expressing themselves, who are shy and ill at ease when they are expressing themselves in class, too often receive little encouragement to improve from the teacher. It sometimes seems to such a student that his classmates are more interested in hearing themselves than in listen-

---

[13]M. Broden, C. Bruce, M. Mitchell, V. Carter, and R. Hall, "Effects of Teacher Attention on Attending Behavior of Two Boys at Adjacent Desks," *Journal of Applied Behavior Analysis*, 3 (1970), 199–203; W. H. Nelson, "Teachers as Experimenters," *Journal of School Psychology*, 7 (1968), 29–34; W. C. Becker, C. H. Madsen, C. R. Arnold, and D. R. Thomas, "The Contingent Use of Teacher Attention and Praise in Reducing Classroom Behavior Problems," *Journal of Special Education*, 1 (1967), 287–307; R. V. Hall, D. Lund, and D. Jackson, "Effects of Teacher Attention on Study Behavior," *Journal of Applied Behavior Analysis*, 1 (1968), 1–12.

ing to him, and moreover, that the teacher is also more interested in listening to herself than in listening to him. So the student may withdraw, drop out, or engage in behavior which will get him the attention that he craves.

In order to change a behavior, one must identify the behavior to be changed. The behavior must be defined in very specific terms, defined so precisely that there could exist a consensus of opinion if a group of people were to all observe that behavior. The more concrete the definition the better the possibility of manipulating or controlling the behavior. After the principal, teacher, parent, or whoever might be involved has observed and defined the behavior they must also be able to communicate the terminal or resultant behavior which is desired. A simple example might be helpful. A parent observes that a child at the age of three does not talk. The parent notices that the child can make a crying response, and that of course the crying response does involve certain sounds. Through successive approximation, that is, reinforcing every response that the child makes that is close to an understandable sound, the child finally begins to make an "ummm" sound. Every time the child makes a closer sound to the "ummm" sound the parents might give the child a pat on the back and at the same time perhaps some candy. If the child's rate of making "ummm" sounds increases, then by definition there is a positive reinforcer in the first instance, and in the second the parent can shape the child into the first word which might be "mom" or "ma." So far the parent has observed the child, begun to modify the child's behavior, and has recognized what kind of sound responses the child can make at this point. The parent must also be able to state in very explicit terms what terminal behavior he wants from the child. In the present example, he wants speech, but speech is a very complex behavior. So the first step of the desired terminal behavior might be words. The next step up the hierarchy might be phrases, and so forth.

Many people that have heard just a bit about behavior modification or contingency usually ask the question, "Yes, but how in the world can you go around giving candy or what have you as reinforcers all the time?" Obviously, you can't and you don't necessarily have to use these particular stimuli as reinforcers. For some people, a pat on the back acts as a positive reinforcer, while for others a pat on the back is a punisher. You first must observe the human being that is involved in order to see what stimuli act as positive reinforcers, which are negative, and which ones act as punishers. There are no reinforcers for all people under all conditions, but there are at least two ways of finding out what will reinforce a particular human being. One way is simply to ask a person, "What would you like to do? What would you like to have?" The second way is by observing what the human being does when he is allowed to do anything he wants. One must remember that any stimulus within the environment has the capability or potential of becoming a reinforcer for a particular behavior.

Negative Reinforcement

A *negative reinforcer* is a stimulus which through its removal from a situation will bring about an increase in the rate of a behavior. Ignoring inappropriate behavior in the classroom is a negative reinforcer. Usually the student is reinforced through teacher attention for appropriate behavior and ignored when inappropriate behavior occurs.[14]

Punishment

Punishment is the presentation of an aversive stimulus contingent upon a response which decreases the rate of the response.[15] Many different kinds of punishing stimuli have been used in the classroom to control inappropriate behavior—verbal reprimand, disapproving looks, or withdrawal of a previously known positive reinforcer[16] are examples.

If a student makes an appropriate response in the classroom and the teacher gives him a piece of candy for this response, and the child does not make the appropriate verbal response again, then it is not a positive reinforcer but perhaps a punisher. From this, one is reminded of the saying, "One person's reinforcer could be another person's punisher."

A punisher may bring about a temporary suppression of behavior, but the suppression is not necessarily permanent. In fact some studies have indicated that after a punishment contingency has been removed, there is a return to a high rate or even a higher rate of response than was previously noticed. Perhaps a good example of this is that when people who have been in a penal institution for a number of years are released, they often return to the very behavior for which they were previously incarcerated. Again, it must be remembered that a stimulus which might be considered punishment for a particular individual could be acting as a positive reinforcer. For instance, in a classroom a child might very well "act up" or disrupt the entire class day after day. And every time the child exhibits this behavior the teacher calls on the child and says, "Johnny, sit down; shut up; be quiet; I'm going to send you to the office; I'm going to send you to the principal," and so on. It might be found that this child disrupts the class at even a higher rate after such admonishments. What the teacher is assuming to be a punisher is really acting as a positive reinforcer for the child.

---

[14]K. E. Allen, B. M. Hart, J. S. Buell, F. R. Harris, and M. M. Wolf, "Effects of Social Reinforcement on Isolate Behavior of a Nursery School Child," *Child Development*, 35 (1964), 511–18; E. H. Zimmerman and J. Zimmerman, "The Alteration of Behavior in a Special Classroom Situation," *Journal of Experimental Analysis of Behavior*, 5 (1962), 59–60.

[15]Meacham and Wiesen, *Changing Classroom Behavior*, p. 212.

[16]Knowles, Prutsman, and Smith, "An Evaluation of the Operant Method of Teaching," pp. 1–100.

Other than punishment what techniques can be used to eliminate undesirable behavior? One method is called *differential reinforcement*. Differential reinforcement means basically that an attempt is made to positively reinforce an appropriate behavior and at the same time attempt to ignore behavior considered inappropriate. For example, while a teacher is talking with a class, a particular child shouts rather than raising his hand. The teacher ignores him. Finally, after some minutes, he tentatively raises his hand. As soon as he raises his hand, the teacher immediately calls on him.

The generalization can be made that it is almost always best to use a differential schedule of reinforcement if one must use punishment. The use of punishment alone has been found, in many laboratory experiments, to bring about emotional side effects which reduce the student's capacity to learn.

Schedules of Reinforcement

Another question frequently asked about behavior modification or contingency management, especially by teachers and administrators, is "How in the world can you reinforce a child when you have thirty-five other children in the classroom at the same time?" Luckily, there is a way of doing this. C. B. Ferster and B. F. Skinner[17] developed a number of schedules of reinforcement. The only schedule alluded to thus far in this chapter is one called *continuous reinforcement* (CRF) where the child is immediately reinforced each and every time he makes a correct response. Fortunately human beings will work very well under delayed reinforcement conditions where reinforcement is not immediate. There are several schedules of reinforcement and quite a few combinations of these schedules.

The first schedule is called a *fixed ratio* (FR) schedule. This schedule is one in which the subject makes the response a specified number of times before reinforcement is obtained. An example of a fixed ratio schedule of reinforcement might be as follows: The teacher might say to her classroom, "When you have completed your ten arithmetic problems correctly you may do whatever you like for five minutes." In this case the child makes ten responses—that is, ten mathematical responses prior to reinforcement.

Another schedule is the *fixed interval* (FI) schedule. When a subject must wait a specified period of time before reinforcement, he is operating on a fixed interval schedule. An example of this schedule is the way salaries are usually paid to teachers and administrators in most public school systems and in the university system. The employee receives his pay at the end of two weeks or at the end of a month. This schedule is not based on the number of responses made, but is based only upon time—how much time

---

[17]Ferster and Skinner, *Schedules of Reinforcement*, p. 5.

has elapsed. One of the common characteristics of the fixed interval schedule is that the subject does not begin to respond until the very end of the schedule. The implications of this for the administrator are intriguing!

Another schedule of reinforcement is the *variable ratio* (VR) schedule. Under this schedule of reinforcement a subject is reinforced after predetermined responses have been made. For instance, if a VR–6 schedule is used, the subject receives reinforcement on an average of every six responses. A good example of a variable ratio schedule in our society is the fisherman. Once in a while the fisherman catches a fish, but he doesn't know exactly when or how often. He may catch a fish once and might not catch another one. He might fish 100 times before he even gets another bite.

Some main points to remember about contingency management are: (1) The teacher and administrator must be good observers of behavior. (2) Whatever is decided upon as a reinforcer should be applied consistently and immediately in the beginning. (3) After the behavior is under control, then the contingency can be stretched, i.e., one can move from a continuous reinforcement schedule to a variable schedule of some type based either on frequency of response or time. (4) When using behavior modification techniques, remember that the subject is always right. The experimenter is the only one that can be wrong. The subject acts in terms of the consequences of its behavior, and if a particular reinforcer does not work or a particular stimulus does not operate as one would have it operate, then the teacher must change and attempt another. If the teacher cannot obtain control of the behavior through operant methodology, the teacher should not say, "Well, that child is lazy; it's the home environment," or the like. All she can really say is, "I do not know the appropriate reinforcer for this particular behavior, but I will continue to try to find it."

The Principal as an Agent of Behavior Change

The principal as chief administrator of a school is in a unique position to bring about behavior changes. He can be considered the third link in a behavior chain which includes students, teachers, and the principal, but the typical principal is usually, and unfortunately, a discriminative stimulus for punishment in one form or another for both teachers and pupils. Generally when a pupil is sent to the principal's office it is for punishment for inappropriate behavior. When a teacher is called to the office it is usually for a work assignment (considered aversive by many teachers), for not having completed some task, or for questioning. On most occasions when a principal visits a classroom—many never do—the teacher feels that he or she is being checked on. One can usually tell whether a principal is an aversive stimulus or a reinforcer for his teachers and students by observing both his and their behavior. If teachers become quiet in the teachers' lounge when he enters or begin to leave then he probably has an aversive effect. Another observation would be the frequency with which teachers and pupils drop in to his office to chat. How much verbal interaction is there in faculty meetings? How often do teachers invite him to their classes? How often do pupils stop by his office to say "Good morning"? How many teachers asked for transfers to different schools in the last year? How often does the principal tell teachers they are late for meetings, school, and so on? These are just a few questions which when answered give some indication of whether the principal is a punisher or a reinforcer.

Reinforcers Principals Can Use With Teachers

There are behavior modification techniques which a principal can use that lead to a more positive atmosphere in a school situation. The principal should first of all be consistent. Too often when a teacher exhibits a behavior on one day, he or she is praised, but on another day he or she may be punished. Secondly, the principal must be willing to change his behavioral methods in relation to teachers, parents, and pupils when he is obtaining poor results.

Most of the reinforcers that the principal has at his disposal could be classified under the broad category of communication. Under this category fall such behavior as praise, memos, and certain gestures such as smiling, frowning, a pat on the shoulder, and so forth. Verbal praise and/or verbal punishment are probably the principal's most frequently used reinforcers. One practical reason for this situation is that these reinforcers are inexpensive. But the principal should also be aware that in order to be effective, the reward or punishment must be administered consistently and quickly. In some instances, the principal praises a teacher for some appropriate behavior weeks after it has been exhibited; it is far better to praise the teacher while the behavior is continuing or at least immediately after the behavior has terminated. Because many situations and opportunities for the principal to praise his teachers exist, there is no reason to wait for the traditional faculty meeting to tell a teacher what a good job he or she has done in the classroom. The principal can give a teacher praise simply by stopping in the classroom unannounced and, in front of the students, complimenting him or her on a job well done, or he might send a short memo to the particular teacher who deserves recognition. If time is of the essence, the principal might simply ask the teacher's friend to relay the message. Another possible means of reinforcing a teacher is to introduce the teacher to dignitaries visiting the school. Too often the principal has his honored guests visit the same teachers in the same classes. If the principal would introduce visitors to teachers who are perhaps not the most effective, poor teachers in the school might become more effective in their classroom procedures simply because they would have the opportunity to gain the principal's attention.

Personal contact may be reinforcing to many teachers. One principal we know operates his school in such a manner that class periods rotate from day to day. Each day during a certain period he meets with a group of teachers from each grade who have their planning periods at that time. He gives his undivided attention to this group of teachers for this period of time. During these small meetings the principal has an opportunity to give praise and, if necessary, reprimand any behavior on the part of these teachers which has come to his attention. Such meetings may also help a new teacher make the transition from the university training setting to the school reality.

The New Teacher

In our society we usually assume that a person who is trained professionally keeps up with and learns new methods of teaching, applying them to the actual teaching situation. It is also assumed that how lately a person has received his training is related to the newness of the techniques he will be capable of applying in a classroom. Unfortunately such data as are available in the field indicate that within a few years the new teacher becomes as inflexible and unadaptable as his older counterpart. One possible way of surmounting this particular problem is to place the new teacher in a team-teaching situation with an older, effective teacher. In this manner the older teacher benefits from the new techniques coming out of the university, and at the same time the new teacher benefits from the older teacher's experience. This method also makes for a smoother transition for the new teacher from the college campus to the school.

The principal's attitude becomes of utmost importance in the new teacher situation. He must have reinforced his teachers enough in the past so that they will not feel insecure when another new teacher joins them. One way of building a nonthreatening environment for the teacher is for the principal to teamteach periodically with different teachers in their classrooms. There are at least two benefits from this situation: (1) Imitation is an excellent way of learning, and (2) the communication between teacher and principal becomes better, since the principal, especially one who has been an administrator for a long time, may have forgotten the problems a teacher encounters in the classroom.

The teacher is obviously an individual and naturally wants to be treated as such. The older teacher in a school setting with years of experience tends to look at the new teacher as still wet behind the ears. The principal must be subtle and creative in handling the relationships between new and experienced teachers in his school. He must reinforce the new young teacher to become both a productive and an innovative teacher, while at the same time reinforcing the experienced older teachers so that they will not feel that they are being put aside. The principal probably already knows what the older teacher's reinforcers are, since he has perhaps worked for him for several years. On the other hand the only probable way of ascertaining what reinforcers will work for the new teachers is observation. Again, communication becomes an important part of the observation procedure. Through conversation with the new teachers the principal may discover that a simple "very good" on an intermittent basis will do wonders for the productivity output of the teacher.

An overall generalization to be drawn from contingency management is "Accentuate the positive and ignore the negative." Often, our society has been based upon aversive contingencies so that the negative behavior is the only behavior to which attention is paid, and positive behavior is somehow or other ignored. Principals in school systems often make this mistake; they rarely positively reinforce their teachers. Instead they pay attention to those negative or inappropriate behaviors exhibited by some teachers which sometimes create all kinds of emotional side effects for the teacher which in turn might very well be taken out on students in the classroom.

Learning Activity Packages

A Learning Activity Package (LAP) is simply an instrument for individualizing instruction. It does not teach the student but rather guides him in learning what he needs to learn. This distinction is important. If the LAP contained all the information, it would merely be the teacher's lecture transposed to written form. All students would still get the same material, in the same way, at the same time. By giving direction to the student rather than information the program for each individual student may be fitted to his needs, abilities, and preferences.

Rationale

The *rationale* is a statement of purpose which explains why the topic covered in the LAP is included in the course of study. By making the topic more meaningful to the student, the rationale can act as a motivating force.

The rationale should relate the present topic to topics previously studied and to those which will be studied later. In this way, the student can see continuity in the topics he is studying.

The rationale should also be short and easy to read. It is written for the student, not the teacher. It and all other parts of the LAP should be free from educational jargon. The statement of purpose should be exactly that. It should not include vague statements such as "It will be good for you to know this."

Performance Objectives

The main topic of the LAP is broken down into smaller areas which, when taken individually, induce study of the topic in an orderly fashion. For each of these smaller areas, the student is expected to obtain a certain amount of knowledge or to learn how to perform a particular task. Since the idea of the unit is to change the student's behavior (so that he can demonstrate his knowledge or perform certain tasks), these smaller areas are stated as behavioral or performance objectives, i.e., expected changes in the student's behavior upon completion of the unit. With behaviorally stated objectives, both the student and teacher can accurately evaluate progress, and the teacher can determine the effectiveness of the instructional program.

These behavioral objectives are stated together near the beginning of the LAP in order to tell the student what he must learn, and what he will be responsible for. If he thinks he knows most or all of the material covered in the LAP, there is little sense in his going through it again.

Pretest

The pretest permits the student to ascertain the extent of his command of the topic contained in the LAP prior to undertaking it. Each question is geared to a particular objective; a test key is included so that the student can evaluate the results. If he passes the test to his satisfaction, then he can ask the teacher to let him take the teacher's own unit test or exemption test (not a part of the LAP). Then, if in the teacher's opinion, the student knows the material covered in that LAP, he goes directly on to the next LAP. If he does not perform satisfactorily, then he must improve on his weaknesses by completing the appropriate sections of the program of instruction before attempting a unit test again.

The pretest also serves another purpose. By pointing out his lack of ability in particular areas of the subject under consideration, the pretest directs the student to activities which will help him in those areas. He will be able to spend his time more effectively in meeting the objectives, and not wasting it by devoting time to areas of the subject in which he is already competent.

Program of Instruction

In the program of instruction, each specific behavioral objective is treated separately or individually. For each specific objective, a variety of media and modes provides the student with alternative pathways to achieving the objectives. With the teacher's assistance, the student selects the path that will best satisfy his needs, abilities, and interests. The choice of media may include readings at different levels with various emphases— films, filmstrips, film loops, slides, audio and video tapes, laboratory experiments, written assignments, and so forth. The LAP may take the form of teacher presentation, group discussion, or independent study. Because the student works mostly on his own, he can proceed through the program of instruction at his personal optimum pace.

The use of an individualized program of instruction does not preclude group activities. The teacher may employ lectures, discussions, and field trips whenever he deems them valuable; students should work together when it is to their mutual benefit.

Self-Evaluation Test

Upon completion of the program of instruction, the student takes a self-evaluation test. The setup is similar to the pretest. Each question is geared to a specific performance objective, and the student is provided with a key so that he can evaluate the results. If he is deficient in one or more areas, the self-evaluation test recycles the student through the appropriate sections of the program of instruction. If the test indicates no deficiencies, he may take the unit test administered by the teacher or teacher-aide. If he is successful, he may proceed to the next LAP. If not, he must be recycled.

In the conventional classroom, the teacher has one major function— to dispense information. This he does largely by means of lecture—by verbal interaction with his class as a whole. This is not the best means of teaching. Studies have shown that students retain 10 percent of what they read, 20 percent of what they hear, 30 percent of what they see, 50 percent of what they see and hear, 70 percent of what they say, and 90 percent of what they say as they do something. With LAP's method of instruction, the student utilizes all of the above modes of learning, but this does not mean that the teacher has little to do under the LAP method. The teacher is more important because his relationship with each student is more personal. He must plan activities that will help the student meet the objectives of the LAP. To do this, he must be competent in his subject area; he must make sure that all necessary materials are available to the student; he must act as a counselor in advising the student on choices available in the LAP; he must aid the student in planning a schedule; he must serve as an alternate source of information for the student; he must stimulate small group discussions; he must supervise a situation in which many different activities are going on at the same time; he must evaluate each student individually and help him in recycling when necessary; and he must be able to instill a sense of responsibility in his students. Under any system of instruction a teacher is expected to do many of these things, but only in an individualized system will he have the opportunity to really do so.

Advantages and Disadvantages of LAP

Because LAP is an experimental concept, it has both advantages and disadvantages. Some of the advantages are as follows:

1. The LAP theoretically eliminates the need for a student to hunt through an unnecessary amount of reading material for the answer to a simple or fundamental question. If *correctly* written, the LAP itself should answer this type of question. If it does not, it should be divided into a number of subtopics, each with its own list of written, visual, and listening aids to help the student find the answers to his questions. The problem here is that this is not always done; many a LAP is written in such a way as to be difficult to wade through.

2. The ideal LAP eliminates the need for teachers to spend much of their time answering questions which could be satisfactorily answered in writing. This enables the teacher to concentrate on meaningful contributions to the students' understanding of the material.

3. The LAP makes it easier to hang onto assignment page numbers, names of films and books, instructions from the teacher, and so on, simply because it is usually possible to find room on the pages of the LAP to write brief but important notes when necessary. This saves much student time and effort, and all but eliminates the need for extra notepaper.

The LAP like any other experimental endeavor in education, has some disadvantages. Some of these are:

1. To many students, the concept of LAP seems to be cold and impersonal. These students sometimes feel as if the LAP is used as a substitute for a teacher.

2. Occasionally when a significant typographical error is discovered in the LAP, students do not hear corrections made by the teacher. Or, if changes are made in which learning aids are used, the student may be absent and be unable to find out the missing information. However, if the LAP is well-written, and if the information is posted on the board or handed out in writing, this problem should not occur.

3. For an average student who needs prompting, there can be a problem. Under the individualized method of learning, a student can slack down on his work and fall behind since he is not on the time schedule in the traditional classroom where work is due on certain dates.

But in spite of the disadvantages, the LAP has proven itself to be a very useful learning tool. It is mostly the teacher's responsibility to construct a well-written LAP using all the available resources to reach every kind of student. It is the teacher who must motivate the student; this can be done with a good LAP which challenges students.

Teaching the Disadvantaged

There are children who come from homes where there is never enough to eat, children who receive little or no encouragement to attend school or to study. These children bring with them patterns of rejection, resentment, and poorly-developed learning skills. School, to many of them, is a prison where they are forced to put in hours every day learning things which have no particular meaning for them and which they feel no need to know.

National recognition was given to the problem of education for disadvantaged children with the passage of the Elementary and Secondary Education Act of 1965. Using funds made available through Title I, educators have been able to spend increased amounts of money on programs for the disadvantaged children.

Many large districts have traditionally spent more money per child for advantaged children than that expended for disadvantaged students, but today the less fortunate students are receiving more attention; more resources are being put into programs to assist them to develop to their fullest potential. A variety of plans is in operation. E. Carlene Crumpton[18] describes a group work project designed to improve the academic level of the pupil by employing some rather unorthodox procedures. Daniel U. Levine[19] suggests criteria for inner-city education which stress (1) the consistency of instructional and managerial practices; (2) the need for disadvantaged students to develop a sense of security and personal attachment to adults; (3) sympathetic guidance; consistent grading policies; (4) opportunity for disadvantaged students to participate in extracurricular and cocurricular activities; and (5) breakdown of the whole school into smaller schools, each of which has its own professional staff and student body.

Many students in our schools already bear the tag of failure. Their parents, their teachers, their peers, have labeled them as "stupid," "dull," "losers." They see themselves as failures too, so they withdraw, perform the bare minimum, or deliberately set unreasonably high goals so that they can punish themselves or those who have failed them. The school should provide a success experience for each pupil; a school has no control over the home environment, but the school does have control over the types of

---

[18]E. Carlene Crumpton, "Share-20: Group Work Treatment," *Educational Leadership*, 28, No. 1 (October 1970), 75–81.
[19]Daniel U. Levine, "Unequal Opportunities in the Large Inner-City High School," *National Association of Secondary School Principals Bulletin*, 54, No. 331 (November 1968), 46–55.

teachers in the classroom, the curriculum offered to students, and the available materials and supporting services. The school can also relieve tension on the part of the student rather than increasing it. The principal should discuss the needs of disadvantaged students with the instructional and counseling staff. He should encourage them to study this area, and make proposals for curriculum revision to serve such students, organize workshops, institutes, and conferences to focus on teaching strategies which could assist each student to learn. Above all he should give the program wholehearted support and encouragement.

Lessie Carlton and Robert H. Moore[20] contend that the assumption that the culturally disadvantaged child cannot make normal progress in school unless home conditions are improved is false. To test this contention they conducted an experimental study in which teachers of culturally disadvantaged elementary children allowed their pupils to select dramatized stories in an effort to improve their reading skills. Initially the children selected their own stories and read alone in books which were made available on many different reading levels. The next step was for students to work together in pairs or in small groups, taking turns reading to each other. Groups were formed according to interest in a particular story, and children selected characters they would portray in the story dramatization. The dramatizations were spontaneous and completely unrehearsed. Among the changes noted in these children's behavior were: A greater willingness to take turns; a preference on the part of some pupils to remain in the classroom and read rather than go outside to play, especially if someone could be found to listen to them read; a greater willingness to talk with visitors or strangers who came to the school; a gain in reading—the first graders in the experimental group gained more than one year in reading over a period of about three and one-half months. They concluded that the culturally disadvantaged child can learn if good teachers are provided with materials and encouraged to employ the best possible teaching methods.

Evelyn Sacadat and Gordon P. Liddle[21] report a study attempted in order to determine whether there were ways to influence children before the basic pattern of failure in school subjects and in social development became ingrained. Children participated in field trips; they attended professional concerts; researchers visited parents to find out about the home situation and to determine the parent's aspirations for their children (this interview was the first contact with a person solely interested in helping the family and the child that many parents had experienced). Informal parent groups began to meet on a bimonthly basis, as well as picnics and family trips which were

---

[20]Lessie Carlton and Robert H. Moore, "Culturally Disadvantaged Children Can Be Helped," *NEA Journal* (September 1966), pp. 13–14.

[21]Evelyn Sacadat and Gordon P. Liddle, "Culturally Disadvantaged," *Illinois Education* (November 1965), pp. 117–19.

arranged by researchers (in one school about 75 percent of the families took a 200-mile trip in school buses each year). A dentist came to talk with the parents about tooth care, while a home economist spoke concerning food preparation and repair of clothing. Newsletters were sent out monthly to keep in contact with the homes and parents, and parents were encouraged to write brief articles for inclusion in the newsletter. Other activities and sidelights were college students working as classroom helpers; girl scouts working on an individual basis with children assigned to them; organization of garden projects; a day camp held at a very nominal fee. The authors indicate noticeable results of the experiment: A marked increase in attendance at P.T.A. meetings; the library was used more frequently by the children; and the parents expressed appreciation for the additional help offered to their children and families.

Ronald H. Silverman[22] suggests that although disadvantaged children often have inadequate backgrounds and skills, they generally seem to be able to perform just as well in art as their more privileged classmates. He suggests that teachers of disadvantaged children should capitalize on art experiences because they may also be useful in overcoming behavior patterns which make it difficult for such disadvantaged youngsters to benefit from their school experiences. Art experiences allow the child to draw upon his own background of experience which will hopefully help the child to recognize that he can use his prior knowledge to assist him in carrying out any current project. Like other classroom experiences, art can serve as a medium to help children secure a clearer picture of themselves and to provide them with an ego-building success experience.

David L. Carl[23] reports on a project at the high school level which brought together teachers of educationally disadvantaged students at the ninth, tenth, and eleventh grade levels, a reading specialist, and a learning disability specialist. The first step in the study was to find the general characteristics and deficiencies of the educationally disadvantaged students in the district. Approximately 15 percent of students were classified as educationally disadvantaged. The characteristics most frequently mentioned were three or more years below grade level in reading; language arts skills below expectation; negative self-image; short attention span; and lack of ability to grasp abstract ideas or symbols. Consultants were brought in, and project members wrote a curriculum program specifically for use with the educationally disadvantaged student which started with small, easy-to-master tasks and then progressed through more difficult assignments.

The social studies and English curriculums were designed to encourage

---

[22]Ronald H. Silverman, "Art for the Disadvantaged," *NEA Journal* (April 1966), pp. 29–31.

[23]David L. Carl, "Project Mobilization—A Suburban Community's Concern for Its Disadvantaged Subjects," *The Clearing House*, 44, No. 9 (May 1970), 519–22.

involvement by stressing the problems, issues, and decisions which the typical student faces. Games, puzzles, role playing, creative arts, dramatic projects, poll taking, and participation in community activities were employed to involve students. The teacher's guides stated skill and instructional objectives to be realized with short-term and long-term lessons. Typical topics for the ninth grade included: Man and Society, Prejudice and Discrimination, and Man and Religion. The social studies unit on prejudice and discrimination explored the nature of prejudice and its effects upon various minority groups. Students studied the biographies of contemporary and historical persons, myths, films, contributions of minority groups to the American heritage, and the works of writers such as James Baldwin, Richard Wright, Langston Hughes, and Arn Bontents to show the literary contributions which have been made by black Americans.

At the sophomore level, units in social studies focused on the methods, reasons, and results of protests in past and present American society; the impact of mass media on thinking and purchasing power; and the consideration of some of the laws which were of interest to teenagers such as arrest and trial, shoplifting, and liability.

The eleventh grade English program focused on man's search for understanding of self, his ability to experience meaningful relationships with other people, and his ability to survive and appreciate his physical environment. The eleventh grade social studies units focused on the working man, consumer education, problems of labor today, the positive and negative effects of automation and specialization in the labor force, and basic principles of economic systems. Field trips were included in all of the curriculums to give the students an opportunity to experience firsthand some of the things that they were discussing—consumer education, reasons for and effect of war on the individual, the group, and society.

Carl suggests that one of the approaches which proved to be extremely valuable was the monthly inservice sessions where evaluations and revisions were made in units of study. He indicates that since the start of the project, the dropout rate has been reduced to less than 1 percent, and that the students in the program have averaged a 1.2 grade level increase in reading. He summarizes the study by saying, "Through *Project Mobilization* teachers have been prepared to meet the needs of the educationally disadvantaged; relevant topics to promote motivation have been constructed; and needed skills for achievement in high school have been introduced and reinforced. The project has proved that it is never too late to aid the educationally disadvantaged!"[24]

Edward S. DeRoche says, "Teaching the culturally disadvantaged is

---

[24]Carl, "Project Mobilization," p. 522.

not easy but neither is being poor."[25] He writes that the culturally disadvantaged youngster has many obstacles to overcome: (1) the English he speaks at home and in the neighborhood is different from that which is spoken in the school; (2) his communication skills are limited because he relies on nonverbal language, yet the school's entire communication system is built upon verbal communication; (3) he has limited understanding of what the teacher is saying or trying to do, and try as he will, it is difficult for him to catch up; there are so many distractions that compete for his attention that very early in his educational career he experiences frustration; (4) he generally has a very poor self-concept, and his experiences in school often merely reinforce his feeling of inadequacy; (5) his values normally conflict with those of the school—which does not mean that his values are poor ones since he has demonstrated his ability to survive in his environment by living according to his values. But it does mean that his values are different from many of those held by the school. DeRoche concludes by suggesting that "The entire school atmosphere should indicate that it is the *best* place to learn about things, where one is taught to think, develop useful skills, to have a chance to contribute and progress according to one's ability."[26]

Selected References

AHRENS, MAURICE R., ed., *Project Ideals*. Clearwater, Fla.: Florida Educational Research and Development Council, 1970.

ALLEN, K. E., B. M. HART, J. S. BUELL, F. R. HARRIS, and M. M. WOLF, "Effects of Social Reinforcement on Isolate Behavior of a Nursery School Child," *Child Development*, 35 (1964), 511–18.

BECKER, W. C., C. H. MADSEN, C. R. ARNOLD, and D. R. THOMAS, "The Contingent Use of Teacher Attention and Praise in Reducing Classroom Behavior Problems," *Journal of Special Education*, 1 (1967), 287–307.

BRODEN, M., C. BRUCE, M. MITCHELL, V. CARTER, and R. HALL, "Effects of Teacher Attention on Attending Behavior of Two Boys at Adjacent Desks," *Journal of Applied Behavior Analysis*, 3 (1970), 199–203.

CARL, DAVID L., "Project Mobilization—A Suburban Community's Concern for Its Disadvantaged Subjects," *The Clearing House*, 44, No. 9 (May 1970), 519–22.

CARLTON, LESSIE, and ROBERT H. MOORE, "Culturally Disadvantaged Children Can Be Helped," *NEA Journal*, (September 1966), pp. 13–14.

CLARK, M., J. LACHOWICZ, and M. WOLF, "A Pilot Basic Education Program for School Dropouts Incorporating a Token Reinforcement System," *Behavior Research and Therapy*, 6 (1968), 183–88.

---

[25]Edward S. DeRoche, "Methods, Materials, and the Culturally Disadvantaged," *The Clearing House*, 44, No. 7 (March 1970), 420–24.

[26]DeRoche, "Methods, Materials, and the Culturally Disadvantaged," p. 423.

CRUMPTON, E. CARLENE, "Share-20: Group Work Treatment," *Educational Leadership*, 28, No. 1 (October 1970), 75–81.

DeROCHE, EDWARD S., "Methods, Materials, and the Culturally Disadvantaged," *The Clearing House*, 44, No. 7 (March 1970), 420–24.

ESBENSEN, THORWALD, *Using Performance Objectives*. Tallahassee, Fla.: Office of Publications and Textbook Services, 1970.

EURICH, ALVIN C., ed., *High School 1980*. New York: Pitman Publishing Corporation, 1970.

FERSTER, C. B., and B. F. SKINNER, *Schedules of Reinforcement*. New York: Appleton-Century-Crofts, Inc., 1957.

HAGERTY, JAMES E., "Individualizing Instruction Through 'Ad Hoc' Grouping," *The Clearinghouse*, 45, No. 2 (October 1970), 71.

HALL, R. V., D. LUND, and D. JACKSON, "Effects of Teacher Attention on Study Behavior," *Journal of Applied Behavior Analysis*, 1 (1968), 1–12.

HOLT, JOHN, *The Underachieving School*. New York: Pitman Publishing Corporation, 1969.

KNOWLES, P. L., T. D. PRUTSMAN, and E. SMITH, "An Evaluation of the Operant Method of Teaching Disruptive and Nonlearning Students in the Classroom," *NDEA Special Project Report*, 1969.

LEVINE, DANIEL U., "Unequal Opportunities in the Large Inner-City High School," *National Association of Secondary School Principals Bulletin*, 52, 331 (November 1968), 46–55.

McASHAN, H. H., *Writing Behavioral Objectives*. Gainesville, Fla.: Florida Educational Research and Development Council, 1969.

MEACHAM, M. L., and A. E. WIESEN, *Changing Classroom Behavior: A Manual for Precision Teaching*. Scranton, Pa.: International Textbook Co., 1971.

NELSON, W. H., "Teachers as Experimenters," *Journal of School Psychology*, 7 (1968), 29–34.

O'LEARY, K. D., and W. C. BECKER, "Behavior Modification of an Adjustment Class: A Token Reinforcement Program," *Exceptional Children*, 33 (1967), 637.

POPHAM, W. JAMES, ELLIOTT W. EISNER, HOWARD J. SULLIVAN, and LOUISE L. TYLER, *Instructional Objectives*. Chicago: American Educational Research and Development Association Monograph Series of Curriculum Evaluation, Rand McNally and Co., 1969.

SACADAT, EVELYN, and GORDON P. LIDDLE, "Culturally Disadvantaged," *Illinois Education*, (November 1965), pp. 117–19.

SILVERMAN, RONALD H., "Art for the Disadvantaged," *NEA Journal*, (April 1966), pp. 29–31.

WILLIAMSON, WAYNE E., "A New Learning Center Thrives in New York," *The Clearing House*, 45, No. 1 (September 1970), 26–28.

ZIMMERMAN, E. H., and J. ZIMMERMAN, "The Alteration of Behavior in a Special Classroom Situation," *Journal of Experimental Analysis of Behavior*, 5 (1962), 59–60.

9

Use of
*Tests in Instruction**

An educational administrator in high office once remarked that two of the most salient forces responsible for the current dilemmas in education are the normal curve invented by Terman and standardized testing. It is fairly common knowledge that the mathematician DeMoivre (1667–1754) first discovered normal distribution. A Belgian astronomer and statistician by the name of Quetelet (1796–1874) was one of the first to make use of normal distribution in social statistics. Standardized tests per se can hardly be blamed for the ills of education. Rather, it is the misuse of both the normal curve and standardized tests by counselors, teachers, and administrators, together with the misplaced expectations for a test score by the lay public which cause problems in education. If a high state official demonstrates such a severe lack of knowledge about tests and their uses, then it is obvious that space devoted here to the issue is necessary information for all prospective school administrators.

By the very nature of his leadership position in the school, the principal must be knowledgeable about tests to the extent that he (1) understands certain basic concepts of measurement, and (2) knows when and to whom to turn for assistance when his knowledge is not enough. More specifically, he should have a sense of history of the testing movement; recognize the need for tests—including an acquaintance with the different types

*This chapter was written by Arthur Mittman, Professor of Education, University of Oregon. The authors have edited it and accept responsibility for its content.

of instruments available and/or useful for certain tasks—know the qualities a test should possess; have some idea as to how to interpret and use test results; and understand the procedures to be followed in selecting a test. Although these topics will be discussed in the remainder of this chapter, it is obviously impossible to give so many topics detailed treatment in a single chapter of a book. The reader is therefore asked to view the discussion as introductory, and is encouraged to pursue the selected references listed at the end of the chapter.

History of Testing in American Schools

Prior to the middle of the 19th century most achievement testing was conducted in the form of the oral examination. In 1845 Horace Mann in Massachusetts raised the valid objection that such a procedure was prohibitively expensive, inefficient, and precluded the ability to make any reasonable comparisons among students. His argument was persuasive, and during the latter half of the century, the essay examination largely replaced oral testing. But studies demonstrated a serious lack of reliability in the essay examination. This factor, coupled with the increase of interest in educational research, led to the development of the objective form of tests. J. M. Rice is generally credited with being the first person to use achievement tests in educational research. Added impetus, given to the testing and measurement movement by the advent of experimental psychology in 1879, continued with the laboratory studies of Wundt in Leipzig, Germany, and Cattell and E. L. Thorndike in the United States.

By the turn of the century, measurement in America was off to a good start. Some authors[1] divide the years 1900–1960 into four equal periods of growth. The first, 1900–1915, is called the pioneering period. During this time the so-called standardized tests evolved partly as a result of the work of Binet and Terman. The United States' involvement in World War I necessitated selective processes which would permit broad experimentation with the newly developed tests. The second period, 1915–30, following World War I was marked by a scramble for the testing market; many tests, both good and bad, were developed and marketed.

As could be expected, this period of rapid growth was followed by a time of critical analysis. People in the field began to raise many valid questions regarding not only the use of objective tests, but also the tests themselves. As a result of these questions, many advances and refinements were

---

[1]R. L. Thorndike and E. Hagen, *Measurement and Evaluation in Psychology on Education* (New York: John Wiley & Sons, Inc., 1964), p. 5.

made in measurement theory in the third period, 1930–45. Also, expectations for tests became more realistic.

The 1945–60 period saw the rapid development and expansion of testing programs. This was due in part to the large increase in the number of school-age children. The increase in federal support for education also provided additional funds for assessment purposes. And the National Defense Education Act, passed by the Congress and motivated by a desire to improve the quality of American education, provided more money for testing.

About 1960 objections to the multiplicity of testing programs were raised, especially from school administrators. The AASA, CCSO, and NASSP formed a joint committee on testing in 1962 to study the problem.[2] More recently, testing programs have been severely criticized on the basis of alleged racial and cultural bias, although research has not confirmed this as fact (from the standpoint of usefulness). In fact, a few studies have even indicated they predict academic success more effectively for minorities than for the general population.

Another feature of the current period is the emphasis on criterion-referenced testing, a statement of the minimal acceptable level of performance. In part the interest in this type of measurement is due to dissatisfaction with norm-referenced testing. To a larger extent, such testing is the result of renewed interest in individualized instructional programs. Programmed materials, computer-assisted instruction, and behavior modification techniques characterize criterion-referenced testing programs. Such techniques and methods require that increased rather than decreased attention be paid to the measurement of achievement.

Some critics have also quarreled over the quality of standardized test items. Others object to testing from the standpoint of the misuse made of test scores, while still others view certain types of testing as an invasion of privacy. (See references at the end of the chapter to Hoffman and Gross.) There is some validity to all of these arguments, because improper uses have occurred. However, these criticisms should not be viewed as blanket indictments of testing and measurement. More and better trained specialists are needed in the schools to prevent malpractice and to assist teachers and administrators with their measurement problems. Advances made in test theory development in the past ten years will hopefully soon be applied to some of the above-mentioned problems, and will in turn enhance the validity of the measurement process.

The period since 1960 has brought forth not only a wealth of testing programs, but also great criticism of them. Many of the criticisms are para-

---

[2]*Testing, Testing, Testing,* AASA, CCSO, NASSP, Joint Committee on Testing (Washington, D.C.: The Committee, 1962).

doxical. On the one hand educators are admonished for using tests, while they are at the same time required to be held accountable—which implies some means of measuring pupil achievement and growth. Furthermore, since 1960 the National Assessment Program (which attempts to show what various age groups *do*—not what they should do) has been instituted. Testing is not dead; the need for valid measurement is more apparent today than ever. But it is incumbent upon those involved in testing to review their practices and products seriously and to come forth with or search out instruments adequate to meet the needs of a particular situation. Tests are useful and essential to many facets of the educational enterprise.

The Need for Measurement in the School

Determination of Present Student Status

Every teacher in every class should possess and make use of information that assesses each child's present skills and knowledge accurately. Most of the materials developed as learning aids are constructed on the assumption that such information is available for use. A teacher and school must accept the child as he is, but in order for the child to be directed toward meaningful learning activity, some idea must be obtained as to what his present skill and awareness levels are. Failure to obtain valid assessments prior to instruction often results in making success in an instructional program a chance event rather than a certain result.

Instruments of assessment must be developed with the objectives of the school's instructional program well in mind. In other words, the question must be asked: What minimum skills are required to pursue a given course of instruction with a reasonable expectation of achieving—at least to a limited degree—the course objectives? If the objectives are known, then an instrument or technique can be built or developed which would enable assessment to be made. If a child who is expected to pursue that specific course of instruction does not have the requisite skills, then either he must be given additional opportunity to develop them, or the course must be changed to incorporate such opportunities. The reader must be well aware by now that such a procedure presumes that it is possible to order the acquisition of certain skills and abilities. This will require careful study and planning on the part of curriculum specialists. Criterion-referenced testing is based on the premise that a hierarchical order and sequence of learning exists.

The process of attempting to determine the status of a student prior to his involvement in a course of study should in no way imply that if the desired minimum skills are already in his repertoire, he will achieve to the same degree as everyone else in the program. Individual differences exist and persist; the role of the educator is to provide for them, not abolish them.

Educational Guidance and Placement

After discussing methods of assessing the current status of a student, we should now look at the differences that exist in the status of individuals at specific times in the educational program. In other words, individuals differ. A major source of criticism of testing has centered around this fact and what is called norm-referenced testing. It is unnecessary to argue about individual differences per se—they are a fact of life. But critics have reason to object to the implications that have been attached to such differences. And although norm-referenced scores are of great importance both to educators and to those interested in the destiny of the students, the worth of an individual should obviously not be construed according to his score on a certain test. Scores on tests are of valuable assistance in decision making relative to the student's educational goals—provided the person using the scores is aware of their limitations.

The abolition of norm-referenced testing would do greater disservice to the student than a service. Decision making should always be based upon as much relevant information as can be gathered together. To completely avoid the use of test scores would be a violation of that principle. It would be ridiculous to have a student embark on a course of study for which he was ill-equipped, and it would be equally foolish to encourage a student to undertake an educational program in which he would be poorly prepared compared to other persons pursuing the same program. By the same token, it might be just as unwise to tell a student he *couldn't* succeed. The best policy seems to be to inform the student as to how those have fared who possessed similar preparation and background at the time they undertook the program. If they have experienced disastrous results, he should be forewarned. For this purpose, test scores of a comparative nature, or referenced to some normative data, can be of great help when discussing educational goals with a student. Wise use of such data is of value in the placement of students in programs.

Evaluation of the Educational Program

The school is asked more and more frequently to be accountable. This may be because the citizenry is better informed, or purely recalcitrant, or perhaps just sensitive about their tax bill. No doubt it is due to a combination of such factors. But in any case, the school should be willing to face the challenge and even welcome the opportunity. Accountability, however, requires careful planning and extensive evaluation. Because the school must collect valid achievement data, more attention will be required to the school's testing program and to the quality of the measures it provides. Hard data rather than a merely descriptive statement about the school program will be necessary. And schools will need to strengthen their research and evaluation functions. The school administrator must delegate these functions, but he will also need to be aware of and sensitive to the work.

Research in Instruction

Historically schools have not undertaken a systematic program of research and evaluation. Most record keeping has been merely a compilation of data for district and state reports. Likewise, educational practices have more often than not been justified on the basis of their longevity rather than by research evidence. In a time of demand for change, the school must be engaged in experimentation, and testing and data collection will of necessity be integral parts of such endeavors.

Improvement of Instruction

The role of testing in instructional improvement is quite obvious in view of the comparison among students mentioned above. Measurement adequate to fulfill many of the school's needs requires great attention to the objectives of instruction in terms of what knowledge and skills students are expected to be able to demonstrate. Therefore, careful measurement will reflect careful course planning and instruction. Similarly instructional programs that result from a careful delineation of objectives provide the bases for good measurement practices.

Reporting to Parents

If parents are to receive comprehensive and meaningful reports relative to their child's achievement, comprehensive measurement practices will have to be used. It is the obligation of the principal to encourage teachers to follow accepted measurement techniques in order to have data available upon which parental reports can be based. Because stereotyped paragraphs which say little and mean less are of little consolation to a parent who is vitally interested in his or her child's education, the reports should and must be based upon valid measurements and observational techniques. The type of report, whether the traditional letter grade, essay report, or some other format, should in no way influence measurement and observational practices. Since the report is designed to transmit valid information to parents, it must be based upon valid data collection techniques. Too often reports are poor because they either transmit too little in the way of substantive information, or because they are based upon insufficient and irrelevant data.

Reporting to Students

Just as it is necessary to use tests and measurements as the basis for reporting a student's progress to his parents, it is equally essential that the student receive regular feedback as to his progress. There is ample support for this view in the literature. Only when both teacher and the student are aware of the student's achievement at a given time is it possible to provide an instructional setting that is compatible with the student's requirements, a setting more likely to elicit a favorable student reaction. For this reason, good measurement practices cannot be left to chance. The teacher cannot expect the student to acquire this insight or knowledge by osmosis. They must be learned.

All of the uses for tests noted here could be attempted to little or no avail if the tests or measurements involved were of poor quality. In the next section a brief outline of the qualities desired in any measuring device will be discussed.

Criteria for Quality Measurement Devices

In discussions of the quality of testing and measurement devices it is necessary to consider three factors—validity, reliability, and usefulness.

Validity

The most important characteristic of a test is how well it measures what it claims to measure. This naturally implies that what the test measures is worthy of measuring. Therefore, before attempting to answer the question, Does it measure what it is supposed to measure? the question, Is what it measures worthy of measurement? must be answered. The person or persons responsible for the construction or the selection of a test must resolve this question at the outset. This mainly involves subjective judgment; it is best resolved by using a panel of experts from the area where the test instrument is to be used. It is this panel which will collectively agree upon the propitiousness of the topics covered and the behaviors to be elicited. When this has been done, the problem then remains of trying to ascertain whether the measuring device succeeds in eliciting the desired behavioral responses.

For example, a group of American history teachers may agree that one of their instructional objectives is to develop their students' ability to understand the implications of a given historical event. If they wish to test the extent to which this objective has been attained, which of the following questions is more valid?

1. When and by whom was the Gulf of Tonkin Resolution passed?
2. Of what importance was the Gulf of Tonkin Resolution to the subsequent involvement of the United States in Southeast Asia?

The second item is preferable, according to the stated purpose, and thus is more valid.

When a test elicits behaviors compatible with the objectives of a course or program of instruction, it is said to have content validity. Such criteria must of necessity be established by careful planning and item preparation. It must also be recognized that a test is valid only for specific purposes; it is not valid in general. A test that is valid for an advanced political science section is likely to have very little validity for an introductory section. Tests for assessing the result of instruction, whether for use with a group or an individual, will be valid only if attention is given to the above considerations during their construction process. The type of validity gained in the building of a test gives it internal validity.

For some purposes tests must be validated externally; performance on a set of questions must be compared with some criterion external to the test. But the location of suitable criteria is the major obstacle in a criterion-related validity exercise, mainly because the criterion used must be relevant, reliable, unbiased, and accessible. Failure to secure a measure that meets these requirements renders external validity coefficients of little merit. The most common example of the use of external validity measurement is the use of tests for predicting future achievement. In this instance a test is said to be valid if it predicts.

From the limited amount of information given here about validity, it can be said in summary that:

1. A test is of little use if it does not serve the purpose for which it is needed.
2. A test valid for one purpose is not necessarily valid for any other purpose—without further evidence.
3. Content validity is established by judging the test against the objectives of instruction; external validity is established by comparing performance on a test with some external criterion, such as subsequent behavior in another setting. This gives the test a predictive quality.

Reliability

A test cannot be completely valid, no matter how relevant it is for a given purpose, if it does not yield consistent results. The scores provided by the test must be reasonably accurate and precise. This means that ideally a student's score on a reading comprehension test should reflect his true ability. But since any set of items which comprise a test is only a sample from the totality of items appropriate for eliciting a specific set of behaviors, the test score will be subject to item sampling error. Likewise at a given time and place a student's response to a given question may vary from the answer he may give at another time and place. The condition of the student and the conditions under which the measuring takes place can also affect test scores greatly. A given score is therefore likely to contain error of this type; random error may infect any measure and is a source for unreliability. Some of these sources of unreliability, such as the daily variations in the behavior of most persons, cannot be anticipated or controlled by either the test builder or the test administrator, but the length of a test and the conditions of administration are controllable. For this reason and for the sake of reliability it is usually better to give as long a test as is feasible within administrative time limits in order to elicit as large a sample of behavior as possible. Likewise, the test administrator should standardize administration procedures so that the test-taking conditions are the same for all persons within a given group and throughout all groups. Close adherence to the directions for administering standardized achievement testing programs is mandatory if the results are to be of any value for normative purposes and/or meaningful interpretation. Any measure of human behavior is of course subject to error, but attention to such things as test length and conditions of administration can minimize certain types of error which contribute to the unreliability of a test.

Reliability is usually reported in terms of numbers ranging from .00 to 1.00. The larger the number the better the reliability, but the magnitude of the reliability coefficient is greatly affected by the variability of the trait or ability being measured in the testing group. Since there are several rather esoteric factors that can influence the magnitude of reliability coefficients, the prospective test user is well advised to not only consult a measurement specialist concerning it, but also to become familiar with the manual prepared and published cooperatively by the American Psychological Association and the American Educational Research Association.[3] Following these suggestions can help preclude the possibility of misinterpretation of the reported reliability data.

In any discussion of reliability, it is necessary to mention the importance of the impact of scoring upon reliability. Throughout this discussion we have assumed that independent scorers would give the same score

---

[3]French, J. W. and William B. Michael, Cochairmen, *Standards for Educational and Psychological Tests and Manuals* (Washington, D.C.: American Psychological Association Inc., 1966).

for a given quality of a paper. Obviously if this assumption is not tenable, the scores yielded by a test instrument would be unreliable. The present widespread use of multiple-choice type questions, matching, and like questions on tests have evolved because of the need to augment objectivity in scoring. The essay type of test makes objectivity in scoring difficult, especially when large numbers of students are tested. But at the same time, this is not to be construed as implying that essay questions can never be scored objectively. However, to do so often involves considerable expense; research evidence indicates that, except in those instances where the purpose of the test is to measure the student's ability to organize his own responses and to express his thoughts in writing, nothing is gained from such expense. In those instances the validity of the essay type question is self-evident, and careful and special effort must be expended in order to secure reliability of scoring.

While discussing the reliability concept, it is also appropriate to mention the reliability of difference scores or gain scores. To completely discuss the problems associated with this topic would require a volume devoted solely to it, but we should here point out that the reliability of the difference between two methods of measurement is considerably less reliable than the reliability of the separate measurements themselves. This is one of the chief problems encountered in attempting to evaluate either the effectiveness of curricular innovations or pupil growth, and it requires great sophistication on the part of the evaluator. Expert assistance should be sought in such cases.

Practical Considerations

Up to this time the discussion of the criteria of the quality of tests has been focused upon the topics of validity and reliability. These are of paramount importance and deserve prime consideration, but concomitant attention must be given to the usability, or practical aspect of tests. A test may be highly valid, that is, relevant for its intended use, and it may produce reliable measures, but at the same time have limited utility. In order for a test to be usable it must—

1. Be easy to administer and score.
2. Be economical.
3. Afford results that are readily interpretable by those who are expected to make them meaningful.

The first requirement is quite obvious. The test should be able to be readily administered by any professional or paraprofessional educator following minimal instruction and adherence to the manual. This implies that the instructions to both the administrator and the student are set forth clearly and succinctly. Following its administration, the test should be scorable—with the guarantee of near perfect accuracy with a minimum of time and effort. In the case of standardized district-wide testing programs, scoring is probably best left to a commercial scoring service, unless the district is large enough to maintain and support such an enterprise of its own.

Secondly, if a test is to be practical for a given situation, it must fit into the school budget, in both the financial and the time-wise sense. With respect to time it is very easy to fall into the situation of being penny-wise and pound-foolish. Because the length of a test is of great significance if it is to yield reliable measures, the person responsible for a testing program must not be dissuaded from securing a valid measure by the arguments of those who resist a certain program on the basis of the time required to administer it.

The final concern from the standpoint of the practical aspects of a test is the matter of ease of interpretation. The score yielded by a test should be able to be made meaningful with a minimum of effort. A carefully prepared and documented manual for interpretation should be available; in the case of standardized tests, it is incumbent upon the publisher to provide such a service. Likewise, when a school or school system embarks upon a testing program, it is the responsibility of the administration to conduct carefully planned inservice training sessions devoted to the matter of test interpretation. Valid and reliable measuring instruments can lead to disaster if the results are misinterpreted and/or misused in reporting the results to parents or students, or if they are placed in the hands of a teacher who has not been trained to use them properly. As stated earlier in the chapter, a great deal of the dissatisfaction with testing is the result of testing malpractice on the part of the schools—due primarily to the lack of personnel trained to handle the test results. Some tests, such as those involving projective techniques and personality characteristics, should be used only in situations where highly trained clinical psychologists are available to interpret the results.

Up to this point we have examined the history of the testing movement, the need for tests in the schools, and the criteria for quality instruments. The remainder of this chapter is devoted to outlining the process of test selection, followed by some guidelines for test interpretation, and finally a listing of some of the responsibilities of the principal in respect to the measurement aspect of the instructional process.

Test Selection

The process of test selection is essentially the same for any purpose, whether it is for nation-wide, state-wide, district, school, or classroom use.

The purpose is to select an instrument which will possess all of the necessary qualities of a test for a specific use. The steps in the selection procedure will be listed in sequence followed by a brief description of the process.

Need the Test Is to Fulfill

This must be carefully and precisely delineated by those concerned. If it is an achievement test, the curriculum objectives, the grade level, the content topics, and so forth must be clearly spelled out, with the thought in mind of the use which will be made of the results.

Search of Available Tests

For this step, the resources most likely to be of assistance are *The Mental Measurement Yearbook*, test publishers' catalogues, and curriculum guides. From these sources a list of possibly suitable tests may be secured and sample sets ordered.[4]

Review of Available Tests

This must be done for each test independently. Each test must be evaluated on the basis of the extent to which it is compatible with the specifications formulated in the first step of the selection process. Special attempts should be made to read the reviews of test and curricular experts found in *The Mental Measurement Yearbook* and the professional journals. Most professional journals have a book and test review section. Prior reviews are usually referred to in the reviewers' statements.

Independent reviews should be obtained from as many prospective users of the test as possible. After these reviews have been collected, a panel of local teachers will have to weigh the evidence, giving particular concern to the criteria questions asked in the manual referred to earlier, *Standards for Educational and Psychological Tests and Manuals*. The selector or evaluator of a test should seek answers to questions concerned with the test authorship, cost, administration, compatibility of the manual with user needs, currentness of the test, validity, reliability, scoring, and scales and norms.

A great deal of information can also be obtained by actually sitting down and taking the test. This process gives the reviewer a feel for the behaviors supposedly elicited by the test items, a good understanding of the level toward which the test is directed, and a sampling of the topics.

Final Decision-Making Process

Following the procedure to here should yield a list of possibilities. From this list the selection committee or selector should make final com-

---

[4]*Mental Measurement Yearbook* (Highland Park, N.J.: Gryphon Press, 1965).

parisons and be able to select a defensible and well-documented recommendation.

The total selection process should be allocated a rather generous amount of time. If a school is contemplating a change in the testing program, a year's advance notice should be given to the committee charged with the responsibility of making recommendations. Likewise when an evaluation is to be made of an existing curricular program, the planning for the evaluation cannot be done in a few days or weeks if anything of merit is to result. Preferably no curricular program should be instituted unless a plan for evaluation has been included. In any case, testing and evaluation merit planning time, and must be accorded such priority if the job expected of it is to get done.

Test Interpretation

Test interpretation is the consummation of everything that has preceded it. Intended uses of the test can be carefully explicated, complete awareness can be evidenced of the criteria for judging the quality of a test, and detailed attention can be given to each step of the test selection process, but it will all be for nothing if interpretation of the results is poorly managed. In other words, the best conceived and executed plan for measurement and evaluation can lead to disaster if misinterpretation and/or misuse are its results.

Extreme care must be taken to look at test results as one step in the total evaluation process, and not to view them as an end in and of themselves. A test score reflects a student's performance at a given time in his educational career. If the test is valid and reliable, it will provide an estimate of the amount of a certain trait or ability he possesses at a specific time. Value judgments about that score must be made in terms of what his status was at a certain time in the past, the educational climate in which he has been involved, as well as any extenuating circumstances that may have influenced his performance. A score should never be interpreted as a measure of a student's personal worth.

In the same manner, normative test data reflect an individual's relative standing in a particular group. If an individual can be legitimately considered a member of that group, then his score provides him and the school with valuable data that can be useful for educational guidance and planning. At the same time there is nothing in a score itself which precludes him from altering his relative position in the future; test scores should not be used in a manner that militates against such a possibility. By the same token, if an individual's behavior has been persistent over a long period of time, it does give some actuarial support to predicting future behavior of the same kind—unless changes can be effected in either the school or the individual that will alter his behavioral patterns. The search for such techniques is the legitimate function of the school. Tests are valuable mainly in describing the present state of affairs and should be viewed in this manner.

The whole area of test interpretation is too complex and too broad to accord it adequate treatment in a single chapter dedicated to the use of tests in instruction. The emphasis here has been to point out some basic concerns. Each test score must be interpreted from the standpoint of the nature and purpose of the test, the type of units or scale used to report the score, and the normative- and criterion-referenced information available. The principal has a vital role to play in this function. It is his responsibility to secure the professional, expert assistance necessary to train his staff for their respective roles in using test data in an appropriate fashion.

In this regard the final section of this discussion deals with the role of the principal in using tests. It is unreasonable to expect the principal to be an expert in educational measurement and evaluation, but it is reasonable to expect him to assume a leadership role in seeing that his school's testing program is operated as an integral portion of the total educational process of the school.

The Role of the Principal in the School's Testing Program

The measurement needs of the school were identified earlier in this chapter as an outgrowth of the need for:

1. The determination of the present status of the student
2. Educational guidance and placement
3. Evaluation of the educational program
4. Research in instruction
5. Improvement of instruction
6. Reporting to parents
7. Reporting to students

If the principal views these as legitimate functions in the total educational program, then he will wish to facilitate and expedite the process to secure the data required to carry them out. Tests play an integral part in each of the seven processes, but only to the extent that they help teachers and administrators secure the information needed to perform these separate but not necessarily independent functions. Initially the principal will wish to secure concurrence with those concerned that these seven functions or a subset of them are beneficial to the school's program. Given that this has been done, the principal should then:

1. Foster and promote a climate or attitude toward the measurement process which is consistent with the educational program of the school. This may mean an inservice program using measurement specialists.

2. Encourage teachers to develop and incorporate good measurement practices into the instructional process rather than considering it as a separate function.

3. Provide clerical and stenographic support to the staff to facilitate such measurement practices.

4. Secure the cooperation of the entire faculty both in studying the needs of the school and in determining what testing program should be developed. This is far better than issuing an edict from the office announcing that certain tests will be administered. Teachers who have a chance to plan the program in the light of their objectives will support it; they may not if it is imposed on them.

5. Provide administrative facilities for purchasing, administering, and scoring tests.

6. Insure that the testing program provides information on the basic needs of children which can be used in both the instructional program and in educational planning. Such a testing program should include instruments which will provide evidence not only on academic achievement but also on general aptitude, student interest, and social and emotional adjustment.

7. The principal should insure that once test results are received, they are used for the designated purposes. The purposes of tests are to provide information on the differing needs of students, to identify the problems students face, to provide information for an overall appraisal of the total school program, and to provide a basis for reports to parents and students.

In conclusion, the use of tests in instruction will be only as effective as the effort that is put forth to make them useful. Testing is only one means to an end. With the principal's support and understanding, it can be made a very effective and valuable process.

Selected References

BLACK, HILLEL, *They Shall Not Pass.* New York: William Morrow & Co., Inc., 1963.

BLOOM, BENJAMIN, ed. *Taxonomy of Educational Objectives—Handbook I: Cognitive Domain.* New York: David McKay Co., Inc., 1956.

BUROS, ASCAR K., *Tests in Print.* Highland Park, N.J.: Gryphon Press, 1961.
———, *The Sixth Mental Measurement Yearbook.* Highland Park, N.J.: Gryphon Press, 1965.

———, *The Seventh Mental Measurement Yearbook.* Highland Park, N.J.: Gryphon Press, forthcoming.

DIZNEY, HENRY, *Classroom Evaluation for Teachers*. Dubuque, Ia.: William C. Brown Co., 1971.

EBEL, ROBERT L., *Measuring Educational Achievement*. Englewood Cliffs, N.J.: Prentice-Hall, Inc., 1965.

ENGLEHART, MAX D., "Improving Classroom Testing," *What Research Says to the Teacher*, 31, American Education Research Association, 1964.

FRENCH, J. W., and WILLIAM B. MICHAEL, cochairmen, *Standards for Educational and Psychological Tests and Manuals*. Washington: D.C.: American Psychological Association, Inc., 1966.

GROSS, M., *The Brain Watchers*. New York: Random House, 1962.

HOFFMAN, BANESH, *The Tyranny of Testing*. New York: Collier Books, 1964.

KRATHWOHL, D. R., B. S. BLOOM, and B. B. MASIA, *Taxonomy of Educational Objectives—Handbook II: Affective Domain*. New York: David McKay Co., Inc., 1964.

LYMAN, HOWARD, *Test Scores and What They Mean* (2nd ed.). Englewood Cliffs, N.J.: Prentice-Hall, Inc., 1971.

PAYNE, DAVID A., ed., *The Specification and Measurement of Learning Outcomes*. Waltham, Mass.: Blaisdell Publishing Co., 1968.

Testing, Testing, Testing, AASA, CCSO, NASSP, Joint Committee on Testing, Washington, D.C., 1962.

THORNDIKE, R., ed., *Educational Measurement* (2nd ed.). Washington, D.C.: American Council on Education, 1971.

THORNDIKE, R., and E. HAGEN, *Measurement and Evaluation in Psychology and Education*. (3rd ed.), New York: John Wiley & Sons, Inc., 1970.

WITTROCK, M. C., and D. E. WILEY, *The Evaluation of Instruction—Issues and Problems*. New York: Holt, Rinehart & Winston, Inc., 1970.

10

Evaluating Student Progress

One of the most persistent traditions of schools in the United States has been that of issuing regular reports concerning the pupil achievement. This is true at all levels—kindergarten, elementary, secondary, and college. In earlier times, marks were given to inform students and parents of the quality of achievement in a particular subject area. Later developments have begun to involve more than just reporting progress in a given discipline for students below the college level. Most school systems have developed evaluation systems designed to reveal not only progress in the various subjects studied, but also attendance and appraisal of the development of the student as an individual.

While teachers have been given the responsibility for judging the achievement of students in a particular subject, others among the professional staff are also concerned in evaluation. Guidance counselors, sponsors of activities, and administrators share in the responsibility. Because the principal must be concerned with the quality of the evaluations made, he must share both in the responsibility for developing the system and in its operation as well.

The matter of evaluation has been receiving increased attention in recent years. Since a student's future may depend upon success demonstrated within the school as judged by the marks he has received, it becomes apparent that evaluations must be made as objectively as possible. They must of necessity prove meaningful to those who must use and interpret them.

New Concerns for Evaluation

Several developments have focused the attention of the teaching profession upon the need for better evaluation of student performance. Sociologists and psychologists have raised questions as to the effects of traditional marking systems upon the self-concept of pupils. National assessment, performance contracting, and the concern for accountability demonstrate the necessity for better procedures of appraising student achievement. Students themselves are increasingly aware of the importance attached to success as indicated by marks assigned in the various classes.

In order to establish more acceptable marking systems and to refine the procedures for making evaluations, there are several problems which must be solved if satisfactory procedures are to be effected. First, the objectives for most subjects are not well-established and are not written to indicate measurable outcomes. Second, subjective considerations enter into the appraisal process. Third, the present emphasis upon individualized learning rejects the tradition of comparing one student's progress with others in the same class and assigning a mark in comparison to the progress of others. Fourth, many schools have not made allowance for modifying the procedures for evaluating performance in classes made up entirely of gifted students.

These are only some of the problems to be considered if better procedures for evaluation are to be established. Because of the importance attached to attaining high rank within a class, many students are discouraged from making choices of subjects that are appropriate to their interests and abilities or which contribute to achievement of future goals. Some educators even feel that there are students who seek "snap courses" or "easy teachers" solely for the purpose of receiving academic honors or high class standing.

Why Evaluation Is Necessary

Public education in the United States is a function of the state, although in recent years the federal government has shared in the process. Increased costs and complex social problems have interested citizens in the quality of available education. Now that there are strong proponents for the doctrine of accountability, schools are being called upon to prove that objectives are being achieved. And the schools cannot ignore this development.

In former years, educational progress was measured chiefly in terms of standard growth in the subjects of instruction. Students were marked in each area of instruction according to an achievement scale ranging from a high of 100 percent to a passing mark of around 65 or 70 percent, according to the passing standard set by the school. Since education is a function of the state, the purpose of education involves not only individual pupil achievement, but also the individual's acquisition of some understanding of preparation for constructive citizenship in a democratic society. For this reason, more than just cognitive learning is involved. Schools must concern themselves with some appraisal of the several aspects of the pupil's development.

Most teachers believe that marks have some effect in motivating pupils to work toward accomplishment of the school's objectives. For most students, the fact that there will be an appraisal resulting in a grade tends to encourage them to make an effort to produce satisfactory results. Although this type of motivation may be negative in nature, some pupils seem unable to be motivated in any other way.

Finally, evaluation plays a large part in determining a student's future school experience and his life occupation. Most institutions of higher education are still selective and require some evidence of a student's performance.

Concerned parents demand periodic and systematic reports concerning the progress their children are making; the process of pupil evaluation also provides for establishing channels of communication with the home.

The Problem of Failure

When a student is judged to be a failure and compelled to repeat a grade or subject in school, both he and society lose. The student loses the chance to benefit from new experiences which repetition denies him. Society's most immediate loss is in the money it costs to have a student repeat his work, but more significant and costly losses occur when individuals fail to make the most of their abilities, and in extreme cases turn to unsocial behavior and delinquency.

It is true that some failure is a normal part of life, and that ordinarily people accept it without serious ill effects, just as they accept degrees of success. When an adult can see the reason for a particular failure and can do something to overcome it, he is usually not affected adversely. In the future, at least he may be able to avoid the situation in which he is likely to fail. However, even with adults repeated failure or occasional disastrous failure can have unfortunate effects on personality and happiness. The same is true for children. A youngster in school can understand and overcome his failure to learn to spell a particular word, but failure for the semester or the year is a disaster that he probably does not understand or know how to deal with. Moreover, for the child the only means of withdrawal from or avoidance of a situation in which he is unsuccessful are socially unacceptable—apathy, classroom misbehavior, truancy, or delinquency.

As conceived by teachers in the past, failure merely meant unsatisfactory progress on the part of students so designated. The only remedy known for failure was to repeat the work of the semester or grade. It seems never to have occurred to the teachers in the past that failure might be relative with the students so judged. Some might almost have passed; others might have achieved very little. In fact, a scale could have been developed for the failing students, ranging from progress just below the passing mark to practically no progress at all. Indeed, it might have been true in some instances that a student who was given a failing mark had actually profited more from the learning experiences of the grade than another student who had received a barely passing mark. The distinction made might indicate the inability of the teacher to recognize sharp differences in the achievement of the students.

The only remedy for inability to progress satisfactorily formerly was more drill and more time in repeating work considered unsatisfactory. Time- and student-tested standards were unknown, and the methods in use then did not permit comparison of results among students or between schools. That in many schools the results of instruction were not commensurate with the time spent became apparent to intelligent laymen who were able to take stock of the progress being made by their own children.

As early as 1894 a journalist named Rice conducted a series of written spelling tests containing a list of common words in a number of widely scattered public schools.[1] The correlation which he found between the test results in the different schools and the time spent to teach spelling in these schools was insignificant. Children in some schools devoting half as much time to spelling as in other schools spelled the list of words equally well. But the findings did lead Rice to prepare articles on "The Futility of the Spelling Grind" which protested the waste involved in teaching spelling. Because of this, educators were in time forced to face the issue of developing better methods of teaching and measuring achievement in spelling. Neither stigmatizing students with failing marks in spelling nor requiring them to repeat the study of the required word lists solved the problems involved. At best a failing mark indicated only a bad state of affairs for the students concerned. The real need was for educational diagnosis and remedial instruction, as well as for different ways of teaching spelling and more refined methods of evaluating progress.

Many years have elapsed since Rice's study, but the successful evaluation of pupil progress is still an unsolved problem. Scientific instruments have been developed, and many principals and teachers now use these instruments in their efforts to evaluate the progress of their pupils. But in spite of such advancement and innovation, schools are still unable to use evaluation to the desired extent. There are those who still believe

---

[1] Joseph Mayer Rice, "Futility of the Spelling Grind," *The Forum*, XXIII, 163–72, 409–19.

that the traditional marking system has considerable validity and practical use in schools; others would dispense with marks and grades. Finley believes that while there has been criticism, traditional grades still represent the best prediction for college success.[2]

Failure in the Elementary School

Traditionally failure in the primary grades has been the most frequent. This has probably been the result of the inability of pupils to learn to read in the school time available. Difference in mental maturity, sometimes described as readiness, is generally given as the reason for disparities in student achievement in beginning reading. Many schools have solved this problem by establishing nursery schools and kindergartens. In addition, the ungraded concept has contributed to the elimination of failure at the elementary level. Progress varies among the students and they proceed upward as required learning is demonstrated. Under such a plan, the students begin with a teacher or team of teachers and remain there during the primary level. Students may be grouped according to levels and changes may be made as the situation warrants.

The content of such subjects as mathematics, language arts, and social studies causes the greatest difficulty for students at the intermediate and upper levels of elementary schools. Many school systems have solved this problem to some extent by attempting to individualize instruction. In such a program, the individual pupil proceeds from one level of accomplishment to the next in a subject. In the past, many pupils have not been promoted from one grade to the next because of failure in one subject. Such a plan would probably find little support from most teachers and educators today.

One additional change which has had considerable effect upon student promotion policy is the development by secondary schools of programs to fit needs of pupils who come from the elementary school. In former years, the secondary school had admission standards that precluded the acceptance of pupils below the secondary level. This change has come about because of a change in a philosophy concerning the role of the secondary school, and because many state legislatures have mandated that students of secondary school age be admitted to secondary schools, and that programs be designed for them.

Failure in the Secondary Schools

There are still failures at the secondary school level. While it is true that the holding power of secondary schools appears to be greater than at any other time, many students do not complete their schooling. A recent

---

[2]Carmen J. Finley, "How Well Can Teachers Judge Pupil Achievement," *California Journal of Educational Research*, May 1966, 126–31.

study reports that the number of high school graduates in the population of youth seventeen years of age was 65.1 percent in 1959–60. By 1968–69, the percentage had grown to 78.4 percent.[3] Although there were more graduates, 21.6 percent still did not finish. While the gain is significant, a considerable number of young people do enter adult life without completing the secondary school.

The problem of eliminating failure in the secondary school may be attacked in several ways. An effective guidance system which functions so that all students who have difficulties may receive assistance from sympathetic teachers, and advice from counselors, is helpful. Special classes for exceptional students, differentiated curriculums, and teaching methods suited to students of various ability levels are also valuable.

The curriculum of the secondary school should be a subject for continuous evaluation and change. The problems and needs of the times indicate the necessity of relevancy. Both personal and societal needs must be considered. The comprehensive school is an institution for all of the children of all the people. Whether the secondary school student expects to participate at a level of higher education or enter directly into productive employment, he has a right to expect that his school experience will contribute to his individual objectives.

Marking Systems

Developing satisfactory ways of indicating pupil progress provides opportunities for experimentation and research at all levels of education. The elementary level has shown the greatest deviation from traditional systems, although a number of high schools are also finding innovative ways to report progress. Few if any plans that have been developed appear to meet the needs of students in all situations. The fact that systems are departing from traditional evaluation methods and that systems are making changes indicates that it is an area of concern. Some progress is being made.

The traditional marking system, one which many schools follow, has the advantage of being understood by teachers, pupils, and parents. It consists of a five-point scale and includes descriptive terms that are helpful in making decisions. The following is an example of such a scale:

A—This mark indicates that the student has given evidence of genuine interest and has achieved in excess of the standards set forth for satisfactory progress.

B—This mark indicates that the student has given evidence of interest by

---

[3]*Digest of Educational Statistics*, U.S. Department of Health, Education, and Welfare (Washington, D.C., 1970), p. 49.

doing work in quantity and quality above the standards established for a passing grade.

C—This mark is a satisfactory passing grade. It indicates that the student has acquired the ability to proceed in the subject and can use the ability where required.

D—This mark indicates that the student has not acquired the ability to proceed efficiently to the next stage of the subject. This is the lowest passing grade. The student's chance of success in the next stage of the subject is doubtful.

F—This mark indicates that little or no progress has been made in the subject. It is a failing grade and is so recorded on the student's cumulative record.

School systems using this traditional plan have usually suggested a percentage for the distribution of marks among the various categories. According to many local schools, the distribution of marks on the five-point scale might be as follows: A: 7 percent; B: 24 percent; C: 38 percent; D: 24 percent; and F: 7 percent. This type of marking system assumes the validity of the normal curve. It is doubtful whether any schools follow this system to the point of awarding as many failing marks as those denoting excellence. In fact, it is probably true that many systems use a five-point system in which the failing mark is used for only the most unusual cases. Further, where grouping is done on the basis of ability, the distribution might not be observed at all.

In addition to reporting academic achievement, many school systems make an attempt to evaluate the student's personal growth. This is usually done by listing and evaluating certain characteristics that have been generally accepted as desirable traits in school age children. The following is representative of traits which might be listed: (1) work habits; (2) relationships with others; (3) citizenship; and (4) use of knowledge and skills. When such lists are used in connection with marking systems, it is usually customary to describe the trait as satisfactory or in need of improvement. While most grading systems indicate some relationship of the individual to the group, the items pertaining to personal growth are concerned entirely with the individual pupil.

Other Types of Evaluation

The Nova nongraded elementary division of Broward County uses a system in which parent conferences are used for evaluation purposes.[4] Two types of conferences are held—one is a group type in which parents are involved in inservice training to make them aware of today's educational

---

[4]Permission received for use of description of student evaluation system of the Nova schools of Broward County.

needs. The other type of conference is individual in nature and includes the teacher team members who work with the child and the child's parents. In addition written reports are sent to the parents at the end of the semester. The written reports indicate the progress made in the various subjects in this way: For each subject a black bar represents the projected goal for the student as determined by his team of teachers. An orange bar beneath the black bar indicates the pupil's progress toward his expected goal. The important aspect of the report is the relationship between the two bars. In addition, the quality and degree of the pupil's performance on an individual personal level is rated as thorough, adequate, or minimal. In order to make the report more meaningful to parents, each subject is described briefly to provide some understanding of the purposes and content of the subject.

The student progress report for the Nova High School, a part of the Broward County Public School System, utilizes the stanine marking method: 9: very superior; 8: superior; 7: very good; 6: good; 5, 4: average; 3, 2, 1: below average; 0: no progress. Grading procedures are in keeping with the alogrithm established by each department. In other words, each department may determine the areas of student performance to be evaluated in addition to the results revealed by the tests. For example, the alogrithm of the academic section may involve: (1) unit evaluation; (2) class assignments; (3) class participation; (4) department section; (5) in-depth study; and (6) comprehensive progress. Instructions are provided for the use of the components of the algorithm. The report to the parent includes an evaluation of the quality of effort, final period grades, and teacher evaluation of social progress which provides for reporting excessive absence, tardiness, and quality of behavior. In addition, a parent conference may be recommended if thought to be necessary. Behavior is evaluated as satisfactory (S) or unsatisfactory (U).

The Shorewood Public Schools of Shorewood, Wisconsin[5] provide an evaluation for each of the following levels: (1) junior kindergarten; (2) senior kindergarten; (3) grade one; (4) grades two and three; (5) grades four, five, and six; (6) intermediate school; and (7) senior high school. The curriculum for senior kindergarten provides for: social, emotional, and creative activities; and physical, intellectual, and work habits. Each of the categories mentioned is described by a number of self-explanatory items. Each item is rated as S (Satisfactory for age level), or N (Needs time to improve). The reports for grades one through six follow somewhat the same format, except that the categories relate to the subjects offered at the particular grade levels. For example, the categories for grades four through six are: arithmetic, reading, English, spelling, science, social studies, work study skills, social attitudes and habits, music, physical education, and art.

---

[5]Permission received for use of description of student evaluation system of the Shorewood Public Schools, Shorewood, Wisconsin.

As with the report forms for kindergarten and earlier grades, each subject contains several explanatory items. For example, social studies contains: (1) assigned work; (2) project work; (3) interest in current events; (4) research skills; (5) maps, charts, and graphs; (6) factual material; (7) oral participation; (8) basic concept understanding. Performance on each of the items for every subject is evaluated as V (Very good); S (Satisfactory); or N (Needs to improve). This system is sufficiently diagnostic to keep parents informed concerning the child's strengths and weaknesses on each of the subject areas.

Pass-Fail Method

One development in evaluation recommended by some educators is the pass-fail system.[6] Although it is in greater use at the elementary school level, not many secondary schools have adopted it. Some plausible reasons for its use are: (1) it is less time-consuming for those who make the evaluation; (2) it may reduce emotional stress for pupils who tend to overemphasize the importance of grades; (3) the element of extrinsic competition is reduced; and (4) under such a plan, the individual student, freed from this element of competition, may spend his time on the subjects he considers most relevant to his life plans.

There are, of course, arguments against the pass-fail method. Because it is less definite in its evaluation, the line between those who pass and those who fail may involve more drastic concern than a system with several categories. It could possibly result in less well-rounded educational experience at all levels. And there is some question as to whether younger children should be allowed to pursue only their current interests and not directed to in-depth study of other areas that may be more important. Finally, those who believe that the traditional marking system is fundamental to good motivation have reason to reject a pass-fail system.

Parent-Teacher Conferences

As pointed out earlier in the chapter, some schools rely almost completely upon direct contact with the parents for reporting pupil progress. Conferences are probably practiced more at the elementary than at the secondary level. Conferences have the advantage of keeping parents more precisely and directly informed concerning the progress of their children. Even though the parent-teacher conference may not be used as the principal technique for reporting progress at the secondary level, it should be used for the students who are experiencing great difficulty. It is the policy of some schools to require notification of parents before a failing mark is

---

[6]*NEA Research Bulletin*, 448, No. 3 (October 1970), (Washington, D.C.: Research Division, National Education Association), 76–80.

issued to students. This provides parents with the opportunity to join the school in encouraging better performance and avoidance of failure. A conference also reduces the shock to parents when the child receives a failing grade. The main advantage of parent consultation is that the parent is recognized as a major partner in the school enterprise.

Some General Considerations

From this discussion, it is evident that there is wide variation in methods of evaluation used by school systems. Tradition and the reluctance of parents and teachers have apparently tended to be a stumbling block in effecting change. However, the interest generated by such developments as individualized instruction, studies in child growth and development, and so forth have led to the conclusion that change will continue. The principal must be prepared to be a participant in developing effective changes.

Some schools have made use of workshops and inservice training sessions to involve teachers and administrators in studying marking systems and other devices used in evaluation. While research is needed to give direction to further change, it is possible to offer some general principles to those who are charged with the responsibility of developing innovative systems.

First, any system of evaluation should consider the objectives set forth by the local school system. The general objectives, usually set forth in printed form, embody the system's philosophy as developed and accepted by the community, administration, faculty, and board of education. Rules and regulations usually deal with policies of promotion, retention, class size, and other matters relating to pupil welfare.

Second, the system of evaluation should be developed cooperatively by parents, teachers, counselors, and administrators. Individuals within any faculty have their own ideas with respect to marking, retaining, and promoting pupils. Parents, too, are vitally concerned with the manner in which their children are judged. It is conceivable that even pupils themselves could participate in considering problems of appraisal.

Third, evaluation should reflect the best that is known in educational practices as revealed by available research. The effect of persistent failure for any pupil has been the subject of considerable discussion, and there appears to be some doubt as to whether too much retention is desirable. Although some still hold that since failure in some areas may be desirable, they agree that some method should be found to reduce the waste that follows repeated failure.

Fourth, the system of evaluation should reveal the progress made by the individual as opposed to that made by the group. Pupils obviously vary in any group. While a test may reveal low standing for the individual's progress in relation to that of the group, it may reveal considerable progress in comparison to his own standing. Any assessment of any individual should therefore reveal progress in relation to his previous standing.

Fifth, any marking scheme that is adopted should be meaningful to those who use it. In other words, if letters or numbers are used there should be adequate explanations for the symbols; these explanations should become a part of students' permanent records. Transcripts containing records of achievement are used by colleges and industry in college admissions and employment in business and industry. Transcripts can serve their purpose only if they are meaningful to all of those who use them.

Sixth, an evaluative system can be improved when the objectives determined for school subjects are defined in behavioral terms. Pupils are entitled to know what is expected of them in the various subjects in which they are enrolled. When objectives are stated in terms of what is expected in the way of performance, progress can be measured with considerably more accuracy. Each student knows with some degree of certainty the knowledge and skills he is to obtain, and the teacher is in a better position to judge student progress because it is much more measurable.

Seventh, any drastic changes that are to be made in the evaluation currently in use should be given wide publicity. This means that teachers, parents, and pupils should be made aware of the change. Some innovative marking systems have failed to gain acceptance because the general public understood neither the change nor the necessity for change.

Eighth, any system of evaluation should be subject to periodic review. Since significant changes and new information in methods, philosophy, and knowledge about education are happening constantly, evaluation systems should be relevant and flexible to change.

One additional matter of considerable importance is that of recording and disseminating material pertaining to pupil evaluation. A pupil's record of achievement and personal growth is of great importance—and private in nature. There have been conflicts between parents (or children) and the school because of unwise use of the information pertaining to records.[7] Every school system should formulate policies regarding use and tabulation of records of school performance. These rules should ensure that safeguards for privacy exist and that the use of records is both ethical and legal.

Selected References

ADAMS, GEORGIA SACHS, and THEODORE L. TORGERSON, *Measurement and Evaluation in Education, Psychology, and Guidance.* New York: Holt, Rinehart and Winston, Inc., 1964.

---

[7] *Guidelines for the Collection, Maintenance, and Dissemination of Pupil Records,* Russell Sage Foundation (Hartford, Conn.: Connecticut Printers, Inc., 1970), pp. 1–48.

ALLEN, PAUL M., "The Student Evaluation Dilemma," *Today's Education*, 58 (February 1969), 48–50.

BARNES, FRED P., "Some Unanticipated Consequences of Testing," *The National Elementary Principal*, XLIX (April 1970), 35–38.

BRODY, ERNESS BRIGHT, "Achievement of First- and Second-Year Pupils in Graded and Nongraded Classrooms," *The Elementary School Journal*, 70 (April 1970), 391–94.

BROOKOVER, W. B., E. L. ERICKSON, and L. M. JOINER, "Self-Concept of Ability and School Achievement," in *Relationship of Self-Concept to Achievement in High School*, U.S. Office of Education, Cooperative Research Project No. 2831, Michigan State University, 1967.

BROWN, DONALD J., *Appraisal Procedures in the Secondary Schools*. Englewood Cliffs, N.J.: Prentice-Hall, Inc., 1970.

CAMPBELL, P. B., "School and Self-Concept," *Educational Leadership*, 24 (1967), 510–15.

DAINES, JAMES R., "Test Difficulty as a Factor in Achievement," *The Journal of Educational Research*, 64 (November 1970), 139–41.

DUNIVAN, LINDELL P., "Grading As a System of Guidance: A Rebuttal," *School and Community*, LVI (May 1970), 31.

EBEL, ROBERT L., *Measuring Educational Achievement*. Englewood Cliffs, N.J.: Prentice-Hall, Inc., 1965.

GEORGE, BRUCE, *Secondary School Examinations: Facts and Commentary*. Elmsford, N.Y.: Pergamon Publishing Co., 1969.

GLASSER, WILLIAM, *Schools Without Failure*. New York: Harper and Row, Publishers, 1969.

GOLD, RICHARD M., and others, "Academic Achievement Declines Under Pass-Fail Grading," *The Journal of Experimental Education*, 39 (Spring 1971), 17–21.

HEADD, IRENE, "The Logic of Grading," *School and Community*, LVII (November 1970), 43.

HIRSCH, JAY G., and JOAN COSTELLO, "School Achievers and Underachievers in an Urban Ghetto," *The Elementary School Journal*, 71 (November 1970), 78–85.

HOLT, JOHN, "I Oppose Testing, Marking, and Grading," *Today's Education*, 60 (March 1971), 28–31.

KARMEL, LOUIS J., *Measurement and Evaluation in the Schools*. New York: The Macmillan Company, 1970.

LAMBERT, PIERRE D., "Student Perception of Failure," *Phi Delta Kappan*, 50 (February 1969), 353–54.

McGUIRE, BRIAN PATRICK, "The Grading Game," *Today's Education*, 58 (March 1969), 32–34.

MOONEY, JOHN, and HELEN MOONEY, "Fail Is a Four-Letter Word," *Catholic School Journal*, 70 (March 1970), 16–17.

PHILBRICK, JOSEPH L., and PATRICK L. O'DONNELL, "Precision in Grading—Panacea or Problem?" *Journal of Educational Research*, 62 (December 1968), 173–76.

PURKEY, W. W., *Self-Concept and School Achievement*. Englewood Cliffs, N.J.: Prentice-Hall, Inc., 1970.

PURKEY, WILLIAM W., WILLIAM GRAVES, and MARY ZELLNER, "Self-Perceptions of Pupils in an Experimental Elementary School," *The Elementary School Journal*, 71 (December 1970), 166–71.

Research Clues, "How Do High School Students React to Pass-Fail Courses?" *Today's Education*, 60 (April 1971), 71.

ROSENTHAL, GERALDINE H., "Where Did the System Fail?" *Clearing House*, 41 (May 1967), 558–61.

SAWIN, ENOCH I., *Evaluation and the Work of the Teacher*. Belmont, California: Wadsworth Publishing Company, Inc., 1969.

STALLINGS, WILLIAM M., JOSEPH L. WOLFF, and MARTIN L. MAEHR, "Fear of Failure and the Pass-Fail Grading Option," *The Journal of Experimental Education*, 38 (Winter 1969), 87–91.

YELON, STEPHEN L., "An Alternative to Letter Grades," *The Educational Forum*, XXXV (November 1970), 65–70.

11

Guidance

From the establishment of the principalship in its earliest form, the school principal has been expected to assume responsibility for student guidance. If a student became a discipline problem for a teacher, it was the principal's duty to give the teacher assistance in bringing the student into line with the purposes of the school. If a student encountered learning difficulties which hindered his progress and baffled his teacher, it was also the duty of the principal to do what he could to help resolve the difficulties for both student and teacher. In addition, many school principals had responsibilities to help students in the complex task of choosing suitable goals and a life work. The principal probably did the best he could to meet the demands of these situations, but for the most part, the basis on which he operated was quite inadequate. Any knowledge of guidance he may have possessed had probably been acquired largely through trial and error.

These principals quite obviously did the best they could to discharge their responsibilities with respect to student guidance. But when their accomplishments are viewed in the light of modern concepts of guidance, it is readily apparent that guidance was at best practiced in only the most rudimentary fashion. The greatly increased number of students enrolled in schools today has resulted in a much more heterogeneous student population with wide ranges in ability, motivation, deficiencies, physical and emotional problems. With these changes in students has come a significant change in the nature of the guidance responsibilities of the principal.

Guidance Role of the Principal

The truly effective school principal today recognizes that his effectiveness is based on some important but simple principles:

1. He has been charged with the management of the school; therefore, he does not need to, nor should he, ask permission to do those things which in his professional judgment are necessary to perform his tasks.
2. He seeks advice but is not bound to accept all of it. He screens the advice he receives through his own judgment.
3. He is prepared at all times to give reasons for a decision he has made.
4. His sole purpose for being in an administrative position is to make the school a place where learning and growth occur.
5. As he reserves the right to make decisions, so he also accepts the full consequences for any mistakes he makes.
6. He is completely honest in all relationships.

If a principal operates according to these principles, he must in all fairness accord the same rights to his associates. He delegates decision making down to the lowest possible operational level by working with his associates in specifying goals and making clear to them that the *means* by which these goals are achieved are left to the judgment of those who are expected to realize them.

In describing the role and characteristics of the administrator, William W. Wayson summarizes these principles quite well.

> The new administrator is not easily classified as either authoritarian or democratic. He certainly is not laissez faire, but tends to calculate his actions in terms of their maximal impact on those whom he is trying to influence. He tends to ignore some of the mythological limits imposed on administrators by narrow interpretations of law, policy, tradition, or senatorial courtesy. He exercises a judicious use of administrative power. Sometimes he directs inflexible demands on staff and he uses all possible sanctions to reinforce them. On the other hand, his reliance on group processes, his faith in staff decisions, his resistance to pressure from higher authorities, and his openness to ideas from all earn him wide recognition for being democratic and humane. He will be described by some observers as ruthless, unethical, and disorganized; by others as understanding, courageous, and flexible.[1]

---

[1] William W. Wayson, "A New Kind of Principal," *The National Elementary Principal*, 1, No. 4 (February 1971), 14. Copyright 1971, National Association of Elementary School Principals, NEA. All rights reserved.

Needs of Students for Guidance

The school which develops an effective guidance program dedicates itself to a policy of treating the students as individuals. This implies that it will consider all the aspects of the student's development—physical, educational, social, emotional, vocational, and recreational. It is necessary for the principal to recognize that these needs may vary in proportion and seriousness from school to school and from community to community; they may also change with new educational developments or with changes in the social order. The guidance program must therefore be evaluated from time to time to determine whether changing needs are being met.

One of the forces which has intensified the demand for expanded guidance services is the increasing number of students enrolled in the schools. Table 9 illustrates quite graphically the great increases in enrollment.

Table 9[2]

Year	Total Enrolled	Primary School or Kindergarten	Secondary Schools	College
1960	46,259,000	32,441,000	10,249,000	3,570,000
1965	53,769,000	35,120,000	12,975,000	5,675,000
1970	58,899,000	36,471,000	15,005,000	7,424,000 (est.)
1975 (est.)	61,858,000	36,088,000	16,310,000	9,459,000
1980 (est.)	67,572,000	40,684,000	15,706,000	11,181,000
1985 (est.)	76,867,000	47,675,000	17,345,000	11,846,000

This increase in the number of young people enrolled at all levels of education results inevitably in a very diverse student body. The goals of the school and the goals of individuals are obviously mixed. Prior to the second quarter of the twentieth century, high school students were a select group—socially and economically—who were destined to hold leadership positions. Advisement then was focused on assisting students to prepare for entry into college. Today's graduates will not only go to colleges but will also go on to community colleges, technical schools, and a large number will want and need jobs. The latter group is particularly difficult to serve because the skilled trades and quasi-professions cannot absorb many young people today. Technological advances have been so great, machines have become so sophisticated and complicated, that industry is unwilling to trust a million dollar machine to an untrained and untried teenager.

---

[2]*The New York Times Encyclopedic Almanac 1971*, 1969, 1970, p. 517.

In an effort to meet the diverse and conflicting needs of all these different students, most schools have expanded their curriculums to such an extent that a boy or girl could spend many years in high school without enough time to enroll in all the courses offered, or to participate in other school activities. Guidance in which courses are to be followed and help in choosing realistic vocational objectives in line with individual abilities are responsibilities the principal cannot overlook. Many young people today have had little or no direct experience with the world of work; consequently, many leave school bewildered by the complex industrial processes and the economic system they observe around them. Assisting young people to make vocational choices is one of the great responsibilities of the schools, and one to which guidance personnel need to pay great attention.

A second factor which magnifies the school's problem in caring for many students with diverse backgrounds is the increased holding power of the school. In 1889–90, for example, the population seventeen years old (the chronological age group which should be completing high school) was 1,259,000. The high schools that year graduated 43,731 students or 3.4 percent. In 1929–30, the population seventeen years old was 2,295,822; 666,904 students graduated from high school—29.0 percent. In 1949–50, there were 2,034,540 young people 17 years of age, and 1,199,700, or 58.9 percent graduated. In 1959–60, out of 3,622,000 17 year-olds, 2,839,000 or 78.1 percent graduated.[1]

Needs of Adolescence

During the past few years the tendency has been growing to recognize the vital role which emotions play in the maturation of the individual. Most teachers are able to identify individuals in their classes who perhaps possess the intellectual capacity to achieve, but because of emotional instability are unable to make satisfactory progress. The school must take into account that the primary need of most adolescents is social acceptance. All young people need to feel that they have importance as an individual; providing adequate social opportunities for personal growth is one phase of guidance activities which cannot be overlooked by any school. The school must in many cases deliberately offer experiences which compensate for the lack of opportunities to develop which many young people experience.

With the increase in the number of working mothers, the home life of many young people has been adversely affected. There is a lack of parental guidance, or whatever guidance exists is erratic. The dinner hour where conversation was accepted and encouraged has been replaced by

[3]*New York Times Almanac*, p. 517.

quick-cook meals hastily eaten in silence or to the accompaniment of the television set. The home is no longer the center for social activities it once was. Outlets for social development are often limited to the recreational center (if the young person is fortunate enough to live in an area that has such a center), or to the theater, or to the street. The modern school must recognize these facts and make provisions in its activities and recreational programs for wholesome developmental activities which will be not only for the students of the schools, but for the community as well. There is no reason why school buildings should not be the hub of community activity during evenings and weekends throughout the year; counseling could be made available to all.

Too many people today get up every morning to go to jobs they dislike because there was no one who was skilled enough or interested enough at some time in their lives to help them discover their talents and chart a program to help develop those abilities. This country has done a magnificent job of developing its material resources, but it has in many ways shamefully neglected the development of its human resources. There is a limit to the supply of natural resources which can be utilized, but the human mind and spirit are almost unlimited and have been virtually untapped.

Much has been written about the problems of personal development facing young people today. Don Dinkmeyer has suggested nine such problems which confront every personality in the process of its development. He suggests that these are actually tasks with which all children need assistance —some to a greater degree than others. He identifies these tasks as learning:

1. A sense of self-identity and self-acceptance; developing an adequate self-image and feelings of adequacy.
2. A giving-receiving pattern of affection.
3. To belong, developing mutuality with others, getting along with peers.
4. To become reasonably independent; to develop self-control.
5. To become purposeful, to seek the resources and responsibilities of the world, to become involved, and to respond to challenge with resourcefulness.
6. To be competent, to master certain tasks, to achieve.
7. To be emotionally flexible, to handle feelings, manage aggression and frustrations.
8. To make value judgments, choices, and accept the consequences of one's decision.
9. To get along with parents and other significant adults.[4]

---

[4]Don Dinkmeyer, "Developmental Counseling: Rationale and Relationship," *The School Counselor*, 18, No. 4 (March 1971), 249.

Need for a Guidance Program

It is for the purpose of assisting students with the tasks of personal development that parents, teachers, and administrators should be concerned with the quantity and quality of guidance programs provided by the schools. And parents, teachers, and administrators cannot alone help pupils to develop their fullest potentials; many professional specialists should be provided by the school.

In reading the literature, there seems to be some confusion as to the meaning of the terms guidance, counseling, and pupil personnel services. There is growing acceptance for the term *pupil personnel services* to refer to the guidance program of a school system. The use of this umbrella term is recognition of the attempt to blend administration, instruction, and counseling. *Counseling* is increasingly being recognized as referring to a face-to-face relationship in which a professional specialist assists a pupil to know himself better, to make more realistic choices and decisions, and to work out courses of action. In addition to the counselors, complete pupil personnel services today include many other specialized personnel: school nurse, physician, psychiatrist, school psychologist, and school social worker or visiting teacher. Sometimes speech correctionists and audiologists are included. It is also becoming more common for special areas of interest such as exceptional child education and research to be included in the pupil personnel services.[5] After all, the major reason for having a guidance program is to assist each pupil to become all that he is capable of.

Guidance in the Elementary School

Elementary schools have been less concerned with developing guidance programs than have secondary schools because there has not been as great a pressure for services for the younger children—an indication perhaps of the widely-held conviction that at those younger ages the home is still the paramount influence in the child's life. Questions about vocational choices, personality development, peer relationships, study habits, and so forth should be handled by the parents. But for years psychologists have been contending that more guidance should be made available to younger children during the formative years in order to minimize the establishment of patterns which will be difficult or impossible to correct later on. They have further suggested that greater attention should be paid to identifying the gifted during the early years so that school programs can be developed which will challenge rather than bore them.

[5]George O. McClary, *Interpreting Guidance Programs to Pupils* (Boston: Houghton Mifflin, Co., 1968), p. 3.

The logical implication of these attitudes is that principals of elementary schools must become, to a much greater extent than in the past, personnel workers with children, and to a much lesser extent general disciplinarians and authoritarian administrators—however benevolent. Obviously they must become students of child development and of the motives which dominate the mental and emotional processes of children. Principals also need some degree of sophistication in the problems of their younger students so that they will select a faculty which shares a common concern for the growth of the children entrusted to their care. The entire resources of the school must be marshalled to help each young person grow and ultimately develop into a mature, responsible adult.

Educators today are more and more concerned that opportunity is available in elementary schools to assist young people in exploring occupational possibilities. Daryl Laramore and Jack Thompson have suggested some exploratory career experiences which could make elementary school children more aware of the world of work. They suggest the following for teachers:

1. Bring into the class people from the community who will be willing to talk to the children about the jobs they hold.
2. Ask students to interview their parents and report what they do in their jobs. In this way students are taught both interviewing techniques and the skills of oral communication. The students can develop a questionnaire which reflects the kinds of questions they have and those things that interest them (appropriate from kindergarten through sixth grade).
3. As a follow-up, invite parents to come to the class, bring in some of the tools of their trades, talk to the children for a short time, and have the children ask them questions.
4. The school is a great resource for occupational information. Invite the different workers around the school to come in and talk about their jobs. (Suggestions are custodians, secretary, cafeteria helpers, nurse.)
5. Encourage students to dream about what they would like to do as an adult. Have them pantomime a job and let other students guess who they are or what they are doing. Encourage them to do research—even as early as first grade. Suggest that they observe somebody working and then act out the job in class. Children interested in the same profession can work together. Those interested in medicine, for example, could act out surgeon or nurse.
6. Ask students in the upper grades who have interesting hobbies to explain them to the other children. Perhaps go a step further and relate different occupations to those hobbies. Lower grade children also often have hobbies such as collecting coins that could be used in such discussions.

7. Upper grade children who have part-time jobs (paper routes, babysitting, yard work) can explain: the satisfaction they get from their jobs; what they like about their jobs; what they don't like; how they are going to spend their money. All speakers that come into the classroom should be encouraged to talk about the satisfaction they gain and the skills they need for their jobs.

8. Have students write a resume of their own skills (weeding, babysitting, cutting grass, ironing) and encourage them to try to sell their skills around the neighborhood. This could begin a discussion on what kinds of skills different grade level children have that could be used to make money. Center another discussion on how children should present themselves for a job.

9. Have discussions in the classroom about the importance of all kinds of jobs and how they relate to society.

10. Have workmen such as auto mechanics or TV repairmen work on small jobs in the back of the classroom. No lecture is involved; merely have the person stay there for a time doing his job in the back of the room. Let the children ask questions when they want to know something. This has been done in schools and has proved very successful.

11. Have students draw occupations they are familiar with. When they are finished, have them describe the meaning of their drawings. Project the student's drawings and read their explanations to the whole class. Discuss the families the occupations belong to, and explore methods of obtaining occupational goals. Ask students to volunteer to gather photographs and other information about the occupations representative of different families and present them in class at a later time.

12. Have the students work on a newspaper. Give each person in the class the opportunity to write something. They can advertise things they want to sell. They can write a story about anything. Have them go through the whole process of collecting the data, writing about it, setting the type if you have a small printing press. Follow up with a trip to a real newspaper plant.

13. Take field trips. Prior to the field trip contact the authority in charge and tell him the kinds of questions the children are likely to ask and the things they might be interested in.[6]

Guidance Duties of Elementary School Principals

The elementary school principal has specific duties relating to the provision of a guidance program for the elementary school. Among these are: (1) Providing leadership in creating a school atmosphere which will contribute toward child development; (2) assisting in planning a guidance

---

[6]Daryl Laramore and Jack Thompson, "Career Experiences Appropriate to Elementary School Grades," *The School Counselor*, 17, No. 4 (March 1970), 262–64.

program which will make an effective contribution to the total guidance offering throughout the school system; (3) establishing administrative provisions for wholesome development through participation in extracurricular activities such as sports, assembly programs, clubs, hobby groups, and civic projects in school and community; (4) helping to adapt the curriculum to the individual needs of students; (5) inventorying the resources of the community which might be tapped to assist the school in carrying out its purposes; (6) being available to pupils in situations other than those requiring discipline; (7) knowing pupils and recognizing them by name; (8) discussing developmental problems, either in general or specifically with teachers; (9) opening the lines of communications with the parents to enlist their support in carrying out the guidance purposes of the school; (10) planning an effective testing program; (11) establishing a systematic cumulative record system and seeing that it is used by the teachers; (12) developing a program for the appraisal of pupil growth; (13) providing for the needs of atypical pupils; and (14) making provision for inservice training for teachers.

The majority of children who come to school bring with them a curiosity, a desire to know, a "reaching out" attitude to others for understanding and acceptance. The bright, clean, well-adjusted youngster normally flourishes in the school environment, but what happens to the dirty or sullen or disinterested or shy or aggressive child? These are the ones who need the most help, but these are also the ones whom we find easiest to reject. The principal, of all people in the school system, can be a positive influence for creating the kind of school atmosphere where wholesome growth and change can occur. If he honestly wants to make the school into a warm, friendly place where all human beings can touch the lives of other human beings in a way that all grow, then he should probably begin with himself. He should ask himself, "How do I really relate to the pupils?"

A study by John D. McAulay reported that in grades 4, 5, and 6 over half of the children sampled had spoken to the principal only when reprimanded. Among these same children, 25 percent did not know the name of their principal. In the primary grades, 63 percent did not know the principal's name, and 86 percent had never spoken to him. The 14 percent who had spoken to him had done so in a negative situation.[7]

The principal who wants to become a more effective leader might assess his positive influence by asking himself some searching questions: Do I threaten those with whom I have contact? (If the principal threatens teachers, then teachers inevitably will threaten the pupils.) Do teachers feel free to ar-

---

[7]John D. McAulay, "Principal: What Do Your Children Think of You?" *National Elementary School Principal*, 47 (January 1968), 58–60. Copyright 1967, 1968, National Association of Elementary School Principals, NEA. All rights reserved.

gue with me about school goals? About the programs designed to achieve the goals? Do I seek advice and reactions from the staff? Does each person with whom I talk leave with a more positive feeling about himself? Do I genuinely like people? Do I *show* that I like and trust them? Do I remember that in any crisis there is not only *danger* present but also *opportunity* to help a person grow, to improve the school atmosphere? Do I show my pride in the faculty, in the pupils, in the school?

Characteristics of an Elementary School Guidance Program

Edgar G. Johnston reports that the characteristics of a good guidance program in the elementary school include the following:[8]

1. The guidance program should be set up to serve all pupils—not just the gifted, the slow learner, or the problem pupil.
2. The approach should be developmental. The central concern should be to help all pupils achieve optimum development.
3. The "center of gravity" should be with the classroom teacher.
4. The function of the guidance consultant is to help teachers understand children better and adapt instruction to their needs.
5. The consultant should work primarily with teachers—individually or in groups. At the request of the teacher, he may spend time with a pupil in individual counseling but will do so only as assistance to the teacher; the continuing responsibility for pupil progress rests with the teacher.
6. A part of the consultant's responsibility may be to meet with parents individually or in groups in order to help them understand their children better. Again, the responsibility for continuing relationships rests with the teachers and the school administrators.
7. The consultant's role is quickly distinguished from that of the visiting teacher and the school psychologists or diagnostician.
8. One function of the consultant may be to assist with the administration and interpretation of tests. It should be recognized, however, that *testing* and *guidance* are not synonymous.
9. A consultant assists teachers and administrators in making decisions about referrals to other specialists or agencies; the consultant is not a therapist.
10. A consultant may initiate meetings and informal conferences with teachers to discuss normal child development and behavior.
11. The consultant may be asked to interpret the school's guidance program to parents and to community organizations.

---

[8]Edgar G. Johnston, "Elementary School Guidance," *The National Elementary Principal*, XLVI, No. 5 (April 1967), 39.

12. The consultant practices continuing evaluation of the guidance program, and with the help of others conducts appropriate research.

Guidance Programs in the Secondary School

Guidance in some form or other is a well-established function in almost all secondary schools, but the activities are extremely varied. In some schools, guidance activities are roughly differentiated into types, such as educational, personal, vocational, social and so forth. Still other schools analyze guidance into specific activities such as providing assistance to pupils in choosing curriculums, overcoming deficiencies, developing special interests, cultivating intellectual interests, imparting occupational information, advising on occupational choice, assisting in securing employment, helping in the choice of a college, and giving assistance to an individual after employment. In some schools these activities are carried on only informally or incidentally by the regular school officers (the principal, deans, teachers) while in other schools, they are formally and systematically under the direction of trained persons who are charged with the responsibility of serving pupils through the different types of specific activities. Guidance is present, but to be of service to students it must be planned.

Anthony C. Riccio and Joseph J. Quarante have suggested that the school which is committed to helping students learn to make appropriate decisions must establish services such as the following to realize this objective:[9]

1. The school must have some means of determining how each student differs from other students in the school on pertinent variables such as abilities, aptitudes, interests, and attitudes. The focus in this service is on acquiring data about the individual; it is referred to as the *appraisal service.*

2. The school must have some means of informing the student about the demands and expectations of his school environment as well as those of the larger society of which the school is but a part. The student must be informed both of scholastic and occupational requirements and of the relationships existing among them. This service is called the *information service.*

3. The school must provide an opportunity for the student to discuss with trained personnel the relevance of the results of the appraisal and the information services to his particular life situation. This service is a *counseling service.*

4. The school must help the student to set in motion the courses of action he has decided to take. This service makes it possible for the student

---

[9]Anthony C. Riccio and Joseph J. Quarante, *Establishing Guidance Programs in Secondary Schools* (Boston: Houghton Mifflin Co., 1968), p. 5.

to be placed in a certain class or on a certain job, as well as to take advantage of a pertinent community resource. This service is called a *placement service*.

5. In addition, the school must also provide some means for determining the effectiveness of the services it is providing. The student is seldom concerned with this *research and evaluation service* (other than as a respondent to questionnaires and the like), but the research and evaluation engaged in by public school personnel play a large role in renovating and modifying the guidance service with which students *are* directly concerned.

Guidance Functions of Secondary School Principals

There is of course wide variation in the kinds of guidance activities which principals perform. In the larger school districts, personnel services specialists are available to assume many of the responsibilities, but in smaller schools, the principal is likely to accept responsibilities for a majority of the guidance duties. In either case, the guidance services will only be as good as the principal permits them to become through his allocation of resources, hiring practices, and support. By virtue of his position as head of the school, the principal must see to it that certain activities are carried out in the interest of establishing and maintaining a guidance program— whether the school is large or small.

Staffing for guidance. Before any guidance specialist is employed, the goals of the guidance program should be formulated and agreed upon. Input for formulating these goals should be secured from teachers, professional literature, consultants, universities, and perhaps from students. When these objectives have been formulated, the task or tasks of the guidance personnel to be employed can be defined and developed. Such tasks are rather readily available in the literature since national and state groups have worked very hard at developing them. Published task descriptions can be used as a basis for developing descriptions of specific tasks to be performed in a particular school or district, but they should not be adopted without modifying them so that they fit the local situation. When these two steps—developing the objectives for the program and outlining the task to be performed—are completed, a search should be instituted to find people who will accept these goals and tasks as their own, and who will commit themselves to carrying out the program as outlined.

There is considerable discussion today that it is desirable for counselors to have had some successful teaching experience and perhaps some work outside of the profession. There is little hard evidence that teaching experience makes a better counselor, but there is general agreement that teachers are more likely to accept the leadership of counselors if they can say, "He's been in the classroom, and he understands our problems." Similarly, the counselor who has had some contact with the world of work will be in a better position to counsel students concerning choice of occupation, getting a job, working with people, and following the student up on the job.

The personal qualities of guidance personnel are extremely important. If they wish to help students become excited about learning, they too must be excited about it. If they believe part of their responsibility is to help the students to make wise choices between alternatives, they must have the ability to make such choices. If they want young people to grow into mature, thoughtful adults, they must be mature too. And if they want to help students to develop a life style that will satisfy them, they must have developed a satisfying life style.

After the staff has been selected, it is important that opportunities be given to them to develop their capabilities even further. They should not only be encouraged to return to universities for further study, but also given the opportunity to attend regional, state, and national conferences. They should be included on the school's committees and involved in research and study projects. And they should always be consulted about student problems which are brought to the attention of the principal. Of all the professionals in the school, the student personnel people should be most closely in tune with student needs, problems, hang-ups, and aspirations.

Establishing techniques and providing devices for obtaining information concerning students. The development and maintenance of a system which can provide information concerning students, for use by staff members, is an undertaking which requires much deliberation. A system may become too complicated to use, or it may prove too time consuming to maintain. An effective record system must contain pertinent information and be available and understood by the faculty as well as by the counselors. Some efficient, usable devices for collecting information are cumulative records, individual folders, objective tests, questionnaires, autobiographies, and interviews.

Most schools have a cumulative record system. Upon entrance a record is begun for each student and his history as he progresses through the school system is recorded upon it. Such cumulative records usually contain standard items such as (1) student's name, date, place of birth; (2) parent's name, occupation, and telephone number; (3) date of entrance; (4) date of withdrawal or graduation; (5) subjects pursued and record of attainment; (6) extracurricular activities; (7) standard test scores; (8) health data; (9) personal characteristics such as responsibility and dependability, social adjustment, influence among peers, and work habits; (10) special interests; and (11) educational and vocational plans.

Many schools now require a birth certificate before enrollment; this permits recording accurate data from the primary source. Photographs are also sometimes made a part of the cumulative record.

Since the cumulative record usually remains with the school as an official record of attendance and achievement, it should be carefully designed and constructed for permanent filing. Accuracy and objectivity in recording information are of utmost importance. Some school systems have two copies of the record, one for safekeeping in a vault, and the other to be maintained by the homeroom teacher or counselor. In addition to these demographic data, the counselors normally have confidential information in their files: interviews with the students which indicate the nature of the problem discussed; personal and social data; occupational information; placement; results of tests; results of parent interviews; and any referrals which might have been made. These records should not be included in cumulative record folders but should be kept in a locked file in the counselor's office. They form the basis for future interviews with the student, and if read before talking with the student on subsequent visits, offer an indication to the student that the counselor remembers quite well what they talked about in previous interviews; in this way he shows he is interested in the student. When a student leaves the school, these personal records should be culled and all records promptly destroyed except grade and test records.

Projecting the guidance organization. Schools which have a limited enrollment—less than 175 to 200 students—may not employ any full-time counselors. In these schools, as indicated previously, the principal is expected to perform guidance functions in addition to his responsibilities for furnishing leadership to the instructional program (discipline, supervision of nonacademic personnel, public relations, and business affairs). He is sometimes able to relieve a teacher from teaching responsibilities to supply part-time counseling.

In larger districts with greater student enrollment (500 or more), the principal is often able to assign discipline and guidance responsibilities to other individuals. Fig. 13 shows a rather typical organization for such a district. Note that the supervisor of guidance is in a staff position. Guidance specialists prefer this form of organization since they do not wish to have any line authority over other individuals. They see their role as representing the students' point of view and student goals rather than institutional goals.

In large schools a typical pattern of organization might be as shown in Fig. 14.[10]

---

[10]Herman J. Peters and Bruce Shertzer, *Guidance Program Development and Management*, (2nd ed.) (Columbus, Ohio: Charles E. Merrill Publishing Co., 1969), p. 57.

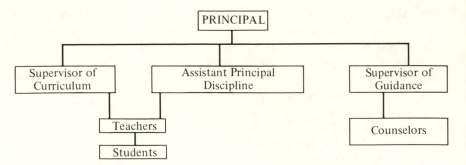

Fig. 13. Organizational structure for guidance services in larger schools enrolling 500 and over students.

In their work on guidance programs, Herman J. Peters and Bruce Shertzer suggest that

in present-day practices, guidance services are usually headed by a director who is responsible for communicating to the staff, central administration, and the public regarding: (1) guidance definition and goals, (2) personnel needs, and (3) selection, assignment, and supervision of guidance personnel, (4) evaluation of and research in the guidance program, (5) needs for physical facilities and budget, and (6) the necessity and program for staff inservice education in guidance.[11]

They go on to suggest that

within the typical school guidance organization, a full-time counselor is assigned 300 to 400 students for whom he is responsible for such activities as (1) counseling, (2) program planning, (3) test interpretation, and (4) educational and vocational planning. Counselors, in addition, serve as consultants to teachers, administrators, parents, curriculum specialists, and others in addition to performing their "counseling roles" with pupils.[12]

Some Characteristics of an Effective Guidance Program

Here are sixteen guidelines which both summarize and redelineate the qualities of a good guidance program structure: (1) Counselors actively seek out students who need help. They do not sit in their offices waiting

---

[11]Peters and Shertzer, *Guidance Program Development*, p. 58.
[12]Peters and Shertzer, *Guidance Program Development*, p. 58.

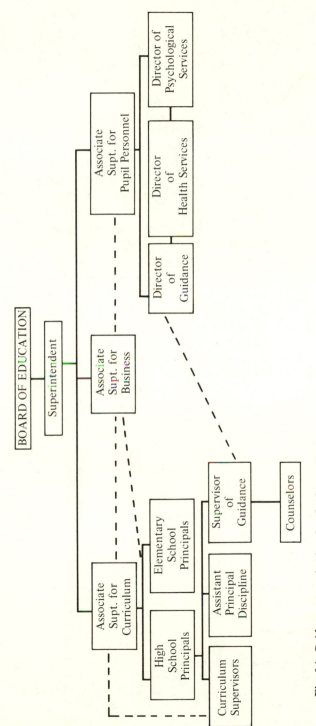

Fig. 14. Guidance organization for the large district.

for students to come to them; they circulate through the halls, in the cafeteria, on the street, in stores, and in the homes. (2) Guidance policies have been clearly established and discussed with guidance personnel and the faculty. (3) Sufficient funds have been provided for the guidance personnel to carry out their responsibilities. (4) Adequate offices have been provided for counselors; clerical help is available. (5) Guidance personnel are actively engaged in institutional research and share findings with the faculty and administration. (6) The guidance program is continually being evaluated and improved. (7) Evidence is regularly presented to the administration on the effectiveness of the guidance program on such concerns as the number and causes of dropouts; follow-up studies of graduates; the effectiveness of the counseling services provided for students; the effectiveness of tests in determining student interests, abilities, and achievements; how these test results were used to improve the learning situation for students; case study reports to the administration listing specific approaches used with students and the results; job placement activities; the effectiveness of the orientation program; the effect of the counseling effort on reduction of incidents in school vandalism; some evidence as to the cooperation or lack of it that exists between guidance staff and instructional staff. (8) An appropriate counselor-student ratio exists (250–300 students per counselor is suggested). (9) Records on each student are complete and up-to-date. (10) The instructional staff understands, supports, and uses the guidance services. (11) Materials, tapes, filmstrips, books, and other references are available to guidance personnel. (12) Occupational information is available in adequate supply and is kept current. (13) An adequate sports program is available. (14) Clubs of sufficient variety and appeal are available. (15) The community is actively involved in the school, attends school functions, has regular conferences with guidance personnel and the instructional staff, and uses school facilities for adult study groups, cultural events, recreational activities, and so forth. (16) The principal understands and supports the guidance program; he expects it to be productive, and receives regular reports as to its effectiveness.

Selected References

DINKMEYER, DON, "Developmental Counseling: Rationale and Relationship," *The School Counselor*, 18, No. 4 (March 1971), 247–52.

McCLARY, GEORGE O., *Interpreting Guidance Programs to Pupils*. Boston: Houghton Mifflin Co., 1968.

PETERS, HERMAN J., and BRUCE SHERTZER, *Guidance Program Development and Management* (2nd ed.). Columbus Ohio: Charles E. Merrill Publishing Co., 1969.

RICCIO, ANTHONY C., and JOSEPH J. QUARANTE, *Establishing Guidance Programs in Secondary Schools*. Boston: Houghton Mifflin Co., 1968.

12

Student Unrest*

The phenomenon of student unrest, doubtless to some extent a reflection of general societal unrest, has reached a new high in secondary schools across the nation, giving many a high school principal his greatest cause for concern. Certainly in any number of areas—particularly in rural sections—the problem is minimal. Most schools throughout the country probably fall into the category described by one principal during a recent survey.

Student unrest is not absent—nor does it interfere with ongoing educational processes. But we are in a period of increasing student awareness, concern, involvement, and activism.

However, in some places the trouble is nothing short of monumental. A school principal, particularly a new principal, must become informed about the nature of student unrest—its extensiveness, its various forms, and the causes that have probably given rise to it. Because there is a definite possibility that a principal may be faced with an immediate conflict, he must know what legal aspects will be involved and what techniques may help to control demonstrations, protect nondissenters, and allow for cool-headed administrative procedures. He will also need to have learned how to regard the situation as an opportunity for a positive, constructive approach; how to reevaluate the school's educational practices in light of the

---

*This section was originally prepared by Margaret Nielsen, Instructor in Education, University of Oregon. The authors have edited the manuscript and accept full responsibility for it.

implications he perceives; and how to prepare to take certain forward steps for the betterment of educational experiences in his school. These concerns, and specific recommendations for meeting them, are the focus of this chapter.

The perceptive administrator must examine his local situation for symptoms of student unrest in an effort to avoid a disruptive confrontation and to lay the foundations for an improved educational institution. He should develop certain strategies and techniques that will make him a more effective principal. Though the strategies suggested in the following pages are not given in rank or time order (in fact, many should be explored simultaneously), they are grouped by large areas for the sake of convenience. The first of these strategies is titled *Get Informed* and the second is *Reevaluate and Implement*.

Strategy 1: Get Informed

Scope of the Problem

A number of studies have been made in an effort to estimate how widespread and serious the problem of student unrest really is. A recent study conducted by the House Subcommittee on General Education indicates that 18 percent of the high schools of the country, private as well as public, had had serious crises during the previous year. An earlier study placed the estimate at 59 percent, but the difference might have been due to definition of the phrase "serious crises."[1]

One study projected that the serious crisis percentage may drop somewhat after reaching a new high because certain complaints about dress codes have now apparently been resolved, and because certain issues on the national and international scenes are no longer as politically explosive as they once were. A more recent study of the New York–Philadelphia area reveals that 91 percent of the students see no lowering of tensions at present. And a report prepared for the U.S. Office of Education by the Policies Institute of the Syracuse University Research Corporation states that 85 percent of 683 schools in 19 large cities responding to a questionnaire had seen "some kind of disruption" in the past three years.[2] Whatever the statistics, it seems clear that few major cities have been able to avoid the impact of rebellion, and countless other towns are just able to suppress it.

Forms the Problem May Take

The forms which unrest may take vary from refusal to conform with regulations on dress codes to mass meetings, picketing, and boycotts; and

---

[1]See *Education U.S.A.*, March 2, 1970, p. 145.
[2]See *Education U.S.A.*, October 12, 1970, p. 35.

from teacher harassment and minor disruption to open rebellion, riot, and arson. An unsuspecting principal may arrive at his building some morning only to find that his office has been taken over by a band of young people and that his chair is occupied by an articulate leader who is ready to set forth a long list of nonnegotiable demands. Student militants resort to a wide variety of activities. Petitions may be circulated, leaflets distributed, underground newspapers published, and community support successfully solicited.

Destructive activism. It is extremely important that a principal distinguish between constructive and destructive activism, between radical activists and moderate dissenters. Destructive activists are extremists who seek impossible goals and offer easy answers. They classify all authority as objectionable, and they defy school rules and civil law. They demand complete freedom for themselves but deny that freedom to others and see no discrepancy in their philosophy. They deplore the use of violence in some situations such as war, but often embrace its use in their own resistance to authority and to established policies.

Constructive activism. Moderate dissenters, on the other hand, are inclined to be sensitive, alert, and highly intelligent students who care about the injustices of society and about the efficacy of the school's instructional practices. They are concerned about the need for the curriculum to relate more specifically to today's problems, for the classroom to improve its learning climate, or for more emphasis to be placed on the personalization of the individual, regardless of background or potential. The thrust of criticism in this group of dissenters is generally directed not so much against persons in authority as against the institution itself and its modus operandi. Such protesters should be recognized and given audience. Their cooperation may be instrumental in effecting valuable educational reform.

Causes of Dissent

This point leads directly into the next area of an administrator's knowledge-ability—the discovery and analysis of underlying reasons for dissent. What makes young people rebel against the status quo? Beyond the age-old restlessness of the adolescent, the long-recognized force of the generation gap, and the healthy desire for conflict, what factors have made the problem of high school unrest the deeply disturbing phenomenon that it is today? What specific circumstances are giving rise to activism in secondary schools?

External factors. It is pertinent to mention here two external sources which have unquestionably had a significant impact upon the high school. One is the fall-out from college campus disturbances; the other is the activity of organized power groups such as Students for a Democratic

Society (SDS). The tendency for high school malcontents to imitate their college brethren is not surprising and needs little analysis beyond recognition of the fact that leadership from college campuses may move in to mobilize the high school student body, taking advantage of any current grievances to emotionalize the situation.

The second factor, the work of power groups, may be more insidious. Most principals are doubtlessly aware that certain agencies have as their prime purpose the instigation and furtherance of anarchy, whether at the societal, the college, or the high school level. In fact, the national council of Students for a Democratic Society (SDS) specifically voted to begin an active recruitment program in the high schools. One officer of that group published a document[3] that set forth the objective of focusing on resistance activity at the high school level. With such militant activists, any administrative decision, even if favorable to a group such as SDS, is actually unacceptable because an administrative decision, regardless of its nature, is to be deplored. The principal's strategy for dealing with unrest may depend to a great extent upon his complete knowledge of these externally-oriented pressures.

Personal factors. What about internal causes of alienation and unrest—personal and school-related factors? There is no single cause, nor even a set of causes, that can be pinpointed.

Many people say that the present generation has been brought up in an environment of permissiveness, and that the high schools and colleges are now reaping the natural consequences—gross lack of respect for authority and open rebellion against regulations. Others say that it is not so strange if, in this age of nuclear technology and desperate personal competition, a fear of the future has sprung up; nor is it odd if the prospect of military obligation with its serious if not tragic implications for the future affects young people adversely. Anxiety is a strong emotional force that vents itself in a variety of ways including the act of striking out at both innocents and authority.

Another personal factor related to alienation is the fact that schools tend to be geared to the needs of middle-class students, with special emphasis upon college preparatory programs. It is natural that this thrust gives noncollege students the impression that they are definitely second-rate, and that blue-collar or quasi-professional jobs for which they should be preparing are looked down upon or, at best, given scant attention. Whereas vocational education courses, including industrial arts and homemaking classes, should have high or at least equal status in the curriculum,

---

[3]Mark Kleiman, *High School Reform* (Chicago: Students for a Democratic Society, 1967).

they are often frankly considered "dumping grounds" for weak students and disciplinary cases. Such inequities, bound to be noticed by the young people (and their parents), may understandably give rise to resentment and rebellion.

Some authorities such as Nathaniel Hickerson of the University of Southern California put the blame for student alienation squarely on the shoulders of the public schools.[4] Reliance on the validity of I.Q. tests, damaging effects of instructional grouping, lack of meaningful motivation, overt and covert prejudice against the economically deprived have loaded the dice against minority groups and so-called slow learners. Hickerson also contends that society, by the exclusiveness of its professional-technical job market, has structured the kind of school which polarizes the have's and the have-not's, and consequently engenders alienation.

The process of growing up has always been a trying experience. A tendency toward rebelliousness naturally characterizes the adolescent period of adjustment from dependency of a child to independence of a young man or woman. Bodily changes and new interests are often bewildering to the adolescent and may result in all kinds of emotional upsets. Obviously such problems are not new. But two pertinent factors are new. One is the current phenomenon of early maturation, especially of city children, as compared to that of yesterday's boys and girls. The other factor relates to today's confusion in standards of right and wrong—standards pertaining to acceptance or rejection of the draft, to sexual conduct, to drug use, drinking, honesty, church-going, and so forth. One bewildered young person expressed it well. "There is less to tie to, less to believe in." Another said, "Adults are hypocritical. They preach one thing and practice something else. They talk out of two sides of their mouths."

School-related factors. Possible school-related causes of student unrest are of even more immediate concern to a high school principal. A revealing study just released in a report by the Center for Research and Education in American Liberties at Teachers College, of Columbia University,[5] shows that in contrast with popular belief that school unrest is due to national policies and racial conflict, it is actually due more to disenchantment with the schools themselves and the lack of choices they provide. Serious accusations leveled by the 7,000 students who made up the population of this study include: (1) schools are undemocratic and unjust, and afford little opportunity for accepted means of conflict resolution such as

[4]Nathaniel Hickerson, *Education for Alienation* (Englewood Cliffs, N.J.: Prentice-Hall, Inc., 1966).

[5]Center for Research and Education in American Liberties, *Civic Education for the Seventies: An Alternative to Repression and Revolution* (New York: Teachers College, Columbia University, 1970).

mediation and arbitration; (2) schools are petty in their rules, and that use of force is typical. In the students' eyes, there is little chance for student contribution to critical decision making, even in those areas which most closely affect their lives. Implications of these findings are that if young people of our nation are to be educated for living in a democratic political system, it is obvious that they should observe and experience the basic principles of that system at work in their schools.

It is possible that alienation and frustration may stem from a poor classroom climate where teachers more often express disapproval than praise or resort to belittling or intimidation or to imposing on students ridiculous, embarrassing disciplinary measures that have no relevance to the offense. The principal may need to look for an even more common but apparently harmless attitude so graphically illustrated recently by the school poster advertising a class:

KNOWLEDGE—Given Away FREE
Bring Your Own CONTAINERS.

Perceptive principals, as well as teachers, have long realized that real education involves not putting knowledge *into* students, but eliciting from them their responses, their inquiry, with special attention to developing individual potential, rather than filling empty vessels.

Perhaps the increase in large classes and the use of technological devices in the instructional program is to blame for a tendency toward depersonalization in the teacher–student relationship. Loneliness resulting from depersonalization may cause a polarization of unhappy defeatists and generate a strong momentum for open protest. The wisdom of Denmark's primary focus in early childhood education—perhaps in all its education, including its famous adult education programs—is an interesting phenomenon. According to the Danish theories, the school must be a happy experience for students. That objective takes precedence over curriculum structure, methodology, and training processes. This thrust may be ignored in American schools.

There is another possible contributing cause of student unrest—an ironical one—about which we might speculate. Perhaps our classroom emphasis toward a questioning attitude has been partially to blame. Maybe the evaluative approach which good teachers encourage at all levels has created a sort of educational boomerang which is returning now to test the validity of the courses, the fairness of examinations, the importance of grades, and other aspects of the system.

Legal Aspects

There are other facets of student unrest besides the scope of the problem and its overt and covert causes on which a principal needs to be well-informed. One important area pertains to the legal aspects of the problem.

An administrator's first reaction to a demonstration may certainly be to "lay down the law," but it is extremely important to know beforehand how civil law limits jurisdiction. Any number of court cases have been cited in *A Pupil's Day in Court*,[6] as well as in other publications, showing that courts may countermand a school administrator's orders and hand down a decision in favor of the pupil. Rulings on hair styles, dress codes, wearing of insignia, and locker privacy have found their way into the courts, and in more cases than not the final decision has been in favor of the pupil and his rights as a citizen.

Help is available for the principal. Excellent guidelines, for example, are set forth in the handbook, *The Reasonable Exercise of Authority*, published by the National Association of Secondary School Principals.[7] Beyond a discussion of suggestions and procedures for controlling and dealing with protests, the booklet summarizes recent court decisions which have caused administrators much grief. It also stresses the importance of knowing when to call in outside help. Of further use are copies of educational and penal codes, which should be readily available to administrators in all secondary schools.

Principals should also be familiar with the statement set forth by the American Civil Liberties Union in *Academic Freedom in the Secondary Schools*.[8] It is based upon the proposition that America must afford each new generation a feeling for civil liberties and that educators have the responsibility for nurturing that feeling by providing exemplary high school communities.

The section on students' rights includes such topics as "Freedom of Expression and Communication" (materials, forums, publications, and so forth), "Freedom of Assembly and the Right to Petition," "Student Government," "Student Discipline" (the right of due process, the role of the police in the schools), "Personal Appearance." The rationale of the pamphlet is summarized in this way:

> The academic freedoms set forth in the student section of this pamphlet must be looked upon as more than a line of defense; they are positive elements in the educational process of a democracy. The spirit of these freedoms should permeate the school and their expression should be actively encouraged by faculty and administration. A school which does not respect civil liberties has failed the community, its students, and itself.

---

[6]NEA Research Division, *A Pupil's Day in Court* (Washington, D.C.: National Education Association).

[7]National Association of Secondary School Principals, *The Reasonable Exercise of Authority*. (Washington, D.C.: The Association, 1970).

[8]American Civil Liberties Union, *Academic Freedom in Secondary Schools*, New York City, 1968.

Such stipulations are documented by reference to the Bill of Rights and the Fourteenth Amendment, as well as by court decisions regarding student rights. (See also *You Have a Right*,[9] a booklet about the rights of high school students.)

In the face of emergencies, a knowledge of these legal matters and the implications they entail will be of inestimable value in making critical, cool-headed decisions and in guiding the staff and student body on a safe course toward a peaceful resolution of the conflict.

Knowledge of the Field

What has worked.   An abundance of articles and treatises describing successful methods and approach to student unrest is appearing in educational literature. The principal should sift out for himself those procedures that seem most feasible and constructive for his own particular situation.

In a study made by the Bureau of Educational Research and Service at the University of Oregon, in cooperation with School Information and Research Service of Seattle, Washington, four guidelines were found that had been of help in alleviating potential problems in selected high schools of the northwest.[10] These guidelines advised administrators to allow:

1. Student involvement in policy making
2. Student-faculty committees
3. Revisions of the school curriculum
4. Establishment of firmer disciplinary controls

Ideas which had not proved quite as useful in these particular schools included the following:

1. Special counseling services
2. Open forums
3. Inservice teacher training
4. Additional school activities

Other sources report how classes may be handled during disruptions, how the staff may be organized for containing the disorder, how parental and school board assistance is recruited, and what kind of punishment is meted out to the disorderly.[11]

---

[9]American Civil Liberties Union, *You Have a Right*, New York City. Write to the American Civil Liberties Union, 2101 Smith Tower, Seattle, Washington, for more information.

[10]George Benson, Kenneth A. Erickson, and Larry McClure, "Student Activism in the Pacific Northwest," *Special Bulletin*, Oregon School Study Council, University of Oregon (February 1970), p. 8.

[11]Leslie K. Browder, "What to Do Before Students Demonstrate," *Nation's Schools* (April 1970), 86–87.

How to handle demonstrations. Though the focus of this discussion is aimed at the constructive approach to problems and at a description of safeguards that may deter serious crises, it is also necessary to consider some precautionary steps which have been found indispensable in dealing with disruptive activities.[12] These are recommendations that all administrators will do well to note—whether they expect to use them or not.

When a demonstration begins, in spite of all attempts to avert it, the best procedures are the following:

1. Utilize every possible channel of communication to and from students to learn of the problem and to provide factual information concerning it.

2. Be sure all students understand that legally they are under direct authority of the school staff; inform them of the means by which violence and vandalism will be dealt with and the sanctions which may be imposed upon them.

3. Identify and communicate with the student leaders of the disruptive activities. Listen to them with understanding. Clarify appropriate channels for grievances. Help them to see the advantages of dealing with their dispute in a positive manner. If necessary, detain the leader or leaders until parents can be contacted. Invite the parents for an immediate conference with you and the student.

4. Establish an interior campus security system using respected members of the school staff.

5. Eliminate from the campus all outside agitation and interference by controlling entrances to parking areas, requiring visitors to have a pass from the office, and asking for police assistance to remove any who loiter without a visitor's permit.

6. Secure the necessary equipment for use by faculty with responsibility for control: cameras (pictures are useful for evidence), communication equipment, printed handouts citing legal authority for administrative action.

7. If in spite of everything, you obviously have a riot on your hands, call the police.

In some states, notably New Jersey, the state board of education requires all school districts to submit a specific plan for coping with potential student disorders. Warnings, notifications, alerts, threats, and protective measures are among the listed plans for action.

It goes almost without saying that a principal needs to act with firmness and coolness, with no thought of acquiescing to the demands of disruptive activists. The need for swift, decisive action underscores the im-

---

[12]Kenneth A. Erickson, George Benson, and Robert Huff, *Activism in the Secondary Schools* (Eugene, Ore.: Bureau of Research and Service, University of Oregon, 1969).

portance of being informed about the possible choices that are open, the legal limitations that are imposed, and the equipment that is recommended.

Strategy 2: Reevaluate and Implement

The astute administrator should be concerned not only about information on the subject of high school unrest, but also about his strategy for dealing with the educational implications of such a problem in his own school. Violent disruption is one thing and peaceful dissent is another. An educational leader must take a firm position in suppressing *destructive activism;* he must also take a positive approach in dealing with *constructive activism.* Quite possibly the administrator who has taken early preventive measures may never have to face the ordeal of handling actual disruptive activities.

Because each community has its own set of values—its own standards of right and wrong—and each school has its own unique characteristics, no hard and fast rules can be laid down as to areas of needed revision or even as to modes of evaluation. Each principal must study his own situation and work out his own approach. Doubtless he will wish to enlist the help of his staff, members of the community, and perhaps representatives of the student body. Some districts, in the interest of complete objectivity, contract for the services of professional survey experts, such as those from nearby universities.

Prime Principles

Regardless of the individual uniqueness of each district or each school, there seem to be three main principles that are good to remember. For one thing, educators will readily admit that schools have been notoriously slow to accept change, to adapt to new developments and opportunities. It is part of the duty of a principal to help his school respond to the dynamics of society without too much external direction or pressure.

Therefore, *do not be afraid of change and experimentation.* No system is sacrosanct. And even failure, if and when it happens, can provide a stimulating learning experience. Besides, the right to dissent is part of our cherished national heritage—our country was founded on the belief in that right, and the independence we enjoy today was secured by means of active demonstration in its behalf.

Therefore, *recognize the constitutional right of free speech,* even among the youthful members of the high school citizenry. Identify it basically as an honorable manifestation of an alert, concerned student body. We may not be sure what the young are saying. They may not even be sure themselves. But we must try to learn together.

Therefore, *find out by some systematic, cooperative plan what both the active dissidents and the "silent majority" of your school are saying—* what they envision as directives for constructive change. A conscientious administrator will help them articulate their choices by having an open mind to positive suggestions and contributions.

Perceived Areas of Student Need

A certain consensus of student needs and desires seems to emerge as broad areas of most serious concern. Students basically want (1) to be heard; (2) to have a piece of the action; (3) to be free to choose; (4) to have an opportunity to "do his thing"; and (5) to be accepted if not loved. Here is a group of human needs which a free democratic society should be trying to meet and to which the schools of America should indeed be dedicated.

It is unfortunate that the very foundations of the public schools should now be under scrutiny by demand of the students rather than by the initiative of educators. A major evaluative study and drastic revisions are now precipitated by strong student dissent rather than by professional acuity and healthy dissatisfaction on the part of school personnel. But educators may take some measure of pride in realizing that schools, to some extent, must have fostered the spirit of free inquiry and helped sharpen students' sensitivity to human values, or those specific desires of free inquiry and value judgment might long since have been phased out.

On the other hand, the schoolroom gap, like the generation gap, has doubtless been a real deterrent. In many places, that gap has not been sufficiently recognized or studied; regimentation, rather than cooperative endeavor, has for too long been the standard for learning.

> Across the generation gap, living persons on the other side look more like abstractions and stereotypes—on one side of the power structure, arrogant, authoritative, stuffed shirts; on the other side revolutionaries, defiant punks, weirdos, teeny-boppers, hippies.[13]

The prime concern of every good school administrator and teacher should be to try to close the generation gap. Students are much more upset about personal and school-related causes than about the Vietnam War, the political situation, the economy, poverty, racial conflict, though these are of great importance to them. Reliable surveys have concluded that certain persistent student demands come out loud and clear. Educators must deal with these demands.

---

[13]Abstracted from *Project Public Information*, May, 1968. See *Quarterly Report*, Oregon School Study Council, 9, No. 2 (1969), 3.

1. We want to be listened to.
2. We want to be involved.
3. We want to make choices.
4. We want to be ourselves.
5. We want to be cared about.

Communication. (We want to be listened to.) Alice Keliher, famous educator known for her special sensitivity to the needs of children, tells of a high school girl who was failing to make a good adjustment in school. That girl's complaint was simply, "I don't know one teacher in this school who has time to listen to me."

Other authorities[14] tell of widespread classroom practices that tend to "put down" the student, allow no time for individual attention, and frighten or silence the students by use of set, one-way, preconceived answers. At a meeting of the Speech Association of America a few year ago, Donald E. Sikkink, Associate Professor of Speech at St. Cloud College, Minnesota, made a prediction about listening in reference to the future of the high school speech curriculum. "The future curriculum will place more emphasis on critical-evaluative listening." It would seem the emphasis on listening should characterize other classes as well.

The teacher's role as listener, as one who encourages open discussion and develops mutual trust, is of paramount importance in setting up effective lines of communication. Because much of the tone of a school is established in the classroom, a good principal should enlist the cooperation of his faculty in fulfilling this important role.

The administrator himself must also go out of his way to communicate. In fact, he should take the lead in the communication process—particularly in listening. He should get out of his office and mingle with students where they congregate, lend an interested ear to their talk, and ask questions in an effort to understand what they are saying and help them articulate their problems. He could set up plans for an open house in his office at least one hour each week, or perhaps design open forums as a supplement to the student government program which would give all students and faculty members a chance to become personally involved in ideas for school improvement.

In other professional fields, a high premium is placed on the art of listening. A doctor, for instance, learns almost as much from what his patient tells him and how he tells it as from examination and tests. A lawyer relies as much on what his client relates and how he relates it as on his own investigation. A counselor or minister can advise his people best by drawing them out and listening sympathetically. A good salesman learns to

---

[14]Charles E. Silberman, from a review of *Crisis in the Classroom in I/D/E/A* (Summer Quarter 1970), p. 1.

listen as well as to talk. By discovering his customers' needs and complaints, he gives better satisfaction. The analogy is obvious. Concerning immediate problems, there is a distinct possibility that the teacher or principal who listens attentively will not only improve his instructional effectiveness but forestall serious student alienation by satisfying an important human need.

While this special emphasis on communication need not entail a commitment for following through, it is quite possible that the strategy of listening may provide new and usable ideas. Psychiatrists are inclined to feel that this is definitely the case and that failure to avert student activism may be the school's own fault. There is a strong possibility that many adults fear that their positions of authority may be usurped and they therefore close their minds to what young people may be trying to tell them.

Involvement. (We want to be involved.) Many a difficult home situation has been solved by student-faculty brainstorming, partially because of valuable ideas that may surface in the process, and partially because the act of sitting down and reasoning with each other tends to satisfy the desire for involvement.

In Lake Oswego, Oregon, for instance, the study of education as a subject was introduced by specifically assigning students the problem of searching for ways and means to improve the high school. After a student school board was elected and a student faculty was selected, a program of extensive research was begun. Committees were set up to scrutinize every facet of school life considered capable of improvement: course content, teaching methods, grading, student conduct, scheduling, school policy, counseling, teacher-pupil relationships. By being truly involved in administrative problems, students began to see education in new ways, and according to reports, "they came up with some sound, well-reasoned recommendations."[15]

From New Trier High School in Winnetka, Illinois, comes a description of a successful student involvement that followed in the wake of an armband incident. After the assassination of Martin Luther King, Jr., many students wore black armbands to school and expressed the desire to become more involved. The administration helped them organize a seminar on the problems of white racism and racial tension, and a door-to-door project selling copies of the Kerner Report. Later a study of this Kerner report was incorporated into a social science course.[16]

Service opportunities both in the school and in the community afford rewarding experiences for high school students who feel that they should

---

[15]"Student Involvement—Roles, Not Goals," Oregon School Study Council, *Quarterly Report* 9, No. 2 (Winter 1969).

[16]Reprinted from the November 1968 issue of *School Management* magazine with the permission of the publisher. This article is copyrighted © 1968 by CCM Professional Magazines Inc. All rights reserved.

be involved, contributing citizens. The Student Service Curriculum, developed in San Mateo High School, California, by Leon Lessinger, is an enviable example.[17] Tutoring elementary school students, working as teacher aides, and assisting in athletics are among possible school activities. Assistance in hospitals, orphanages, and other institutions and agencies provides numerous possibilities for community service.

In Wilson High School in Portland, Oregon, short-term mini-courses on subject matter not usually available in the regular curriculum are sometimes taught by students with special competencies in an area. Also a comprehensive student activity program in this school apparently affords opportunity for involvement and for recognition of individual achievement. Both of these objectives are strong forces much to be encouraged in any human relationship. In another Oregon school, faculty and students together make up a screening committee for deciding on the acquisition of library books and audio-visual aids.

Enlistment of student ideas on school regulations may yield surprisingly effective results. Sometimes, as in the matter of dress codes, involving student opinion can solve the problem with little further trouble. More than one administrator has reported that once the student conduct committee decided that bermuda shorts, for example, might be worn to school the fad suddenly declined in favor, and students felt the issue became unimportant! Besides, when put to the test young people are often more exacting in their standards of behavior than are teachers and principals; desire for peer approval is a strong motivating force.

In Firestone High School, in Akron, Ohio, the student council has been replaced by a twenty-member student-teacher coalition—half students, half teachers—elected by students and faculty. This democratic group, which legislates on broad areas of mutual interest, is even empowered to override the principal's veto (by nine-tenths majority). The coalition has increased communication among all elements of the school population and serves as the main medium for solving differences.[18]

Because the curriculum has been the target of so much criticism by the public and by dissidents, the area of curricular change is in many places the focus of greatest concern. "Relevancy" in the curriculum has become a familiar demand at both high school and college levels, and many students feel strongly the need to become involved in making suggestions for curricular changes. They are especially repelled by the rationale of teachers and administrators who contend that they must "cover ground," or that they must provide a "balanced" curriculum.

With knowledge now doubling in volume every ten years or less,

---

[17]Erickson et al., *Activism in the Secondary Schools*, p. 35.
[18]Rick Sutton, "An Experiment in Freedom," *Student Life Highlights* (October 1970), p. 3.

naturally a sort of desperation is felt by teachers and curriculum planners in their efforts to keep abreast of available materials. The dilemma is just as great as to wise instructional practices that facilitate "covering ground" without sacrificing the human element.

In an effort to involve students in curriculum planning, an increasing number of schools are opening their curricular revision committees to students who have demonstrated high maturity levels. One result is that a wide variety of new types of courses has sprung up ranging from modern jazz to the humanities, from auto mechanics for girls and cooking for boys to oceanography and aerospace studies.

Student membership on the advisory committee which is charged with the establishment of general school policy is not unusual today. The Portland, Oregon, board of education, for example, has recently appointed two high school students to each of three area advisory committees. Thus, a body which originally was composed of only teachers and administrators, and which later added citizens from the community, is now expanded to include a fourth dimension—representation from the student body.

Students in many schools throughout the nation are getting a piece of the action in some form or another. How that involvement achieves results in student and staff satisfaction remains to be seen. Jim Ylvisaker, specialist in social science education in the Oregon State Department of Education, believes that the responsible citizen views himself as a participant in, rather than a spectator of, the political and other civic processes that define American democracy. It is clear, he feels, that schools must discover the best mode of education to prepare for such responsibility, and that the values that guide behavior are best learned by appropriate student involvement in the decision-making processes of school life, grades 1 through community or junior college.

An opinion poll[19] conducted by the editorial staff of *Nation's Schools* indicated that 51 percent of the schoolmen surveyed approved greater student participation.

Making choices. (We want to make choices.) While most students may be unwilling or unable to describe alternative choices for resolving the high school conflicts they face, there is considerable evidence of disenchantment with the schools over the lack of choices they afford. What the American Association of School Administrators (AASA) calls the "cells and bells" approach should be examined for its outmoded structure and the possibility of providing students with more self-direction. When one considers the fact that adult life consists of one long series of choices, from the least important daily decisions to the once-in-a-lifetime matters of monumental significance,

---

[19]"Special Report: Student Involvement—Channeling Activism into Accomplishment," *Nation's Schools* (September 1969).

the imperative for guidance and instruction in making wise choices looms large.

Choices students could make might include decisions on teachers, courses, study time, study place, grade or no grade, credit or no credit. Student choices could help decide books to read, questions to ask, experiments to make, community resources to explore, audio-visual equipment to use, projects to undertake, study contracts to sign, research to pursue, skills to practice, schedules to follow, papers to write, poems to compose, pictures to paint, exercises to do, and so on ad infinitum. When one of the school's *philosophical objectives* is to recognize and satisfy the need for making choices, the list of educational opportunities is endless.

This principle of choice making underlies most of the successful teaching which has been done in the nation's Job Corps program, where the student body is made up entirely of "turned off" youth. Certain tasks and courses, individually selected by the student himself, reveal the need for other skills to be mastered and other information to be acquired. Though great stress is placed upon the making of realistic choices, the practical reason behind most requirements soon becomes obvious to the student and he sees that his study has relevance. More schools should for this reason free themselves from rigid, organizational patterns.

The program known as independent study which began at the college level is now gaining widespread acclaim in secondary schools in some areas, particularly in those schools which have established instructional materials centers easily accessible from all classrooms. Some centers are equipped with student carrels as well as a wide variety of software and hardware—books, magazines, pictures, graphs, tapes, films, records, transparencies, and film strips.

William M. Alexander and Vince A. Hines of the University of Florida, who conducted research on independent study, give this definition and evaluation.

> Independent study is learning activity largely motivated by the learner's own aims to learn, and its rewards lie within its intrinsic values. As carried on under the auspices of secondary schools, such activity is somewhat independent of the class or other dominant group organization . . . and utilizes the services of teachers and other professional personnel primarily as resources for the learner.[20]

Their study, based upon findings from over 300 secondary schools, predicts great potential for this methodology, and reports such teacher and

---

[20]William Alexander and Vince A. Hines, "The Nature of Independent Study in Secondary Schools," *Theory Into Practice*, Ohio State University (December 1966).

student comments as "change in attitude toward school"; "opportunity to work with highly respected and competent teachers"; "improved self-concept"; "personal satisfaction"; "a sense of increased prestige"; "intellectual stimulation"; and "increased self-reliance and independence."

For students at Winston Churchill High School in Eugene, Oregon, independent study has for several years been an accepted program, utilizing unscheduled time for work in fifteen resource centers spaced conveniently throughout the building. The school is moving toward a concept of personalized instruction and independent learning.

Self-direction is a comparable type of classroom methodology based on a student's discovery of his present achievement level and on his established goals without the pressure of time limits. Resources on a personal-choice basis are provided both inside and outside of the classroom. Evaluations are made by the teacher and pupil together.[21]

The Metropolitan Learning Center in Portland, Oregon, is based upon guidelines of extensive self-direction as well as student initiative. Portland's Adams High School, recently cited nationally for its innovative practices, offers wide choices through modular scheduling as well as a variety of approaches in its general education classes.

In *Pre-Tech*,[22] a program for eleventh and twelfth grade students being offered in the San Francisco Bay area, students get two years of math, science, technology lab, drafting, and English in high school, then have these choices: admission to a junior college or technical institute; acceptance into an applied engineering program at San Francisco State or California Polytech; enlistment in a technological program in the armed services; employment right after high school in a firm where additional technological experience could be obtained. This program gives the student a wide variety of choices, important decisions that will influence his entire life.

A sobering corollary that must be stressed in a discussion of the importance of offering choices to high school students lies in the axiom that governs all freedom in a civilized society—namely, that freedom entails responsibility. The tenets set forth by our founding fathers, delineating the right to life, liberty, and the pursuit of happiness, did not constitute a right to libertine living. Neglect of the imperative of self-discipline could be fatal to the orderly operation of a school, to say nothing of damage to the success of an individual's educational program. Furthermore, the extension of student choice in a school carries with it a considerable extension of faculty and administrative responsibility. But the overall challenge of increased

---

[21]Zilpha W. Billings, "Self-Selection Classroom," *Today's Education* (October 1970).

[22]Information may be obtained from Portland School District 1, 631 N.E. Clackamas Street, Portland, Ore., 97208.

responsibility is certainly in keeping with the basic educational objectives. Student and administrative responsibility may be the key to averting open destructive dissent.

A strong counseling program, based on a person-to-person approach, is of infinite value in making the free-choice programs into practical, working arrangements. The success of an effective guidance program depends to some extent on a reasonable pupil-counselor ratio. And not only should counselors be specially trained and fully credentialed, they should also be skilled and knowledgeable in presenting possible alternatives, and in guiding each student in areas where he flounders. Here is an excellent opportunity for providing desirable human relationships, and they may prove to be strong preventives to student alienation.

Self-concept. (We want to be ourselves.) Closely associated with a person's desire for an audience, for involvement, and for freedom to make choices is each individual's need to find himself and be himself. In fact, this area is so definitely related to the foregoing considerations that one is hard pressed to find the distinguishing limits of each.

Perhaps the chief characteristic of any person's desire for identity is that the search and discovery of that identity is more uniquely individual, and more distinctly indicative of the kind of person he is and wants to be. The desire for self is a product of individual talents and interests, as well as of a native drive to develop those gifts. It is subject to individual inherent short-comings, as well as to a sensitivity to motivating forces and external incentives.

Do some high schools still refuse to put mirrors into restrooms for fear the students—especially girls—will linger too long? Headstart teachers install a full-length mirror in their classrooms in order that disadvantaged children may have a good look at themselves and begin to develop a positive self-image.

Many a youngster—notably of the minority groups—doubtlessly reaches high school with little of a positive self-image. A big question for all adolescents is "Who am I? And why?" It is part of the school's task to help construct a good self-image and assist the child to realize he has certain special gifts which are uniquely his own—physical, intellectual, and social talents—which he must try to develop. In too many classrooms and offices the student's self-image is not only ignored, it is demeaned. To be guilty of "putting out a person's light" or crushing his spirit is to commit a very far-reaching sin. We are even told in the Bible that "it is better for him that a millstone were hanged about his neck and he were cast into the sea." (Mark 9:42).

Jack Frymier's article, "Teaching the Young to Love," calls attention to this unfortunate situation.

Studies also indicate that youngsters who come from lower income homes receive less physical attention, less eye-to-eye contact, less verbal attention from their teachers than do youngsters from advantaged homes.[23]

Psychologists tell us that while most people desire positive recognition and acclaim, they will try for negative recognition rather than being ignored. That point may be the clue to some serious student confrontations. A few years ago a high school senior in a large school system was permanently expelled from the cafeteria because he was caught, for the third time, matching pennies. On remonstrating the severity of the penalty and lack of administrative understanding which it reflected, a teacher was told, "But John is belligerent and impossible. He is one of the most serious nonconformists in school. He even refuses to wear a belt." John's brother was a big football hero; John felt he was a "Nuthin'." But he was gaining attention through breaking the rules.

There is much to be said for a cooperative approach. Marie Fielder, director of Inservice Education Collaborative at the University of California (Berkeley), has made some helpful studies in conflict interaction using a team of adults and youth who, for the most part, were disenchanted underachievers. Highly successful results were apparently effected in various areas of school conflict through a diversified team approach.[24]

Acceptance. (We want to be cared about.) One of the most persistent demands that we hear in the voices of the young may sometimes be partially covered by rather rough deportment—indicating the desire for acceptance and openness. This need is instinctive in human nature. According to psychologists, a child comes into the world ready to love and be loved, *expecting* to be loved and expecting to give love in return. Educators should recognize this important fact and grasp its strong potential and implications for learning. The traditional school system and its tendency toward strict regimentation, together with contemporary instructional practice and its increasingly impersonal approach, may be serving as dampers on this motivating force. By such practices they may be creating in children and youth the negative forces of rebellion.

This thought certainly ties up with the previous points considered—notably with the desire for a positive self-image. Ronald Rousseve, Professor of Education at the University of Oregon, states that each person in his continual search for an answer to "Who am I?" needs to be freed from

---

[23]Jack Frymier, "Teaching the Young to Love," *Theory Into Practice*, Ohio State University (April 1969).

[24]Marie Fielder, "Diversified Team Approach to Conflict Interaction," *Educational Leadership* (October 1969).

the inhibiting frigidity he may previously have acquired in order to take the first important step toward self-realization and trust.[25]

The adult who is trying to help an adolescent must become involved in him and his individual problems; he must show him that *somebody cares about him, likes him as he is,* understands him, and believes in his possibilities. Only then can the adult begin to clarify for him his possibly distorted perceptions of reality, guide him in his choice of options and in his quest for personal identity. The immature or rejected person must have strong, supportive warmth all the way in order to build up his confidence.

A number of high schools, taking their cue from some universities like the University of California at Santa Cruz, have set up smaller units within the larger structure of the school in order to offset the impersonal, institutionalized set-up. Of course the human element is dependent on the personality of the teacher or the counselor, and is still paramount. A new organization, no matter how carefully mounted to provide for individual attention, may still be oriented to curriculum or structure; the teacher may still be no more human in his approach than a computer or a television set. Unless the teacher (or principal or counselor) is motivated by a personal desire to reach out with warmth and to care for that boy or girl, the design will fail to achieve its prime purpose—no matter how noble its intent.

Educational literature, even biographical information of famous men and women, is full of examples of successful (and unsuccessful) approaches to youngsters regarded in some way as atypical—withdrawn, recalcitrant, underachieving, nonconventional. Consider three such approaches, one to an elementary youngster, one to a group of high school boys, and one to a college freshman.

Harold D. Drummond, now Professor of Elementary Education at the University of New Mexico, tells this incident from the days when he was a second-year elementary principal.[26] Butch, a sixth-grade show-off, had been sent to him regularly for disciplinary purposes nearly every day all year. No amount of talking, no kind of punishment, had helped. On this particular day, in a moment of bewilderment, Mr. Drummond asked what turned out to be the catalytic question, "Butch, who are your friends?" The ordinarily cocky expression on Butch's face vanished. The super-confident youth became a child. He covered his face with his hands and wept. "Nobody," he mumbled, "I ain't got no friends." From that moment on, the principal became his friend. He reached out with warmth to help the boy,

---

[25]Ronald Roussève, "Encounter, Confrontation, and Emergence: An Approach to Counseling in Secondary Schools," *Oregon Education,* 43, No. 7 (December 1968), 22–23.

[26]Harold D. Drummond, "I Don't Have Any Friends," *Theory Into Practice,* Ohio State University, (December 1969).

finding or inventing a multitude of responsibilities and rewards. Butch went on to become a high school football hero and is today a successful farmer. He could have become a misguided or hostile activist.

The second approach: In a panel discussion on school dropouts held in a metropolitan area recently, four youths were questioned about their unhappy school experiences. At first, among others there were several questions concerning the difficulty they had had passing their courses. Answers varied: "I hated the stuff." "I hated the teacher." "When I asked teacher what the stuff meant, she'd say, 'Read the book.' But that was it—I couldn't understand the book." Then, toward the end of the discussion someone made this contribution, "I'm sure there were some positive aspects to your high school experiences. Didn't anyone give you encouragement, praise, friendly advice, a helping hand, or make you feel good about school?" All four dropouts replied, "Nobody."

The third incident:[27] This one is not about a potential activist or an actual dropout, but about a man who went on to become a professor of education at Indiana University, Harold G. Shane. It all happened because of a kindly professor at Ohio State University 35 years ago. Harold, then a college freshman, stood at Professor Orville Brinn's desk at the end of the class period, patiently waiting for the girls of the class to finish their inquiries. When Brinn finally turned to Harold, he said, "Why don't we go across the street for a cup of coffee?" In writing about this moment as a turning point in his life, Dr. Shane says, "I can't tell you how impressed I was to have a senior professor express that much interest in the company of a beginning student from upstate Ohio. I can't remember what we talked about, except that Dr. Brinn was friendly and supportive."[28]

Friendly and supportive. Perhaps those are the key words, what high school youth are hoping the school faculty will be. Perhaps that desire for the human approach is the overriding motivating force that underlies all human behavior, whether aggressive or submissive or conforming.

Conclusion

In this period of social turbulence, where campus unrest is surely one manifestation, every school principal will inevitably have to face the situation realistically—neither making a mountain out of a molehill nor playing ostrich—either of those roles could be disastrous. Certainly to be thoroughly forewarned, the astute administrator should lay down for himself

---

[27]Harold G. Shane, "A Cup of Coffee," *Theory Into Practice*, Ohio State University (December 1969).

[28]Shane, "A Cup of Coffee," p. 321.

certain guidelines for positive procedures. But building upon his knowledge of the situation at hand and upon his acceptance of sound educational principles, he should also evaluate his school for ways to improve it and for ways to involve his students and teachers in constructive, cooperative endeavor with special emphasis upon creating warm, open, human relationships. Much depends upon his strong leadership, possibly in handling a serious crisis, and surely in responding to the long-range challenges that may make or break the morale of his school.

Edwin Schneider, former principal of Lincoln High School in Portland, Oregon, is exemplary of such leadership. He is one of those principals who believes that activism is basically a good thing—good for the students in getting them involved in social, economic, political, and educational issues, and good for the school as a whole in its opportunity for promoting change. But his strategy for handling a disruptive display of activism is also commendable: he kept the lines of communication open to all students, he avoided alienation by distinguishing between issues of major and minor significance, and he explained reasons for his actions by means of an address to the student body. That address answered well the activist appeal to the principle of "student rights."

> The phrase, "I have my rights" is one of the common phrases to be heard in our society when an individual faces any kind of limitation on his actions. . . . What's wrong with saturating our environment with an emphasis on "liberty and the pursuit of happiness"? It is that without counter-balancing emphasis on responsibility to society and on restraint, the simple concern for unbounded freedom contains the seeds of self-indulgence, license, disregard for the rights of others—the very seeds of destruction of an ordered law-abiding society.

Schneider went on to challenge the student body with responsible behavior, with keeping the faith, and with their cooperative efforts to improve the school.

> Lincoln High School has been a great school. . . . I charge you, individually, to follow its tradition and to work with us in maintaining a spirit of learning, of understanding, of cooperation, of not assuming that with a little learning we have found all the answers. I challenge you to leave this morning with a new determination to grow and to develop the attitudes and patterns in school which will be your most important tools for meeting the future.[29]

---

[29]Kenneth A. Erickson, *Student Activists and Oregon High Schools* (Eugene, Ore.: Oregon School Study Council, University of Oregon, 1968).

Selected References

ALEXANDER, WILLIAM, and VINCE A. HINES, "The Nature of Independent Study in Secondary Schools," *Theory Into Practice*, Ohio State University (December 1966).

American Civil Liberties Union, *Academic Freedom in Secondary Schools*. New York City, 1968.

BENSON, GEORGE, KENNETH A. ERICKSON, and LARRY McCLURE, "Student Activism in the Pacific Northwest," *Special Bulletin*, Oregon School Study Council, University of Oregon (February 1970).

BILLINGS, ZILPHA W., "Self-Selection Classroom," *Today's Education* (October 1970).

BROWDER, LESLIE, K., "What to Do Before Students Demonstrate," *Nation's Schools* (April 1970), 86–87.

Center for Research and Education in American Liberties, *Civic Education for the Seventies: An Alternative to Repression and Revolution*. New York: Teachers College, Columbia University, 1970.

DRUMMOND, HAROLD D., "I Don't Have Any Friends," *Theory Into Practice,* Ohio State University (December 1969).

ERICKSON, KENNETH A., *Student Activists and Oregon High Schools*. Eugene, Ore.: Oregon School Study Council, University of Oregon, 1968.

ERICKSON, KENNETH A., GEORGE BENSON, and ROBERT HUFF, *Activism in the Secondary Schools*. Eugene, Ore.: Bureau of Research and Service, University of Oregon, 1969.

FIELDER, MARIE, "Diversified Team Approach to Conflict Interaction," *Educational Leadership* (October 1969).

FRYMIER, JACK, "Teaching the Young to Love," *Theory Into Practice*, Ohio State University (April 1969).

HICKERSON, NATHANIEL, *Education for Alienation*. Englewood Cliffs, N.J.: Prentice-Hall, Inc., 1969.

KLEIMAN, MARK, *High School Reform*. Chicago: Students for a Democratic Society, 1967.

NEA Research Division, *A Pupil's Day in Court*. Washington, D.C.: National Education Association. Updated yearly.

National Association of Secondary School Principals, *The Reasonable Exercise of Authority*. Washington, D.C.: The Association, 1970.

Review of Charles E. Silberman's *Crisis in the Classroom*, in *I/D/E/A* (Institute for the Development of Educational Activities), (Summer Quarter, 1970).

ROUSSÈVE, RONALD, "Encounter, Confrontation, and Emergence: An Approach to Counseling in Secondary Schools," *Oregon Education*, 43, No. 7 (December 1968).

"Special Report on Student Unrest," *School Management* (November 1968). Entire issue.

"Special Report: Student Involvement—Channeling Activism into Accomplishment," *Nation's Schools* (September 1969). Entire issue.

SUTTON, RICK, "An Experiment in Freedom," *Student Life Highlights* (October 1970).

13

Pupil Personnel Concerns

The educational and social reforms which resulted in greatly expanded guidance programs during the 1960s will probably seem minor in comparison to the changes which will occur during the 1970s. In addition to the sociological and psychological aspects of change, the anticipated reduction in poverty and the growing demand for universal education will place tremendous strains on educational resources. In order to survive institutions of learning will have to take the initiative in the change process. The internal disruptions in schools today are only a hint of the chaos which awaits them if they do not adapt.

The most probable agents of much of this reform are pupil personnel organizations. The training of guidance workers makes them particularly able to cope with change and innovation, and their influence should not be restricted to the classic boundaries of guidance services, but should follow the recent trend described by Douglas D. Dillenbeck as a "movement toward a central position in the school's educational program."[1] This necessitates a growing concern on the part of the principal for the proper utilization of these services. He can no longer consider the guidance department as an adjunctive facility, a luxury not vital to his school's survival. The viability of the institution may well depend on integrating pupil personnel services into the heart of the educational process.

The question still remains concerning the present and future concerns

---

[1] "The Future in Guidance, Psychological Services and Testing," by Douglas Dillenbeck. From the book *High School 1980* edited by Alvin C. Eurich. Copyright © 1970 by Pitman Publishing Corporation. Reprinted by permission of Pitman Publishing Corporation, pp. 218–25.

of guidance services. Because the actual organizational areas have already been discussed, the central concerns of this chapter are the problems and forces with which the organized groups must deal. Different authors have taken varying approaches to this question. James R. Brough[2] has investigated the self-expressed problems of junior high students through the questionnaire method. His results show that students place great emphasis on academic shortcomings, though this may be the result of the nature of an inschool questionnaire and the nature of his subject population—an upper-middle-class, white, suburban group. Jack M. Thompson[3] has surveyed the guidance literature to discover pertinent problems and issues. He has identified seven major problems, among which are role conflicts, lack of empirical data, and the lack of new ideas.

Thompson's use of review of the literature as a method of delineating guidance concerns has been employed in this chapter—but in a broad sense. Besides writings in the guidance area, publications relating to all areas of education have been analyzed. This is consistent with the belief in the broad application of pupil personnel services and its future as an integral part of educational progress. The classification system presented here should be considered only an organizational device through which discussion of the subject may be accomplished. Obviously there will be considerable overlap between categories, due to the broad nature of the subject matter, and in any one specific situation, perhaps another classification scheme may be more appropriate. But the arbitrary nature of the system should not limit its effectiveness as a tool of analysis.

The areas of pupil personnel concern have been broadly grouped into four categories: *Community-Centered Concerns, School-Centered Concerns, Student-Centered Concerns,* and *Guidance-Function-Centered Concerns.* The object of the chapter is to identify and discuss problems within these categories and to relate them to the school's role as an agent of change.

Community-Centered Concerns

A Changing Society

It seems sufficiently clear that the world, Western society in particular, has entered into an era of radical change. The factor which has possibly evoked the most extreme reactions is that of overpopulation. The current

---

[2]James R. Brough, "The Junior High Schooler: His Concerns and Sources of Help," *The School Counselor,* 13, No. 2 (December 1965), 71–76.

[3]Jack M. Thompson, "Current Issues and Problems in Elementary School Guidance," *The School Counselor,* 13, No. 2 (December 1965), 77–81.

world population is over three billion people, and according to United Nations reports, this figure will rise to four billion by the year 2000.[4] Besides the obvious result of overcrowding, we will experience rising pollution, declining natural resources, declining public services, and perhaps declining standards of living. The demands on education will be overwhelming. Along with this and resulting from it, will be a spectre of urban decay. Schools in the city are finding themselves with a growing lower class population. As the white middle class flees to the suburbs, the ghetto will continue to inbreed without sufficient heterogeneity of peer contacts to provide any constructive, upward societal models. And as city schools fail to cope with a rapidly diminishing tax base, the urban child will suffer.

The growth of technology and automation may be one of mankind's few hopes. Yet paradoxically this contains an inherent problem which contributes to social disruption: many people find themselves obsolete in their *youth*. The number of unskilled workers grows as education fails to adapt to the need for life-long training. And there are few places for the unskilled in a technologically-oriented society.

Another force which has the capacity for both salvation and destruction are the new media. The communication industry has awakened interest in many areas which need attention, but at the same time, people are poorly equipped to integrate and cope with the exponential growth of information. Once again education must intervene and provide the training necessary to help in forming the adaptive reactions needed with rapid progress. Closely related to the multiplicity of communications is the smothering fact of government expansion. Bureaucratic inefficiency which often contributes to the lag between technological and cultural developments shows few signs of self-correction at this time.

One wonders if education can effect changes in such situations. There are no easy solutions, no magic formulas. Proper utilization of all resources is the only response which schools can make. It is only too apparent that they have often failed to do so, becoming, in fact, contributors to confusion and decay. Educational leaders who cannot react to needed innovations are not leading; they are committing the future to a state of continuing unrest.

Changing Values

As we experience radical change in technological areas, we find that we are unable to find stability in our value systems. Though less obvious than the physical factors and results mentioned above, the question of

---

[4]Clifford Earle, "Overpopulation: New Threat to Survival," in August Kerber and Wilfred R. Smith, eds., *Educational Issues in a Changing Society* (Detroit: Wayne State University, 1968), pp. 35–39.

morality is no less important. What one generation finds important is often discarded by the next, and as a result, communication becomes more difficult and resolutions of crises are impeded.

Basic to our changing values is the disintegration of the family. The new nuclear family of parents and children is frequently a social isolate, forced to deal with increasingly complex problems, but with decreasing emotional support for its members. As the family life deteriorates, so do many long-held beliefs concerning authority. Today's youth no longer categorically accepts the wisdom of family, community, and national leaders. They wonder about war and the necessity of dying for what often seems to them vague and disputable purposes. They question the existence of a segregated society, and they find that authority-dispensed drug information is both incorrect and hypocritical in an alcohol-consuming nation. They doubt the validity of a morality which declares all but marital sex a sin.

These are all drastic changes in beliefs, yet they may be secondary to another fact: a weakening of the Puritan ethnic with a concomitant rise in a true Christian ethic. Many of our youth are no longer career-oriented, success-consumed. They find worth and happiness in other features of existence besides labor and money. We have long professed to be living the Christian life, and have impressed our children with the need to love and honor their fellow men, but many parents react with shocked disbelief when their children actually follow such teachings; they actually find it more rewarding to help the human condition than to compete for the affluent life.

The question still remains: Is it within the role of education to teach values? It might be more valid to ask whether it is possible to ignore values during the educative process. The answer to the latter question is *no*. To avoid dealing with values is to not only endorse the current system, but also to abdicate the goal of education of the total person. This is not to suggest that each teacher should attempt to impress his beliefs on his students. It is only the educator's place to stress the worth of the individual; not to comment upon every law and custom, but to train flexibility, so that each person may adaptively develop his own pattern of responses. The enemy of education is dogma; the closed-minded citizen today lacks the primary tools of survival.

As a leader, the principal must impress his teachers with open-mindedness. He should find and dedicate his counseling staff to such an ethic. Their basic philosophy should be one of individual growth and development; because of this, they can be utilized in matters pertaining to values. The integrity of the school and the integrity of the student are not incompatible. All resources must be directed toward achieving cooperation.

Racial and Cultural Concerns

As a result of the civil rights movement and federal court decisions, the schools must confront a problem which many of them have avoided for years. The need to deal with racial and cultural minorities is often the most difficult aspect of the principal's job. As a highly visible arm of the school administration, he frequently finds himself between opposing forces, unable to satisfy either side. This problem will in all likelihood persist in varying degrees for a number of years. Today's principal must develop successful practices for resolving racial and minority conflicts if he is to ensure his school's survival, and aim for the goal of educating the total student as an intellectual and social being.

Among the specifics of culturally-centered difficulties are dealing with disputes over busing, confronting confused parents, mediating between opposing student forces, and resolving staff frictions. The pupil personnel worker functions in numerous ways which may be of assistance. As a school psychologist, he can develop a testing program which is minimally discriminative against any group. As a human relations consultant, he can provide group experiences leading to a reduction of inaccurate social, cultural, and racial perceptions. One of the counselor's primary goals should be the improvement of human communication. Research and program development to discover new instructional methods can decrease the gap between middle-class students and those with more limited backgrounds.

Basic to the counseling function is the building of self-concept and feelings of personal worth within students. In dealing with culturally deprived youth, guidance must consider the problem of ethnic differences between counselor and student. There is a trend toward using people of similar backgrounds to counsel disadvantaged or minority pupils. One study specifically tested the preferences of disadvantaged students for counselors of their ethnic group.[5] Results indicated that pupils should have a choice of counselors, that minority guidance workers should be provided, and that counselor training must include classes in subcultural differences. These results do not mean that only Blacks should counsel Blacks or only Mexican-Americans should work with Mexican-Americans. In the process of building cultural equality, the need for societal integration must not be neglected. Appropriate models of other cultures are necessary for a child to learn to be accepting and open. Though over-correction of previous wrongs may be a temporary necessity, long-range goals must be

---

[5]Richard J. Stranges and Anthony C. Riccio, "Counselee Preferences for Counselors: Some Implications for Counselor Education," *Counselor Education and Supervision*, 10, No. 1 (Fall 1970), 39–45.

for the reduction of ethnocentrism on all sides. Cultural integrity can be preserved within a framework of cooperation.

The Demand for College

The higher education goal has become standard in our society, and is rapidly rising among many minority groups. The reasons vary from a desire for improved economic conditions, to a search for identity, to attainment of higher status. Whatever the reason, the general public as a whole is greatly concerned with college education.

Probably the greatest factor in the recent acceleration of the higher education trend is the establishment of an open-door policy in our collegiate institutions, particularly in the community colleges. The Carnegie Commission's call for universal access to postsecondary education has put pressure on two-year colleges to provide diverse learning programs to fill the needs of all citizens. This burden is also felt by schools below college level. They too must prepare students for a broadening range of educational opportunities.

The sequence of events leading to enrollment in college traditionally begins in the ninth grade. Yet recent events indicate that this process must be extended further down, even into the elementary schools. In many areas of the country, this will involve attitude change. Those who previously considered high school graduation the ultimate goal should be made aware of the new possibilities open to them. They should be informed of the wide scope of higher education in addition to the liberal arts programs available. Optimally, each school district would have a coordinated program from the elementary level through twelfth grade to disseminate such information.

Vocational Concerns

The educational system of the United States is primarily designed to prepare the student for continued schooling not for the world of work. Not until near the end of graduate school does future employment become a major objective of training. This obsession with nonvocational concerns is even more clearly illustrated by the fact that the majority of testing programs are designed to predict success in *further educational undertakings*. Noncollege-preparatory students are aware that most schools consider them of secondary importance and have a weak curriculum in vocational areas. As a result, they often become discipline problems or dropouts. A recent study showed that much delinquency is system-generated because of inadequate vocational counseling.[6] The researchers found that boys low on the socioeconomic scale tended to have unrealistic occupational aspirations. Their subsequent failures led to discontent and antisocial behavior. Proper guidance could channel these youths into areas in which success is feasible, and could direct them to the necessary training.

Another factor which points out the need for adequate job counseling is the changing nature of the American labor scene. During the 1960s, there was a shift from a majority of workers in production roles to a majority in service and distributive positions. It is estimated that technological development will require the average person to change his job four or five times during his life.[7] Work has become more than a survival function; more people are demanding psychological and emotional fulfillment from their jobs.

Vocational counseling cannot be divorced from educational guidance. If employment is believed to be more than the mere performance of certain duties, the schools must include a total curriculum of preparation for life—an interrelated program of future possibilities. The cooperation of both educational and industrial institutions is necessary, and education must take the initiative in achieving cohesiveness of purpose.

The Dropout

Unrealistic occupational aspirations among lower socioeconomic students can lead to dropping out of school; this is but one aspect of the problem. When a student withdraws prematurely from school, the waste of resources affects every citizen. Of course, the greatest loss is to the student whose personal development is restricted.

The extent of the dropout problem is illustrated by these figures: About 25% of secondary school populations withdraw prior to graduation.[8] In addition more than 80,000 young people who rank intellectually in the upper quarter of their age group drop out of school each year. These students fall within normal limits of mental health, and are frequently independent, self-assured, and cheerful. Why do they fail to complete school? One finding indicates that the school's pressure for conformity

---

[6]Morris A. Forslund and Lenton Malry, "Social Class and Relative Level of Occupational Aspiration: Implications for Delinquency and Education," *National Association of Secondary School Principals Bulletin* 54, No. 349 (November 1970), 106–15.

[7]Grant Venn, "Vocational Education for All," *National Association of Secondary School Principals Bulletin*, 51, No. 317 (March 1967), 32–40.

[8]Joseph L. French, "Characteristics of High Ability Dropouts," *National Association of Secondary School Principals Bulletin*, 53, No. 334 (February 1969), 67–79.

creates blocks for them. A more flexible and diverse educational program, coupled with individual counseling for those who are potential withdrawers, could reduce the number of dropouts. But prior to this, students with potential must be identified. The literature abounds with studies of dropout identification; one study found eleven variables to be predictors, including arithmetic achievement, age, socioeconomic status, father's occupation, and I.Q.[9] It is a reasonable assumption that possible dropouts can be identified accurately prior to the ninth grade.

Those geographical areas which have a high withdrawal rate should develop methods for dealing with their problems. Early identification is preferable to after-the-fact attempts at correction, but this requires coordination of school and community efforts, since the latter pays a high price for educational failure. Continued awareness among teachers and counselors concerning predictive factors and means of prevention is vital. It is not to be assumed that once a student has dropped out he is lost. The French study mentioned above included contacting a number of dropouts to serve as subjects, and interestingly enough, several returned to school soon after.[10] Such individuals as these must not be allowed to drop out of contact with educational institutions. The schools should be a primary source of information concerning job opportunities; they should also be the center of retraining efforts.

The Draft

In addition to educational and vocational planning, male students are faced with an added decision concerning the draft. Because the status of military service is in a condition of constant revision, draft laws have changed considerably in recent years. At the present time there are tentative plans to create an all-volunteer army.[11] This would place much of the problem in the realm of employment possibilities.

In the absence of nonconscriptive armed forces, however, the counselor must deal with a subject which has strong emotional overtones. In addition to keeping current on changing laws, he must be aware of the feelings of many students about serving in the armed forces. No matter what his own beliefs are, the guidance worker has a growing obligation to provide his students with all pertinent information concerning the draft.

Military recruiters also find themselves in a difficult position. They are attempting to glamorize the services and revamp their unpopular image.

---

[9]Harvey Eugene Walters and Gerald D. Kranzler. "Early Identification of the School Dropout," *The School Counselor*, 18, No. 2 (November 1970), 97–104.

[10]French, "Characteristics of High Ability Dropouts," p. 79.

[11]"Volunteer Army—When?" *U.S. News and World Report*, February 24, 1969, pp. 56–57. Copyright 1969 U.S. News & World Report, Inc.

Yet they meet with increasing protest from student groups who object to their presence on campus. The counselor must be careful to remain objective when dealing with the draft, for he is caught between opposing forces. He must provide both information concerning alternatives to military conscription and information about the services without violating any laws or unethically influencing any students. In such a situation, it might be best for advisors to act as a referral service for both the armed forces and draft counseling organizations. Counselors would then have to inform pupils of such possibilities and perhaps arrange for the dissemination of information. The school's role in this area is not entirely clear, but that is no excuse for it to avoid the issue. Each community must assess the situation independently.

Community Relations

There are few schools in the United States with planned programs of public relations. Even large districts with adequate facilities to allow for such projects tend to neglect this important area.

Education is under pressure from many sources. Church and civic groups, militant minorities, self-proclaimed moralists, right- and left-wingers—all have attempted to influence educational practices. The public appears to be past the stage where they are willing to blindly endorse and fund any project. They have demanded relevance and practicality in education, and they are demanding increased accountability. As a result, the schools find new bond issues defeated, see parent support become minimal, and discover a lack of coordination between them and other community organizations.

Minor attempts to relate to the outside world are primarily through parent-teacher groups, home visits by the classroom teacher, and annual parent's nights at the school. Unfortunately, these efforts usually reinforce the image of educational plants as specialized institutions, emphasizing the schooling function, a one-dimensional concept. The recent trend toward the creation of community schools is a major step in changing this image. In such programs, the school does not shut down at 3:00 P.M., but provides a variety of services including classes for adults, enrichment activities, and community cultural events. The public must begin to perceive its schools as multipurpose, locally-involved institutions.

Another necessity for improving relations is the development of in-service training to provide familiarity with local subcultures. Desegregation of school staffs has resulted in unfamiliarity on the part of many teachers with their students. While desegregation has positive aspects such as growing intercultural acceptance and the availability of a wider range of adult models, there are dangers because of inadvertent breaches of social mores, and misinterpretation of both verbal and nonverbal communications. The pupil personnel worker can be of assistance in these inservice sessions.

School-Centered Concerns

The General Curriculum

Curriculum improvement is an area for which the guidance worker is particularly suited, since his training has been directed toward several aspects of the learning process. Yet there are few principals who properly utilize this available talent. The counselor can be of benefit in the innovation, implementation, evaluation, and correction of the curriculum.

A first step in forming a relevant curriculum is knowing the strengths and weaknesses of the pupils. Guidance personnel can perform this service with a program of diagnostic testing. Closely related to the evaluative process is the counselor's advisement function. Here the students' abilities are weighed along with his educational goals, personal needs, and the availability of programs. The more diverse the curriculum, the more the need for advisement. For example, the Brigham Young University Laboratory School has been experimenting with a program of flexible scheduling to allow high school students to progress at their own speeds.[12] Each student is evaluated and placed in an appropriate curriculum—some are even allowed to attend university classes. Obviously this program requires extensive testing and advisement.

Perhaps the most important theoretical contribution made by the behavioral sciences to the area of curriculum is learning theory. Their contributions have led to such techniques as programmed instruction and performance financing, both of which are based on principles of reinforcement. Learning theory, if it is considered a flexible tool, may be applied to nearly any classroom setting without altering the basic program. And many counselors know how to use learning theory as a tool. In the future learning theory specialists may well become the most vital part of the guidance program. Besides the new techniques mentioned above, other new methods are continually offered to the schools. Guidance personnel can serve to evaluate these new programs as a part of their research function.

Educators are well aware that in addition to the cognitive areas of the curriculum, affective influences must be considered. A student's emotional state can alter his learning process, and it is as a personal adjustment

---

[12]Joe Wittmer, "The Effects of Counseling and Tutoring on the Attitudes and Achievement of Seventh Grade Underachievers," *The School Counselor*, 16, No. 4 (March 1969), 287–90.

counselor that the guidance worker frequently gives indirect aid to the classroom teacher. But this role should not exclude his helping the student. Since the instructor must be aided in gaining psychological insights into the emotional make-up of his pupils, inservice programs including teachers in the guidance process can accomplish a great deal.

Special Programs

Special programs are directed to the gifted student, the underachiever, the mentally and physically handicapped, and those students with more serious emotional problems. Estimates of the number of exceptional children in our schools range upwards from a minimum of 8%.[13] Since these pupils require curricula geared for their particular difficulties, it is in this area that school counselors have been broadly used in the past. The astute principal will continue to draw on the expertise of his guidance staff to improve these services.

The most common special programs in our schools are those for the educable, or mildly retarded pupil. The basic requirement of these children is an environment structured to their particular needs. (This is also vital to the physically disabled.) Handicapped pupils must be allowed to meet with success in this altered setting; all efforts must be aimed at avoiding failure experiences. Programs must have the services of a guidance expert to ensure that the environment is appropriate and flexible enough to react to changing demands. In addition to a proper environment, those with motor or sensory disabilities often benefit from the conditioning responses and counseling which help them to accept their problems.

When dealing with emotionally disturbed students, a school counselor may need the assistance of a trained psychologist. If the pupils' problems are less serious, counseling for better self-concept and improved interpersonal relations is often the treatment. These students should not be overly segregated to avoid reinforcing their image of themselves as "different."

Education research has long been concerned with the underachiever, but the effects of counseling with this group are contradictory. For instance, improved academic performance through counseling was reported by M. H. Thelen and C. S. Harris[14] while Winkler et al.[15] found no sig-

---

[13]Lloyd M. Dunn, *Exceptional Children in the Schools* (New York: Holt, Rinehart, and Winston, Inc., 1966), p. 17.

[14]M. H. Thelen and C. S. Harris, "Personality of College Underachievers Who Improve with Group Psychotherapy," *Personnel and Guidance Journal*, 46, No. 6 (February 1968), 561–66.

[15]Ronald C. Winkler, John J. Teigland, Paul F. Munger, and Gerald D. Kranzler, "The Effects of Selected Counseling and Remedial Techniques on Underachieving Elementary School Students," *Journal of Counseling Psychology*, 12, No. 4 (Winter 1965), 384–87.

nificant improvement. In view of the conflicting reports, further research is needed, yet counseling has been effective in some cases, and should be a part of programs with the low achiever. One type of guidance, developmental counseling, which focuses on changing specific coping behaviors, shows promise with this group.[16]

Dealing with the gifted, on the other hand, has proven a difficult problem for school officials. These children often go undetected because they are seldom a disruptive element for the teacher—they do not fail, and neither are they behavior problems. In addition, education has been concentrating on the low achiever and the retarded, and has few resources and programs for creative or brilliant pupils. This is a great waste of natural resources, and if at all possible, the principal should include programs for such individuals. Even without special programs, the guidance staff can work with the teachers to encourage freedom of expression and imaginative problem solving.

The newest subject of concern for pupil personnel is the problem of learning disabilities. These students are of adequate intellectual ability, but have one or several learning areas in which they function poorly. They require a specialized curriculum which deals with their weaknesses and helps them develop compensatory strengths.

Extracurricular Programs

The student personnel worker views the out-of-class environment as a means of contributing to the growth of the students and the faculty. He must frequently take the lead in encouraging appropriate use of extracurricular activities. Extracurricular programs have specific purposes for the counselor, including improved student relations, improved student-faculty relations, and growth of student self-concept.

If the principal and guidance staff view their extracurricular programs as constructive, they can structure them to accomplish their desired goals. One often-neglected factor is total faculty participation. Pupils see their instructors as more complete individuals instead of one-dimensional figures when they are participating together. Accompanying the use of large numbers of faculty should be an attempt to involve as many students as possible; this requires a broad range of activities to include a variety of student interests. Pupils should be allowed a voice in choosing activities, and should be given responsibilities in the administration of the programs. In large schools it may be necessary to divide into subschools, or schools-within-schools to give equal opportunity to all.

---

[16]Ronald L. Benson and Don M. Blocker, "Evaluation of Developmental Counseling with Groups of Low Achievers in a High School Setting," *The School Counselor,* 14, No. 4 (March 1967), 71–76.

If the principal has sufficient resources, it might be advisable to assign one or more full-time staff members to extracurricular activities. These programs can be a vital factor in the mental health of the school community.

Orientation

Orientation programs should concern and deal with entering classes, transfer students, and parents of new pupils; and they require the cooperation of the whole school staff. Though they involve many mechanical functions, orientation has a definite place in the guidance program. If students and parents are smoothly integrated, the school will function efficiently, but if students get off to a confused start, the whole year may have negative associations.

Orientation should begin before the actual start of school. Information programs may be arranged with the cooperation of feeder schools, and printed materials may be mailed to the homes of the expected enrollees—for students and parents. One helpful device is the school handbook. Since all pre-entrance programs should be aimed at preparing the student to emotionally accept the change in environments, information should not be overly detailed, and lengthy lists of rules should be avoided.

After students have entered the school, there are various orientation programs which may be employed. A class assembly is one popular method, a tour of the school is another. It is advisable to include older students in these activities, perhaps to the extent of assigning all new pupils to a "big brother" or "big sister." If this is done, upper-classmen should be prepared for their roles. Above all, the guidance department must take the primary role in this and other programs.

Howard L. Blanchard stresses the orientation of parents.[17] He suggests a group meeting at a time convenient for both fathers and mothers where every staff member is present, and understands his role in assuring parents of the quality of the school. This does not mean that school problems are to be hidden; but honest, direct responses which communicate a sense of commitment are needed. Those who deal with parents agree that cooperation from the home is vital. A good orientation program can pave the way to a long, profitable relationship between parents and faculty.

Discipline

School counselors are usually involved in the disciplinary process. And though the problem of behavior control is far too complicated for

---

[17]Howard L. Blanchard and Laurence S. Flaum, *Guidance: A Longitudinal Approach*, (Minneapolis, Minn.: Burgess Publishing Co., 1968), pp. 53–55.

adequate discussion in this section, some basic concepts and techniques may be profitably considered.

Probably the greatest misuse of a counselor occurs when the principal uses him as a punishing agent. This is not only an unsuccessful practice, but it also destroys the basic guidance function of nonpunitive assistance in growth and development. The counselor should be protected from such a role, even though he may contribute in numerous ways to behavior management. As a disciplinarian, however, his worth is negated.

The causes of misbehavior are many, including broken homes, social unrest, changing values, and racial friction. These and other outside influences are not the prime concern here since the focus of this section is the school's control of student disruption. To effect positive change with misbehavior problems, many researchers are utilizing group counseling.[18] Such attempts may be aimed at prevention, or working with those who show signs of becoming discipline problems. They may be corrective, attempting to help children acquire more adaptive behaviors. Of course in most instances such counseling would also be interested in promoting self-confidence and better interpersonal relations among those with behavior problems.

The newest approach to discipline has been offered by learning theorists. These researchers recommend the shaping of adaptive, positively-valued behaviors through the application of contingent reinforcements.[19] Such an approach considers behavior as possessing neither good nor bad. Behaviors are evaluated as to their adaptive or maladaptive results, and basic to the theory is the belief that all behavior is caused and only persists if it is rewarded. The role of the behaviorist is to discover the reinforcements which maintain certain actions, and then to restructure the situation to reward new, appropriate behaviors while diminishing the old. Behavior modification should be considered a tool, not a mechanistic philosophy of life. It is not a panacea for all discipline problems, but it is the most successful technique we have today.

The principal should have some familiarity with the above methods, and those on his staff concerned with management of behavior should be well versed in their applications.

Staff Relations

It seems unnecessary to stress the fact that there is a connection between positive staff relations and a smoothly functioning school. In

---

18Eugene W. Kelly, Jr., and Doris B. Matthews, "Group Counseling with Discipline-Problem Children at the Elementary School Level," *The School Counselor,* 18, No. 4 (March 1971), 273–78.

19John D. Krumboltz and Carl E. Thoresen, *Behavioral Counseling: Cases and Techniques* (New York: Holt, Rinehart and Winston, Inc., 1969).

today's educational milieu, with desegregation changing the homogeneity of many faculties, the principal must use all his resources to promote understanding and cooperation among his staff.

Unfortunately, one typical school problem is friction between the principal and the director of guidance services. This results from personality conflicts, threats to authority, acts by the principal which block fulfillment of pupil personnel objectives, and failure of the guidance leader to include the principal in his decision process. The key to a good relationship between these two is frequent and clear communication. Both must realize that a lack of cooperation is harmful to them, to the staff, and especially to the students they serve. Power struggles must be prevented; they are never constructive.

In regard to other staff relationships, the principal should employ his full range of human relations skills. Among the techniques which are useful are discussion groups (with and without the principal), in which teachers are encouraged to express opinions freely without fear of disapproval or censure. Together with this, the principal should include teachers in the decision-making process and continually demonstrate his willingness to tolerate legitimate dissent. Relations among teachers may be enhanced by a more recent method, the T-group.[20] This is a part of the laboratory method which resulted from studies at the Research Center for Group Dynamics. The National Training Laboratories utilize the laboratory method, developed under the auspices of the National Education Association. Laboratory training in human relations may require the assistance of special consultants, and is designed to help each individual realize his own growth potential and increase his ability to work more effectively with others.

Perhaps the most effective procedure for promoting staff cooperation is the establishment of a grievance expression machinery which deals with problems in a rapid and equitable manner. If such an avenue is not provided, dissatisfaction and disruption have no outlet other than the school itself. The principal must anticipate staff problems and prepare for their consideration if he wishes to avoid internal dissent.

Teacher Militancy

Teacher militancy is closely related to staff relations, and many of the suggestions made concerning the latter apply here. But teacher militancy is more than a question of relationships. It results from a mixture of unionism, professionalism, and the rising cost of living. One writer forecasts a long-term trend toward a gain in teacher power and a loss in the

---

[20] L. P. Bradford (Ed.) "Group Development," No. 1 in Selected Readings Series. Washington, D.C.: National Training Laboratories, National Education Association, 1961.

power of principals and superintendents.[21] This could lead to equality in the educational structure, and could well be beneficial.

Unfortunately, present conditions in bargaining are not conducive to improving education's public image or to encouraging cooperation among members of the profession. An example of this situation is the unionized teacher's strike in Newark, N.J. Friction between this group and the school board led to "near guerrilla warfare" and prevented any discussion of reform.[22] There has been lack of faith on both sides—epitomized by the discovery that a teacher's lounge in Carrollton, Michigan, had been "bugged" by the school superintendent.[23]

In many cases, the question of militancy is out of the principal's domain, but there are certain areas where he may either agitate or calm a troubled situation. The main problem is dealing with militant teachers within each school, and once again the counselor may be of assistance with his skills as a human relations consultant. The principal and the guidance personnel should make an effort to remain neutral, if at all possible. Care must be taken to ensure the rights of all parties concerned. While organizers should be given times and places for union work, and bulletin boards should be made available, those teachers who do not choose to join the organization must be likewise protected. Channels for dissent *must* be provided if conflict is to be minimized.

The Team Approach to Guidance

Most contemporary educators give at least lip-service to the team approach to school guidance. In reality, little effort is given to improve the guidance-oriented activities of all staff members. To restrict pupil personnel services to a counselor or school psychologist is a waste of an opportunity. The classroom teacher spends far more time with students than does any guidance worker, and in many cases he sees a broader range of pupil behaviors, not just the testing or counseling session. Therefore at the very least, the teacher must be considered a primary source of information about each child. It would be an excellent use of time to devote several faculty meetings or inservice sessions to the subject of behavior observation. One of a school's most valuable assets is a trained observor in the classroom.

The broadest application of the teacher's guidance role is his part in the homeroom. Here he devotes time each day to a discussion of individual and group problems. Even if such discussion is not feasible, the teacher

---

21David Storm, "Changing Balance of Power in Education: Teacher Militancy," in August Kerber and Wilfred Smith, eds., *Educational Issues in a Changing Society* (Detroit: Wayne State University Press, 1968).

22"Savage Strike in Newark," *Time*, April 19, 1971, p. 66.

23"Bugging the Bargainers," *Time*, November 7, 1969, p. 45.

can help provide many pupil personnel services including data collection, parent conferences, and participation in counseling sessions. The teacher should further establish a positive, accepting atmosphere in the class which allows the student to approach him with his problems. Although counselors and teachers frequently have friction between them because of a variety of reasons including different goals and criteria for student success, role misunderstandings, and lack of communication, the burden for improving these relationships must fall on the counselor, since this is his area of expertise.

One innovation which could improve the counseling activities of the entire staff is the creation of a school guidance committee. This group should include counselors, administrators, faculty, and students. It should be responsible for such parts of the school guidance program as enrichment, student-faculty relations, and procedures for student discipline and appeal. If pupils and teachers help create the rules and activities, they will be more likely to support them.

One further suggestion is the use of subprofessionals for certain guidance duties. In pupil personnel services, there is still a shortage of professional staff. It is sometimes advantageous to employ people without advanced degrees in positions such as testing officer, interviewer, and information specialist. The duties of the first two subprofessional jobs are self-explanatory, but the responsibilities of the latter include data gathering and tabulating. The principal should not be averse to utilizing subprofessionals who are trained for specific guidance areas.

Accounting

Student records and attendance might seem a rather safe area, yet there are numerous pitfalls. The major problem concerns the use of students' records and the legal rights of pupils. Issues relating to this are discussed in the previous chapter's section on civil rights and due process.

Another concern is pupil attendance. Truancy should be approached as a maladaptive behavior frequently maintained by conditions in school and at home. A student may have little control over his truancy because of parental, social, or classroom influences. A classroom which is nonrewarding, boring, or oppressive, a home which forces the student to carry responsibilities beyond his years, or degrading social conditions can all lead to a reduction in school attendance. Though the school is legally responsible only for dealing with the actual truancy, the principal should consider it his ethical responsibility to investigate the entire situation. The antiquated truant officer image has generally been replaced by a social worker. In any instance, those trained in pupil personnel work should handle this type of problem.

The guidance staff should be included in collecting basic student records. They may wish to add other informational devices or forms which may aid the performance of their duties. They may also suggest nonthreatening methods of data collection to avoid alienating students and parents. Guidance workers should be consulted in issuing work permits and releases, as well as in matters of suspensions and expulsions. Since these latter actions can be crucial to a child's future, they should not be handled in a preemptory fashion solely for reasons of punishment. There must be a consideration of goals for both the pupil and the school, and both should understand why such actions are taken.

Student-Centered Concerns

Civil Rights

There is a decided trend toward enlargement of the civil rights of public school students. As a result, the authority of principals and teachers has been somewhat narrowed. The recognition that pupils have constitutional rights to perform certain behaviors which the schools, as government agencies, may not restrict has been substantiated. Many of these behaviors may be personally repulsive to administrators, but limiting them often limits freedom, which often has negative aspects in a learning situation. In addition, removing restraints has a positive effect upon student maturation and societal involvement.

George Triezenberg has summarized the results of recent legal decisions.[24] The Supreme Court has indicated that the schools are no longer "sacred cows," and that their disciplinary actions must meet the test of due process. Education is no longer a privilege, but a right of all citizens.

Basic to much of the debate over civil rights is freedom of speech. Student organizations and publications have become more out-spoken and have met with varying degrees of suppression. School leaders must realize that because this constitutional guarantee is vital to the continuance of a free democratic society, they cannot deny any citizen the right of expression. There is, however, confusion in the courts on certain aspects of obscenity and violence. The principal should consult both his legal and guidance experts when dealing with such matters.

Authority must derive from acknowledged rules of conduct. Internal order is a necessity, but it cannot exceed the bounds of recognized power. The more citizens accept an authority as legitimate and equitable, the easier is regulation of behavior. Principals must tread carefully in matters of individual freedom. Students are not a subclass of citizens. As the Gault

---

[24]George Triezenberg, "How to Live With Due Process," *National Association of Secondary School Principals Bulletin,* 55, No. 352 (February 1971), 61–68.

decision of 1967 states, "Neither the Fourteenth Amendment nor the Bill of Rights is for adults alone."[25]

Student Unrest

The student protest question is central to the previous discussion of civil rights. Due to the extensive ramifications of such protests, this book has devoted an entire chapter to consideration of the area, but here are briefly mentioned some of the basics of the problem.

In 1969, more than 2000 high schools experienced various forms of protest, from walkouts to sit-ins to boycotts to outward violence.[26] Few sections of the country avoided all turmoil, though schools in large urban centers had the most difficulties. Educators see a number of reasons for this, including boring and irrelevant curricula, lack of student involvement in decision making, and poor human relations efforts by school staffs. In addition, protests have gone beyond educational dissatisfaction and into the realm of social protest—students are concerned about numerous issues from pollution to minority oppression. Those who wish to affect changes in society can only do so within the context of their personal environment, so that the school has become the center of student activism, much as the ghetto has borne the protest of most black residents.

This is not to say that all protest is justified; certainly some of it is not. It is unfortunate that many leaders see all pupil disruptions in a negative light. They must learn to discriminate between constructive and destructive protest; the task is often difficult. Educators cannot respond in a shallow fashion if schools are to survive.

Some have stated that "the system" is theoretically incapable of change and must be radically altered so that it can cope with future developments.[27] This is a powerful indictment, and should be seriously considered by all educators. The evidence is incomplete; it cannot categorically be claimed that because a system has not responded adequately, it does not have the capacity to do so. Once again, the principal should utilize all resources to deal with the problem in his own set of circumstances.

Dress and Hair Regulations

The current era of disruption and protest has many causes. The wise administrator is alert to issues which contain the roots of student activism,

---

[25]Morris J. Clute, "Rights and Responsibilities of Students," *Educational Leadership*, 26, No. 3 (December 1968), 240–42.

[26]James E. House, "Can the Student Participate in His Own Destiny?" *Educational Leadership*, 27, No. 5 (February 1970), 442–45.

[27]Jack R. Frymier, "Why Students Rebel," *Educational Leadership*, 27, No. 5 (January 1970), 346–50.

and he works to institute procedures which tend to de-fuse potential problems. This requires anticipation and a willingness for innovation. Protest frequently involves basic issues of societal and individual dissatisfaction, as well as major questions of rights and responsibilities. Despite this schools are too often obsessed with matters of relative unimportance which have little bearing on the learning process. These minor points may lead to altercations which drain the energies of all involved and mask truly crucial questions. Such is the status of regulations concerning the personal appearance of students. To enforce strict rules of dress and hair styles is on a par with concern over gum-chewing. Both are factors of aesthetics and individual expression, and are not related to improved learning conditions—except in a negative sense. When there are attempts to impose standards of clothing and hair length upon students, the result is to reinforce their image of the school as an oppressive institution.

It sometimes seems that education's priorities are inappropriately ordered. It is much easier to devote attention to such obvious factors of conduct as student appearance than to devote time to less obvious but more important factors as individual learning styles. As a straw man issue, the problem of dress only diverts energies from more worthy concerns. Public schools have limited techniques of behavior control. To apply them to minor issues only weakens their effectiveness in matters of importance. And as in all cases of individual development, the principal will find the pupil personnel worker of assistance in deciding on priorities and expenditures of all school resources.

Drug Use in School-Age Populations*

All laws which can be violated without doing anyone any injury are laughed at. Nay, so far are they from doing anything to control the desires and passions of men that, on the contrary, they direct and incite men's thoughts the more towards these very objects; for we always strive toward what is forbidden and desire the things we are not allowed to have. And men of leisure are never deficient in the ingenuity needed to enable them to outwit laws framed to regulate things which cannot be entirely forbidden. He who tries to determine everything by law will foment crime rather than lessen it.

—Spinoza

At no other time in history has it seemed more appropriate to say the more we gain, the more we lose. Ecological balance, balance of power,

---

*This section was written by Dennis L. Ekanger, former Project Director, White Bird Sociomedical Aid Station, Inc., Eugene, Oregon. It has been edited and approved by the authors.

balance of payments, space races, Vietnam, peace talks, urban crises, and youth and drugs constitute problems of this sort. Not just a few youth in scattered pockets or subgroups here and there are using drugs, but increasing proportions of youth in every sector of the United States are indulging. And youth can no longer be singled out as *the users* because drug use and misuse cuts across all strata of our culture, from the young to the old, from the wealthy to the poor, from the politically respected to the politically apathetic, from the silent majority to the verbal minority. Drug use (both legal and illegal) is nearing a social *norm*. American chemical optimism grew up with television and through the years has gained indirect though not intentional medical endorsement. Failure to comprehend these factors has led to dysfunctional understanding, poor program designs, and misplaced priorities.

Public schools today are all having to face the reality of student drug use. Students in almost every school argue with the authorities over the decision to use or not to use certain illegal drugs. For some students the decision is not too difficult, for others there is more pressure. But for many their decision may result in tragedy. Drugs have become an integral part of much of the youth social sphere, and these drugs are for the most part illegal. Allan Cohen puts the attitude very succinctly when he says, "It may be that the primary question among youth presented with the opportunity for experimentation is no longer 'Why?' but 'Why not?' "[28]

It is a highly conservative estimate that *at least* 15 percent of the students in every public secondary school in America have had intimate experience with some form of illegal drug (excluding alcohol and tobacco). And more significantly, a much larger proportion of secondary school students defend the rights of those who use drugs to do so, or do not rule out the possibility that they may use the drugs at some future time.

The single greatest obstacle to dealing effectively with the current drug problem is the hysteria and emotion attributed to the unknowns and dangers of illegal drug use. When one uses the terms "drugs" and "youth" together it has a certain electric or magic (or black) effect. It is a feared combination. But among the school population, most youth—users and nonusers alike—do not voice or show nearly the concern and distress about illegal drug use and misuse as the adult populace does. It is this emotional reaction from adults which makes it difficult for the schools to even acknowledge to their constituent public that they have drug use problems among their students. It has been easier, and politically safer, for schools to deny such reports, or in many larger metropolitan schools where this is more difficult to avoid, to shun any responsibility for such problems.

---

[28]Allan Y. Cohen, "The Journey Beyond Trips: Alternatives to Drugs," *Journal of Psychedelic Drugs*, 3, No. 2 (Spring 1971), 16–21.

The quicker this forced duplicity in the schools is corrected, the sooner the necessary coordinated adjustments and solutions will be possible. As Allan Cohen has stated in reviewing drug education efforts, "Educational honesty and credibility must be maximized in the same way that legislators should make drug use a public health and not a criminal concern."[29]

Compounding Factors to Youth Drug Use

An individual uses drugs because he wants to, and in most cases enjoys them to the point of his own perceived or reactive limits. He will continue to use them until he finds something more satisfactory.[30]

Many reasons have been given for the use and misuse of drugs both by youth and adult populations. Most of these explanations have attempted in theory to isolate a "type" or "specific cause." Predictably, studies abound stating and specifying conclusions about personality and socio-cultural factors of drug use. The importance of these studies rests on their ability and accuracy to identify implications for preventive and educational directions. But is there a type? Can one "predict" use? More importantly, does it help to talk in such terms? Added understanding and increased awareness, in our opinion, has not greatly increased from such research endeavors.[31] And more clearly, we do not think that human needs, mixed with the present social, environmental, and cultural dynamics, are clear cut. The problems of drug use and misuse cannot be reduced to a set of simplistic variables which can be dealt with individually. On the contrary, it is a labyrinth of labyrinths. Defining the specifics will not advance us any faster to a resolution of the whole problem.

But schools and school personnel undoubtedly ask, "Shouldn't we seek a solution to the problem?" Our opinion is a resolution, not in terms of isolating a cause—researching it—but in actively seeking with students alternatives—not solutions—to getting high chemically. Principals should not seek a solution, nor expect to find an answer or a group of answers. The use of drugs among school-age youngsters and the adult population today is a reality; they are going to continue to use drugs. And there are certain things that a principal may do that will further *increase* the possibility of their continued use or enhance it!

Schools, more than any other single institution, need to be assertive, aggressive, and willing to take the necessary risks in exploring nontraditional approaches to dealing with drug and other types of problems. The

---

[29]Cohen, "The Journey Beyond Trips," p. 20.
[30]Cohen, "The Journey Beyond Trips," p. 17.
[31]Cohen, "The Journey Beyond Trips," p. 16.

more students feel locked out of participating in the solutions to our local and national problems and crises, the more frustrated, alienated, bored, and adult-rejecting they become. As this occurs, drug use and abuse among them will increase as a symptom of these depersonalizing processes.

In this respect, the public schools as reactive rather than proactive institutions have the potential to contribute to the continuance of drug use among adolescents. Schools have in this way become a part of the problem—not a part of the solution. Today's young people, having grown up with the tension of possible atomic disaster, nerve gas disaster, ecological disaster, racial disorders, political double-talk, and having had less financial difficulties than the previous generations, are experiencing and have experienced tremendous social pressures to correct these huge problems and seek solutions to them. The sense of urgency underlying youth reactions to situations is oftentimes missed or incomprehensible to adults. It is not difficult to understand that with problems of such magnitude plaguing them, youth find mathematics, history, and physical education irrelevant, to miss the mark. And it is getting more difficult to either ignore the young people's cultural observations, or to dispute their feelings about such issues—nor should we try. Upon close examination they have solid justification for their feelings.

Regardless of the true nature of the matter, as long as a growing segment of the student population feels strongly that the school processes are largely irrelevant or that schools have incorrectly ordered educational priorities, then to some degree this view will have truth to it—a self-fulfilling prophecy. When students reject the institution, its values and merits, they seek other pursuits. If they are forced to be in school, these other activities may include escapism while in school. Students taking this self-chosen, yet circumstantially enhanced, course of action do so because they decide to. Solutions to the symptom problems which accompany this trend must focus on the motivational aspects of this rebellion. Endeavors must center on abuse and misuse among youth drug users, and priorities given to different abuse behaviors. Efforts toward developing alternatives to drug use must realistically suggest more than simply a substitute, they must suggest rather something *better*. To accomplish this necessitates a sensitive, flexible, clear picture of where kids "are at" in order to realize these programs.

Most authorities, along with most parents, have generally not listened or communicated effectively with youth. What has been heard and seen in most cases is *what* they are saying—not how or why they are saying it. Most young people today are very idealistic and compassionate. And perhaps ironically, their particular brand of humanism is an active extension of the spoken ideals of their parents. Frustration and tension build when they seek ways of implementing these ideals and are shuffled aside, ignored, or denied active participation in tasks they correctly identify as meaningful, want to make contributions toward, and feel strongly about. If these outlets are stifled, these tensions must naturally be either sublimated, rationalized, or driven into the psychic underground possibly to surface in another form.

Although schools confront these frustrations early, since a majority of a student's waking hours is spent there, they are usually late and respond in an all too often pacifying manner. It is not surprising to find that more and more attacks are being leveled at the relevancy of the schools and the structure itself. The times are tense, the issues often heated, and the emotional investments high, and youth naturally are the first to respond to the effects of these pressures. The key is channeling this energy, emotion, and tension constructively. The school can help young people to safely test and use these deep-felt concerns to their advantage and in the best interests of others around them—without destroying the spark of idealism, or alienating them so much that they try to escape or drop out.

In effect what is happening as these alienating and distancing processes continue is that more youth are saying to older people, "We do not believe in your attitudes, values, and priorities to the same degree you do." This leads to decreasing effort at school as students become even more deeply convinced that they are being kept from active participation in meaningful change and activity. At this point many give up, sit back, play a waiting game, watch the very slow process of needed change on crisis issues, and become more critical and apathetic as time passes. More distance occurs, allowing more freedom to criticize and less desire to participate constructively.

Program Development Considerations

In designing an educational attack on youth drug use, the important factor for schools to consider is the spark of interest and curiosity present in all young people. What we are now seeing is that many of them have either extinguished the spark or have had it snuffed out. Once this has happened in a school setting, it becomes more and more difficult to rekindle motivation; it may even be impossible.

Examples of the most promising curriculum and program designs currently in practice combine youth participation with a coordinated comprehensive effort by the schools, community, and parents to provide alternatives to the depressant spiral of dropping out. Such efforts are coupled directly with an up-dated, accurate, educational effort presenting known facts about drugs, and focusing upon the decision-making process and attitude formation process inherent in drug use/abuse. The programs deal with respect for chemicals, personal respect, constructive/destructive behavior, peer group flow and pressure, and the realities of the culture students have inherited.

Most preventative efforts against drugs of the past have not only failed miserably, but in many cases have backlashed, creating more distance, mistrust, discouragement, and alienation. In dealing with youthful unlawful drug users, strong legal sanctions, informers, incarceration, educational scare techniques, and so forth have been clearly ineffective control methods. What resulted from these and other efforts was an intense polarity with strongly entrenched sides facing each other, neither willing to move, and each determined to win, despite the potential social damage to the individual or the social community.

The new drug education focus is on unraveling confused misinformation, misconceptions, and faulty logic systems. As the errors are corrected, more accurate information is gathered. New educational approaches are beginning to correct the mistakes of the past and are taking a closer and more realistic look at the drug scene as manifested in the hallways, rest rooms, and parking lots of our public schools.

If we admit to the logic that people take drugs because they *want* to, we also are forced to realize that people will only stop using drugs when and if they want to. From this logic comes another problem: better educational programs, equipment, and information will only play a part in the individual's decision to use or not to use drugs. Older, more erroneous models were based on the premise that individuals could be frightened away from drug use and experimentation. Frankly, both models are only partially accurate. Earlier programs such as misinformation, scare tactics, and hidden goals not only alienated students from the educational institution, but also placed the instructor in the frustrating position of not knowing what his students knew from experience. Much of the old drug education curriculum was very poor and not based on realistic field-tested and research-substantiated knowledge. The new programs, if simply based on the concept of providing accurate information, will not include the necessary variables of attitude formation, motivation, and decision making as an active process in drug use consideration, nor will most of them deal with the compounding variables—alienation and disenchantment.

Complementary and integral to these revised drug education programs, active behavioral alternatives and youth-initiated projects have found young people not only willing to work—and work hard and long— but have also found them to be cooperative and eager to develop and learn the necessary skills to continue the projects. Crash pads, youth hostels, switchboards, religious projects, co-ops, ecology projects, free clinics, political action groups, and a score of other such programs have been enthusiastically received and supported by today's youth.

Administrative Considerations

It is essential in program development that considerations be based on intimate understanding of the dynamics of youth drug use and abuse and the underlying dynamics of the drug scene. Unless this is so, there is a chance that it will backfire. Therefore, before any school administration develops policies and programs to stop student drug abuse, a word of caution is appropriate. Administration must ask itself, "Are we sure our appraisal of our local needs is accurate? Do we have articulate student-trusted staff to assist us?" If the answers are no, possibly doing nothing for the moment is better than simply doing "something" and hoping it is in the right direction. Calling in students, asking for professional assistance—from those working with drug-using populations—and finding out those persons on the staff the drug-using students trust are good starting points. In these respects, common sense is your best guide. In terms of experimental programs, no one project seems to have an edge over any other in the United States.

Specific considerations for curriculum design and programs should include:

1. Accurate appraisal of your school's drug use and abuse populations
2. Appraisal of the school as a conducive system for growth and development (the degree of sensed antagonism and alienation of students by particular school policies)
3. The involvement of students in planning, implementing, and coordinating drug education programs
4. Inclusion of adult drugs-of-choice in discussion and presentation of materials (up-to-date and accurate)
5. Focus on use/misuse, attitudes toward chemical ingestion, decision-making process, motivation to use or not use, and factors which inhibit this
6. Involvement of representatives from the community actively dealing with drug abuse (courts, public and mental health officials, physicians, attorneys, and police) recognizing their expertise and limitations
7. Involvement of the counseling staff and selected teachers in the design of the program
8. Involvement of students in the ongoing evaluation of the program
9. A coordinated, concerted effort including primary and secondary schools

In preparing school personnel for handling drug education programs, the National Drug Education Training Program has stressed

First . . . the awareness that the drug problem is a concern not only of the school but of the whole community. All segments of the community should be actively involved if there is to be a solution to the problem.

Second . . . the need to provide school personnel who are in direct contact with youth, with the information, understanding, and skills to deal with the problem. Accurate up-todate information about drugs and drug use is one aspect of the need. Just as important is the necessity to help teachers and parents develop the insights, skills, and techniques which are effective in dealing with the attitudes, values, life-styles, and problems of contemporary youth. Adults must learn how to listen to and communicate effectively with youth and, in so doing, will need to reexamine their own values.

Third, and perhaps most important . . . the continuous involvement of youth in the planning, the implementing, and evaluating of a drug education program.

Fourth . . . the need for continuing cooperation at all levels—federal, state, and local. This is basic to the achievement of the goal of reaching virtually every teacher and school administrator in the country by June of 1971.[32]

Administrative Policies

Many school districts today are in the process of reviewing and, if necessary, developing administrative guidelines and policies related to drug abuse control which consider the occasional user, the chronic user, pupils suspected of possession, and pupils suspected of selling or furnishing drugs to others. A fine example of a sound administrative program is found in the Drug Abuse Committee, Thornton Township High School, Harvey, Illinois, of June 1971.

Confidentiality

It is the policy of District 205 that all professional staff, when approached by a student regarding the use of drugs, be encouraged to involve himself with the student in order to explore the situation. It is believed that discussions with a student should be treated with various degrees of confidence depending on the seriousness of a student's involvement with drugs. Although it is generally believed that teachers, counselors, and administrative personnel are not legally protected if they withhold knowl-

[32]David E. Smith, M.D., and David J. Bentel, *Fourth Annual Report to the Legislature—Drug Abuse Information Project* (San Francisco: University of California, December, 1970), p. 49.

edge about a student's drug problem, the Illinois School Code states the following:

> Discretion . . . 2-201. Except as otherwise provided by statute, a public employee serving in a position involving the determination of policy or the exercise of discretion is not liable for an injury resulting from his act or omission in determining policy when acting in the exercise of such discretion even though abused.
>
> Negligence . . . 2-202. A public employee is not liable for his act or omission in the execution or enforcement of any law unless such act or omission constitutes willful and wanton negligence.

The following recommendations are suggested for teachers, counselors, and administrators if approached by a student about a drug problem:

1. The teacher, counselor, administrator should involve himself at length with the student about the problem; for example, he should:
   a. Try to learn the extent of the problem.
   b. Try to help the student understand the problem.
2. The teacher should contact a resource person for specific information or send the student to a resource person, school nurse, counselor, or dean of boys or girls.
3. If the student's drug problem is serious, the teacher should:
   a. Try to convince the student to tell his parents.
   b. Try to convince the student to contact a drug abuse center.
4. If there is a direct danger to the health and safety of the student, it is recommended that the teacher contact the parents of the student, or someone else in authority, even if done without the student's consent. (Since teacher, counselors, and administrators are not legally protected if they withhold knowledge about a student's drug problem, the teacher could be held responsible in case of serious injury or death.)

Persons Under the Influence of Drugs

Persons under the influence of drugs should be sent to the school nurse for medical care. This condition should be reported to the student's counselor and respective dean. Extensive counseling should be given the student to determine the cause of his behavior and help the student so that the situation does not occur again. Parents should be included in the counseling session after the problem has been defined. Whenever a teacher suspects drug abuse, *someone* should be notified to obtain help for the student.

1. Obvious disruptive behavior, possibly caused by the use of drugs, should be treated as any other type of disruptive behavior. Depending on the

seriousness of the situation, these steps should be taken:
a. Notify the nurse.
b. Notify the dean, counselor, and department chairman.
c. Parents should be notified by the dean.

2. Obvious nondisruptive behavior which leads the teacher to suspect drug abuse should be treated in the following way:
   a. Notify the nurse and counselor as to noticeable changes in behavior that lead the teacher to suspect that the student may be taking drugs.
   b. In reporting such students, teachers are advised not to state or accuse the student of taking drugs because of liability laws and reputation of the student.
   c. Nurse and the counselor of the student should have conferences with the student to determine, if possible, what the problem is and whether the parents need to be notified immediately.
   d. Parents should be notified as to the problem and as to what assistance can be given depending on the case. Student and/or parents should be advised of agencies and community organizations which might be of assistance.

Persons Possessing Drugs in School

Drugs should be confiscated and turned over to the police to verify that the drugs are illegal. If they are, the student's name should be turned in to the police, student's counselor, and dean. Disciplinary action should be taken along with extensive counseling.

A teacher, or any other employee of the school, should report to the deans any substance thought to be drugs, confiscate the possible drugs, place them in an envelope marking where they were found, have the student report to the dean, and the dean, in turn, should notify the police if the quantity is sufficient to constitute a breach of the law. All items which may possibly be drugs should be turned over to the police.

Persons Pushing Drugs in School

Persons pushing drugs and the drugs should be turned in to the police. If the drugs are verified as being illegal, and if the person is a student, he should be expelled.

1. The deans should be notified of any person or persons suspected of pushing drugs and the reasons for such suspicions. The deans should:
   a. Investigate the suspicions by having the individuals watched.
   b. Check with the police to see if the individual is a known pusher.

Role of the School Nurse

The role of the school nurse is that of a resource person to have available information for interested students. Nurses should recommend medical, sociological, and psychological resources for assistance when needed by students who are using drugs. The nurse should hold conferences with the student and refer the student to a counselor, if extensive counseling is needed.

Role of Teachers, Counselors, and Deans

The role of teachers, counselors, and deans should be that of advisors. They should help the student using drugs to understand his situation and attempt to help him solve his problems, if possible. If the situation is serious, the student should be advised where to go for help. A list of drug agencies serving the community should be available to the student desiring such information.

Teachers, counselors, and deans should be concerned primarily with the student's sociological and psychological needs through extensive counseling of any involved student. The teacher should be involved with such counseling if the student shows confidence and trust in that teacher by approaching him for help. Anyone dealing with students concerning drugs should be honest as to their own knowledge of drugs. Teachers, counselors, and deans should serve as resource persons and have information or sources of information for students who need assistance. The dean will also act as a disciplinarian in serious cases such as using drugs in school or pushing drugs in school.

Written Reports

A high school employee should not diagnose or accuse any individual of using drugs. A description of behavior or personal appearance should be used rather than a statement that the person uses drugs.

Possible General Symptoms of Drug Abuse

1. Sudden changes in behavior, such as:
   a. A decline in the level of attention to school work
   b. Loss of interest in sports and other activities
   c. Staying out of school.

2. Disinterest in the opposite sex.

3. Moodiness.

4. A tendency to sit looking in space. Called by addicts "goofing," it could be caused by use of heroin, barbiturates, or both.

5. Sudden carelessness in appearance; especially if he or she has been neat in the past.

6. Drowsiness and idleness.

7. A tendency to laugh too much or to laugh at things no one else thinks are funny.

8. The appearance of intoxication without the odor of alcohol.

9. A "hopped-up" appearance; bright shiny eyes, when usually he looks like a fairly calm person.

10. Mixing with new companions who drink and smoke and look for fun in questionable places; staying out much later than usual; giving evasive answers when questioned about his whereabouts.

11. Loss of appetite, perhaps with a rapid loss of weight, or just the opposite—a sudden increase in appetite or an unusual desire for sweets.

12. Changes in the size of the pupils of the eyes not accounted for by changes in light intensity.

13. Desperation for money; you can't understand why he needs it.

14. Staying alone too much of the time.

15. Possession of pills, capsules, or injection equipment.

16. Hallucinations or convulsions signal immediate medical attention.

Specific Symptoms of Drug Abuse

1. Redness and watering of eyes (glue sniffing)

2. Running nose (heroin, morphine, codeine)

3. Constant licking of lips to keep them moist resulting in chapped raw lips (amphetamines)

4. Drastic loss of weight (heroin, opium)

5. Sunglasses worn at inappropriate times and places hiding dilated pupils (LSD)

6. Staggering, disoriented behavior (barbiturates)

7. Red, raw nostrils (sniffing cocaine)

8. Profuse perspiration and body odor (amphetamines)

9. Long sleeve garments worn constantly to hide needle "tracks" (heroin or methedrine)

10. Tremor of hands (amphetamines)

These are a few of the signs that may indicate that a young person could be abusing drugs or using narcotics. While these symptoms are not proof of drug abuse (most could occur for several other reasons), they should serve to alert parents and friends that a problem may exist. *Remember—even if a young person develops these symptoms, it does not mean he is under the influence of drugs.* It could be any number of reasons. Counselor should notify parents as to possible health hazards indicated by any of these symptoms and recommend a medical examination if there is no apparent reason.[33]

A second example of a comprehensive statement of administrative guidelines developed by a local school district is a publication entitled *Drug Abuse Control—Administrative Guidelines,* published by the Los Angeles City Schools in 1970. Keeping in mind that it reflects California state laws, it poses the following considerations:

Question. What is the relationship between legal action involving the juvenile and action to be taken by the local school district?

Considerations. When the use or sale of drugs by a juvenile brings that youth within the jurisdiction of the juvenile court and the probation department, the courts may impose disciplinary conditions of probation upon the juvenile. *Simultaneous disciplinary action by the local school district may have the effect of placing the juvenile in "double jeopardy"* or may be in direct conflict with probationary conditions imposed by the court.

Long term suspension or expulsion may unduly deny the juvenile access to an education and access to the rehabilitative atmosphere possible in the school setting. Banishing a student from school could encourage him to develop associations with other out-of-school potentially delinquent youths.

Question. What is the legal obligation of school personnel if students are found who possess, use, or sell narcotics?

Considerations. Any case involving *confiscation* of narcotics requires reporting to law enforcement for obvious reasons including the fact that possession by a school official could lead to his personal citation on a misdemeanor or felony charge.

Generally speaking, *observation* of use, possession, or possible influence carries a moral obligation to report, while reporting cases of *rumored involvement* must be decided on the basis of careful evaluation of the reliability of sources of information.

Juvenile officers of local law enforcement agencies should be consulted regarding desirable procedures in handling drug involvement cases.

Question. Is the decision to suspend or expel a student for use of

---

[33]Unpublished report of District 205—Drug Abuse Workshop Report. Courtesy of District 205, Harvey, Illinois.

narcotics basically different from the decision to suspend or expel for other reasons?

Considerations. Most districts have policies which provide for collaboration of counseling, attendance, welfare, and other administrative staff in decisions regarding appropriate disciplinary action for infractions of school rules. The primary focus of such policies tends to be upon the welfare of the individual student, while recognizing the importance of the welfare of the students generally. These considerations are also applicable in the case in which the student has used or possessed narcotics.

Question. Can the school staff obtain help for the student from community resources outside the school?

Considerations. Referrals from school staff may be made to community agencies such as child guidance clinics, mental health facilities, Big Brother organizations, Family Service Agencies, recreation and group work agencies. Pupils and their parents may be referred. The school's concern for the adolescent who is exposed to drugs is shared by most community agencies and many of them have instituted special treatment programs.

Question. To what extent should decision making regarding individual case disposition be shared?

Considerations. "Discipline," regardless of infraction, is often a matter of heated controversy. Put drugs and narcotics into the picture and reason is sometimes lost to emotional and, perhaps, damaging reaction.

Administering a policy can become an agonizing proposition for the individual. Thus, a district may choose to consider making provision for a representative professional disciplinary committee empowered, through policy and by virtue of the referral process, to make suggestions and recommendations to the person(s) initiating a referral.

Question. What are some of the alternatives now utilized by school districts in handling narcotics cases?

Considerations. Some districts restrict school disciplinary action to those cases directly related to the school. Offenses occurring away from the school activity are left to law enforcement. Other districts—particularly smaller districts—have adopted policies covering involvement at school "or elsewhere."

Often transfer to a different educational setting is deemed advisable. This may be to another regular school or to a special school such as continuation school. In some instances, interdistrict transfers are considered beneficial in changing the school orientation of the pupil.

In all cases, consultation with parents and representatives of other involved agencies is essential. Referrals to other community agencies for assistance may be advisable. Such agencies are enumerated above.

In summary, recognizing that an individual's involvement with narcotics may range from simple personal experimentation to gross engagement which adversely affects others, a flexible policy will allow for the employment of alternative disciplinary efforts or dispositions. These include (1) appropriate counseling by school personnel; (2) consultation with family; (3) referral to out-of-school agencies for professional help; (4) school and class adjustment transfers; (5) utilization of district pupil personnel services for testing and possible referral to other community agencies; (6) referral to law enforcement; (7) severance from school attendance (suspension or expulsion).

Such alternatives may be utilized separately or as a combination of acceptable procedures. They may be written into policy as *required sequential steps* for handling cases involving narcotics or as *suggestions* to be considered in any individual case.

If, in the final analysis, severance from the public schools of the district is contemplated, compilation of accumulated evidence, including a case chronology, should be standard procedure. It is obvious that much of these matters is contingent upon state law and local policies, but the above program is exemplary of some of the questions now being raised about school boundaries, jurisdiction, and choice of action.

In conclusion, several points should be stressed. Each community has its own unique drug problem(s) and interrelating variables (economic, educational, supply and demand, and so forth.) Trends within the drug scene indicate that drugs-of-choice gradually change from year to year, and that the sophistication of the general populace will be a determining factor for sophistication of drug use/abuse among students. The dynamics of the new drug scene cannot be simplified and segmentized, but apparently from observation, young people are being turned off in slowly increasing numbers. They are using drugs—it is becoming a very integral part of their social reality—and they will also continue to use drugs. As this increases in the schools, the schools themselves may become a more active contributor or deflector of drug use. Only a concerted effort on the part of all schools, the community, and the state can provide a successful program to confront the difficulties.

In terms of recent experimental programs dealing with drug education, it is not yet clear which approaches show the most promise. Revision and up-dating of older methods and materials is clearly necessary, because up to now the program goals of prevention have been a dismal failure. With the old approaches, the problems were oftentimes compounded—as is exemplified in the credibility and communications gap presently being felt between youth and adult populations. In correcting these shortcomings, the first ventures must begin with these results.

The role administration takes in these developments will be of the utmost importance. Cautious and careful consideration and attention must be given to details and miracles must not be anticipated. It is wiser to consider doing only a little to begin rather than simply doing "something" and having it compound the problems. The middle-class white youth drug movement of epidemic proportions has succeeded in creating a totally new cultural dilemma. The largest obstacle in rationally dealing with the problems is the hysteria currently connected with it. As this emotionalism hopefully ebbs with time, we will see many of the mystiques and tragedies evident now gradually decrease and more effective, knowledgeable action taken. In this last respect possibly youth themselves are further along than the adult population would give them credit.

Selected References on Drugs and Drug Use

BECKER, H. S., "Becoming a Marijuana User," in *Outsiders: Studies in the Sociology of Deviance*. New York: The Free Press, 1963.

BLUM, R., et al., *The Utopiates*. New York: Atherton Press, 1964.

CLAREY, J. T., *The College Drug Scene*. Englewood Cliffs, N.J.: Prentice-Hall, Inc., 1969.

COHEN, ALLEN Y., "Relieving Acid Indigestion: Psychological and Social Dynamics Related to Hallucinogenic Drug Abuse," Bureau of Drug Abuse Control, 1968.

——, "The Journey Beyond Trips: Alternatives to Drugs," *Journal of Psychedelic Drugs*, 3, No. 2 (Spring 1971), 16–21.

DeROPP, ROBERT S., *Drugs and the Mind*. New York: Grove Press, Inc., 1957.

Directory of Drug Information Groups. Beloit, Wisconsin: Student Association for the Study of Hallucinogens.

FORT, JOEL, *The Pleasure Seekers*. Indianapolis, Ind.: The Bobbs-Merrill Co., Inc., 1969.

KAPLAN, JOHN R., *Marijuana, The New Prohibition*. New York: Field Enterprises Educational Corp., 1970.

KITZINGER, ANGELA, and PATRICIA J. HILL, *Drug Abuse: A Source Book and Guide for Teachers*. Sacramento, Ca.: California State Department of Education, 1967.

LEWIS, DAVID C., "How the Schools Can Prevent Drug Abuse," *National Association of Secondary School Principals Bulletin*, 54, No. 346 (May 1970).

LINDESMITH, A. R., *Drug Addiction: Crime or Disease?* Bloomington, Ind.: Indiana University Press, 1961.

——, *The Addict and the Law*. Bloomington, Ind.: Indiana University Press, 1961.

MENNINGER, KARL, *The Crime of Punishment*. New York: The Viking Press, 1966.

MEYERS, FREDERICK H., "The Pharmacology of Marijuana," *Journal of Psychedelic Drugs*, II, No. 1 (1968).

National Clearinghouse for Drug Abuse Information, P.O. Box 1701, Washington, D.C., 20013.

SMITH, DAVID E., *The New Social Drug: Cultural, Legal and Medical Perspectives on Marijuana*. Englewood Cliffs, N.J.: Prentice-Hall, Inc., 1970.

SMITH, DAVID E., and DAVID J. BENTEL, *Fourth Annual Report to the Legislature, Drug Abuse Information Project*. San Francisco: University of California, 1968.

SOLOMON, D., ed., *The Marijuana Papers*. Indianapolis, Ind.: The Bobbs-Merrill Co., Inc., 1966.

"A Study of More Effective Education Relative to Narcotics, Other Drugs, and Hallucinogenic Substances," Progress Report Submitted to the California Legislature. Sacramento, Ca.: California State Department of Education, 1969.

YABLONSKY, LEWIS, *The Hippie Trip*. Racine, Wisconsin: Western Publishing Co., Inc., 1968.

————, *The Tunnel Back: Synanon*. New York: The Macmillan Company, Publishers, 1965.

Religion

Just as the topic of religion is the most emotionally-tinged of all civil rights areas, so religious questions in the public system of education provide administrators with a thorny dilemma. They must balance those groups who fear that school authorities have denied them their right of personal belief against those who maintain that the school sponsors religious practices against their will.

The First Amendment guarantees freedom of religion in two ways. It bans the establishment of religion by Congress—church and state are to be separate. In addition, the Free Exercise Clause guarantees that each person may choose his own form of religious observance. Both of these constitutional points have been the subject of a number of legal cases.

C. A. Hollister and Peter R. Leigh have reviewed recent trends in religion cases court action.[34] They note that religious instruction by professional clergymen on school grounds has been disallowed, but if conducted off campus, or if voluntarily held by students, it is permissible. Schools cannot sponsor devotional exercises during school hours (this includes literary recitations of a religious nature). Interestingly, some

---

[34]C. A. Hollister and Peter R. Leigh, "The Student's Freedom of Religion," *National Association of Secondary School Principals Bulletin*, 55, No. 352 (February 1971), 37–45.

citizens have objected to patriotic ceremonies on the basis of religious freedom. These protests have referred to the national anthem, the flag salute, and the pledge of allegiance as violations of their rights. As yet there is no clear statement of legality on these points, though there are indications that no student may be compelled to participate in such ceremonies.

The principal should note that this is not purely a matter of student rights; teachers have also objected to both religious and patriotic displays. Growing activism and concern for individual rights augur an increase in similar issues. The need for legal advice and administrative support is obvious, but beyond this there is need for a philosophy which includes acceptance of all personal credos and practices which contain provisions for the exercise of such beliefs. Principals, counselors, and teachers must cooperate in arrangements to develop an environment in which all have freedom to worship as they wish and to avoid certain religious ceremonies.

Nutrition and Health

School health services typically include a number of activities. An emergency nurse service protects against unexpected injury and illness while regular vision, physical, and dental screenings deal with the preventive aspects of health. The school environment is checked for possible hazards, and immunization programs guard against various diseases. In addition, most schools include some type of health education.

These are all positive practices. Yet schools must not disregard the subject of nutrition if health programs are to be complete. There is growing evidence that nutrition is a vital factor for an educational system concerned with total student development. One authority states the problem in this way: "In recent decades, early malnutrition sufficient to impair growth in experimental animals has repeatedly and conclusively demonstrated its effect on their subsequent learning, memory, and adaptive behavior."[35]

If there is doubt as to the existence of nutritional deficiences in United States children, there is a wealth of evidence to substantiate this sad fact. For instance, an article in the *Nutrition Program News*, published by the U.S. Department of Agriculture, shows that between the ages of 12 and 14, approximately 10% of males and 30 percent of females had serious deficits in calcium, a mineral crucial to bone and nerve development. In addition, over 30 percent of children were below the recom-

---

[35]Nevin S. Scrimshaw, "Infant Malnutrition and Adult Learning," *Saturday Review*, March 16, 1968, p. 64.

mended daily requirement of another important mineral, iron.[36] Another author has pointed to the poor quality of much of our food, referring to modern bread as "the flimsy staff of life."[37]

School lunch programs have corrected nutritional lags in some children, particularly those in poor communities, but additional efforts are required. The principal should incorporate sections on nutrition in his health education units. Both he and those who evaluate student abilities must be aware of the connection between nutrition and learning, emotional stability, and motivation. If there is suspicion that deficiencies exist, referral to the appropriate agency should be made.

The Self-Concept and Emotional Development

Traditionally school counselors have worked in the area of student self-concept. However, guidance personnel have been reluctant to deal with those problems believed to be of a deeper emotional nature. They have only recently accepted a broader role in the mental health field, and this is fortunate, for the dividing line between the two types of problems has frequently seemed artificial. Human behavior is difficult to separate into healthy and sick classifications. The particular culture or subculture usually sets limits for what is considered deviant, but the definition is frequently vague. The counselor should consider himself part of the total community mental health effort; in this light, he is involved with all degrees of student emotional difficulties. Only the extent of his training should be considered, and even within these limits he has far more latitude than was previously accepted. Apart from individual psychotherapy, which has dubious value, he may employ such techniques as developmental counseling and behavior modification, or he may serve a supportive role in a long-range therapy program.

Attention should also be given to those factors which may hinder personal development. Among these is the punitive nature of instructional procedures which foster failure-avoidance responses instead of success-seeking patterns. Another negative feature is labeling. Applying generic terminology can lead to a fatalistic acceptance on the part of the student of his condition, often restricting the growth of a good self-image. Researchers frequently find the students' parents to be emotionally damaging influences; such disturbed relationships have an obvious effect on matura-

---

[36]Lillian J. Fincher and Marjorie E. Rauschert, "Diets of Men, Women, and Children in the United States," *Nutrition Program News* (September-October 1969), p. 4.

[37]John Lear, "The Flimsy Staff of Life," *Saturday Review*, October 3, 1970, pp. 53–54.

tion. One other situation is the increase in youthful alienation, resulting from a lack in personal contacts. It is becoming more and more common to hear students protesting their feeling of anonymity, the belief that they are no more than an identification number.

There are many other causes of personal imbalance; the above-mentioned are only a few of the more prominent ones. Considering these few, what can be done to reduce their impact? To begin with, there is a need to restructure schools from settings of failure into sources of success. Too many pupils study from fear of poor grades, rather than enjoyment of the learning process. This can be changed in each school to some degree. Educators cannot afford to wait for large scale operations, the problem is too acute.

The school must provide more individual contact between student and staff. This involves more than guidance personnel; teachers and administrators are far more important in this matter. Teachers should be trained to be aware of the warning signs of personal difficulties, to make vital contributions in the role of sophisticated observer. When preventive measures are not sufficient, the counselor must assume responsibility for appropriate treatment, including both referral and therapeutic functions. He should be the school mental health coordinator, and it is up to him to initiate programs of education and remediation.

Pupil Personnel Service Concerns

The Role of the Counselor

Of all pupil personnel workers, the counselor has the most undefined position. By comparison, the role of the school psychologist or school nurse is well delineated. As a result the counselor frequently allows himself to assume functions of record clerk or substitute teacher. This is not only the fault of the incorrect expectations of others; it also stems from the counselor's own confusion as to his role and his desire to please others.

The American Personnel and Guidance Association has stated that "the major responsibility of the counselor is to assist an individual through the counseling relationship to utilize his own resources and his environmental opportunities in the process of self-understanding, planning, decision-making, and coping with problems relative to his developmental needs and to his vocational and educational activities."[38] But this definition is too broad to answer the question of the counselor's role. What is included

---

[38]American Personnel and Guidance Association, "The Counselor: Professional Preparation and Role," in George E. Hill, *Management and Improvement of Guidance* (New York: Appleton-Century-Crofts, 1965), pp. 106–10.

in "counseling relationship," for instance? Almost any activity could be justified as contributing to the student's ability to "utilize his resources and his environmental opportunities." Perhaps the most serious failure in this statement is the absence of any precise, well-defined goals.

In practice there are four general models of counseling: (1) the classic counseling role, which primarily includes individual guidance; (2) the psychologist which centers upon the testing and appraisal of student abilities and personality development; (3) the counselor as a consultant, guiding other educational workers to aid their pupils, consulting with teachers to help them understand the nature of learning, student development, or their own behavior, consulting with administrators leading to inservice programs, research, and the restructuring of the school environment, guiding parents in their relationships with their children and in understanding the school program, consulting with curriculum specialists to help them discover negative learning elements and future requirements; and (4) the counselor as a social worker, working with students, homes, communities, and parents in an effort to improve the total milieu of the pupil.

There has been some controversy about the counseling as opposed to consultation roles; some educators see them as incompatible. But they both have a place in the pupil personnel program. Counseling is a psychological approach which involves direct contact, while consultation is more sociological, dealing with relevant social variables affecting student development.

Another controversy has developed around the amount of social involvement which those in the behavioral sciences should have. The traditional passive, impartial role has been favored, but more recently there has been a trend toward activism among professionals. This is probably a positive factor in the acceptance of greater responsibility on the part of guidance personnel for student behavior and social conditions.

Whatever role the counselor assumes, it should be determined by the particular setting and resources he encounters. The only absolute criterion of counseling activities must be their effects on the students. Within this limitation, the principal and counselor can develop a guidance model jointly.

Counseling Techniques

The counselor's choice of role is the prime determinant of his techniques, although other factors include theoretical background and practical experience. The main controversy here is the use of verbal or action-oriented devices.

Verbal techniques may be of the individual or group variety. The best-known school of thought is client-centered or Rogerian counseling. Many guidance workers have adopted this approach, which focuses on relationship variables and personal insight on the part of the client. The central concern is the development of an empathetic, accepting environment which allows the counselee to work out his problems on his own terms. The counselor avoids intervening in matters of values and decision making; his function is to assist the client to help himself. Despite widespread use of client-centered counseling, however, there is no valid evidence that it is especially effective. Research has been inconclusive and often contradictory.[39]

The other major counseling technique is that of the Skinnerians or behavior modifiers. This group derives its treatment methods from learning theory and operant conditioning examples. They are not concerned with underlying causes, but focus on changing of overt behavior patterns—the cause and symptom are one and the same for all practical purposes to them. In educational settings, these people are usually described as contingency managers. They attempt to redesign the school environment in order to reinforce or strengthen appropriate responses. To do this, they arrange various forms of reward for behaviors which are considered socially adaptive. Instead of making individual contacts, they usually act as consultants for the classroom teacher. Research on these techniques has been generally supportive and impressive.[40] An additional positive factor is the applicability of behavior management to large groups. Considering the shortage of school counselors, this is a most important variable.

One additional point in the controversy over technique: "Talking to children in the privacy of the counselor's office is largely a waste of time, no matter what the counselor's theoretical orientation . . . treating the problem by removing the child from the situation to talk to him appears to be somewhat absurd."[41]

Testing

Evaluation procedures in educational systems are of two general types—psychologically-oriented testing of such variables as intelligence, personality, and psycho-linguistic ability and school-wide testing programs. Most of the former's assessment is performed by a school psychologist and is based on referrals from teachers. The purpose of the second type of tests

[39]Theodore C. Alper and Gerald D. Kranzler, "A Comparison of Behavioral and Client-Centered Approaches for the Behavior Problems of Elementary School Children," *Elementary School Guidance and Counseling*, 5, No. 1 (October 1970), 35–43.

[40]Jay M. Toews, "The Counselor as Contingency Manager," *Personnel and Guidance Journal*, 48, No. 2 (October 1969), 127–34.

[41]Alper and Kranzler, "Behavioral and Client-Centered Approaches," p. 41.

is varied. They may be used to examine the success of the curriculum, appraise student progress, or to determine teaching styles.

No matter the goal of testing, proper interpretation of results is critical. Those involved must consider such variables as validity and reliability, and take into account the population on which the test was standardized. Care must be given to avoid generalizations from limited data, usually occurring when a test is used on an inappropriate group— a common problem in today's integrated schools.

Probably the greatest sin in any evaluation is the practice of labeling, and this is particularly true with psychological assessment. I.Q. scores are frequently discussed as if they were entities, instead of representations of hypothesized abilities. Students lose their identities and become "110s" or "86s." Applying labels serves to disguise the actual behavior being measured. A person is not a "schizophrenic," though he may exhibit behaviors which are classified as "schizophrenic." Alternatives to I.Q. type tests are procedures yielding profiles of student abilities which are directly related to the learning process and can be used for prescriptive purposes.

In the area of school-wide assessment, the problem is often one of cultural discrimination. Minority groups object to such tests because they are often based on middle-class values. In addition, the limited background of many youngsters immediately handicaps them when competing with children from better environments. Particularly discriminative is the paper-and-pencil evaluation of language skills.

Putting the whole situation in proper perspective, it should be stated that tests are not inherently unfair; they are merely psychoeducational tools. Only in their application do they become good or bad. If a test is used with an appropriate group, is well-designed and interpreted, and serves a specific goal, it has worth. In this sense, the objections of minorities are particularly accurate. The typical, improper utilization of testing is indeed discriminative. Hopefully, devices will be developed which accurately assess the learning abilities of all groups. The pressing need for new tests is obvious.

Research

Possibly the most neglected function of guidance services is research. Considering the confusion and controversy within education in general, and pupil personnel services in particular, this lack is unfortunate. Research by counselors is usually confined to graduate school papers and theses. The reasons for this are partially related to the personal needs and expectations of those who enter the field. (After all, it is called *Counseling and Guidance*, not *Research*.) Another limiting factor is the difficulty of performing rigorous studies within a school setting—a result of the failure to differentiate between basic and applied research. Experimental methodology has contributed to an attitude of rigidity in many counselors, and the improbability of maintaining strict, laboratory standards has been a psychological obstacle to progress. Greater emphasis must be placed on field studies which yield answers to practical problems and produce change of some kind.

Research may center on a number of areas. Studies can explore pupil achievements, aspirations, self-concepts, learning styles, and dropout rates. They may investigate school characteristics such as the general curriculum, instructional styles, quality of teaching, staff attitudes, and remedial programs. Inquiries may extend into the community to discover economic and social variables which affect the school, and perhaps even more pertinent for guidance researchers would be studies of the value of counseling procedures. The list is endless; countless factors need examination.

There is no problem in finding areas of concern, but there is a great problem implementing the necessary research. The need is for a systematic program on a district-wide basis. In small school districts, a cooperative venture could be arranged with either adjoining districts or those with similar populations. In any case, such coordination is needed to avoid duplication of effort and sloppy experimentation. This should not discourage individual work; it does suggest optimal utilization of resources.

Ethical and Legal Responsibilities

For both practical and philosophical reasons, pupil personnel services should take more interest in developing adequate guidelines for those who are legally and ethically vulnerable. Counselors in particular are highly susceptible to such problems because of the personal nature of their work. Counselors should be accorded rights of privileged communication on an equal basis with psychiatrists and lawyers, because counselors are open to libel and malpractice actions, while the school district is immune, and are therefore the obvious target of parent grievances. The intimacy of the counseling relationship is essential for the development of trust and confidence, yet intimacy has potential for a future invasion of privacy. Though care may be taken in the release of school files, they are still considered public records and may be legally scrutinized by the courts. School officials should be aware of this, and limit counseling folders to broad descriptions of student progress. Personal interview notes, on the other hand, probably will not be requisitioned if kept apart from the usual cumulative records. To further protect himself, the counselor should avoid duties for which he is not adequately trained, and consider the purchase of malpractice insurance.

Guidance personnel have a more pleasant part in the legal matters in the role of expert witness. When testifying, the counselor should expect to be carefully questioned about his preparation, experience, and competence. He functions best as a friend of the court, unidentified with either disputant. Limitations must be admitted, and all opinions require a thorough estimation of the relevant facts. The lay nature of juries may be an important factor—overly sophisticated terminology may confuse and alienate jurors.

The primary ethical consideration for guidance workers is their responsibility to their clients—this must come before all other factors. For instance, there is no reason to reveal past antisocial behavior, except in cases of valid danger to others. The needs of the school are secondary to the well-being of the student. There is a necessity for a strong widely-accepted and widely-enforced code of counseling behavior. One set of standards with this potential has been offered by the American Guidance and Personnel Association,[42] the principal and counselor might do well to utilize these guidelines.

New Developments

Another responsibility of the guidance worker is to keep abreast of current changes in the field. If he is employed by a large school district, there may be a specific agency concerned with discovering, exploring, and disseminating new information. If it is his individual duty to do so, he will find the best sources to be research publications and professionals journals. Some of these are the following:

> *The Review of Educational Research.* Every three years an issue is devoted to guidance and student personnel. Besides this, each issue contains selected summaries of research on a broad range of topics.
> *The Encyclopedia of Educational Research* includes rigorous summaries of major or particularly representative studies.
> *The Journal of College Personnel*
> *Counselor Education and Supervision*
> *Vocational Guidance Quarterly*
> *The Personnel and Guidance Journal*
> *The School Counselor*
> *Rehabilitation Counselor Bulletin*
> *Elementary School Guidance and Counseling*
> *The Journal of Counseling Psychology*

Among other recent developments is the use of subprofessionals with

---

[42]American Personnel and Guidance Association, *Guidance*, pp. 106–110.

limited training as guidance assistants.[43] These support personnel perform a variety of tasks and free the counselor from pursuits such as record-keeping and information-gathering. Another burgeoning area is the employment of video aids in school counseling.[44] Other innovations include the "two-headed counselor" technique, which applies the skills of two counselors with one client,[45] and procedures adapted from the behavior modification field. An example of the latter is *fading*, a term which refers to the gradual withdrawal of guidelines and stimulus support to condition independence of actions.[46]

Improvements in the guidance field may be expected to continue to increase in the coming years. Those whose knowledge is not current do a disservice to themselves, their profession, and especially their clients.

Selected References

ALPER, THEODORE C., and GERALD D. KRANZLER, "A Comparison of Behavioral and Client-Centered Approaches for the Behavior Problems of Elementary School Children," *Elementary School Guidance and Counseling,* 5, No. 1 (October 1970), 35–43.

American Personnel and Guidance Association, "The Counselor: Professional Preparation and Role," in George E. Hill, ed., *Management and Improvement of Guidance.* New York: Appleton-Century-Crofts, 1965, pp. 106–10.

BENSON, RONALD L., and DON H. BLOCKER, "Evaluation of Developmental Counseling with Groups of Low Achievers in a High School Setting," *The School Counselor,* 14, No. 4 (March 1967), 215–20.

BLANCHARD, HOWARD L., and LAURENCE S. FLAUM, *Guidance: A Longitudinal Approach.* Minneapolis, Minn.: Burgess Publishing Co., 1968, pp. 53–55.

BROUGH, JAMES R., "The Junior High Schooler: His Concerns and Sources of Help," *The School Counselor,* 13, No. 2 (December 1965), 71–76.

CARLSON, JON, and C. ROY MAYER, "Fading: A Behavioral Procedure to Increase Independent Behavior," *The School Counselor,* 18, No. 3 (January 1971), 193–97.

CLUTE, MORRIS J., "Rights and Responsibilities of Students," *Educational Leadership,* 26, No. 3 (December 1968), 240–42.

---

[43]Leo Goldman, "Help for the Counselor," *National Association of Secondary School Principals Bulletin* 51, No. 317 (March 1967), 47–55.

[44]Charles W. Ryan and Russell A. Whitman, "Video Aids in School Counseling: Some Practical Innovations," *The School Counselor,* 18, No. 1 (September 1970), 69–74.

[45]Bert M. Hoenigmann, "The Two-Headed Counselor," *Personnel and Guidance Journal,* 48, No. 2 (October 1969), 144–46.

[46]Jon Carlson and C. Roy Mayer, "Fading: A Behavioral Procedure to Increase Independent Behavior," *The School Counselor,* 18, No. 3 (January 1971), 193–97.

DILLENBECK, DOUGLAS D., "The Future in Guidance, Psychological Services and Testing," in Alvin C. Eurich, ed., *High School 1980*. New York: Pitman Publishing Corp., 1970, pp. 218–25.

DINKMEYER, DON D., "Developmental Group Counseling," *Elementary School Guidance and Counseling*, 4 (1970), 267–72.

DUNN, LLOYD M., *Exceptional Children in the Schools*. New York: Holt, Rinehart and Winston, Inc., 1966.

FINCHER, LILLIAN J., and MARJORIE E. RAUSCHERT, "Diets of Men, Women, and Children in the United States," *Nutrition Program News* (September-October 1969), p. 4.

FORSLUND, MORRIS A., and LENTON MALRY, "Social Class and Relative Level of Occupational Aspiration: Implications for Delinquency and Education," *National Association of Secondary School Principals Bulletin*, 54, No. 349 (November 1970), 106–15.

FRENCH, JOSEPH L., "Characteristics of High Ability Dropouts," *National Association of Secondary School Principals Bulletin*, 53, No. 334 (February 1969), 67–79.

FRYMIER, JACK R., "Why Students Rebel," *Educational Leadership*, 27, No. 5 (January 1970), 346–50.

GOLDMAN, LEO, "Help for the Counselor," *National Association of Secondary School Principals Bulletin*, 51, No. 317 (March 1967), 47–55.

HOENIGMANN, BERT M., "The Two-Headed Counselor," *Personnel and Guidance Journal*, 48, No. 2 (October 1969), 144–46.

HOLLISTER, C. A., and PETER R. LEIGH, "The Student's Freedom of Religion," *National Association of Secondary School Principals Bulletin*, 55, No. 352 (February 1971), 37–45.

HOUSE, JAMES E., "Can the Student Participate in His Own Destiny?" *Educational Leadership*, 27, No. 5 (February 1970), 442–45.

KELLY, EUGENE W., JR., and DORIS B. MATTHEWS, "Group Counseling with Discipline-Problem Children at the Elementary School Level," *The School Counselor*, 18, No. 4 (March 1971), 273–78.

KRUMBOLTZ, JOHN D., and CARL E. THORESON, *Behavioral Counseling: Cases and Techniques*. New York: Holt, Rinehart and Winston, Inc., 1969.

LEWIS, DAVID C., "How the Schools Can Prevent Drug Abuse," *National Association of Secondary School Principals Bulletin*, 54, No. 346 (May 1970), 43–51.

RYAN, CHARLES W., and RUSSELL A. WHITMAN, "Video Aids in School Counseling: Some Practical Innovations," *The School Counselor*, 18, No. 1 (September 1970), 69–74.

STORM, DAVID, "Changing Balance of Power in Education: Teacher Militancy," in August Kerber and Wilfred Smith, ed., *Educational Issues in a Changing Society*. Detroit: Wayne State University Press, 1968.

STRANGES, RICHARD J., and ANTHONY C. RICCIO, "Counselee Preferences for

Counselors: Some Implications for Counselor Education," *Counselor Education and Supervision*, 10, No. 1 (Fall 1970), 39–45.

THOMPSON, JACK M., "Current Issues and Problems in Elementary School Guidance," *The School Counselor*, 13, No. 2 (December 1965), 77–81.

TOEWS, JAY M., "The Counselor as Contingency Manager," *Personnel and Guidance Journal*, 48, No. 2 (October 1969), 127–34.

TRIEZENBERG, GEORGE, "How to Live With Due Process," *National Association of Secondary School Principals Bulletin*, 55, No. 352 (February 1971), 61–68.

VENN, GRANT, "Vocational Education for All," *National Association of Secondary School Principals Bulletin*, 51, No. 317 (March 1967), 32–40.

WALTERS, HARVEY EUGENE, and GERALD D. KRANZLER, "Early Identification of the School Dropout," *The School Counselor*, 18, No. 2 (November 1970), 97–104.

WINKLER, RONALD C., JOHN J. TEIGLAND, PAUL F. MUNGER, and GERALD D. KRANZLER, "The Effects of Selected Counseling and Remedial Technique on Underachieving Elementary School Students," *Journal of Counseling Psychology*, 12, No. 4 (Winter 1965), 384–87.

WITTMER, JOE, "The Effects of Counseling and Tutoring on the Attitudes and Achievement of Seventh Grade Underachievers," *The School Counselor*, 16, No. 4 (March 1969), 287–90.

14

Managing Extracurricular Activities

History of Extracurricular Activities

Although organized extracurricular activities in American public schools are largely the product of the second quarter of the twentieth century, there was probably never a time when similar activities were not associated with youth and their training. E. D. Grizell has shown that such activities first appeared in the schools of Greece.[1] Individual sports such as running were common, but little was done with team games. The beginning of student participation in student affairs, now the rule in American schools, began in Greece. Management of affairs was entrusted to students more frequently than is the present custom in the United States. English secondary schools have long stressed activities; dramatics, forensics, publications, and student government all had some place in early English schools.[2]

Although athletics were not particularly important in the early American schools, football was popular at Exeter as an intramural sport. In fact, the first interscholastic football game took place in 1878 between Exeter and Andover.[3] Some dramatic and forensic activities were also incorporated in some American high schools in the early nineteenth century.

---

[1]E. D. Grizell, "The Evolution of Student Activities," *Educational Outlook,* I (November 1926), 19–31.

[2]Grizell, "Student Activities," p. 20.

[3]Grizell, "Student Activities," p. 24.

School Publications

Early manuscript papers containing school news and student literary efforts were usually read in general assemblies, a practice which is not uncommon even now. When papers were first inaugurated, the paper was read or told as a class project. The first printed paper, *The Student Gazette*, first appeared on June 11, 1877, and was published each Wednesday by the students of the William Penn Chapter School of Philadelphia.[4] The most successful venture in high school journalism before the Civil War was the *High School Thesaurus* published by the Worcester, Massachusetts, High School; it began in 1859 and continued monthly until 1862.[5] Extracurricular activities in journalism were thus not widespread before 1900.

Interest in student government—or, as it is now called, student participation in school activities—was considerable in the early American schools, but few details have been published about it.

Early Activities

Although organized extracurricular activities in the American secondary schools are a fairly recent development, isolated examples of them have been reported prior to 1920. Galen Jones, in an investigation of the relations of the extracurricular activities to the curriculum in 269 secondary schools which he studied, found some activities had been established as early as the five-year period 1870–1874.[6] By 1880 according to his data two schools had inaugurated football, four held assemblies, two had homerooms, and one had established track and one field, one a newspaper, one a baseball team, one debating, and one an honor society.[7] One-fourth of the schools which replied to the study had football teams by 1897, and half of them had football by 1907. Other activities which were established relatively early were the assembly, baseball, track and field, basketball, and the yearbook. Musical activities, except the band, were established by 1920 in 50 percent of the schools.[8]

The investigation by Jones is interesting because it is the only quantitative study of extracurricular activities which goes back beyond 1900. An examination of Table 10 indicates that the median year for estab-

---

[4]R. L. Boyle, "Student Publications," *National Association of Secondary School Principals Bulletin*, 184 (February 1952), 59.

[5]Grizell, "Student Activities," p. 31.

[6]Galen Jones, *Extra-Curricular Activities in Relation to the Curriculum* (New York: Teachers College, Columbia University, 1935), p. 17.

[7]Jones, *Extra-Curricular Activities*, pp. 17–20.

[8]Jones, *Extra-Curricular Activities*, p. 18.

lishment of activities falls between 1923 and 1924. Prior to 1900 activities were mostly regarded by school officials as dangers to the education program; efforts were made to suppress them. Coaching or sponsoring such activities was not considered a fit occupation for teachers. Boys were often expelled for playing football; learning was a full-time occupation, not to be interfered with by "outside activities."

From 1900 to the time of World War I, activities were tolerated but not accepted. Many administrators considered them a sort of necessary evil in the school program. During this period coaches and sponsors frequently were not full-time resident members of the faculty, although employed and paid by school boards. (Incidentally, this practice, especially with respect to dramatics, has not entirely disappeared from smaller high schools; it is not recommended as an educationally desirable practice.) Facilities provided for the activities were for the most part inadequate.

Developments Since 1920

In the decade following 1920, and through the 1930s, extracurricular activities became an integral part of the educational program. The attention to child growth and development, the appreciation of social goals in education, the decline in the opportunity for young people to have remunerative employment, and the development of commercial forms of entertainment have all helped to develop and expand the extracurricular program in the schools. During this period of activity growth, studies were made, speeches given, articles written, and buildings constructed. Sponsor qualifications were established, and public relations programs were inaugurated. The high school football team became the darling of the sports-minded adult population. The high school principal often became more interested in the "a cappella choir" than in the academic program.

By mid-century, some school personnel felt that extracurricular activities had gained too much interest and attention. This was certainly not true if the feelings and beliefs of the students who were enrolled had been polled. The period from 1920 to 1950, then, represented a growth in the way activities were accepted and fostered as an integral part of the program.

Definition of Extracurricular Activities

It is not entirely easy to define extracurricular activities, but there is general consensus that activities for which credits are given, which are on the time schedule, and for which there is a generally recognized body of literature are curricular; those which are excluded by this definition are

Table 10

	Year Reported When Activity Is First Allowed			
Activity	*25 Percent of Schools*	*50 Percent of Schools*	*75 Percent of Schools*	*Number of Schools Reporting*
1. Football	1897	1907	1919	147
2. Track and field	1902	1910	1921	139
3. Basketball	1907	1912	1920	152
4. Baseball	1902	1913	1924	110
5. Assembly	1902	1915	1924	105
6. Yearbook	1907	1915	1920	152
7. Magazine	1900	1916	1928	66
8. Debating	1910	1919	1924	128
9. Dramatics	1910	1919	1924	145
10. Boy's glee club	1912	1920	1926	158
11. Girl's glee club	1912	1920	1924	159
12. Chorus	1915	1920	1925	124
13. Orchestra	1915	1920	1924	166
14. Newspaper	1916	1921	1926	179
15. Recreational clubs	1914	1923	1926	82
16. Band	1919	1923	1927	168
17. Outside agency clubs	1918	1924	1926	101
18. Homeroom	1920	1924	1928	109
19. Student Council	1920	1924	1928	132
20. Departmental clubs	1921	1924	1926	111
21. Tennis	1920	1925	1930	140
22. Swimming	1920	1926	1930	66
23. Handbook	1922	1926	1930	99
24. Honoring clubs	1923	1926	1928	107
25. Hockey	1924	1926	1929	41
26. Special-interest or hobby clubs	1923	1927	1931	79
27. Golf	1925	1929	1931	115
28. Wrestling	1928	1930	1932	56

[9]Adapted from Jones, *Extra-Curricular Activities*, p. 17, and rearranged in the order in which they were established in 50 percent of the schools which maintained the activity.

extracurricular.[10] Thus the homeroom, about which exists voluminous literature but for which credit is never given, and although it is on the time schedule, is extracurricular. The band, which has a vast musical and pedagogical literature, and which is ordinarily on the time schedule as a credit course, is curricular. In general, there has been a movement toward making many activities curricular rather than extracurricular. However, whenever an activity such as the band becomes a part of the curriculum, a number of extracurricular activities always develop, such as a woodwind sextette or a brass quartette, which meet out of school time and without credit.

For our purposes of discussion, extracurricular activities will include athletics, class organization, clubs, contests, homerooms, honorary activities, music, publications, speech, social activities, student participation in school control, tours, and out-of-school experiences, even though credit may be given for some and others may meet during school time.

The problems of administration and supervision are the main topics treated in this chapter. Specific activities will be discussed in the next chapter. Methods of financing and accounting for extracurricular activities are treated in the chapter on business duties. It is the purpose of the following discussion to show conditions as they are and to suggest how the principal may best conduct approved activities.

Present Status of Extracurricular Activities

There is no clear-cut picture of activities in the secondary schools at the present time. Some activities have found their way into extracurricular programs largely as the result of insistence on the part of students, teachers, and community groups, with a minimum of centralized direction. As a result many administrative problems exist which need to be solved.

Most school workers accept activities as an integral part of the program, but the practices show differences of opinion on the way in which activities should be carried out. Should the activities be inaugurated by students or administrative officers? Should some be compulsory and others elective? Should there be an activity period, or should the activities be scheduled after school? Are sponsors to be paid an additional sum for their duties? What qualifications should sponsors possess? Are there to be any limits on the number of interscholastic games or the conditions under which they are played? How much responsibility should students have in the development and carrying out of a program? What is to be the policy with respect to finance? What evaluative criteria are to be

---

[10]Jones, *Extra-Curricular Activities*, pp. 24–32.

applied to the program? Should every teacher have a part in the development of the program? These and many other questions plague the busy school administrator; in this chapter we shall outline some guides for finding the answers for a local school.

Values in Extracurricular Activities

The exhaustive pioneer study of extracurricular activities was carried out by the National Society for the Study of Education under the direction of Leonard V. Koos in 1925.[11] Values most frequently mentioned were training in some civic-social-moral relationship, fitting the school to the needs of the adolescent, training for leadership, and improving discipline and school spirit.

Values to Students

J. Lloyd Trump made a study of 3,525 secondary school students.[12] These students rated the values of activities in the following order: (1) developed friendships; (2) became more interested in school; (3) learned how to win and lose in sportsmanlike manner; (4) developed greater loyalty to the school; (5) discovered worthwhile things to do in their free time; (6) developed friendly relationships with teachers; (7) became more willing to accept criticism; and (8) gained valuable information that had never been received in a curricular course.

Personal Satisfaction

In Illinois, 6,817 high school students were asked by Earl G. Pogue to rate the following six types of activity in order of personal satisfaction: (1) extraclass activity, (2) school subjects, (3) activities centering around the home, (4) activities centering around noncommercial agencies (the church, Y.M.C.A., and the Boy Scouts), (5) activities centering around commercial agencies, and (6) unplanned peer-group activities. The results indicated that Illinois high school students uniformly rank extracurricular activities above regular school subjects in terms of personal satisfaction. Extracurricular school activities rated second only to commercial activities,

---

[11]Leonard V. Koos, chairman, *Extra-Curricular Activities*, National Society for the Study of Education, Twenty-fifth Yearbook, Part II (Bloomington, Illinois: Public School Publishing Company, 1926).

[12]J. Lloyd Trump, *High School Extracurriculum Activities: Their Management in Public High Schools of the North Central Association* (Chicago: University of Chicago Press, 1944), pp. 112–13.

Table 11[13]

RANK ORDER OF SATISFACTION OF
VARIOUS TYPES OF ACTIVITIES AS
DETERMINED BY THE MEAN OF
RATINGS BY THE PUPILS

	School												
Activity	A	B	C	D	E	F	G	H	I	J	K	L	M
Commercial	2	2	3	1	2	1	1	2	1	1	1	1	2
Extraclass	1	1	1	4	1	2	3	1	2	3	2	5	5
Home	3	3	2	3	3	3	2	3	3	2	3	2	1
Noncommercial	4	4	4.5	5	5	5	5	4	4	4	5	4	3
Unplanned	5	5	4.5	2	4	4	4	5	5	5	4	3	4
School Subjects	6	6	6	6	6	6	6	6	6	6	6		6

Code: 1 = greatest satisfaction; 6 = least satisfaction

when data from thirteen schools were considered, and in five of the schools they were considered of greater satisfaction than commercial activities.[14]

Since the foregoing data are representative of many other studies, it is clear that students value extracurricular activities quite highly. Whether the potential values of activities are realized or not depends almost entirely on how the program is managed.

Participation in Activities

Extent of Participation

The study made by Trump mentioned above reveals the extent of participation during a twelve-month period in the extracurricular activities of 3,581 students in grades 9–12 in five secondary schools having membership in the North Central Association of Colleges and Secondary Schools.[15] Approximately one-fourth of the students did not participate in any activity during this period. Thirty percent of the nonparticipants were boys and 20 percent were girls. The range in activities in which students participated was from one to sixteen. Boys on the average participated in 1.1 activities, while girls participated in 1.7. Participation increased from grade to grade; 59 percent of freshmen participated, 67

[13]J. Lloyd Trump, "Extracurriculum Activities: Some Principles of Management," in *The American Secondary School*, Paul B. Jacobson, ed. (Englewood Cliffs, N.J.: Prentice-Hall, Inc., 1952), p. 213.

[14]Earl G. Pogue, "Participation in Extra Class Activities as Related to Socio-Economic Classification," (Ed.D. dissertation, University of Illinois, 1949), pp. 47–52.

[15]Trump, *High School Extracurriculum Activities*, p. 76.

percent of sophomores, 77 percent of juniors, and 83 percent of the seniors were involved in some activity.

Other data compiled on seventeen types of activities for thirty-two small secondary schools, fifty-eight medium-sized high schools, and thirteen large schools showed that a student in a large school is less likely to participate in some extracurricular activities than one in a small school. Trump also found that participation in interscholastic athletics is proportionately much greater on the part of juniors and seniors. Conversely in intramural athletics, participation is greater on the part of freshmen and sophomores. Participation in club activities reached a peak with juniors in small and medium-sized schools, but peaked with seniors in larger schools. Participation in social events was about equal among all the groups for which the events were planned.[16] These findings are further confirmed by a study of participation of senior high school students in two high schools in Eugene, Oregon. L. F. Millhollen found the number of activities participated in per student in the larger school was 3.3 and in the smaller one was 3.9.[17]

Principles of Management

The rest of this chapter consists of a list of principles which can help guide the management of extracurricular programs.[18]

Principle 1

Voluntary student participation in extracurricular activities should be encouraged so that a large percentage of students may benefit from the experiences. A school should attempt to supply the needs of all of its students, although this is not always the case because participants come from the middle and upper and lower socioeconomic levels. Athletics for boys and club activities usually have more participation from lower economic groups, while government service, dramatics, and committee work tend to be more popular with students from the middle and upper class backgrounds. This is not surprising when one considers the cost involved in participating in some activities. The incidental costs vary from school to school depending upon established policy; they may range from a low of fifty dollars to four or five hundred dollars per year. Formal dances,

[16]Trump, *High School Extracurriculum Activities*, pp. 78–84.

[17]L. F. Millhollen, Jr., "The Role of Parents' and Pupils' Opinions in the Improvement of Extra-Class Activities," (Ed.D. dissertation, University of Oregon, 1952), p. 49.

[18]J. Lloyd Trump, *High School Extracurricular Activities*, pp. 18–40. These principles of management (pp. 317–33) are a rearrangement and restatement of those found in Trump's book.

class jewelry, and graduation expenses add to the cost in the upper secondary grades. It is good policy for individual schools to study the costs for local students and take measures to see that a complete educational experience is provided without undue hardship to the individual student.

There are significant individual differences regarding the leadership opportunity provided for students. Of the 3,581 students in Trump's investigation, 85 percent of the boys and 86 percent of the girls said they had had no leadership opportunity involving election to a major office during the past twelve-month period. With respect to minor offices, 79 percent of the boys and 78 percent of the girls had held no minor offices.

Of the students included in Trump's study, 1,628 indicated reasons why they did not belong to activities they would like to join. The following reasons were given: (1) lacked necessary ability or skill; (2) lacked time because of out-of-school activities; (3) lacked time because of out-of-school work; (4) participation would interfere with regular school work; (5) memberships were secured by election; (6) were prevented by school regulations; (7) lacked money; and (8) were opposed to the way the activity was being carried out.

It is also clear from the study that more activities should be provided for lower classmen, and that activities should be planned for students with fewer abilities, skills, and resources. For example, if there is a band, there should also be a second band. If there is a football team and enough boys to fill its ranks, there should certainly be a junior varsity and perhaps a sophomore team as well. More activity should be scheduled during the school day, and dues, assessments, special requirements for clothing or equipment, and other expenditures should be reduced to a minimum or eliminated. The program of extracurricular activities should be reexamined and perhaps revised so that everyone who wishes to participate in it may do so. Millhollen also concluded that family income was related to the number of activities in which students participated, and that students from the lower income groups participated in the smallest number of activities. Millhollen also found that three-fifths of those parents and students whom he studied felt that the cost of activities was excessive; one-tenth had no opinion.[19]

The effects of participation. In the past it was assumed that participation in activities lowered scholarship. The evidence in the interim has not proved this to be true; studies show that there are no discernible harmful effects of participation in extracurricular activities. The findings of these studies, however, must be classed as indicative rather than conclusive; the findings could possibly have been chance or coincidental.

If a principal concludes, as the evidence seems to indicate, that

[19]Millhollen, "Improvement of Extra-Class Activities," p. 50.

athletes do as well in school as can reasonably be expected, he should be careful not to claim too much. There is no objective evidence that athletes would not have done better had they not participated in activities, but the experienced school administrator knows that in many cases the desire to participate in athletics is the urge which has prompted some boys to do better academic work.

Control of participation. From the evidence presented, it seems questionable for principals to play a large part in limiting participation in activities. Because instances have been reported of students who participated in ten or more activities, including football captaincy, editor of a major publication, several committee memberships, and clubs, the control of participation should aim to distribute extracurricular opportunities widely among students, even though it may mean curtailing the privileges of a few. If the results of participation are beneficial—and the authors contend that they are—the school administrator then has the responsibility for distributing participation among a large percentage of the pupils— without making participation compulsory. In cases where compulsion has been tried, it has usually been abandoned rather quickly.

Methods of controlling participation. There is serious question as to the advisability of limiting participation in extracurricular activities to students who have passing grades, or exclusion from them as a means of enforcing scholarship regulations. Participation in extracurricular activities has probably motivated some pupils to keep up their grades; many may have benefited from participation had they not been excluded by scholarship requirements. If the activities are to be of value to as large a percentage of the total enrollment as is possible, scholarship requirements cannot be justified. But this statement must not be interpreted too broadly. For example, participation in interscholastic events and election to such offices as captainships, editorships, or student council presidency may well be limited to those who maintain scholarship standards; but participation in intramural athletics of all kinds, in club programs, or any activity confined to the school should be open to everyone enrolled there.

Methods of controlling participation are justified insofar as they protect those who would take part to excess, and as they tend to distribute participation more widely.

The practices of 901 secondary schools which reported to Trump favored the method of guiding choices shown in Table 12. In the majority of schools, sponsors and faculty members assisted students in selecting activities along the lines of their abilities and interests. Slightly over half the schools urged students to consult the sponsors of the activities, and slightly less than half of the schools had the counselors give advice to students regarding appropriate activities. Furthermore, sponsors and faculty members tried to influence students to elect activities in which they needed

Table 12

Number of Schools Reporting

Steps Taken	Small	Medium	Large	Total
Sponsors and members make an effort to secure new members with ability along the lines of the activity.	139	282	89	510
Students are urged to consult sponsors in order to find out more about different activities.	119	293	77	489
Students are advised by counselors as to appropriate activities.	105	237	67	409
Sponsors and members make an effort to secure new members who are in need of training along the lines of the activity.	64	141	38	243
There is no specific school policy with respect to assisting pupils in choosing activities.	57	128	30	215
Students are strongly urged to visit different activities until they find one of special interest.	41	95	32	168
Activities selected by a pupil must be approved by his counselor or homeroom teacher.	37	98	21	156
Others.	4	7	3	14
Total Number of Schools	257	519	125	901

training. In order to facilitate choices, the students were strongly urged to visit different activities until one of special interest was found. A little more than a third of the schools had no policy with respect to regulating participation, and nearly one-sixth of the schools required students to secure the approval of the counselor or homeroom teacher in selecting activities.

Stimulating participation. One of the administrative problems in connection with extracurricular activities is securing the participation of students who can profit from them but who have not demonstrated much interest or proficiency regarding them. Only 27 percent of the sponsors in the schools Trump studied made an effort to secure members who had little ability in the activity which they sponsored. In all too many cases, the ability to perform a specific activity is a prerequisite for membership. Such conditions are most prevalent in large schools, where the number of activities per hundred pupils is smaller than in small schools, and where, consequently, there are more competent students for each activity. The logical solution is a larger number of activities to meet the varying abilities to be found in students of an individual school.

The activity period. Participation in activities is controlled by the arrangement of the schedule in some schools. The principal may set aside a period during or after school when all clubs may be scheduled to meet. Such a procedure automatically limits participation to the number of activities for which there are separately scheduled periods.

Principle 2

Advising students regarding entrance into extracurricular activities should be one of the functions of the guidance service of the school. There is disagreement among educators with respect to the amount of control to be exercised over participation in student activities, but there is no disagreement over advising students in the selection of activities. Some methods which have been used to advise students are assemblies, homeroom discussions, planned publicity in the school and community, newspapers, special exhibits, information in the student handbook, and the publication of special extracurricular bulletins. In addition, informal conversation between pupils, teachers, and counselors is an effective method of acquainting people with activities.

Based on the experience of the authors, special guidance publications on the extracurricular offerings of the school is the most desirable method of information for students. Of the 901 schools which reported their practices to Trump, 196 prepared special bulletins to familiarize students with school activities; 324 published a student handbook which gave an account of the activities sponsored by the school. Both are extremely desirable practices. A special guidance bulletin issued for discussion in homerooms before activities are chosen in the fall tends to make activities more readily available to everyone.

Point system. Used quite extensively a quarter of a century ago, the point system, where a number of points were allowed for each activity, and a total was set beyond which no student could go, seems to be giving way to a system of controlled activities, where there are limitations so that no one may have more than one major and one minor activity at any one time.

Principle 3

Records of extracurricular activities, including an evaluation of student participation, should be made a part of the permanent record. Records of participation in activities are generally not kept as much as are scholarship records, but since activities constitute an important part of the educational program, a record of participation and achievement should be kept just as carefully as achievement in classroom work or the scores on achievement and psychological tests.

Students, parents, employers, and college admission officers often need to know much more than the mere fact that a student joined one or more activities. All of them should know what happened as the result of that participation. Records of participation, collected from the sponsors, should be as routine a duty as the collection of marks from classroom teachers. Whether the report on pupils is the anecdotal type, paragraph summary, or letter grade type will depend on the philosophy of the school, the clerical help available for recording information on the permanent record, and the space available on the record. Certainly the principal should take steps to provide adequate records of participation if the school does not now have them.

Principle 4

A training program for all officers and members of each extracurricular organization should be undertaken. Group activities may be more effective if all of the persons involved receive training for their respective roles—whether president or group leader, recorder or secretary, treasurer, group observer, consultants, or members.

Student leaders need help in such matters as planning meetings, conducting discussions, and organizing groups for action in a democratic manner. Some schools have organized leaders' clubs under the direction of a social studies teacher. Recorders need instruction in keeping minutes; such instruction might well be given by a member of the English faculty. Similarly, the student treasurers should be assembled and given instruction on finances by a member of the business department, the principal's secretary, or the extracurricular finances supervisor in the school.

Group observers (or persons who help evaluate the group process) should also be given training by some faculty member who is familiar with the techniques. Observers are relatively infrequent, both in student and adult groups. Students and sponsors also need instruction regarding the role of consultants in group activities. Group members themselves need training with respect to the difference between effective and ineffective participation. Role playing may be used to illustrate such behavior as interrupting, nonparticipation, talking too much, and other characteristics of poor group membership.

While we do not have statistical evidence on the extent to which leader training is being conducted, we do know that more and more forward-looking schools are providing such training.

Principle 5

Well-qualified sponsors should be carefully selected and inservice training programs devised for them in order to create more effective sponsors. Slightly more than one-fourth of the sponsors interviewed said that they had received specific training, but these were primarily athletic coaches and speech and music instructors. Eighty-five percent of the sponsors indicated that they were teaching in a subject area closely related to the activity they sponsored. That was the most frequently mentioned qualification. However, fewer than half of the sponsors indicated that they had gained experience by participating in that activity in college.

It seems reasonable that the training programs in colleges need to be revised to provide preparation for sponsorship activities. A corollary is that an inservice training program should be designed to help teachers who are sponsors become more effective. This too seems to be a developing practice in forward-looking schools. Those who hire personnel need to keep in mind the qualifications for sponsors and take them into consideration when appointing teachers to vacancies.

Inquiry among the North Central Association schools revealed an interesting difference between the selection of athletic and nonathletic sponsors. Athletic coaches were most frequently appointed by the superintendent of schools, while nonathletic sponsors were most often chosen by the principal. This difference in practice appears open to question if all types of activity are to receive the same appraisal by the school.

Another issue on which there is a difference of opinion is the extent to which student wishes are considered in the selection of a sponsor. Whenever possible, it seems desirable to consider student opinions.

Principle 6

Sponsorship of extracurricular activities should be considered in planning the total work load of teachers. Because many schools do not have a well-defined policy governing the extra-class load of teachers, there has been a tendency to assign activity sponsorship with little consideration for the extra duties involved. Teachers who are very popular with young persons and consequently in demand as chaperons, club sponsors, and so forth may accept more hours of extra duties than is wise. And the question of salary differentials is closely associated with the work load.

Should coaches of athletic teams, band instructors, and other persons be paid higher salaries than other instructors with comparable training and experience? It depends on individual district policy. Some argue that the salary differentials are necessary to compete with other school districts in hiring outstanding, successful teachers.

Studies should be conducted in local school systems to find out the number of hours required to sponsor different activities and the relative amount of responsibility involved with specific programs. For example, it apparently requires from 400 to 500 hours to coach a varsity basketball team; these hours should be added to those spent by the coach in preparing for and teaching classes, grading papers, preparing reports, counseling students, serving on committees, and so forth. This total number of hours should then be compared with those of other faculty members for whom similar calculations have been made. If a basketball coach works more hours than other persons, his work load should be lightened or he should be paid extra salary based on the number of hours worked. In general it is likely to improve staff morale if the one with the heavier load works fewer hours and is paid the same sum as other teachers; it may very well improve instruction. If this kind of a study is undertaken, it should be done by members of the staff who participate in activities; all who are sponsors should participate.

Not all teachers can be expected to be sponsors. Teachers who are not sponsors may be assigned to other duties for which they are suited, and in this manner the work load is equalized so that those who are the effective sponsors are not penalized for their ability.

In recent years most schools have solved the problem of developing a schedule by listing the amounts (established by a representative faculty committee) to be paid the sponsors of various activities. In other systems, an index schedule for each activity is established, and the extra pay is then based upon the actual salary of the coach or sponsor. While the extra pay principle may not be professionally sound, many boards of education have adopted the plan because released time is more costly than paying a modest amount for the extra service.

Principle 7

Activities should be managed so that sponsors are to the largest degree possible free from community pressure. One of the problems frequently associated with sponsorship of extracurricular activities is the existence of community pressure for success not encountered in other phases of the school program. If a community is more interested in the percentage of victories in football or a state championship in basketball, the coach has an unenviable lot. In many communities, the band takes precedence over club activities, or livestock judging may be more important than good instruction in mathematics.

There are several ways of minimizing community pressures. Undoubtedly the fundamental method is through increased community participation in policy making for the school system. As more and more persons become involved in discussing the aims and objectives of the professional staff, greater understanding and appreciation of the total program including athletics or music will develop. Other ways of reducing pressure include (1) expanding the programs so that more students and teams play regularly in interscholastic competition; (2) placing athletics on the same basis as nonathletic activities; (3) eliminating admission charges to students; and (4) providing strong support for the faculty and administration in an effort to preserve a well-balanced program.

Administration and Supervision

Principle 8

In developing policies for the management of extracurricular programs, the following principle of management applies. A planning body representative of the interested groups—teachers, students, and community—needs to be organized to advise the board of education regarding policies for the extracurricular program, and to insist on their implementation. The board of education is of course legally responsible for the program, but it has so many other responsibilities that it cannot, in most cases, develop the recommendations which can be thoughtfully prepared by a representative group specifically charged with such a responsibility. Certainly students from the student council should have the largest part in planning the program, together with teachers and school administrators.

Some persons may think that creation of such an organization for extracurricular policy-making is needlessly complex. This criticism need not apply in actual operation if the involvement is taken seriously. There is no good reason why some of the evils attached to an extracurricular program cannot be eliminated, and desirable moral and financial support obtained. The groups need not meet after preliminary policies are adopted. The administration of the policy is a time-consuming job, to be done by paid employees. But the policy group should meet from time to time to reexamine its policies and hear reports from administrative officers in charge of their execution.

Principle 9

The responsibility for the management of the extracurricular program rests with the principal, although in many cases it can be delegated to a director of extracurricular activities. But obviously if extracurricular activities are to be properly supervised, someone must be responsible. In a small school, the task is generally the responsibility of the principal, while in the large schools there is a tendency to appoint a director of activities. The director should be released from about half of his regular teaching load in order to devote himself to the direction and supervision of the program in the school enrolling 1000 students. Many schools have a director of activities either on full-time or part-time basis; more schools are moving toward this objective. The duties of the director are to initiate, correlate, and supervise activities. He doesn't keep accounts or do other necessary clerical work—the position is professional and administrative in every sense of the word. The director should have qualities of leadership, personality, and sympathy, as well as sound technical knowledge of activities and activity programs and their place in the scheme of education. The qualities necessary for a good director are broader than those listed for a sponsor.

Principle 10

The administrative relationships in athletic and nonathletic activities should be the same. Although this principle seems reasonable, in practice there are many violations of it. Administrative relationships in appointing, supervising, and dismissing the coach of athletic activities are not the same as in other activities. Budgetary provisions may sometimes vary—athletics may be expected to be self-supporting, while other activities receive partial subsidy from tax funds. For these reasons, the director of athletics may not be administratively responsible to the director of extracurricular activities. Based on the authors' experience, it is our judgment that all activities be subjected to similar administrative control.

Principle 11

Extracurricular activities should be given adequate support from tax funds by the board of education. While most school systems do not know what the program of activities costs, either to taxpayers or to the school, they do know that costs absorbed by tax funds include the use of buildings, supplies, and equipment, salaries of the teachers and sponsors, the cost of hiring bus drivers, and sometimes transportation. The costs to the individual activity members include admission charges, dues, special clothing, and the like.

Students should not be prevented from participating in extracurricular activities because of cost. In view of the fact that there is undoubtedly a positive relationship between dropping out of school and family socioeconomic status, and since the cost of participating in extracurricular activities is relatively high, it appears that more extracurricular costs should be paid from tax funds. There seems to be little justification for paying the cost of algebra and United States history from tax revenue while expecting basketball to be self-supporting. Most people would agree in theory, but in practice it is not yet possible, except in the wealthier and more forward-looking communities, to make the athletic program free to all.

A few boards of education have made student admission to all athletic contests free, and a few schools have adopted this policy. It is to be hoped that more schools will follow this lead so that all students, regardless of family income, may participate in school activities.

Principle 12

Procedures in receiving, spending, and accounting for activity funds should teach students correct attitudes and habits in handling funds. Activity funds are legally under the control of the board of education and should be subject to the same control exercised over all funds thus administered. Generally funds for athletics have been more carefully accounted for than in any other part of the extracurricular program, probably because more money has been involved. At this point, we will merely say what we say in the chapter on business functions—that in handling activity funds there should be an auditable record for every transaction.

Principle 13

Continuous evaluation of individual activities in the total program should be done on a systematic basis. Many devices have been used to evaluate the effectiveness of the program, but probably the simpler way is to analyze the extent of student participation in a specific program. This kind of study will be more effective if the data show participation by sex, grade level, socioeconomic classification, geographical location, and scholastic achievement. Studies of opinions of appropriate persons, such as sponsors, relating to the program may be valuable, as will opinion polls of students on an anonymous basis. Studies of the opinions held by parents, alumni, and other groups toward student activities are also useful in appraising the quality of the program.

Nature of the Extracurricular Activities Program

Principle 14

The aims of different activities should be clearly defined so that later evaluations may be made in relation to the accomplishment of the stated purpose. In considering the nature of the program, attention should be given to the purpose, balance in the offerings, ways in which new activities are started and existing ones continued or abandoned, time of meeting, and types of programs carried on by different organizations. For example, in holding a school dance, what is supposed to happen—in terms of behavior change—to the chairman, to those who serve on committees, and to those who attend? Unless the aims are clearly stated, it may be impossible to evaluate the contributions of various activities or to evaluate the total program.

Principle 15

The activities program should be characterized by a vertical and horizontal balance in offering. Horizontal balance implies the necessity of providing a broad variety of activities to keep any one activity from over-shadowing another. Vertical balance implies the necessity of providing similar activities for students of various interests and abilities.

A school which supplies only opportunities for participation on the football team, and lacks adequate building, coaching, or equipment facilities for persons talented in other areas such as music, fails to provide horizontal balance in the activities program. A study should be made to see that horizontal balance exists in the programs in the school. The principle of vertical balance is violated when a school offers a given activity on a selective basis, but does not provide a similar activity for those who do not possess sufficient ability to participate in the elective activities. What evidence has been presented tends to indicate that both horizontal and vertical balance is violated in many schools.

Principle 16

Procedures for the inauguration of new activities should be characterized by definiteness in responsibility, ease of operation, and relevance to student wishes. Both students and faculty ought to know exactly how a new activity can be started; this is part of the responsibility of the guidance bulletin. One method by which the results can be achieved is to vest all chartering of new activities in the student council. Whenever a given number of students, say eight or ten, wish to start a new activity, they may petition the council for a charter. Before the charter is granted, the students must be required to show very clearly the purposes of the activity, the time and place of meetings, persons eligible for participation, facilities required in terms of building space and supplies, and the name of the proposed sponsor. Such a petition should bear the approval of the principal or director of extracurricular activities, and should indicate the willingness of the sponsor to accept responsibility for the group. The student council would then be expected to assist the petitioning group in complying with the requirements and obtaining the charter. The student council should publicize these procedures from time to time so that all concerned are familiar with them.

Principle 17

Participants in extracurricular activities should be asked at the end of the season or year for recommendations relative to the continuing of their particular activity. Unless participants are asked for recommendations, some activities may be continued year after year mainly because of the wishes of some sponsor or a small clique of persons in the school. Changes in procedure or program may be warranted because of experiences during the past season or year, and unless suggestions are systematically sought and recorded through some form of opinionnaire, there is no effective way of evaluating the programs.

The director of extracurricular activities and a group from the student council might be wise to evaluate all activities and bring to the attention of the council those which should be discontinued, or indicate areas where there seem to be needs for additional activities. There are no persons better qualified than the members of the Spanish Club to indicate what ought to be done the coming year, or what should be curtailed or eliminated in their club. And there is probably no one who can better suggest what needs to be done in the development of a baseball program than those who have participated in the event.

The Schedule

Principle 18

The scheduling of extracurricular activities should receive the same careful attention accorded other phases of program development. When a large number of activities are scheduled during a single activity period, students may necessarily have conflicts and may be denied participation. Or when activities are scheduled at the close of the school day, students who work or who are obliged to travel long distances may be prevented from participating. Activities scheduled on week nights cause some students either to lose sleep or to stay away from the activities. And sometimes activities are held at places where it is difficult for all students to attend.

When all these factors are recognized, the director of activities will have the possible responsibility of lengthening the schedule of the school day, week, or year. Participation by students in out-of-school activities, including work experience, should be recognized; activities should be scheduled at times to allow for maximum use of school facilities.

School organization for extraclass activities generally follows one of three patterns: (1) the activity period, which is intended to provide for most extraclass activity within the daily schedule; (2) the core program, which consolidates most of the extraclass activities with class activities; or (3) the before- and after-school program, which provides for most of the activity outside of the regular program.[20] The school activity period may be a regular period of thirty-five or forty minutes, or it may be staggered throughout the day, meeting, for example, from 8:40 to 9:20 on Monday, from 9:40 to 10:20 on Tuesday, and so on throughout the week. As an illustration of this, Tompkins quotes the following:

> The school day has five one-hour periods, of which four are regular class periods, and one is an extra period. The extra period occurs once on Monday, Tuesday, Thursday, and Friday, and is used for additional curriculum experiences for pupils; the free period comes at the third period on Wednesday, and is an activity period. The free period on the first and third Wednesdays of the month is devoted to organized clubs and a variety of activities, such as plays, rifle competition, photography, nature study, and dancing, many of which extend beyond the school day and outside the school walls. On the second Wednesday the free period is set aside for assemblies, and the fourth Wednesday is devoted to class meetings, student council meetings, homeroom guidance, and planning for the annual senior class excursion to Washington. All of the activities are regarded as of equal importance for the class at work in achieving the objectives of the school.[21]

In the Millhollen study mentioned previously, four-fifths of the parents and nine-tenths of the students believed that some activities were worth including in the school day; only one-eighth of the parents thought that activities should be totally excluded from the school day. Activities which the respondents believed should be included in the school day were assemblies, student council, school newspaper, yearbook, debate or speech practice, and music rehearsal.[22] There were very few who believed that club meetings, intramural athletics, athletic practice, or preparation for parties should be included in the school day.[23] In discussing methods for including activities in the school day, both parents and the students favored

---

[20]Ellsworth Tompkins, "The Relation of Activities to the Curriculum," *National Association of Secondary School Principals Bulletin*, 184 (February 1952), 13–14.
[21]Tompkins, "Relation of Activities," p. 8.
[22]Millhollen, "Improvement of Extra-Class Activities," p. 97.
[23]Millhollen, "Improvement of Extra-Class Activities," p. 97.

shortening the class periods or eliminating one class on the day of the activity and rotating the periods so that all classes would be affected in the same way.[24]

Planning Activity Programs

Principle 19

The activities program should be characterized by active participation on the part of the membership. Sometimes a small group takes the responsibility for planning of the program; this is particularly likely to be true in club programs. It may result in a sterile program, interesting only to a few specialists and the sponsor, or it may result in rather boring speakers from outside organizations or listening to monotonous reports from one or two members. Unless there is a committee to help plan the program, and unless the active participation of the entire group is secured, there is likely to be dissatisfaction. Doing, rather than listening, should characterize the activity program.

Activity programs should be planned to include services to school and community. Young people should have experiences that demonstrate the role of organized groups in a democratic society.

Principle 20

Contest participation among groups should be on the basis of educational merit rather than because of pressures from the community sponsoring the organization or from other sources. In the survey of activities in the North Central Association done by Trump, the most frequent reasons for inaugurating contests were (1) that neighboring schools were doing so, (2) that students in the school demanded them, (3) that an aggressive principal or director of activities wanted them, (4) that the state college or university had sponsored a contest, (5) that a service club had sponsored an essay or poster contest, or (6) that some teacher saw an opportunity to add to his prestige or professional position by inaugurating a contest. It is readily apparent that not all of these reasons are desirable or valid.

Night football is almost certain to produce more revenue and permit larger attendance than afternoon games, but are the educational purposes of football better served by night contests? There is certain to be a greater policing problem, there will be the problem of drinking in the stands, and there are almost certain to be complaints about students being out at late

---

[24]Millhollen, "Improvement of Extra-Class Activities," p. 99.

hours. In an increasing number of communities, the matter has been settled at the turnstiles rather than at meetings because the receipts are larger.

Bands and orchestras are sometimes encouraged to travel long distances to participate in state and regional contests. Parents or interested citizens may be willing to defray the expenses, but are the educational purposes of instrumental music better served by participating in such state and regional meets? In general, the festival type of gathering, representing a reasonable area or region, is much preferred to the state or regional contest.

Principle 21

The purpose of participation in a contest should be strictly adhered to, or contests should be changed to make them harmonize with stated aims. It is quite apparent that both worthwhile and unworthwhile results may come from participation in a contest. Does charging student admission at an interscholastic activity achieve the purpose of the contest? Does scheduling four, eight, or ten teams in interscholastic athletics provide a greater realization of the purposes in scheduling than two? Does the practice of entering essay contests improve the writing of the students? These kinds of questions must be asked when deciding whether or not a contest should take place.

The problem of contests has become so great that the National Association of Secondary School Principals has developed a committee which approves some national contests and not others. In October of each year, a committee (first organized in February 1942) publishes in the association's *Bulletin* a list of those approved contests. The committee recognizes two kinds of contests in the nonathletic area—those originally set up by school staff members as constructive educational programs, and those originated, organized, and promoted by persons outside the school educational staff. The first kind usually grew into state and regional competition, such as festivals and tournaments, and is now generally confined to groups of schools within a single state. School administrators are included in the planning stages of such contests, and they must be approved by the state activities association.

The outside of the school type of contest is not planned to be coordinated with the school program, but is promoted by commercial firms, patriotic organizations, colleges, and universities. Although the motives and purposes of these contests may be commendable, the plan of participation is often faulty and conceals the chief underlying purpose. To make the contest more attractive and appealing, prizes and awards are usually promised the winner. Many of these contests are not approved by the national committee.

In an earlier day there were national contests in athletics, particularly in basketball, but these have been discontinued because of the activities of the state athletic associations and state activities associations.

Principle 22

The school should accept responsibility for the physical, mental, and moral well-being of the students participating in interscholastic contests. Participation in interscholastic contests takes students away from the home community, sometimes on long trips that keep them away from home overnight or until late at night. It is a generally accepted practice that students must travel to and from an activity in transportation furnished by the school, or be dropped from the activity, unless the student's family personally drives a student to the event. Some schools will not allow the student even to ride with his parents to a scholastic contest. Another responsibility of the school is to require students to make up work missed while participating in contests. Insurance should also be provided covering possible accident to players in interscholastic contests.

Principle 23

Awards, other than scholarships, for participation in contests should be intrinsic rather than extrinsic. Some states have requirements that no award with a value of more than one dollar, except those given them for the finals of interscholastic contests by the state associations, may be given to any individual. Such rules are desirable. There have been incidents in the past where students were awarded sweaters or gold watches of high value. Awards should consist of school letters, medals, banquets, and sometimes sweaters for interscholastic athletics. Certainly there can be no quarrel with scholarships for prowess in particular events, if the scholarships are equally available to all persons.

Activities in Elementary Schools

Activities are rapidly becoming a part of the elementary school too. Because activities at the secondary school level have come into the schools from outside the curriculum, although often related to it, they have been designated as extracurricular activities. In the elementary school, these activities tend to become a part of the curriculum. Since the activities are likely to be much more closely articulated with the curriculum at the elementary level, some authors have suggested the term *cocurricular activities*—those school-sponsored activities which require administrative provision and organization in a somewhat different way than typical classroom activity.

Many of the activities at the elementary level are similar to those at the secondary level. For example, there are bands, orchestras, and choral groups. In addition, some elementary schools have rhythm bands. There are performing groups which include pageants, puppet shows, assemblies, and plays. Service organizations such as the safety patrol, library assistants, and Junior Red Cross exist. The athletic opportunities available emphasize intramurals. Many elementary schools have their own newspapers; they are usually of the mimeographed type. Student councils can also be effective at the elementary level.

It is important that activities in the elementary school be kept appropriate to the characteristics of pupils of that age group. Concerning parties and social affairs, some pupils and even some parents desire to duplicate activities at the secondary level. Most boys at the elementary level are not ready for sophisticated dances and dating affairs. To prevent events of this kind parent education groups should be oriented to the purposes of the program and their cooperation solicited.

As at the secondary level, selecting a sponsor is an important consideration. F. Neil Williams has suggested that the sponsor should have enthusiasm, feel that the activity is worthwhile, have an adequate knowledge of the area, possess an interest in individuals, and have an awareness of problem areas likely to develop in the activity.[25] The contributions of the sponsor are many, but one of the most important is that of creating an attitude upon the part of students that school is meaningful.

Evaluation of Activities

Appraisal by Public School Graduates

In his study, Trump received 435 replies from an inquiry addressed to the alumni of five high schools, in which the graduates were requested to check 22 possible benefits from participation in extracurricular activities, indicating those which they believed to have been of greatest value to the students. Examination of the values attributed to activities shows that the most frequently mentioned benefit was the formation of new personal friendships, which may not have been formed through association in classes. Opportunities for developing friendly relations are greater in activities than in class work because the activities involve voluntary cooperation in the pursuit of common interests to a greater extent than is provided in most classes.

The same list of values was submitted by Trump to 3,525 students in the North Central Association high schools. It is not surprising that

---

[25]F. Neil Williams, "The Student Activities Sponsor," *School Activities*, XXXIX, No. 8 (April 1965), 3–4.

the students in this group placed first the same value which was given top rating by the alumni of the original five schools. The value given second place by students—"made school seem more interesting"—supports the contention of the proponents of extracurricular activities in secondary schools, namely, that a program of activities makes school a more real experience and enhances work in the classrooms.[26]

Evaluation of Reasons for Participation

In order to secure further information on participation, Trump secured answers to a questionnaire from 994 parents and 214 faculty members in several public high schools regarding the benefits they believed students received from participating in activities. The benefits believed to be most important were (1) developing new friendships; (2) making school more interesting; (3) having something worthwhile to do in leisure time; (4) causing students to be more tolerant of the opinions and wishes of others; (5) teaching the students how to win and lose in a sportsman-like manner; (6) creating greater loyalty to the school; (7) developing poise and social contacts; (8) causing the students to become more willing to accept criticism from others; (9) developing more friendly relations with teachers; and (10) creating greater interest in regular school subjects.[27] The judgments of the faculty members were very similar to those of the parents, but not all of the values were given in the same order.

Millhollen also made a study of the opinions of parents and students in two high schools in Eugene, Oregon, relative to the emphasis on activities. He found that parents and students in both high schools, in from one-half to three-fourths of the cases, thought the emphasis on activities was about right, although one-sixth of the parents thought that clubs, music activities, interscholastic athletics, and dances were given too much emphasis. Half of the students thought dramatics did not have enough attention, and one-third thought that dances and parties had too little emphasis, while one-fifth felt that music and intramural athletics were not emphasized enough.[28] Very few parents or students thought that there had been excessive participation. Forty percent believed their children had not participated as much as they should have.[29]

The benefits claimed (by more than 50 percent of the students) for participation in extraclass activities were (1) interest was broadened and extended; (2) ability to work with others was improved; (3) self-confidence was increased; (4) they had learned to speak and feel at ease

[26]Trump, *High School Extracurriculum Activities*, pp. 113 and 115.
[27]Trump, *High School Extracurricular Activities*, p. 118.
[28]Millhollen, "Improvement of Extra-Class Activities," pp. 42–43.
[29]Millhollen, "Improvement of Extra-Class Activities," p. 44.

in a group; and (5) needs for socialibity were helped.[30] About three-fifths of the parents and three-fourths of the students were of the opinion that extraclass activity did not interfere with class work,[31] and over three-fourths of those who answered believed that extraclass activities had little or no effect on grades.[32] Parents and students at both schools agreed that about seven out of ten students felt that they belonged, and that only one in ten felt that he was an outsider or could not get into an activity.[33] Two-thirds of the students and four-fifths of the parents were satisfied that responsibilities outside the school made little or no difference in the extent to which students took part in school activities,[34] and two-thirds of the parents and students believed that lack of skill or ability had no effect on participation, and only one-tenth believed that this kept students out of activities, dramatics, music, and athletics.[35] This was also most likely to be true in dancing.

Undesirable Outcomes

Trump asked 3,525 students, 214 faculty members, 435 alumni, and 994 parents concerning the undesirable outcomes of participating in extracurricular activities; eight were recognized as being harmful to students. The control of activities by a small group or clique was considered objectionable by nearly 20 percent, while neglect of regular school work, jealousy among participants, overemphasis of winning in games and contests, time and effort demanded by activities out of proportion to the value received, inferiority feelings developed on the part of some students, excessive costs, and the interference in activities by nonschool personnel were the undesirable outcomes which were designated by other responses. As long as such problems are unrecognized and unsolved, the serious challenge to the value of extracurricular activities exists.[36]

Although parents and students were overwhelmingly in favor of student participation, Millhollen found six criticisms of extraclass activity which were frequently mentioned. (1) Activities were not conducted so that all members could take an active part; (2) activities resulted in cliques; (3) activities did not do enough to encourage students who were not in activities to take part in activities suited to their needs and abilities; (4) not enough training was given to develop leadership; (5) publicity given to opportunities available in activities was inadequate; (6) insuffi-

---

[30]Millhollen, "Improvement of Extra-Class Activities," p. 92.

[31]Millhollen, "Improvement of Extra-Class Activities," p. 52.

[32]Millhollen, "Improvement of Extra-Class Activities," p. 55.

[33]Millhollen, "Improvement of Extra-Class Activities," p. 58.

[34]Millhollen, "Improvement of Extra-Class Activities," p. 72.

[35]Millhollen, "Improvement of Extra-Class Activities," p. 78–80.

[36]Trump, *High School Extracurricular Activities*, p. 116.

cient opportunity was given for students to learn the skills and to develop the abilities needed in some activities.[37]

Other Considerations

Extravagant claims for participation in activities have been made, but there is some evidence that there are many schools where students are not fully utilized in helping the school to realize its greatest potential. A recent study by Stephen K. Bailey has revealed that only half of the schools examined used students in forming student conduct policy.[38] While it is probably questionable whether students should be involved in disciplining other students, it does seem entirely proper for students to be involved in a consideration of policy which so greatly affects them.

Another work by Ackerly, sponsored by the National Association of Secondary School Principals, deals with the matter of the reasonable exercise of authority.[39] This document gives recognition to recent court rulings that have had considerable impact in the general operation of schools. While some of the recommendations and implications have been dealt with in other sections, it is important that school administrators are aware of their significance.

1. Before it can be recognized as a school group and be given use of school time and facilities, the club must be approved, in accordance with established criteria, by the principal or some other designated school official.

2. Membership must be open to all students except where the purpose of the club requires qualifications (a French club, for instance).

3. The club must have a faculty sponsor or advisor selected and approved according to agreed-upon procedures, and club activities will not be permitted until a faculty sponsor has been selected.

4. Clearly improper purposes and activities are not permitted and if persisted in will be cause for withdrawing official approval of the group.

5. School groups, either continuing or *ad hoc*, are not permitted to use the school name in participating in public demonstrations or other activities outside the school unless prior permission has been granted by the designated school official.

While most of these recommendations pertain to school clubs, the document also offers valuable information pertaining to many other school activities.

---

[37]Millhollen, "Improvement of Extra-Class Activities," p. 106.

[38]Stephen K. Bailey, *Disruption in Urban and Public Secondary Schools* (Washington, D.C.: National Association of Secondary School Principals, 1970), pp. 43–44.

[39]Robert L. Ackerly, *The Reasonable Exercise of Authority* (Washington, D.C.: National Association of Secondary School Principals, 1969), p. 13.

Not even their most ardent supporters expect extracurricular activities to develop by themselves all the desirable character traits for young people. Nor are activities expected to serve as a panacea for whatever ills may be ascribed to the schools by either friendly or unfriendly critics. Throughout this chapter we have asserted that activities have values; extravagant claims of their benefits harm the orderly development of activities more than they assist it. There is danger, too, that school principals and enthusiastic sponsors will become complacent about these values, forget the possible shortcomings, and overexpand the program. The activity program is an integral part of the school program, and employing the principles of management enumerated in this chapter will tend to stabilize and improve the program.

Selected References

ALLEN, J. E., "Student Unrest in High Schools," *Journal of School and Society,* 98 (February 1970), 75–76.

ARMSTRONG, R. L., "Comparison of Student Activity Involvement," *Journal of American Indian Education,* 9 (January 1970), 10–15.

BEAVAN, K. A., "Students Unite in City High Schools," *Times Education Supplement,* 2811:1086 (April 1969).

BOUTWELL, W. D., "Our Leisure-Time Education," *Education Digest,* 35 (December 1969), 25–27.

COLLINS, D., "Providing Recognition for the Seldom Recognized," *School Activities,* 40 (May 1969), 17.

DRAAYER, D. R., and P. A. TEAGUE, "Student Lounge or Study Hall: How Are Grades Affected?" *Clearing House,* 44 (November 1969), 141–44.

FLICKINGER, K. E., "Student Lounge for the Small High School," *National Association of Secondary School Principals Bulletin,* 54 (October 1970), 50–55.

FREDERICK, ROBERT WENDELL, *Student Activities in American Education.* New York: Center for Applied Research in Education, 1965.

HALL, J. TILLMAN, *School Recreation: Its Organization, Supervision, and Administration.* Dubuque, Iowa: W. C. Brown Company, 1966.

HEARN, ARTHUR C., *Evaluation of Student Activities.* Washington, D.C.: National Association of Secondary School Principals, 1966.

HONN, F. R., "Tomorrow's Students," *Journal of Secondary Education,* 44 (May 1969), 237–40.

"How Student Involvement Pays Off," *School Management,* 14 (March 1970), 29–32.

JOHNSON, W. T., "Youth Organizations Aid in Teaching," *Agricultural Education Magazine,* 42 (October 1969), 102.

KLEINERT, E. JOHN, "Effects of High School Size on Student Activity Program," *National Association of Secondary School Principals Bulletin*, 53 (March 1969), 34–46.

KRARUP, AGNES, et al., *The School Day Begins: A Guide to Opening Exercises, Grades Kindergarten–12*. (3rd ed.), New York: Hobbs, Dorman and Co., 1967.

MCGREW, J. B., "Student Participation in Decision-Making; Report on a Conference," *National Association of Secondary School Principals Bulletin*, 54 (March 1970), 124–33.

MEEHAN, M., "Come Early and Stay Late," *School and Community*, 56 (April 1970), 20–21.

MILLER, H., "Santa Barbara Has a Student School Board," *American School Board Journal*, 157 (May 1970), 29.

MUSE, W. V., "Management Skill in Student Organization," *Personnel and Guidance Journal*, 48 (June 1970), 842–47.

National Education Association, Research Division, "Salary Schedule Supplements for Extra Duties, 1968–70." NEA Research Division 1970-R 4: 1–68.

NELSON, C. L., "Delegate Responsibility, A Necessity for Leadership Development," *Agriculture Education Magazine*, 42 (November 1969), 118–19.

RIZZO, M. E., "Active Activities Program," *Clearing House*, 44 (November, 1969), 182–84.

ROBBINS, JERRY H., and STIRLING B. WILLIAMS, JR., *Student Activities in the Innovative School*. Minneapolis: Burgess Publishing Company, 1969.

SAXE, R. W., "Manifest and Latent Functions in Educational Activities," *National Association of Secondary School Principals Bulletin*, 54 (January 1970), 41–50.

"Schoolmen Split Over Student Involvement; School Administrator's Opinion Poll," *Nation's School*, 84 (September 1969), 47.

STROUP, HERBERT, *Toward a Philosophy of Organized Student Activities*. Minneapolis: University of Minnesota Press, 1964.

"Student Involvement: Channeling Activism into Accomplishment," *Nation's School*, 84 (September 1969), 39–50.

"What Happens When Students Criticize: Montgomery County Student Alliance," *Nation's School*, 84 (September 1969), 59–60.

15

Extracurricular Activities—
Some Representative Programs

In the preceding chapter we indicated that extracurricular activities include student government, school assemblies, school clubs, class organization, honor societies, social activities, speech and dramatics, music, out-of-school experiences, publications, and athletics. In our opinion, because student participation in the management of activities is of prime importance, it will be discussed first.

Student Participation
in the Management of School Affairs

The Student Council

Student participation in the management of school affairs has replaced the term student government, prevalent in educational literature for many years. The student council has been in existence for almost a half century and has the strong support of the National Association of Secondary School Principals. While no one knows exactly how many student councils are in existence today, thousands of schools make use of its services and the number is increasing. The 1970 National Association of Student Councils Yearbook reported an increase of 627 councils for the forty-six states which reported. Of this number, 195 are classified as new councils.[1]

---

[1]*The 1970 Student Council Yearbook*, National Association of Student Councils. Washington, D.C.: National Association of Secondary School Principals, 1970, pp. 101–20.

When the student council idea was new and student participation was much less frequent than it is now, there was considerable use of the term student government. This term was always something of a misnomer because there never was, and never can be, such a thing as student government. The faculty and the principal have legal responsibilities which cannot be abdicated, but students may participate and assist in the administration of the school and can gain valuable experience in the process. The faculty and the head of the school must be ready to assist the student council in its operation. It may be necessary in some cases to decide against or to use the veto when the student council decides upon an activity that may be illegal or one that is prohibited by the rules and regulations of the board of education. When a council is sponsored by a good advisor, it should not be necessary to oppose its proposals. There should be a continuous effort to maintain mutual understanding and a good working relationship between the council and the school principal, although the principal should probably not serve as the sponsor.

Purposes of a Student Council

It has been pointed out that there are several objectives that have been considered traditional for student councils.[2] (1) To promote good citizenship; (2) to promote harmonious relationships; (3) to coordinate activities; (4) to instill proper attitudes; and (5) to provide a means for student expression. There are other objectives that may be equally or more important than these. In the midst of drastic social change, every school is faced with the results of these changes. Attention to the problems as they arise and anticipation of those that may be a cause for future concern should be of interest to school administrators and student council. The council has a basic interest in the total school experience, and should try to create an atmosphere in the school that both fosters respect for the individual and is a guiding force in making the school an example of the best in democratic living. If the members of the council are truly representative of all the students within the school it can be effective in developing an *our school* concept.

Organization of a Student Council

A student council is an organization of students elected by other students to represent them and to speak for them in the activities of the school. It knows and makes known to the administration the wishes of the student body, and it directs various student campaigns, conducts drives to

---

[2]*The 1967 Student Handbook*, National Association of Student Councils (Washington, D.C.: National Association of Secondary School Principals), pp. 11–12.

improve the schools, and finds activities within its ability to perform. The council is more and more becoming a directing force in the activities of the school; it can be and often is an excellent means of training students in democratic living. But no council worth having will run of its own momentum. The faculty and the principal, or his delegated representative, must guide the council until it becomes a vital and functioning organization. The council cannot be successful if it is considered a place for dumping the details of school administration for which the principal has no enthusiasm. Neither should the student council be composed of a hand-picked group of students, such as are generally looked upon by the student body as the principal's stooges.

Principles of Organization

The operation of the student council is usually outlined in a constitution. Writing a new constitution or revising an existing one is a good experience for students. The National Association of Student Councils provides samples of existing constitutions for schools which have not yet written a constitution. Some schools examine those in operation in other school systems to gain new ideas and to evaluate their own. In addition to the constitution which provides the framework of the organization, bylaws are adopted to govern its operating procedures.

If the council is to succeed, it must fill a need in the lives of the students. It cannot be dominated by the principal, the sponsor, or the faculty. Councils are most effective when they deal with specific problems in need of solution, such as human relations, sportsmanship, school assemblies, dress codes, and student conduct. Newly organized councils should be advised to deal with a problem of immediate concern that has possibilities for immediate solution. By demonstrating effectiveness in its formative stages, the council's standing in the school can gain prestige and support and thus be a more effective organization.

The council should be chosen from the school in such a way that every student feels that he is represented. The homeroom has often been chosen as the unit of representation. Other systems have used clubs, class organizations, and the like to constitute the membership. Whatever plan is adopted, there should be safeguards to see that there is adequate representation for all students. If the school population is made up of pupils of different races, different cultural backgrounds, and widely separated socio-economic levels, the council representation should reflect these differences. No method of grouping should destroy the representative nature of the council.

The council should not be too large. If representation is by home rooms, a large school might have a membership of two hundred. A council of that size could not be effective without some internal organization, such as an executive committee. The committee would function for the council and report directly to it. A council numbering more than thirty students should probably have such an arrangement. To be effective, however, it is necessary to develop safeguards to ensure that the executive committee acts in accordance with the wishes of the entire council.

Internal Organization

The officers designated by the constitution—usually president, vice-president, secretary, and treasurer—should be elected. Committee organization will probably best care for the duties of the council; such committees should consist of student representatives from the council, the student body, and faculty representatives. These committees should have definite duties and should report to the council at appropriate intervals.

If the council is to hold an important place in the life of a school, elected officers should be presented to the student body and installed in a dignified manner at an all-school assembly. The way in which this is done varies; each school should develop a ceremony of its own. No matter what ceremony is adopted, the assembly at which officers are inducted should be one which recognizes the presidency of the council as the most highly honored position in the school.

Standards for a good student council are (1) that it has clearly defined powers and responsibilities—which it understands; (2) that it practices accepted democratic principles in its operation; (3) that its constitution and bylaws are carefully and democratically conceived; (4) that it is supported by the faculty and the principal, who are sympathetic to its role; (5) that it has a sound functioning organization; and (6) it has prestige, serves the school willingly, and enlists the ready cooperation of the student body.

Activities Performed by the Student Council

The type and number of the student council's activities depend upon the local situation. *The Student Council Handbook* represents an excellent source for offering suggestions of suitable activities. In surveying the literature in this field, it becomes apparent that there are certain activities that most student councils sponsor.

Most councils sponsor social activities. All schools need to provide opportunities for students to meet in social and recreational situations. Since the council is representative of all the students in the school, the social activities should be planned to meet all their needs.

Councils also develop orientation activities. These activities are designed to acquaint new students with the school organization and to inform them concerning the opportunities available for participation. To assist in orientation procedures, a handbook is usually developed and used in orientation procedures. Student councils charter school clubs. Most council constitutions outline procedures for establishing and facilitating the operation of clubs of various types. Councils work at providing services too. There are many areas of the school's operation that benefit from the volunteer services of students. One example is providing a lost and found service. Another might be organizing host services to school visitors.

Extracurricular finance is another of the council's duties. Some schools give the council wide latitude in managing funds, while others center this responsibility in a business office. Whatever method is used, it appears that when the source of the funds rests with student contributions and effort, the allocation and management of them should rest largely with the students (under proper guidance). Student councils often sponsor forums. In recent years much has been said concerning the relevancy of the school to students. Many schools now sponsor sessions in which student representatives and faculty members, including administrators, have the opportunity to express concerns and discuss problems. The objective is to create an atmosphere of mutual respect.

It is impossible to make specific recommendations concerning activities for a given school in a specific location. A successful activity in one may fail in another because of the local situation.

Managing Finances

As has been pointed out, the amount of responsibility given to students for handling money matters varies greatly from school to school. If most funds are provided by the board of education to support the school activities, the finances are probably a function of the business office. But even in situations of this kind students do have an interest in how funds are handled and alloted and may serve well in an advisory capacity. When the funds that subsidize the activities are collected from students or accrue as a result of their activities, the students should play a major role in apportioning funds and in devising ways for ensuring sound financial management.

The development of the activities budget represents a vital learning experience for students. While pupils will probably not do any actual handling of the money, many situations will arise where the exercise of their good judgment will be of prime importance. It is not uncommon for the annual activities budget in large secondary schools to exceed $100,000. Despite the size of such sums, there are usually more requests for funds than the budget can supply. It then becomes the duty of the council to decide upon fair and proper allocations.

Most school systems use forms, often developed locally, to facilitate sound business practices. Where this has not been the practice, it should be the council's function to develop or secure them. They may be obtained from other school systems or developed by using the suggestions in the *Student Council Handbook*.

The Council Handbook

Source of Funds

Since activities are a part of the total school curriculum, they should be supported by the board of education in the same manner in which curricular experiences are provided. Many boards provide funds for some activities, but most student bodies must rely upon their own resources to provide operating funds.

A second source of funds is the money taken in the form of gate receipts from athletic or dramatic performances. Certainly money earned from athletic or dramatic activities should not be taken away and divided equally among all activities, but spectators do attend such events partly because the participants represent the school. Some schools attract thousands of people to events and take in quite a bit of money. Perhaps a small percentage of these revenues could be placed at the disposal of other worthy activities with less drawing power. For example, school plays and athletic contests, which are generally well-patronized, could carry on without harm, and the council would have funds with which to sponsor worthy but low-income activities. But above all, until the council has some control over the purse strings, it cannot become the center of the life of the school.

The Activity Ticket

A growing number of schools have adopted an activity ticket, which admits students to all school activities, and sometimes include the yearbook and the newspaper. In some schools the ticket may be sold for a fixed fee, say, $5.00, but may also be available on a weekly payment plan for a thirty-six week program. Where the activity ticket has been inaugurated, it is customary for the council to receive legislative control of the funds and to appropriate the funds among those activities which need support. The main benefits claimed for the activity ticket are that it interests a larger percentage of students in activities; it provides a basis early in the year for organizations to plan their programs, since they will know what money is available; and it provides an equitable distribution of finances among the organizations.

Other Considerations

Many states and regions have conferences for the purpose of exchanging ideas, discussing common problems, and reporting promising innovations. One of the outcomes of such experiences should be improved leadership at the local level. There is no "blueprint" that can be used for the local situation; every student council must develop its operation for the local scene.

The council idea is not restricted to the secondary level. There are many successful organizations at elementary and middle school levels. While the activities differ with different age groups, the basic purposes remain the same. Councils provide a voice for students, and they are instrumental in serving to satisfy the legitimate needs and desires of the student body, but they will never be effective if they are regarded as groups which deal with insignificant matters and serve as a "rubber stamp" for the administration.

In earlier years, student councils did attempt to regulate conduct through the student court. Placing the disciplinary function of the schools in the hands of a student court is a questionable procedure, and it should never be placed in a position of regulating conduct within a given classroom. But this does not mean that the quality of student conduct cannot be a matter for their concern. The creation of a school profile that reflects a wholesome climate for learning experiences should be a goal of an effective council.

The School Assembly

The school assembly is a development from the religious exercises commonly found in academies and colleges, but the public school assembly is an educational exercise. (Recent rulings have indicated that religious exercises are inappropriate for public schools.) School assemblies have become a part of the operation of most schools because they make definite contributions to the quality of educational experience. Principals are generally emphatic in feeling that regular assemblies are necessary.

The frequency of assemblies varies from school to school. It seems that there should be an assembly each week of the school year with the exception of those weeks marking the beginning and ending of school and during the weeks when examinations are given. The length of the assembly also is dependent upon the local situation, but it is difficult to conduct an adequate assembly in less than forty-five minutes. On the other hand, no assembly should be convened for more than one hour. The time during the day for holding assemblies also varies from school to school. The least desirable time for holding assemblies other than "pep" sessions seems to be the end of the day.

Purposes to Be Served

A variety of purposes may be served by the school assembly. Four possible purposes are: (1) to inform, (2) to educate, (3) to entertain, and (4) to recognize. Assemblies of an informational nature include orientation programs, presentations of societal problems, governmental issues, and current affairs, while programs on drug abuse, international relations, and the like provide information on broad problems of interest to education. Some assemblies organized for the purpose of entertainment such as talent shows and dramatic and music presentations, are usually enjoyable because they amuse and entertain. It is also appropriate to recognize those within the school who have achieved honors in various ways, including athletics. When properly organized, recognition programs do not have to be dull or uninteresting.

Developing Assembly Programs

In the past many schools have relied upon commercial enterprises to furnish ideas and talent for programs. Most of these programs were designed to be entertaining, but they did not contribute very much to the educational program of the school. Recently the responsibility for the production of assembly programs has been shared by students and faculty; a representative committee plans the programs and secures the talent to execute its ideas.

One other idea that has worked well in some schools is to center this responsibility in a given class; the class in creative writing for example. The materials produced for the assembly form the basis for the written materials. Developing creative ideas for programs is educationally sound. Under such an arrangement, it is necessary to make sure that all departments within the school have representation in the class. Further, the class should be under the direction of a teacher with some enthusiasm for the project. Class members themselves appear only occasionally, if at all, since they have had the benefit of developing their ideas for the assembly and giving them reality in the presentation. But whatever plan is used, both students and faculty should be represented and assemblies be well planned in advance.

Another additional thing to be kept in mind as assemblies are planned is that there is always the need for scenery, lighting effects, and stage management. A good plan is to center this responsibility in another group which is interested in arts and crafts, or is perhaps a specific class in the industrial arts department. Or it could be a division of students from the dramatic department. By working closely with the students planning the assemblies, the background for the assembly can be enhanced and the over-all quality improved.

Types of Programs

Assembly programs serve many purposes—some are traditional in nature, such as observance of special holidays. In some schools assemblies for special holidays are stereotype presentations and hold little interest for the general student body, but they need not be so. A patriotic program might be presented in which the central attraction on the stage might be a huge picture frame. Characters from past history, costumed by their time, might give short speeches which would have been appropriate to them. It could be made evident that our past leaders were concerned with social problems and political issues. Such a program could be made to come alive with proper planning. Likewise, a department of the school could be given a program in which a foreign language could be given the spotlight. The French club could be featured in a cabaret setting with appropriate entertainment.

There is almost no limit to the ideas which creative students under the leadership of a talented teacher can develop. The traditionally dull assemblies featuring awards or honor days could be made interesting and appealing to students. A guiding principle to be followed is that of planning well in advance and making adequate preparations for staging the production. Any innovative school will find little need for professional talent from the outside to present programs if they utilize the talent they have to present programs that probably have more appeal than the "canned programs" which come from the outside.

Administering Assemblies

Since school assemblies are student centered it is appropriate that the presiding officer be a student. It could be the president of the student council, or the president of the senior class, but whoever presides, the faculty advisor should give special attention to advising him on such matters as handling large groups of students, introducing speakers, and announcing programs.

In some schools, the principal chooses to be the presiding officer, but it would be a better plan for him to assume the role of spectator. This does not mean that he should never appear at an assembly; he might well be allotted one full assembly program to make a presentation, providing all students the opportunity to know him and to learn his special concerns.

Seating arrangements sometimes present special problems. In elementary schools and middle schools, it is a good practice to have students seated by grades or classes with teachers seated in the groups. At the secondary level, many schools have found it advantageous to allow students to seek places in the auditorium under the guidance of an ushering committee which is responsible to the student council. Some students, even in the best regulated schools, occasionally violate proper standards of conduct. One very effective treatment for misbehavior is to revoke the privilege of attendance temporarily and to segregate the offenders for a time in an adjoining room where the program can be heard without the opportunity to fully participate. Some schools provide music during student entry and exit, but it is advantageous in any case to adopt regular procedures for administering the assemblies.

Because of the variety of programs provided, advanced notice concerning the content of the program should be provided. It is proper to attempt to establish a mood for viewing the program. Since students are accustomed to hearing radio programs and seeing television programs, they constitute a more sophisticated audience. These programs have the benefit of professional talent and staging, and while school programs cannot always have the same degree of perfection, they can be well accepted for their high quality.

Evaluating Assemblies

One way of maintaining assembly standards at a high level is to make continuous evaluations. The group responsible for the activity should develop a format for appraising each performance; the evaluations should consider stage arrangements, audience reaction, effectiveness of speaking, and the degree to which the purpose of the assembly was accomplished. Evaluations should be preserved for the future use of those responsible for assembly programs.

Clubs

Organized clubs are characteristic of student life from elementary school through college, and exist in adult society as well. Many students who are not interested in other activities find satisfaction in belonging to a club. Through club membership an individual makes new friends, finds people of similar interest, and participates in a common activity. Clubs have been classified as (1) student government and school service, (2) honorary organizations, (3) social and moral clubs, (4) subject matter clubs, (5) publications and journalistic clubs, (6) dramatic clubs and literary societies, (7) musical clubs, and (8) special interest clubs.

Examples of School Clubs

Mathematics and science clubs. With the advances in science and technology, there has been increased interest in study groups which do extensive work in these areas; special projects and research are part of the activity.

Language clubs. These clubs are usually an outcome of study of such foreign languages as Latin, Spanish, French, and German. Practice in using the language, learning songs, listening to tapes or records are all club activities. Very often meals are served which might be typical of a meal produced by the people who speak the language represented by the club.

Current affairs and history clubs. Societal conditions, political issues, and the world situation have interested young people to an extent not reached before. Round table discussions held on issues and visits to governmental units are activities of these clubs. Some have even made trips to visit the United Nations.

Health and physical education. One of the most successful clubs in many schools is the Girls' Athletic Association. Since most schools do not permit participation in interscholastic contests, girls participate freely in an athletic association of their own. For boys, lettermen's clubs exist in many schools and provide social as well as athletic participation.

Clubs and the Curriculum

There are many examples of close relationships between the club and the curriculum. Radio clubs have been formed as a result of the technical aspects of radio in science classes. Rock clubs sometimes emerge from considerations of geologic formations in general science classes. The teaching profession has attempted to recruit competent students to consider teaching as a vocation by encouraging the formation of chapters of the Future Teachers of America. The National Education Association is offering strong sponsorship for this organization in the belief that it represents an excellent way of attracting career teachers. The local chapter of the F.T.A. often assists in remedial programs and provides clerical service to teachers. In some cases, their efforts are comparable to those of employed paraprofessionals.

Basic Considerations Which Affect Clubs

There are many benefits from participation in clubs. The following criteria for judging a club embody the basic problems with which a principal must be concerned.

1. Is the club program headed by a capable sponsor?
2. Are the club offerings varied to meet local needs?
3. Is the program dignified by a definite place in the daily program?
4. Is the club sponsored by competent faculty members—trained, interested, enthusiastic, cooperative?
5. Is membership limited to students of like interests with the ability to profit from the experience?
6. Are self-perpetuating organizations excluded from the sponsored list?
7. Are definite and worthwhile purposes required before a club is chartered and approved?
8. Are offerings limited to local facilities and actual needs?
9. Are all offerings authorized by a local authority?
10. Is there general participation by the student body scheduling the club meeting?

Club programs are gradually becoming part of the daily schedule—either through the regular class periods or, more frequently, through an activity period—rather than being forced to meet after school. If the principal and faculty believe in the educational value of clubs, and if the student council has something to do with chartering clubs, there can be little justification for not providing time for meetings during the school day. The frequency of club meetings varies greatly—the model practice is weekly. The next most common interval is every two weeks. The average length of life of clubs has been found to be five years, but for special interest groups, the average may well be less than half that. This indicates that special interests change from time to time; clubs organized to care for student interests disappear as that interest wanes. Some persons have objected to clubs on the ground that students tend to join those their friends are members of or sponsored by popular teachers, but this objection is not well founded. If the students, at the time of joining activities, do not know one another, they should have an opportunity to become acquainted through the pursuit of common interests and through cooperative effort to the realization of common goals.

The Homeroom

Strictly speaking, the homeroom is not an extracurricular activity, but its organization occupies a fundamental place in the operation of activities. The homeroom is basically a method of accounting for students and assisting the group guidance program, as well as a means of facilitating the administration of the school. In the homeroom, the daily bulletin is read and announcements made. It is here that records of attendance are kept and minor disciplinary problems handled. In many cases, particularly in the elementary grades, the homeroom sponsor teaches a part, or all, of the daily program of the students who are enrolled.

In the homerooms campaigns—such as are periodically sponsored by the yearbook—and drives for the Red Cross or another worthy purpose, such as the sale of activity tickets, may be carried out. Representatives to the student council are elected from the homerooms. The student council representatives, in return, report to the homeroom on the activities of the council—assembly, budget, clubs, corridor traffic, or whatever is discussed by the council.

From the standpoint of extracurricular activities or general school organization, there is no best way to organize homerooms. The prevailing practice is to group students by grade, and scatter them alphabetically.

Many teachers and principals look upon the homeroom as a necessary nuisance. When properly planned for, and when its organization and management contribute to a given student's well being, it can perform a significant role in making the school experience relevant and significant.

Class Organizations

Some school principals feel that a well-organized homeroom system obviates the necessity for grade or class organization. Certainly there are doubts as to the effectiveness of class organization, but if the enrollment is large, the business of the class cannot be carried out efficiently except by committee action. The factor which should determine whether classes are to organize formally is the amount of activity which they are allowed or expected to sponsor. If the class is to sponsor social events, or if there are other activities which need to be cared for, class organizations can be valuable. In addition, such organizations make it possible for more students to hold positions of leadership and receive training in group procedures.

Financial Problems

Most class organizations have some kind of structure for the collection of dues. Some have held that this places too much of a burden on certain students. This is a serious consideration and should be handled in such a manner that no student is embarrassed by the obligation. In some cases, classes participate in money-raising ventures to finance social events, publications, gifts to the school, and trips. While this can be overdone, there are many projects that do not necessarily entail an additional financial burden to the community and which are constructive activities.

Class rings and official clothing for graduation may also constitute an expense to students. Many principals would like to eliminate such purchases, but they find local tradition too strong to discontinue the practice. One means of lowering the cost of class rings and pins that has worked satisfactorily is to adopt standard jewelry that may be purchased at retail stores upon presentation of an identification card by the student.

Honor Societies

Excellence in scholarship has always been given a high priority in most school systems. The first honor society aimed to promote high scholarship in the American secondary schools was Phi Beta Sigma, founded in 1903 at the South Side Academy in Chicago. This society continued when the Academy became a part of the University of Chicago High School in 1904. In 1921 the Department of Secondary School Principals National Education Association founded the National Honor Society, today sponsored by the National Association of Secondary School Principals. Thousands of high schools maintain local chapters and hundreds of thousands of students have become members. There are other national organizations, among which are National Thespians, the National Forensic League, and Quill and Scroll.

Certain commercial firms, in an effort to sell insignia, have conceived the idea of fostering additional organizations which purport to be national in scope. So far none of these have been conspicuously successful, but the effort is a commentary on the effectiveness of the national organizations, particularly the National Honor Society. The advantages that accrue to the school from having a chapter of an honor society are that students with particular talents are given official recognition, and chapter members are often dedicated to render service to worthwhile school endeavors such as assisting in tutorial service, assisting in the library, and so forth.

It is important to establish standards and to develop objective techniques for electing students to honors groups. There have been problems when the student body and parents were given the impression that only conforming students and teacher's pets could be selected. This difficulty can be avoided by spelling out conditions for membership and providing general information concerning selection to those concerned.

Social Activities

While there is probably no school where there is a complete absence of social events sponsored for the students, at the same time, in no school are the social events extensive enough to satisfy the desires of some students and parents. Social affairs may be sponsored by clubs, classes, or other organizations. Some are limited to special groups; others are planned for the entire student body. Activities may include open houses following athletic events, afternoon dances, mothers' teas, father and son nights, semiformal evening parties, costume parties, and so on.

The objectives of the social program center around several aims, among which are (1) to develop poise in social settings; (2) to provide wholesome opportunities for informal associations between members of the opposite sex; (3) to develop good interpersonal and group relations; and (4) to satisfy the recreational needs of children and youth. Social affairs, when properly organized, can increase mutual respect and create favorable attitudes in students of different racial and socioeconomic backgrounds.

Planning School Parties

Parties are more successful if they are planned under the direction of a social committee and sponsored by a member of the faculty. The social committee should conduct affairs of general interest and make suggestions to those in charge of the parties for special groups. For parties to be maximally successful, the age level of those in attendance should be considered, and the activities planned should be sufficiently varied to meet the needs of the participants. If dancing is to be featured for some, games or activities should be planned for those uninterested in dancing.

The committee should also set standards for conducting parties, including such items as decorations, costs within the limits of the funds, and checkups on the return of materials borrowed within the school. Standards for decorum may also be worked out and inaugurated by the social committee. If dancing is to be a featured attraction, opportunity must have been previously provided to learn to dance through the physical education classes or during the noon hour.

School policies relating to dances need to be carefully determined in advance. Standards for invitations, dress, decorations, chaperons, pay for the orchestra, opening and closing hours, leaving the dance, and the building in which the dance is to be held must be thought out and announced in advance.

The problem of guests who are not enrolled in the school is always a difficult one. In small communities, the intermingling of out-of-school youth and students may have some plausible reason, but in an urban area it can become a difficult situation. In either case, supervision is more difficult, even though invitations have been approved in advance. In general since the difficulties outweigh the benefits, many schools do not approve out-of-school guests.

Students in many communities are cooperating with adults in establishing youth centers and providing recreational opportunities for young people. Square dancing has become a popular activity in some of these centers. Such opportunities are particularly advantageous for those who are ill at ease with members of the opposite sex, and square dancing places the emphasis upon group activity rather than upon the couple. Furthermore, less popular and less attractive young people may find it easier to secure partners in the square dance setting.

Additional Considerations

Parties at the elementary level and at the middle school division are probably best held in the afternoon. This arrangement is not always pleasing to them, but it has much to recommend it. Secondary school functions often take place in the evening, although informal mixers may take place in the afternoon. If parties are held in the evening, a reasonable closing hour should be established and parents should be informed of it.

School parties should be held in the school building, although some functions, such as picnics, cannot ordinarily be held on the school grounds. If social affairs are held away from the school, the question of cost, dangers to be encountered, and the like should be carefully considered and discussed with the prospective participants in light of recommendations of the social committee. They must also see that the plan is carried out "until the last cup is washed and put away."

Speech and Dramatics

Debate

Debate as an activity was among the first to be used by educational institutions. It later became less popular because teachers who specialized in speech felt that debating often tended to develop superficiality, insincerity, and glibness. And in some cases the desire to win was so heavily emphasized that it was not uncommon to find debate coaches writing set speeches and planning rebuttals to such an extent that the students did very little except to repeat what the coaches had prepared. Modern methods of training sponsors have eliminated many such problems with coaches, and debate is again playing a prominent role in many school activity programs. Experience as a member of the debate team is considered valuable in preparing for an active role in citizenship, and is extremely helpful to those who find satisfaction in politics. The National Forensic League has been a constructive force in developing good programs for debate.

Speaking Contests

Many national organizations have organized contests for students of school age. While it would be a mistake to use the entire time of a speech club to prepare for one event, it is possible to make such a club effective by providing broad experience in all types of presentations. The custom of having students memorize dramatic, oratorical, or humorous selections and polish them under the direction of a coach so that they may excel in interscholastic competition has little to recommend it.

Extemporaneous speaking provides excellent training, because in preparation students read widely, usually on contemporary affairs, then shortly before the performance draw topics by lot and give a brief speech. This procedure gives excellent training in organization and presentation. It should be emphasized that speech activities should be used for developing effective speakers for all situations, not just for those designed to win contests—although a contest may be a suitable motivating activity.

Dramatics

Children of all ages enjoy dramatics, whether the performances are impromptu or planned. While it is desirable to feature the best actors in "star" productions for the public, it is also desirable to provide opportunities for those who wish to participate and to learn acting techniques. There are many opportunities for the dramatics club to make appearances, such as short plays for assemblies, activity meetings, noon time entertainment, and community meetings, as well as more formal presentations for the school and public.

More than acting is involved in dramatics. Groups must plan and manage lights and properties. Another group must take care of printing and distributing tickets and account for the proceeds to the business office. In some schools it is customary to have two casts for all major productions; if two performances are planned, this method allows everyone in both casts to participate. It also prevents postponement of the production in case of illness of a participant shortly before the performance.

Participation in dramatics is a wholesome activity and should be made available to all interested students. Meetings should be scheduled so that members of music and athletic groups have an opportunity to participate. Such an arrangement reduces the stigma that arises when only star actors are chosen for the leading roles in productions. And it is possible to plan activities for the entire year.

Members of a dramatics club could be divided into various groups who are assigned to specific objectives. These groups could be: (1) a play reading group in which suitable plays of different length and type would be studied for their suitability; (2) a play acting group in the process of rehearsing for the production; (3) a make-up group, which would be receiving practice in the use of "creating characters" to play various roles; (4) a business group, which would concern itself with techniques of ticket selling, printed program production, and advertising; (5) a scene and properties group, which would study stage sets, costuming, and lighting. By providing students with experience in all these areas, many worthwhile learning experiences are available, and such experience makes the job of the play coach easier. Students come to understand, too, that dramatics involve more than acting.

To be most effective, dramatic programs should be continuous and representative of the experiences provided. Planning the program for the year in order that definite times for performances are included in the school calendar is advisable. Any year's program could include such types of performances as a classical play, a comedy, a musical show, a talent night, and an evening of one act plays. The value of such a schedule could be the development of aesthetic appreciation, effective cooperation with the music department, recognition of individual talent through individual or group performance, and extensive possibilities for wide participation.

Some schools have failed to promote dramatic activities because of the lack of facilities. While a good auditorium equipped for flexible stage arrangements is desirable, it is possible to have a good program without such a facility. Many schools—even those with a modern auditorium— use the theatre-in-the-round concept. Performances can also be given in areas that seat no more than 100 spectators, thus making use of cafeterias, study halls, or rooms accommodating large student groups. The dramatics coach should be sufficiently competent to adapt a presentation to this type of setting.

The selection of plays sometimes constitutes a problem for schools. The coach of the play and the students, with the advice of the principal, should consider the suitability of a play in the light of community standards and backgrounds. There are some national organizations including the National Thespians which assist in promoting and improving dramatic presentations.

Music

In many schools music activities have been placed on the time schedule and credit is given toward graduation for membership in the group. Even in such schools, time is spent in activities outside of regular music classes. There may be a music appreciation club, dance bands, a woodwind sextet, a bugle corps, and many other special groups. Most schools are moving toward a point of view which regards music as an experience for a very large percentage or, if possible, for all of the students enrolled in the school. The cost of participating in music activities constitutes a problem to many students; instruments, music, supplies, uniforms or special dress, and transportation are all expensive. Moreover, practice time may prevent students from working for money.

Individuals and organizations in music frequently receive invitations to perform in public. Such appearances provide the school with an opportunity to build goodwill in the community, as well as to provide valuable services. The music program should be planned to produce favorable attitudes on the part of the community, but this does not mean that only the most talented students should perform. Adults are interested in efforts of young people in the process of developing.

Music Contests

Contest participation for musical organizations has sometimes resulted in interference with the development of a broad type of program. In general, contests are less desirable than music festivals, where groups from various schools play together, and are not judged on a competitive basis. Special types of festivals include not only band and large instrumental groups, but also vocal groups, solos, ensembles, string groups, and other combinations.

Need for Direction

Music groups are sometimes asked to provide background music or to provide selections at conventions and conferences. If this practice is followed, the group should have an opportunity to perform when the audience has been assembled and ready to give full attention to the performance. Likewise, many community groups often make last minute calls for band programs or choral presentations as an afterthought to give variety to their projects. It is the principal who must give protection to the school musical organizations in these matters.

School Publications

In many schools journalism has become a major activity. A variety of publications, used not just for purposes of communication, provides a means for students to experience seeing their literary contributions in print. In some cases, graphic arts classes become involved in printing the school's publications. Careful consideration should be given this activity in order to avoid difficulties.

The School Newspaper

School newspapers range from daily newspapers published in the printshop and written by the newswriting class to simple publications written by members of the class and produced in a manuscript edition. Between these extremes are the mimeographed paper issued irregularly or infrequently, the column or page in the local community paper, and the weekly school paper. In the lower grades, an informal paper may be read to students or written on the blackboard by the teacher. The cost of these publications varies from almost nothing to several thousand dollars.

The Purpose of the School Paper

The purpose of the paper is to meet the needs of the students within the school, and is also a valuable source of information for the community. It should publish news items concerning the various departments of the school using short stories, essays, and editorials. Most papers also provide space for the views of individual students.

The school paper represents an avenue for producing high morale, for making students aware of the school's activities and operation, and for making the school come alive to both students and parents. Forward looking schools use the newspaper, adequately covering school affairs, and in a wholesome fashion, to create a favorable public opinion. Because vulgar language, gossip items, and rumors have no place in the paper, censorship becomes an important consideration. This is usually not a problem when the students have been in a class in newswriting where in-depth consideration is given to reporting and newswriting. Where this is the case, the sponsor will experience little difficulty and the principal will never need to serve as censor.

In schools where strong censorship is exercised, the newspaper is likely to be considered as a tool of the administration and not a medium for expressing student ideas. The general rule to follow is that of holding to the normal rules for responsible journalism. When this is not done, an "underground press" may develop. Many principals have resorted to extreme measures in prohibiting this type of publication, but such action is not recommended. It is fairly well-established that such publications cannot be banned when the normal rules for journalism are observed. However, it is possible to restrict the time and place of distribution.[3]

Many schools have used a class in English, newswriting, or journalism to sponsor the school newspaper. This practice has much to recommend it because the teacher is usually well-qualified to give expert advice and to create favorable attitudes toward the purposes of the paper. In some cases, a class in the business department cooperates in the handling of the financial side of the publication. Whatever method is used, the direction given to publications cannot be half-hearted or be given by people who have little knowledge of the field.

---

[3]Robert L Ackerly, *The Reasonable Exercise of Authority* (Washington, D.C.: The National Association of Secondary School Principals, 1969), p. 17.

Considerable assistance to newspapers can be obtained from national agencies; among the oldest of these is the Columbia Scholastic Press. Some universities also specialize in furnishing expert evaluation of publications. A publications sponsor should utilize such agencies as sources both for effecting improvement and for setting up high but attainable standards.

The Annual or Yearbook

The yearbook is usually a considerable undertaking, and is found almost entirely in senior high schools, sometimes the work of a class in the English department. In the past these publications were printed by letterpress, but photo-offset is being used more and more. Although detail may be lost in the pictures, photo-offset permits greater variety of layout for the available money. Such publications, often costing several thousand dollars, are of course impossible to produce except in schools where a large number of subscribers may be secured. Many school administrators have opposed the annual because of its cost and because they have felt that it is just another book. But it has been shown that high school graduates prize their annuals highly and refer to them frequently for a few, or occasionally more, years after graduation.

Since annuals are desirable memory books and historical records, the main objection raised against them is their cost, but this objection can be met satisfactorily if the school wishes to do so. Small schools have produced inexpensively mimeographed annuals with snapshots of seniors and important events. The cost of yearbooks is dependent almost entirely on the number of pages and the number of photoengravings, and both of these factors are subject to control. A stock cover, rather than one prepared for a particular annual, will also reduce cost.

Solicitation of advertising in school annuals is a very undesirable practice, since the money secured is really a donation. Allowing students to solicit this so-called advertising for the yearbook is equivalent to giving approval to begging. It therefore seems desirable to produce inexpensive annuals whenever at all feasible, since the annual is an historical record prized by the graduates, and its planning and publication offer opportunities for splendid educative experiences. One safeguard with respect to quality is the practice of submitting the yearbook to a national agency for evaluation.

The Handbook

Handbooks are ordinarily published by the school in an effort to assist new students in becoming acquainted with school opportunities and procedures, as well as to review them for students who are already enrolled. Some of the handbooks are used as a basic reference in orientation or core courses for first year students.

Handbooks are made in a variety of sizes, from the popular pocket size to the 8½-by-11-inch size. They may be mimeographed or reproduced by a lithographic process. They may be revamped and issued each year, or a supplement may be issued annually, while the complete book is revised only every three to five years. Such items as school organization, program of studies, school song, cheers, attendance regulations, directory of the building, lunchroom regulations, history and traditions of the school, and use of the library are usually found in the handbook. In addition, the principal may want to include other items he considers pertinent. Frequently, the handbook is sponsored by the student council.

Sometimes a student directory is included with the handbook; if this is done care should be taken to ensure that those who do not wish their names and addresses to appear are given the option. In some cases, commercial agencies have obtained such handbooks and used them for purposes unrelated to school matters.

The handbook is usually financed through sale to students at a small price. But since the purpose of the handbook is to orient students, at least one copy should be issued to every student without charge. Where the student council has funds, they may underwrite the cost of publication. In other cases, the board of education may pay for the handbook.

Intramural Sports

It is natural and normal for young people to play. Few deny that there are benefits to be derived from properly developed and carefully supervised intramural and interscholastic athletic competition. But many school principals have felt that intramural athletics are much more valuable than interscholastic programs, since they do not attract so much attention, and in addition offer the possibility of greater student participation. Others are equally emphatic in asserting the superior values of interscholastic sports. The different manner in which the programs are administered in the individual school probably accounts for the disagreement.

The Program of Participation in Intramurals

The program of intramural sports has developed almost entirely since 1925 and is now quite extensively employed in the American schools. It is not at all unusual to find 75 percent of the boys and girls in a junior high school, or more than 50 percent of the total enrollment in a senior high school, engaged in one or more parts of the intramural athletic program. The most common sports included in junior high school programs are basketball, field and track, and baseball. Tackle football is not generally approved at a junior high school level unless very careful efforts are made to see that the teams are evenly graded as to weight and that complete protective equipment is furnished. In the senior high school, the same sports are common, but tennis gains in popularity, as does golf. For girls, basketball and volleyball are the most frequently played sports, but tennis, field hockey, and softball are gaining in popularity.

There has been the opinion among educators that sports should be developed which have a carryover to adult life; however, the nature of the adolescent does not make this entirely possible. The more active and competitive sports appeal to adolescents, although in some schools it is possible to encourage horseback riding or swimming, and in certain regions skating and other outdoor winter sports are popular. Fly casting, horseshoe pitching, social dancing, archery, hiking, and other sports are possibilities for both individuals and groups. Each school must develop a program which fits the needs of its location, facilities, and student population.

Administering Intramural Sports

The most frequent basis for selecting pupils for participation in intramural athletics is enrollment in a particular grade. Other frequently used bases are enrollment in physical education, enrollment in homerooms, height, weight, and age. Each of these bases can be defended, but the main purpose of any grouping in intramurals is to arrange groups which are nearly equal, so that close competition may result. The exponent system by which age, weight, and height are given separate values in determining student classification for intramural sports has much to recommend it.

Financing Intramural Sports

Ordinarily intramural sports are financed by the board of education out of funds for physical education activities, because the intramural sports program is considered an extension of the physical education program. Infrequently, the support for intramural programs, particularly if football is included, comes from the interscholastic program. There is also a tendency for support of intramurals from the board of education in larger and more forward-looking schools.

In those schools where the interscholastic program is financially successful and the board of education funds have not as yet been secured, there is every reason to use the interscholastic funds to underwrite the cost of intramurals. In other schools, where the student council has legislative control of the funds, it is possible to secure some of the available funds through the student council.

Relation to Physical Education

It has been stated before, and is reemphasized here, that the relationship between intramurals and physical education should be close, with each strengthening the other. Skills, knowledge, and attitudes acquired in physical education can be used and made permanent through the intramural program, while the benefits of the sports program motivate work in physical education for both boys and girls. In turn, those who prove to be star performers in the intramural program can ultimately gravitate to the interscholastic program, which then becomes the crown of the athletic-intramural program. The intramural program in most schools exists for those who are interested in the activities, but they do not, nor should they, exist as training exercises for the interscholastic squads. The proper articulation between interscholastic, intramural athletics, physical education, and health work needs to be developed even further by properly trained staff members who have had training in all phases of the program, so that all parts of it receive equal emphasis.

Supervision of Play Activities

There is a definite trend in elementary schools toward supervising the play periods rather than allowing the noon recess and after school hours to be used for free play. In most schools it is necessary to use the regular classroom teachers to supervise play activities either for their classroom group or to take charge of all groups in rotation. It is the principal's duty to build a favorable sentiment among the regular teachers toward the supervised play period. But a more satisfactory program results when competent physical education teachers are employed to direct both the instructional activities in the gymnasium and the supervised play periods. Such arrangements have been made in a number of schools and will no doubt continue to increase in number.

With the recent emphasis upon the necessity of allowing teachers more planning time, the tendency in this area has been to use paraprofessionals for such matters as playground direction and supervision. When the rules of the board of education approve such a practice, it is highly desirable to use this type of supervision.

Intramural and Interscholastic Contests in Elementary Schools

Free play and intramural sports are being used increasingly as part of a program for good mental hygiene in children at all levels. With such a conception comes the obligation on the part of the administration for introducing as large a percentage of pupils as possible to participation. Intramurals are usually restricted to pupils in the fourth grade and above; segregation of sexes is made above the age of ten. There is, however, some experimentation going on with mixed play groups at higher age levels. It is entirely possible that such a program could become popular.

Interscholastic athletic contests are more popular than are intramural contests in elementary schools. Baseball, basketball, and track are the most popular sports. The fact that these sports are sponsored does not prove that they are more desirable than intramural activities.

Opinion is divided as to whether interscholastic activities are appropriate below the senior high school level. While it is possible that intramural sports can furnish all the competition necessary below high school, some elementary schools and many middle schools do have interscholastic competition. In such cases schools should see to it that the equipment is of high quality and that the pupils are under the direction of a coach with a sincere concern for the welfare of his athletes.

Because of the rapid physiological changes which occur as children grow, particularly in the circulatory system of the body, care should be taken to see that overexertion does not occur. Omitting exhausting interscholastic competition will help safeguard the health of elementary and junior high school children. Interscholastic tournaments to determine the best individual or team are not uncommon in the elementary schools, but such contests are likely to be even more strenuous and undesirable than interscholastic contests. A far more desirable practice is to initiate a play day when children from the community, and adults too, may come together for mass participation in athletic games, stunts, and rhythms. No individual or team championships need be determined; everyone may participate in activities which appeal to him and which are best suited to his needs.

It is just as important that intramural games at the elementary school level be as well officiated as at any other level so that the spirit of good sportsmanship may be developed among the participants. The principal, or the director of intramural athletics and physical education, if there is one, should develop a competent, voluntary, nonpaid staff of officials. Ordinarily these could come from the faculty or from nearby secondary schools where competent performers in the intramural program can be secured and taught to officiate properly.

Interscholastic Athletic Contests

Athletic contests are the most spectacular member of the extracurricular family. Crowds estimated as large as 100,000 persons have attended most of the high school championship football games in Chicago. The number of people who attend the finals of a state basketball championship tournament is many times limited only by the size of the gymnasium or the auditorium in which the contest is held. And in many schools it is literally true that interscholastic athletics is "big business." Under such conditions it is inevitable that abuses and infractions of desirable practices should occur. At the outset let us say that interscholastic athletic competition for girls is not generally encouraged. Only a few smaller schools allow such programs.

Administration of Interscholastic Athletics

Public high schools participate extensively in tournaments, in addition to regularly scheduled contests. National tournaments for public high schools are no longer held, and there is a feeling among high school administrators that state tournaments, or championship contests, should not be held. State football championships are being eliminated by many high school athletic associations in those regions where weather conditions have not already done so. But state championship contests in basketball are likely to continue for some time, because the receipts are needed to finance the activities of the state associations. Until schools are willing to tax themselves instead of those who attend the state basketball tournaments, tournaments will continue. When tournaments are played in large centers of population, they may become sources of interest to "sporting" elements and gamblers. This attention is as unfortunate as it is unwanted, for sooner or later it is certain to result in some unpleasantness, if not outright scandal.

In place of state-wide contests, district or league tournaments or championships are being held more frequently. They are less expensive in school time, distance to be traveled, and physical strain to participants. All high schools now belong to a state high school athletic association or to the High School Activities Association, which imposes stringent regulations and generally provides an insurance program to insure students against injury.

State associations have made notable changes in the administration of athletics during the last three decades. They have adopted eligibility rules concerning age, scholarship, and residence, eliminated undesirable practices, required a strict physical examination so as to protect the health of the participants, and raised the conduct of interscholastic sports from the disreputable status formerly existing in some schools to an almost universally respected condition. State associations are also evaluating the services of officials and recommending proper fees. The evaluation and compilation of a list of competent certified officials is one of the services which will do much to further the tone of athletic contests. Competent officiating, based on examination and evaluation, is indispensable in developing proper attitudes among the players, friendly attitudes among schools, and tolerance on the part of spectators.

Interscholastic Relations

In general, high school boys exhibit good sportsmanship to rival teams and individuals, but some administrators practice sportsmanship on a much lower level. In schools which endeavor to secure wholesome interscholastic relations, good results usually follow.

Treating the visiting teams as guests and meeting them on arrival, arranging tours through the city, lunch with the home team after the game, and other courtesies have been used to advantage. School assemblies, at which the matter of proper conduct at games is explained or dramatized, also proves helpful. Even in communities where good sportsmanship is practiced by the students, it is not unusual to find that the adults exhibit poor sportsmanship. Probably the most effective way of developing proper attitudes among the adults is through the students, through direct contact with parents in conversation, or through printed or duplicated statements which describe the aims of the program and the ways in which adults may help foster them.

If proper relationships can be established through the press, it should prove helpful in securing better sportsmanship from adults. Incidentally, good press relationships will prevent overemphasis on the exploits of star athletes and will tend to keep the stars from evaluating themselves so highly that it causes trouble.

The problem of judging the success of the school in terms of athletic victories is a difficult one. It is not unusual to find that coaches are hired and fired on the basis of their ability to promote winning teams. Successful coaches have, in some instances, been rewarded with administrative positions because of their success. While many coaches have become successful principals or superintendents, coaching service and success do not prepare a person for the professional duties of either of these offices. In some instances constituted administrative officers have been dismissed because their ideals of the conduct and administration of interscholastic athletics did not coincide with the community's desire for winning teams. A strong extracurricular program and continuous growth of the kind of school news which school patrons wish to hear about a school should help to overcome the tendency to judge the success of the school only in terms of interscholastic athletic victories.

Safety in participation in athletics is a problem which cannot be overlooked. The following suggestions are basic to safeguarding students from injury in interscholastic athletics:

1. Well-trained coaches who are more interested in the welfare of boys than in winning games should be employed.
2. Adequate and properly fitted equipment should be provided for all who practice for participation—if such equipment cannot be furnished, the sport should be abandoned.
3. The school should be large enough to furnish an adequate number of

reserves. For schools which are too small to permit regular football, six-man teams have been found useful.

4. Under no conditions should games be played unless conditions are safe. Playing football on frozen ground has no place in high school athletics.

5. Adequate training periods should precede the scheduled event—ordinarily at least three weeks of practice is advisable.

6. A sufficient number of competent officials adds to the safety with which athletic contests may be conducted.

7. School administrators should seek fair competition—ordinarily small schools should not compete with large schools, either to receive large financial returns or to increase the prestige of the school.

Most schools now provide insurance programs against injuries, so that boys whose parents are poor can afford to participate in sports. Unfortunately, not all schools finance this protection from school funds or from the income of athletic contests. The insurance should be provided without cost to the individual concerned.

Other Activities

It is impossible to describe all the activities found in today's schools. Any program for the local school should be designed to fit activities to extend the interest and experience of its students in many ways. Some sponsor excursions to places both near and far. Other schools have made wise use of other community organizations to benefit the local school population.

Tours and Out-of-School Experiences

It is increasingly common for students to make trips to visit some educational activity or to make a longer tour to visit other schools, industrial enterprises, or perhaps the national capitol in Washington, D.C. Such excursions are planned to motivate, supplement, and vitalize the curriculum; to develop desirable character traits; and to provide an opportunity to satisfy the urge to travel. The school trip should be the result of a need on the part of some class or group.

Trips can be made by private automobile, bus, train, or airplane. If a trip is to be of any great length, it is necessary to secure parental and community support. It should also have the approval of the board of education, and adequate insurance provided to care for any emergencies. Types of trips are: (1) the bus trip within the radius of the community; (2) longer trips to other communities or schools; (3) camping trips; (4) trips for the purpose of making music presentations; and (5) trips of historical significance. The principal should be aware of the school's responsibilities for any of these excursions and should organize the trip with the thought of providing proper safeguards and chaperonage.

Cooperation with Other Agencies

Many communities have organizations to assist in promoting wholesome activities for youth. Among these are the American Junior Red Cross, the Boy Scouts, the Girl Scouts, Camp Fire Girls, 4-H Club, Future Homemakers of America and the Hi-Y Club. While the list is not inclusive it is representative of the many organizations that have appeal to youth. It is the responsibility of the principal to cooperate in the interest of the welfare of the students, and to see that the activities conform to the purposes of the school program.

In recent years, student groups have cooperated with other agencies in such matters as conservation, beautification, ecology, and the like. Participation in such ventures represents a good learning experience and prepares students for accepting responsibilities for mature citizenship.

The discussion of representative programs indicates steady growth in the orderly management of school activities. Informal and formal organizations, such as state high school activities associations, set standards or offer suggestions for improvement. As the activities program has become an integral part of the school's offering for young people, it was inevitable and desirable that standards should be set and programs improved, and there is every reason to believe that representative programs will be improved and extended in the coming years.

Selected References

"Administrator's Forum: Problem; Student Editor Charges Unfair Censorship," *School Management*, 13 (December 1969), 144.

ARMSTRONG, R. L., "Student Council: Whither Goest Thou?" *Clearing House*, 44 (May 1970), 553–55.

BIXLER, F. M., "What Is a Good High School Newspaper?" *English Journal*, 59 (January 1970), 119–21.

DIVOKY, D., "Underground or Independent High School Press," *Catholic School Journal*, 70 (February 1970), 16.

GORTON, RICHARD A., "Student Activism in the High School: The Underground Newspaper and Student Dress and Appearance," *High School Journal*, 53 (April 1970), 411–16.

GREENWALD, M., "Junior-High Production of the School Yearbook," *School Shop*, 29 (November 1969), 47–48.

"Guidelines for the Appraisal of Travel-Study Tours for Secondary School Students," *National Association of Secondary School Principals Bulletin,* 54 (November 1970), 116–22.

HIXSON, CHALMER G., *The Administration of Interscholastic Athletics.* New York: J. L. Pratt, 1967.

HOFFMAN, K. E., "Suggestions for a Young Marketer Program," *American Vocational Journal,* 44 (October 1969), 54–55.

HOLLAND, R. G., "High School Press Revisited," *College and University Journal,* 9 (Spring 1970), 31–34.

"How Free Should the High School Press Be?" *Today's Education,* 58 (September 1969), 52–54.

HUNDLEY, E. J., "Community School and Hospital Future Nurse Endeavor: North Shore High School Future Nurses' Program," *Journal of School Health,* 40 (June 1970), 291–92.

Joint Committee on Physical Education and Athletics of the American Association for Health, Physical Education, and Recreation, the National Collegiate Athletic Association, and the National College Physical Education Association for Men, "Professional Preparation of the Administrator of Athletics," *JOHPER,* 41 (September 1970), 20–23.

KLEINDIENST, VIOLA K., and ARTHUR WESTON, *Intramural and Recreation Programs for School and Colleges.* New York: Appleton-Century-Crofts, 1964.

LAVENBURG, JACK, "An Analysis of a Student Council Workshop As a Training Institution for High School Leaders," *Educational Leadership: Research Supplement,* 3 (January 1970), 385–88.

MCCURDY, D. W., "Student Commons in High School: Why Not?" *Education,* 89 (February 1969), 215–16.

MCGIFFIN, VIDA B., and ORISSA FROST KINGSBURG, *Creating the Yearbook, School, College, University.* New York: Hastings House Publishers, Inc., 1962.

MCGUIRE, T. C., "Help Your Student Council Justify Its Existence," *Journal of Secondary Education,* 45 (April 1970), 152–54.

National Conference on Intramurals, Michigan State University, *Intramurals for Elementary Children, School and Community Programs for Grades Four, Five, and Six.* Chicago: Athletic Institute, Publishing Division, 1964.

National Conference on Intramurals, Michigan State University, *Intramurals for the Junior High School.* Chicago: Athletic Institute, Publishing Division, 1964.

National Conference on Intramurals, Michigan State University, *Intramurals for the Senior High School.* Chicago: Athletic Institute, Publishing Division, 1964.

"Sanctioned Critics: New Responsibility for Underground Papers," *Nation's Schools,* 84 (September 1969), 43.

SCHMIDT, E., "Needed Now: Truly Representative Student Councils," *New York State Education*, 57 (January 1970), 4–6.

SCHWERTLEY, D. F., "Little League Can Hurt Kids," *Today's Education*, 59 (May 1970), 40–41.

SOLBERG, J. R., "Interscholastic Athletics: Tail That Wags the Dog?" *Journal of Secondary Education*, 45 (May 1970), 238–39.

"Student Major Clubs Chartered by AAHPER," *JOHPER*, 41 (May 1970), 83.

SULLIVAN, R. J., "Overrated Threat: What to Do about Underground Newspapers," *National Association of Secondary School Principals Bulletin*, 53 (September 1969), 36–44.

VAN POOL, G. M., "Student Council Crisis," *Momentum*, 1 (April 1970), 56–59.

WAGONER, J. L., JR., et al., "Student Relationships and Activities in Desegregated Schools," *High School Journal*, 54 (December 1970), 188–201.

WEBER, L. J., "Inequities in Athletics," *Clearing House*, 45 (November 1970), 177–80.

YUHASZ, L. S., L. SPRING, and R. BECKER, "Dance for Sixth Graders," *Instructor*, 79 (June 1970), 13.

16

Teacher Personnel Problems

Just as the school's major function is to provide learning experiences for children and youth, so administration's major function becomes one of selecting and developing professional personnel. This has always presented a difficult problem at all levels of education, but now in light of new developments in teaching techniques and changed societal conditions, the task of staffing is more challenging than ever. In addition, planning for continuing career development for new staff members as well as for those already on the faculty is a major concern.

Teacher Supply and Demand

In pioneer times the teacher was a person who took up teaching almost as a last resort occupation or as a part-time vocation. Dissatisfaction with the quality of education caused public leaders to recognize the importance of a supply of teachers properly prepared for teaching as a profession.

Massachusetts was the first state to establish a publicly supported normal school for the professional preparation of teachers. Opened at Lexington in 1839, the Lexington Normal School provided one year of training, including a comprehensive review of the common branches of learning; instruction in advanced subjects, such as mathematics, bookkeeping, general history, natural philosophy, and astronomy; training of a professional character in the principles of piety and morality; instruction in the science and art of teaching; and supervised practice in a model school.

371

Between 1839 and the Civil War, twelve such schools were established in eight different states. By 1885 a total of 117 public normal schools had been established in thirty-four states with thirty-six private schools distributed through eighteen states.

Until the past two or three decades teacher training was centered in public and private colleges and normal schools organized for the specific purpose of preparing students for teaching. This is no longer the case since these institutions have tended to become more concerned with liberal arts. And most colleges and universities have added departments of colleges of education. In fact, institutions that do not offer complete teacher preparation programs do offer courses in education for students who plan teaching careers. Many community colleges, for example, do offer such courses.

Teacher Supply

At the present time there appears to be a surplus of teachers. A survey made in 1970 reported the general conditions for forty-nine of the fifty states as follows:[1] (1) some shortage of applicants in two states; (2) in thirty-five states, some shortage of applicants in certain subject areas and an excess in others; (3) a sufficient supply of applicants to fill positions in seven states; (4) one state, some excess of applicants; and (5) a substantial excess of applicants in four states.

There were expected to be 114,390 elementary school teachers and 167,802 prospective secondary school teachers completing at least their bachelor's degrees in time for entry into the teaching profession for the 1971 session.[2] While data for 1961 revealed that 53,634 students became eligible for teaching certificates at the elementary level and 85,427 qualified for teaching in secondary schools.[3] The increase during the past has obviously been considerable.

The various states that supplied information concerning the teacher supply for the year 1970–71 also reported that they had had extreme difficulties in filling positions in the following areas: elementary librarians, special education, industrial arts, remedial reading, speech correction, teaching the educationally disadvantaged, girls physical and health education, and mathematics. Sixty-seven large school systems surveyed at the same time indicated similar difficulties.[4]

Not all of the teacher education students become available for teach-

---

[1] Research Division, National Education Association, *Teacher Supply and Demand in Public Schools*, (Washington, D.C.: The Association, 1970), p. 7.

[2] NEA, *Teacher Supply and Demand*, p. 8.

[3] NEA, *Teacher Supply and Demand*, p. 5.

[4] NEA, *Teacher Supply and Demand*, p. 7.

ing positions; the number who actually enter directly into teaching in the subsequent session after they qualify has been from 74.1 to 83.2 percent for elementary teachers and from 62.3 to 69.2 percent for secondary school teachers during the past ten years.[5] Determining the teacher supply is further complicated by the fact that there are large numbers of teachers who reenter teaching after leaves of absence or other reasons.

Teacher Demand

The demand for teachers in the United States is the number of vacancies to be filled in a given year, but such figures do not include the number needed to replace unqualified teachers or the number needed to relieve the overcrowding that is still typical in many school systems. According to estimates, 95,800 elementary and 105,300 secondary, or a total of 201,100 teachers were needed to satisfy the demand for the school year 1970–71. The Research Division of the National Education Association has estimated that 446,500 teachers would be needed under a "Quality Criterion Estimate." In other words, to create a desirable educational climate for all children, almost twice the number of positions are needed.[6]

There are several factors which should be considered in estimating teacher demand in a particular school. Among these are (1) rate of turnover, (2) teacher load, (3) class size, (4) special services offered, and (5) type of staff organization. The problem of matching supply and demand throughout the profession is further complicated by other factors. One of these factors is that the positions to be filled and the persons qualified to fill them may not be in the same geographic or employment area, that a considerable number of those eligible have other employment goals, and that salaries may not be at a competitive level.

Impact of Teacher Supply

For many years, there was a shortage of teachers, which resulted in employment of substandard teachers to fill vacancies. In addition, the problem of teacher turnover has even in normal times caused some difficulties. Such matters as salary schedules, tenure, working conditions, and community attitudes bring about turnover, but the inadequate supply of teachers is the major reason. As long as demand greatly exceeds the supply, a strong competition for competent teachers will exist and will keep the rate of turnover much higher than is conducive to the best interests of the school and the teaching profession.

The teacher surplus situation has not been present long enough to

---

[5]NEA, *Teacher Supply and Demand*, p. 8.
[6]NEA, *Teacher Supply and Demand*, p. 33.

make definite predictions as to its effects on schools and the profession. However, it is possible to make some assessment of what is likely to occur. First, a surplus of teachers will make it unnecessary to employ candidates with substandard preparation. Second, the opportunity to employ fully qualified teachers should bring positive benefits to school systems and to students in particular. Third, there may be efforts to employ beginning teachers for the first year on an intern basis. While such teachers would be fully qualified for certification, the teaching load could be lightened during the first year, and more supervision provided to further career development. Fourth, it appears that there would be less teacher turnover. With more competition for existing vacancies, there is less likelihood of change for the mere sake of change.

Fifth, institutions accepting teacher education students will have an opportunity to establish higher standards for admission. In the past, there had been a feeling that youth who could not meet the requirements of schools of engineering, medicine, and science were acceptable in teacher training. This should not be true when the supply is sufficient to meet the demand. Finally, the profession will be urged to exert more influence in determining teacher education programs and in deciding upon standards for teacher certification. It may also be necessary for the profession to take a strong stand to counter efforts that may be made in some areas to prevent further up-grading of salaries. If teaching is to maintain definite professional status, salaries must be kept in line with the requirements for training and experience. Professional associations will undoubtedly be aware of their responsibility in this matter.

Teacher Supply in the Future

In the past the number of young people who desired to pursue teaching as a career was insufficient. There should be some effort to encourage men to enter the teaching profession, because there are no differences in teaching effectiveness based on sex differences. Even though salaries are improving, there is still an inadequate number of men teachers, particularly at the elementary level. Since 1961–62, the available statistics show that men have represented less than half of the number of persons expected to complete teacher education at the secondary level.[7] The number at the elementary level would be an even lower figure.

While the state and the profession itself can do much to recruit promising young people for the teaching profession, principals and teachers share the responsibility for providing information pertaining to the advantages of teaching. Future teacher organizations give opportunities to students to become acquainted with what is entailed in the profession.

---

[7]NEA, *Teacher Supply and Demand*, p. 17.

Many of the frustrations that formerly made teaching unattractive are disappearing. There are fewer economic problems and better social conditions for teachers. Higher education institutions can contribute by raising standards for admission, improving the curriculums, and stressing innovative instructional techniques.

The general public seems to have become aware of the necessity for good teachers and improved educational techniques. The principal and his teaching staff, through their contacts with pupils and school patrons, can do much to improve public opinion toward teaching and to provide young people with an unbiased view of the opportunities and satisfying experiences of a teaching career.

Staffing the School

Most large school systems and many smaller ones have established personnel departments to facilitate recruitment and selection of teachers. This process represents a year round operation; recruiting is no longer a seasonal matter. Personnel departments collect data on potential candidates for positions, visit teacher training institutions, arrange for interviews, recommend for appointments, and prepare contracts when final selection has been approved. In the larger systems, a pool of teachers is made available from which each principal may make his selection. In smaller systems the local principal may have the responsibility for the entire process.

Locating Candidates

Most institutions that offer teacher training programs also maintain placement bureaus which are organized to provide services to school systems in need of teachers. It is common for a recruiter from a school personnel office or a member of the administrative staff to visit the placement office to discuss vacancies and to interview prospective candidates. If the recruiter does not have the authority to do the hiring, he may invite the likely candidates to make a trip to the local system for final interviews. Another method of locating candidates that is often overlooked is the existing staff of the local school. In many cases, local staff members know of good teachers in other areas and they would be happy to assist in recruiting them.

Administrators who have vacancies to be filled should provide position specifications describing the vacancies. Specifications should include such matters as training required, personal qualifications, responsibilities, experience, and so forth. Placement offices can render more effective service if such information is provided along with notifications of vacancies.

Collecting Information

The use of application blanks in securing information about prospective teachers is virtually universal. The application blank is usually designed to secure such information as: (1) personal data—age, marital status, place of birth, address, and telephone number; (2) educational training including high school data and college degrees; (3) types of certification held, including subject area qualification; (4) record of teaching experience; (5) record of other types of employment; (6) professional references and character references; and (7) health status. Some systems also ask for a short biographical sketch. If a photograph is desired, it should be optional, not required.

The interview presents another opportunity to secure information about prospective teachers. The interview is often conducted by the principal, and if the system has a personnel department, a representative of that office should be included. It is wise also, if possible, to include the department chairman. To be effective, the interview must be well planned, and the applicant must feel that he has a fair chance and sufficient time to present his qualifications. Those who conduct the interview should establish criteria upon which evaluation is to be made; criteria may include personal appearance, mental qualities, poise, scholarliness, and so on. After the interview, the evaluation should be summarized and kept for comparison with the records of other candidates.

Some systems have followed the practice of attempting to observe candidates who appear to be most promising while they are in the classroom. Because of the difficulties involved in this procedure, the practice will probably not become universal. And a single observation may not be sufficient to form a valid judgment.

Selection

The final step in teacher recruitment is actual employment. The local board of education usually establishes procedures for issuing contracts in conformity with state legislation which are legal and therefore binding. The board of education is the ultimate authority as the employing agent. Successful and unsuccessful candidates should be notified as to their status. In some cases, the unsuccessful candidates are given the option of keeping their applications on file for future consideration.

Orienting New Teachers

As soon as contracts have been signed, teachers new to the system should be supplied with information and materials pertaining to the new

assignment. Most systems require that new employees report a day or sometimes a week prior to the opening of school for the purpose of orientation.
Orientation may be conducted on a system-wide basis to acquaint new
members of the professional staff with rules and regulations. Some time
should also be allotted for orientation at the building level. With proper
planning, orientation sessions may relieve the beginner of the frustrations
characteristic of a new assignment and result in a more effective start for
the new teacher.

Teacher Salaries and Other Benefits

No school system can be effective unless the compensation structure
is such that good teachers can be recruited and maintained by the system.
Compensation must be such that the objectives of the system can be realized through the efforts of competent personnel working in an atmosphere
conducive to the best professional efforts. In earlier times, teachers had
to be satisfied with meager paychecks and few or no collateral benefits.
Fortunately, the situation has changed. Salaries are much higher and there
are many other benefits in addition to the annual salary.

Salaries

Among the influential provisions which retain superior teachers in a
school system is an adequate salary schedule. In past years, teachers were
employed by individual bargaining, but teachers today are employed and
paid on the basis of a formally adopted salary schedule. The earliest pay
schedules differed greatly from the ones in use now; they often contained
features which discriminated between men and women and paid higher
salaries to those who taught in the upper levels of the school. For example,
a first grade teacher with training and experience identical to that of the
secondary English teacher was likely to receive a much lower salary. This
situation was intolerable and has largely disappeared.

In preparing the salary schedule, it is advisable to involve many
people including representatives of the teaching force, the school administration, the board of education, and the community. Many factors need
mutual consideration to establish a satisfactory schedule: basic data on
the cost of living in the community, salaries paid in comparable communities, relative ability of the community to support its schools, and individual training experience. The community should be aware of the process
followed in developing the schedule. Sentiment can be created for it
through newspaper reports, parent-teacher discussions, and presentations
before local community organizations.

The single salary schedule is utilized in most school systems. This type of schedule is nondiscriminatory in that all teachers with identical training and experience receive the same remuneration regardless of sex or teaching level. An outgrowth of this principle has been the development of the index salary schedule. In this schedule the chief item for negotiation is the base or starting figure. The increments that come as a result of further training and experience are determined on a percentage basis. The salary schedule illustrated in Table 13 is one example.

In the table below, $8,000 is the base starting salary for a teacher with a bachelor's degree and no experience. As the teacher gains more experience and receives additional professional training, the salary increases in accordance with the index determined for additional experience and training. A teacher on the fifth step of the schedule and the holder of a master's degree would receive a salary of $10,400. The index itself is a matter for local consideration by teachers, administrators, and the board of education. Some schools develop schedules which recognize additional inbetween steps, such as a bachelor's degree plus fifteen hours, and a master's degree plus fifteen hours.

The table also shows that teachers who do not advance beyond the bachelor's degree stage receive no further increments after the ninth step and those who stop at the master's degree level do not proceed beyond step

Table 13

INDEX SALARY SCHEDULE

Step	Bachelor's		Master's		Master's + 30 Graduate Hours		Master's + 60 or Doctor's	
1	(1.00)	8,000	(1.10)	8,800	(1.20)	9,600	(1.30)	10,400
2	(1.04)	8,320	(1.14)	9,120	(1.24)	9,920	(1.34)	10,720
3	(1.10)	8,800	(1.20)	9,600	(1.30)	10,400	(1.40)	11,200
4	(1.15)	9,200	(1.25)	10,000	(1.35)	10,800	(1.45)	11,600
5	(1.20)	9,600	(1.30)	10,400	(1.40)	11,200	(1.50)	12,000
6	(1.25)	10,000	(1.35)	10,800	(1.45)	11,600	(1.55)	12,400
7	(1.30)	10,400	(1.40)	11,200	(1.50)	12,000	(1.60)	12,800
8	(1.35)	10,800	(1.45)	11,600	(1.55)	12,400	(1.65)	13,200
9	(1.40)	11,200	(1.50)	12,000	(1.60)	12,800	(1.70)	13,600
10			(1.55)	12,400	(1.65)	13,200	(1.75)	14,000
11			(1.60)	12,800	(1.70)	13,600	(1.80)	14,400
12			(1.65)	13,200	(1.75)	14,000	(1.85)	14,800
13			(1.70)	13,600	(1.80)	14,400	(1.90)	15,200
14					(1.85)	14,800	(1.95)	15,600
15					(1.90)	15,200	(2.00)	16,000

thirteen. To receive the maximum, the teacher would need to have sixty hours beyond the master's degree and to remain for the fifteen years.

Salary Trends

While it is true that teacher salaries are still inadequate in view of the training necessary for effective teaching, there is evidence that considerable progress has been made. In 1964–65, in systems enrolling more than six thousand students, the average beginning salary for teachers with a bachelor's degree was $4,707.[8] During the year 1970–71, the same teacher would earn $6,850, or an increase of 46 percent. The average beginning salaries for master's degree teachers have increased 49 percent, or from $5,085 to $7,599, during the same period.

There is general agreement that the maximum attainable salary should be considerably higher than the beginning minimum salary. Some writers have suggested that it should be approximately double. Some systems have provided supermaximums for select teachers due to special training and competence. Others have utilized the merit pay principle. The length of time required to reach the maximum is a matter of debate; most feel that it should be reached within a reasonable length of time, not to exceed ten or twelve years.

Teacher Retirement Plans

Plans for teacher retirement have been in existence for more than a century. As early as 1949, retirement laws had been enacted in all the states. Advantages of developing such plans include the protection of families, attraction of capable young people into the teaching profession, increased efficiency while in service, improved morale, and so forth.

An examination of recent legislation reveals that state legislatures are continuing to improve the retirement systems in many states.[9] Recent action taken has involved increasing benefits, providing for early retirement, giving death and survivor benefits, and giving postretirement benefits.

The following principles are generally considered fundamental to an adequate retirement system:

1. *Membership should be required of all teachers entering the profession.* When retirement systems were first developed, it was usually customary to give the teachers the option of participating.

2. *The costs of the system should be shared both by teachers and the public.* The sums deposited by teachers and the public during the period of service should be approximately equal.

---

[8]*NEA Research Bulletin*, 49, No. 1, 10–13.
[9]*NEA Research Bulletin*, 48, No. 4, 108–13.

3. *Deposits by the teacher and payments by the state should be concurrent with service.* The teacher's contributions and the state's payments to the retirement fund should be made regularly and concurrently during the teacher's period of service.

4. *Individual accounts should be kept.* The retirement board should provide an account for each individual teacher. Sums deposited in that account by the teacher should be held in trust.

5. *Retirement system funds should be on a reserve basis.* An adequate and actuarially sound reserve fund should be created to guarantee that the necessary money to pay the benefits will be on hand at the time of retirement.

6. *There should be periodic actuarial investigations.* The purpose of such investigations is to insure the financial soundness of the system.

7. *Disability should be a part of the system.* A retirement allowance should be provided for disabled teachers after a reasonable period of service.

8. *The accumulated deposits of the teachers should be returnable in case of withdrawal or death prior to retirement.* Teachers leaving the service before the regular retirement age should retain rights to all moneys accumulated in their accounts. Accumulated deposits should be returnable upon withdrawal from teaching service, or on death prior to retirement.

9. *Upon retirement a choice of options should be allowed.* The teacher should have the opportunity to elect the manner in which he will receive the benefits presented by the accumulated value of his deposits and the state's payments.

10. *There should be reciprocal relations between states.* Provision should be made for cooperative or reciprocal relations among the retirement systems of the different states.

11. *Both the teacher and the public should be protected.* Retirement ages and rules should be defined and administered so as to retain teachers during efficient service and provide for their retirement when old age or disability makes satisfactory service no longer possible. The retirement allowance should be sufficient to enable the retiring teacher to live in reasonable comfort, thereby removing the temptation to remain in the classroom beyond the period of efficient service.

12. *A retirement board should control the system.* The administration of the retirement system should be in the hands of a retirement board whose make-up is carefully prescribed in retirement legislation. Both teachers and the public should be represented on the administering board.

Teachers in former years were reluctant to retire because retirement pay was much less than the salaries received while actually engaged in teaching. Most states now have set a mandatory retirement age and are providing larger pensions. Some states have incorporated federal Social

Security as a part of the retirement plan. There are some differences of opinion with respect to the long-range effects of the plan.

Teacher Tenure

The first tenure laws came into being more than sixty years ago. While the movement has been somewhat slow, most teachers are now protected by tenure laws. A part of the reason for its lack of acceptance was the feeling that it was practically impossible to dismiss ineffective and incompetent teachers, but because of the harsh and unfair treatment given many teachers, tenure legislation became a necessity. Most laws now make provision for orderly dismissal of teachers for such matters as gross immorality, criminality, insubordination, demonstrated incompetency, and so on.

It becomes the responsibility of the principal to judge whether or not a teacher attains tenure. During the probationary period, there is ample time to determine whether or not the teacher is worthy of tenure. When a teacher is clearly not effective, tenure status should be denied, but evaluation must be objective, a matter of record, and there must be evidence that an effort has been made to provide supervision which would help a teacher to be effective.

Leaves of Absence

One of the benefits to members of the teaching profession in recent years is the granting of leaves of absence for several purposes, among which are provisions for sick leaves, sabbatical leaves, and for meetings and conventions of professional significance.

In every occupation much time is lost from work by personal illness. It is probably true that teachers tend to be absent from their regular employment somewhat less than the average for all employed groups. Many states have made it mandatory that sick leave be provided at full pay, while other states leave the matter to the local board of education. The amount of time provided varies from state to state and ranges from twenty days in one state to an indefinite or unlimited amount in others.[10] Most states require a minimum of ten days annually.

The practice of giving sabbatical leave has been gaining momentum in recent years. Boards of education have used this as one way of stimulating staff career development. School systems which use the plan usually establish definite rules and regulations for its operation; such matters as time needed for eligibility, number of sabbaticals to be granted during a given year, amount of salary to be prorated for the leave, purposes for

[10]*NEA Research Bulletin*, 47, No. 2, 43–44.

which the leave is granted, and time allotted for the leave are generally covered in the rules. In addition, there is usually a stipulation that those who take sabbatical leave must give some guarantee of returning to their positions for a given period of time.

Most school systems encourage faculty members to attend summer schools, conventions, and seminars devoted to professional improvement. The manner in which these activities are encouraged varies from system to system. In some cases, there is financial remuneration, while most schools provide substitutes for the days missed for participation in professional meetings.

Providing Substitutes

In all schools it is necessary to secure substitutes for teachers who are absent because of personal or family illness, personal reasons, such as attendance at weddings or funerals, or visiting days. It is general practice that teachers who are to be absent call the central office as far ahead of the absence as possible to allow for sufficient time to arrange for a substitute. After calling the central office, the teacher should immediately notify the principal. Substitute teachers should of course possess the same qualifications as regular teachers.

A pool of substitute teachers consisting of retired teachers, teachers who desire only part-time work, and young persons waiting appointment as regular teachers may be recruited. The principal should not only prepare a bulletin outlining necessary procedures to orient substitute teachers, but also visit the classroom to observe how well the substitute is doing. On the basis of his observations he may advise the central office of the relative competence of various substitute teachers. It is also advisable to ask for a report of the substitute's observations and experience in the classroom.

While it is generally agreed that the substitute teacher does not equal the services of the regular teacher, the principal can be helpful in improving substitute service with proper planning and supervision. It is common practice in some schools to include substitute teachers in orientation programs, social occasions, and professional seminars. This practice is recommended because it is evidence of the importance the school attaches to substitute service.

Merit Pay

The matter of merit pay has been a subject of considerable discussion and debate for many years. Though advocated by many boards of education, it has not won the approval of professional associations. Those who serve on boards of education are usually familiar with systems that pay according to the quality of work performed. They believe that effective teachers should be given higher salaries than those who are considered marginal. Professional organizations have maintained that there are no evaluation systems in existence that can definitely determine effectiveness and that the end result of merit pay schedules is dissatisfaction and low morale on the part of the teaching staff.

It is true that many of the means employed in evaluation have proved to be unsatisfactory. The reasons are not difficult to find. Some of the methods have been borrowed from civil service and business administration and have not been adapted to the evaluation of teaching. Such means of evaluation—some kind of rating scale—have been arbitrarily adopted in some cases by boards of education and imposed upon unwilling subjects who have had no voice in the preparation of the evaluation instruments or their use. As a result, many teachers feel quite antipathetic toward the evaluation of merit. Furthermore, the type of rating frequently employed has been done so unscientifically and used so unwisely by some school officials that the teachers in these school systems have come to regard rating either as a policy to be opposed or an evil to be endured. The mental attitude of teachers toward merit evaluation under such conditions is naturally hostile, and unfortunately, improvement in attitude can scarcely be expected until teachers concerned actually experience the benefits from evaluation.

The recent attention given to the subject of accountability makes it clear that there is considerable internal and external interest in finding definite ways to measure the effectiveness of the school's operation. Taxpayers are interested in knowing whether the input into the school system is resulting in satisfactory output. The involvement of commercial enterprises with the business of education through performance contracting is additional evidence that achievement and teaching methods are of prime concern. These developments are causing the profession to give attention to the necessity of demonstrating beyond reasonable doubt that the schools are effective and that new methods may be needed to prove it. A further development may be a renewed interest in merit pay.

Although there is much professional opinion to support the merit principle, there is still much to be done to enlist the support of the teaching staff. Evaluation must be done by those who can conduct it with a high degree of competence and objectivity. Furthermore, teachers should be included when methods of evaluation are developed.

The following principles may well constitute the basis for dealing constructively with the problem. First, any system planning to adopt the merit pay principle should have a good basic salary schedule. Some systems in the past have announced schedules with very high maximums for those who achieve merit. But because the number who could attain it was very small, this is a misuse of the principle. Second, criteria should be established outlining the items to be considered in the determination of merit, and teachers should have a share in determining the criteria. Third, there should be no limit to the number of teachers entitled to merit raises. The system can never be acceptable if a mere fraction of the staff have the possibility of attaining merit. It is reasonable to expect that 50 percent of any staff should attain merit pay. Fourth, those who are made responsible for making the evaluations should be identified and made known to the staff. Fifth, the staff and community should be informed of the schedule and made aware of its provisions. Sixth, the method should be placed under continuous study and changes made when conditions warrant them.

When members of the profession are convinced that a merit schedule results in an improved educational experience for children and youth, it will be accepted, but experience and research are necessary to ensure proper development and operation.

Teacher Morale

A school cannot be an effective organization unless teachers find satisfaction in their work. It is a major responsibility of the principal to create a school climate which is conducive to a high degree of teacher satisfaction. Because many principals have looked upon the teacher as a hired hand, antagonism toward this attitude on the part of teachers resulted in dissatisfaction and militancy. The main concern of the principal is the welfare of the student, but he also has the responsibility for realizing that the teacher also has definite needs. In some cases, it is impossible to meet the wishes of teachers without violating some of the rules and regulations established for the operation of the schools. It is his function, then, to resolve these competing forces. One way of doing this is to make full use of the faculty in the determination of policy and the resolution of difficulties. Teachers in today's climate not only expect this sort of treatment, they demand it.

Negotiations

Teachers have always been concerned with salaries and working conditions. In the past, most of these problems have been solved by administrators and boards of education, and some enlightened administrators and boards of education have always involved teachers in considering these matters. But in recent years teachers have not been content to leave these concerns to other hands. They are ensuring their right to participate through the process of negotiations. A volume of the American Association of School Administrators lists the following as prime reasons for teacher dissatisfaction and militancy:[11]

---

[11]*The School Administrator and Negotiation* (Washington, D.C.: The American Association of School Adminstrators, 1968), pp. 22–23.

Discontent with traditional methods of teacher involvement in educational decision making.

Mounting class sizes and crowded classroom space.

Social change, pupil mobility, racial unrest, and concurrent changes, especially in urban communities.

Necessity to "moonlight" to make ends meet.

Frustration with traditional instructional methods and materials, which clearly do not meet the needs of pupils having learning difficulties.

Insensitive administrative procedures and overpaternalistic personnel practices.

Cleavages between teacher groups and contests for organizational power and status.

Increase in number of new teachers coming from labor union families and backgrounds.

Increased educational level of teaching staff.

Increased awareness of recent research on personnel practices.

Reaction against oversupervision or inappropriate supervision.

Whatever the causes for the new militancy, it is evident that teachers are no longer satisfied with being consulted; they wish to participate in making decisions that will affect them.

The Principal's Role

It is impossible to deal adequately with the principal's role in negotiations in a text dealing with general administration, but every principal should familiarize himself with the problem. The effects of the negotiation process are so far-reaching that the principal must play an active role. Although there has been a tendency to ignore the principal or relegate him to the role of onlooker, he must be represented in any negotiation team. Traditionally most principals have desired to be closely allied with the teaching staff, but the realities of the present situation place him as a part of administration. This does not mean that it is necessary that he become an adversary of the teaching staff. When properly handled, negotiations can bring benefits to a school system. The process may be time-consuming, but the principal must take the time to be an effective participant, and to insure that all participants share in the decisions.

One of the principal's most important responsibilities is to acquaint himself with the items to be negotiated. As the leader of his school the principal knows that there are areas of responsibilities that cannot be negotiated. The National Association of Secondary School Principals has proposed the following criteria for use by the school principal:[12]

---

[12]Benjamin Epstein, *What Is Negotiable* (Washington, D.C.: The National Association of Secondary School Principals, 1969), pp. 21–28.

1. No item should be considered negotiable which could be decided on the basis of the results of scientific investigation, evaluations of experimental efforts, or other devices used by professional expertise to determine what is best for the education of pupils.

2. No assignments of professional personnel should ever be made on the basis of automatic rotation or of any so-called "equitable" distribution of classes grouped according to levels of pupil ability or disciplinary difficulty, nor should assignments, transfers, or promotions of teachers be determined on the basis of seniority.

3. The principle of accountability is one which should never be overlooked in determining the negotiability of any item.

4. Whenever, in any negotiation, there is a possible conflict between the interests and needs of the child and the organizational demands of teachers, the resolution of any differences must in every case be in favor of the child.

5. No educational policy making is sound which involves school board members and teacher organization negotiators exclusively and omits administrators.

6. It will be to the interest of teachers' organizations to avoid negotiating petty items which in the eyes of school boards, administrators, the general public, and a great many of their own teacher members raise doubts about their professional zeal.

7. Finally, there is no point in seeking to negotiate items that are beyond the power of a school board or administration to grant.

It is evident from a discussion of problems involving teaching personnel that the principal is involved continually in situations that require him to be a master in the field of human relations. The decisions he makes usually involve the welfare of human beings. He cannot avoid the responsibility for taking steps to create a favorable work climate for teachers. Neither can he overlook his duty to provide a school that will be accountable for the quality of the educational experience available to children and youth.

Selected References

ALLEN, DWIGHT W, "Differentiated Teaching Staff," *New York State Education*, 57 (December 1969), 16–19.

————, "Differentiated Staffing: Putting Teacher Talent to Work," *Pennsylvania School Journal*, 118 (December 1969), 100–102.

BISHOP, LLOYD K., and PATRICK W. CARLTON, "Staff Differentiation: A Model for Developing Professional Behavior," *The High School Journal*, 7 (April 1971), 422–31.

BOWMAN, GARDA W., and GORDON J. KLOPF, *New Careers and Roles in the American School.* New York: Bank Street College of Education, 1968.

CALDWELL, BRUCE A., "Differentiated Staffing: Who Is Labor and Who Is Management?" *Educational Technology*, X (December 1970), 59–60.

CARLTON, PATRICK W., and HAROLD I. GOODWIN, *The Collective Dilemma: Negotiations in Education.* Worthington, Ohio: Charles A. Jones Publishing Company, 1969.

CHAMBERLIN, LESLIE J., *Team Teaching: Organization and Administration.* Columbus, Ohio: Charles E. Merrill Publishing Company, 1969.

CHAPLIN, WAYNE, "Merit Pay Is Alive and Well in Wisconsin," *The American School Board Journal*, 157 (July 1969), 13–15.

DAVIS, DONALD E., and NEAL C. ERICKSON, JR., *Critical Issues in School Personnel Administration.* Chicago: Rand McNally and Company, 1968.

DAVIES, DON, "The Teacher Numbers Game," *American Education*, VI (October 1970), 7–8.

DOYLE, WALTER, "The Supervisor's Role in Negotiation: A Critique," *Educational Leadership*, 27 (February 1970), 475–80.

FRANKLIN, MARIAN POPE, "Nongraded Schools," *Educational Forum*, XXX (March 1965), 331–34.

GANERKE, WARREN E., *Legal and Ethical Responsibilities of School Personnel.* Englewood Cliffs, N.J.: Prentice-Hall, Inc., 1959.

GIBSON, R. OLIVER, and HEROLD C. HUNT, *The School Personnel Administrator.* Boston: Houghton Mifflin Company, 1965.

GREENE, JAY E., *School Personnel Administration.* Philadelphia, Pa.: Chilton Book Company, 1970.

HANLON, JAMES M., *Adminstration and Education: Toward a Theory of Self-Actualization.* Belmont, California: Wadsworth Publishing Company, 1968.

JUSTIZ, THOMAS B., "A Reliable Measure of Teacher Effectiveness," *Educational Leadership: Research Supplement*, 3 (October 1969), 49–55.

KRUMBEIN, GERALD, "What Differentiated Staffing Will Cost," *The American School Board Journal*, 157 (May 1970), 19–24.

MOORE, HAROLD E., *The Administration of Public School Personnel.* New York: The Center for Applied Research in Education, Inc., 1966.

OLIVERO, JAMES L., and EDWARD G. BUFFIE, eds., *Educational Manpower: From Aides to Differentiated Staff Patterns, Bold New Venture.* Bloomington, Ind.: Indiana University Press, 1970.

OWENS, ROBERT G., *Organizational Behavior in Schools.* Englewood Cliffs, N.J.: Prentice-Hall, Inc., 1970.

PERRY, CHARLES R., and WESLEY A. WILDMAN, *The Impact of Negotiations in Public Education: The Evidence from the Schools.* Worthington, Ohio: Charles A. Jones Publishing Company, 1970.

STEIG, LESTER R., *School Personnel and In-Service Training Practices*. West Nyack, N.Y.: Parker Publishing Company, 1969.

STOCKER, JOSEPH, and DONALD F. WILSON, "Accountability and the Classroom Teacher," *Today's Education*, 60 (March 1971), 41–56.

TYLER, RALPH W., "Testing for Accountability," *Nation's Schools*, LXXXVI (December 1970), 37–39.

VAN ZWOLL, JAMES A., *School Personnel Administration*. New York: Appleton-Century-Crofts, 1964.

17

Records and Reports

The development of the school office and the office functions of the principal have tended to centralize and to expand school records and reports. In earlier times when principals were head teachers and building administrators, the responsibility for records rested largely with the individual teacher. In fact, there were few records besides the teacher's class register. Just as the completion of the register at the end of a semester or school term was usually regarded as the teacher's report, so the duty of the teaching principal was to keep his own register and to collect the registers of other teachers when requested by the superintendent or board of education.

Administrative Forms in Secondary Schools

The release of the principal from teaching and his consequent assumption of managerial and supervisory duties led to the multiplication of records and reports for which he was responsible. The principal became jointly responsible with the teachers for all the pupils of the school. Administrative forms, designed to facilitate teacher communication with the principal, were devised and they later became matters of office record. The data contained in the forms frequently became a subject for study and report.

The earliest forms called for periodic reports on attendance, punctuality, conduct, and class progress of pupils. The principal summarized these items of information for all the teachers of his school and reported the data to the central office.

Other forms were devised by individual principals as a means of collecting data needed in the administration of their schools. In city school systems, administrative forms were devised by the central office and distributed to the local principals with the idea of facilitating the collection of data needed in preparing reports. Because few school systems can devise all the forms needed by individual principals in routine administration, the administrative forms in use in local schools in a school system at any time consist both of those common to all the schools and of those developed by individual principals as needed in carrying out administrative duties.

Scope of Forms in Use

A study of the administrative forms in use in any given school would reveal the types of office duties which are subject to record and report in that school. These forms naturally vary from school to school, since the principals of the schools differ in their conceptions of office duties. The size of the school also influences to some extent the number of administrative forms in use; larger schools require more forms than the smaller schools.

An informal study revealed that the ten forms used most often in approximately 100 secondary schools were (1) student administration; (2) health, safety, and welfare; (3) student guidance; (4) permanent records; (5) extracurricular records; (6) test and examination records; (7) financial accounting; (8) school supplies and equipment; (9) student activity funds; and (10) teachers' personnel records.

Analysis of the lists of forms reported in use by these schools reveals that some principals have used an excess of forms in high school administration. In doing so they have complicated administration and made the forms difficult for their staff members. The clerical task of collecting and tabulating the data on the forms may become burdensome to the secretarial staff, and the responsibility for interpreting the findings may so absorb the time of the principal that he has no time for rendering services of much greater importance to the school.

The principal should be certain that the forms used in his school facilitate administration and can be justified by the functions they serve. In general most administrators employ too many rather than too few forms. Caution must be exercised to eliminate the collection of unnecessary data through useless forms. The remedy for collection of unnecessary data is to send back to those who make reports the significance of the findings. In schools that employ many forms in administration, it is very easy for the principal to become an expensive head clerk concerned with seeing that the forms are properly filled out, tabulated, and filed, rather than with other more pressing duties.

Typical Forms

Office forms used to facilitate administration are summons to office, visitor's card, telephone call slip, report of article lost, report of article found, special excuse card, car license record, report of accident in classroom or on grounds, honor point record, teacher's tardiness, report of monthly fire drill, teacher's check-in list at end of year, trip expense report, and refund order. Forms of this kind keep the principal informed regarding the activities of his school, and serve as the basis for the study of practices and the modification of policies. They are transient rather than permanent records.

Forms should be used to facilitate administration and to allow time for the most important function of the principal, the improvement of instruction. The fact that this does not always result is illustrated by the Reavis study of the forms used in taking, administering, and recording attendance in twenty-seven secondary schools. He found 145 different forms used, which he classified into nineteen types designed to facilitate the administration of absence, tardiness, and attendance data. The nature of these forms is indicated in Table 14.

Reduction in Number of Forms Needed

From this study of the 145 attendance forms used in the twenty-seven secondary schools, it was concluded that the excessive use of forms as administrative devices unduly complicated attendance administration in some of the schools without improving the results. Reduction of the nineteen types to four types would simplify and improve attendance administration. Examination of the four forms recommended shows that adequate records of attendance can be secured without an excessive expenditure of time on the part of teachers, clerks, and the administrative head of the school. The form in Fig. 15 is to be filled out by teachers each period of the day, while Fig. 16 is to be used by an attendance clerk, an assistant principal, or any qualified member of the staff assigned to do so by the principal. Fig. 17 is to be compiled by a clerk for the benefit of the attendance administrator or the principal. Fig. 18 constitutes the annual cumulative attendance record of each pupil for the year, and is to be prepared and kept by a clerk with administrative supervision.

Administrative Forms in Elementary Schools

Many office forms which serve a variety of purposes are necessary in the efficient operation of elementary schools. Table 15 lists the different

Table 14

TYPES OF FORMS USED IN THE
ADMINISTRATION OF ATTENDANCE IN 27
SECONDARY SCHOOLS AND NUMBER
OF EACH TYPE IN USE

	Number of Schools Using Form
Daily report of absence	20
General readmission with disposition of case to be checked	16
Absence permit	15
Report of pupil absence or tardiness	13
Readmission of pupil to classes after absence, without excusing the absence	12
Report of pupil absence by periods	12
Special form used in checking attendance	8
Readmission of pupil to classes after absence for which he is excused	7
Yearly record of attendance	7
Report made to attendance officers	6
Monthly report of attendance and absence	5
Report on attendance for first two weeks of term	5
Readmission without conditions	4
Reports to parent on absence of pupil	4
Statistical reports of attendance	3
Weekly reports of absence	3
Notice to pupil to return admittance slip	2
Notice to teacher or adviser to investigate the absence of a pupil	2
Notice to teacher to explain failure to make absence report	1

forms, classified as to function, used in a group of elementary schools in over 100 cities. As is seen in this table, no type of form was common to all the schools studied, but the highest frequency of use for any type of form was found in the permanent record for individual pupils—although this record was not kept by all the schools. (The fact that some of the schools did not keep a permanent record form for each pupil does not mean that the essential data were not kept on some other form.)

Great Variation Among Elementary Schools

Obviously the persons responsible for the preparation of these forms varied greatly in their conceptions of the data needed in school records and reports. For example, fifty different items of information were called

School Heading

PERIOD REPORT OF ABSENCE

Date _____   Teacher _____

Name of Pupil	Period	Class

Note: Indicate minutes lost by tardiness as T-10.

Fig. 15. Form recommended for reporting period absence.

Table 15

PUPIL RECORD FORMS USED IN
ELEMENTARY SCHOOLS IN 114 CITIES

Classification	*Number*
Permanent records	74
Periodic reports to parents	73·
Teachers' periodic reports	72
Miscellaneous	67
Pupil attendance	62
Current health reports	53
Teachers' reports of scholarship	50
Principals' reports	45
Transfer cards	44
Registration and enrollment cards	44
Office cards	28
Admission, discharge, and promotion cards	22
Occasional reports to parents	21
Census cards and records	18
Teachers' annual reports	17
Certificates of promotion	14
Total	704

School Heading

DAILY SUMMARY OF ABSENCE

Date _____

Name of Pupil	1	2	3	4	5	6	7	8	Cause	Ex.	Not Ex.

Fig. 16. Form recommended for use in summarizing daily absences.

```
┌─────────────────────────────────────────────────────────────┐
│                                                               │
│                       School Heading                          │
│                                                               │
│                    ADMISSION NOTICE                           │
│  ═══════════════════════════════════════════════════════════  │
│                                                               │
│                                                               │
│      Admit  _____         │
│                     ┌─────┐                    ┌─────┐        │
│          Absence    │     │       Tardiness    │     │        │
│                     └─────┘                    └─────┘        │
│                     ┌─────┐                    ┌─────┐        │
│          Excused    │     │      Not Excused   │     │        │
│                     └─────┘                    └─────┘        │
│    Remarks:                                                    │
│                                                               │
│    Date  _____      Signed  _____    │
│                                                               │
└─────────────────────────────────────────────────────────────┘
```

Fig. 17. Form recommended for reporting admission of pupil after absence.

for in the permanent record form, but only one item was common to all the forms studied. Four items—(1) the name of the pupil, (2) scholarship record by subjects, (3) date of birth, and (4) attendance record—were common to 50 percent or more of the permanent record forms. The form showing the greatest agreement in items of information was the "periodic report to parents." In seventy-three such forms, only two items had a frequency of mention of 100 percent while fourteen items a frequency of mention of 50 percent or more. Twenty-three items were mentioned in fewer than 10 percent of the seventy-three forms studied.

From this study, it is apparent that the forms in use in elementary schools are loaded with items of information that meet with very slight agreement among persons responsible for their preparation. Although it is generally necessary for the elementary principal to use some or all of the forms adopted by his central office, he is not required to use a form for which he alone is responsible if it calls for the recording of information that is never used. Good practice requires that the office forms pertaining to the records of students be carefully studied by the principal with a view to justifying them on the ground of functional use and information they contain.

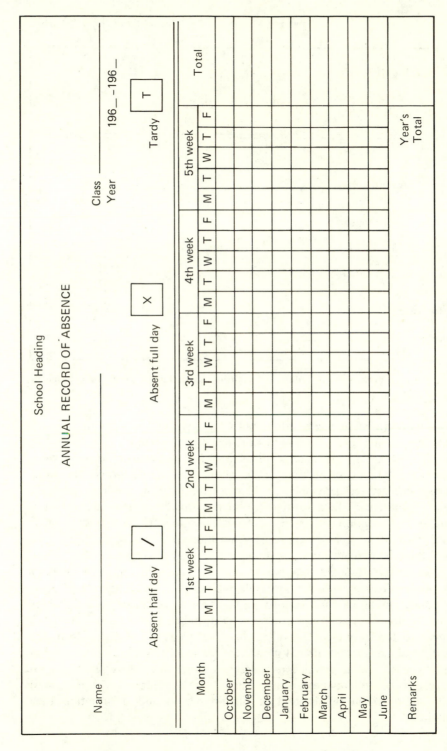

Fig. 18. Form recommended for use as an annual record of attendance and absence.

Records Pertaining to Students

Forms Used in Recording Attendance and Performance

In most states it is the principal's legal duty to keep records pertaining to pupil attendance; he is held responsible by the local school authority for this duty. Although important as a means of accounting for the child's presence in school, the attendance record is by no means as valuable as records of educational progress. Most schools today—regardless of level—keep records which appraise the progress of their pupils. These appraisals are contained in office records which are prepared and kept as necessary duties by the school staff. These records often include (1) data regarding personal and family history of each student, educational background, standardized tests results, and medical inspection; (2) systematic reports and measurements at regular intervals; and (3) such special reports as the needs of any individual case may require from time to time.

Regular Collection of Information

The personal and historical data considered vital to his complete understanding should be collected at the time the student presents himself for admission to the school. This occasion is the best time to impress upon both parent and child the importance of the educational contract implied when the school accepts a student. If students and parents are required to furnish the information desired by the school as a part of the admission procedure, they must understand that the school takes seriously its obligation to provide suitable education for its students. They will also probably assume a better attitude toward the requirements which the school imposes. The information called for should concern the future progress of the student and should be held in confidence by the school.

Unless the school takes pains to gather facts which enable it to understand its students, it cannot provide guidance. The school should prepare to appraise new pupils as soon as possible after they are admitted. In order to provide suitable and profitable work, and to direct the efforts of its students to success, the school must determine as accurately as possible the educational status of its students.

The personal data secured as a part of the admission procedure enable the school to guide its students at the time of admission. The school does not have to wait for maladjustment and failure before it begins to assemble information regarding the student. In the light of its initial appraisal, the school may direct its students so that much of the maladjustment which often results from aimless floundering is avoided.

Information Essential to Educational Diagnosis

If problems do occur, the first step in a diagnostic study, an appraisal of the educational status of the student at the date of his admission to school, has been met. If nothing had been done before to the appearance of the maladjustment to determine the educational status of the student, a real emergency would exist which would require a great amount of preliminary work before diagnostic study could be undertaken. Of course, it is not always possible to obtain a full case history at the time of a student's admission to school, but an effort should be made to assemble important personal and educational information.

After a student's initial appraisal, the school should measure his accomplishments from time to time to determine the quality and quantity of his progress. Such measurements should be periodic, a part of regular school procedure. Monthly, bimonthly, quarterly, or semester reports are essential in appraising the work of students. Such reports both provide accounts of progress and constitute points from which each new advance is made. The history of the student's education will be written very largely in terms of the periodic accountings which the school makes. If the record is made in terms of marks only, the interpretation will be subject to the variation inherent in grading symbols lacking precise definitions.

Anecdotal Reports

To avoid the vagueness inherent in marks and tests, anecdotal statements of the individual student's progress should be made a part of the records. An anecdotal record is a written statement regarding the behavior of a student or an account of a particular learning experience filed as a part of the student's cumulative record. The account may be written by a teacher, parent, attendance officer, psychologist, or other cooperating staff member, or by the principal himself. The record should report actions which cannot be adequately portrayed by the marks incorporated in the cumulative record. The anecdotal statement is supplementary to the regular cumulative personal or scholastic reports; these are incidental rather than permanent records.

Such statements can be secured at the time of the periodic appraisals if the teachers have actually made an inventory of the student's progress for the time in question. The statements should be of a descriptive nature and should contain facts rather than opinions, although qualitative ratings of personal traits and characteristics may also be made from time to time so that the social and personal maturity of the student may be evaluated.

Examination of many of the anecdotal reports filed in the cumulative folders of students would reveal all too much trivial comment, which is interesting enough but of little or no value in diagnosis or remedial treatment of a problem. The warning therefore stands that administrative officers must assist those who submit anecdotal statements to recognize the kind of information which makes the reports valuable as records of student progress. One such aid is "A Guide to the Use of Anecdotal Reports," published by the Bureau of Reference, Research, and Statistics of the New York City Public Schools.

Special Reports

Whenever an instructor notices that a student is showing signs of unsatisfactory progress or maladjustment, the principal should provide a special report form so that proper staff members may be directed to assisting and guiding the student to more satisfactory behaviors This report, like the anecdotal comments, should be descriptive in nature and should contain concise statements of facts rather than expressions of opinion. The receipt of such a report by the administrative officer is to be regarded as a timely warning that this student is likely to become a problem. The symptoms which the special report reveals should be checked promptly, and an effort should be made to correct or to remedy the conditions underlying them. So that cases of this type may not be overlooked, special reports may be called for in the middle of each semester for all pupils whose work at that date is below credit level. The mid-semester report should indicate the respects in which the student is failing to do satisfactory work and should characterize his attitude toward study. In addition, the administrative officer should take the initiative whenever information indicates a potential problem in maladjustment by calling for special reports from all members of the staff who have any contact with the student. The reports should deal with the present status of the student and indicate the areas where his learning and conduct are unsatisfactory.

Case Conferences

When the data assembled from special reports for a student require extra consideration, the principal may call a conference of interested persons—teachers, counselor, psychologist, and school social worker—for group study. In this conference, suggestions may be offered for further study or for remedial treatment. A report of the conference may be prepared for the cumulative record of the student and for consideration with the parents if a parental conference is necessary. The findings of the study may warrant contacting social service agencies and possibly clinical assistance.

Permanent Student Records

In an intensive study we did of office forms used in the administration of students by twenty-six secondary schools, 556 different forms are on file. These forms were classified into forty groups according to the administrative function indicated by the title of each form. The groups and the number of forms found in each group, as well as their scope, are shown in Table 16.

Table 16

TYPES OF FORMS USED IN THE
ADMINISTRATION OF PUPILS IN 26
SECONDARY SCHOOLS

Function of Form	*Number of Different Forms*
Accident, report of	2
Admission and registration	15
Aid	3
Attendance, administration of	143
Change in marks	2
Class record book	4
Class schedule of pupil	17
Conduct report	12
Cumulative academic record	17
Cumulative personnel record	13
Cumulative academic and personnel record	5
Elective cards	14
Extracurriculum activities	10
Guidance	10
Home visitation	3
Honor pupils	5
Interest questionnaire	3
Library records	7
Locker records	14
Manual of information	5
Music records	3
Physical and health records	36
Pupils' pass and permit forms	19
Pupil pledges	2
Report cards	11

Functions of Form	Number of Different Forms
Report to principal of unsatisfactory work of pupil	4
Schedule changes	10
Special report on pupils failing or incomplete	13
Special report to parent on work of pupil	8
Special request by pupils	7
Study hall records	7
Study helps	3
Summons forms	4
Supplementary reading record	6
Teacher's class reports	24
Teacher's reports to adviser	3
Transcript of pupil's record	4
Transfer forms	5
Withdrawal cards	5
Miscellaneous forms	78

The findings clearly show that secretarial assistance in tabulating and filing the records and in preparing reports for the information of the principal is much needed. It is also evident that the forms used in high schools as well as elementary schools are in need of simplification. The problem of revising and shortening the forms becomes almost crucial when the principal is responsible for handling the mass of record material without clerical aid. Relief is often sought in teachers who can take some time from teaching to help with records.

The Cumulative Record

The cumulative office record for individual pupils is a development of recent years in both elementary and secondary schools. An effort made by the National Education Association in 1912 to encourage schools to keep cumulative records of all pupils was accompanied by two model forms prepared by the Committee on Uniform Records and Reports of the National Education Association and widely distributed by the United States Bureau of Education.[1] Further attention was given to the matter at the annual meeting of the Department of Superintendence in 1925, when a committee was appointed to revise the forms prepared by the 1912 committee. The results of the new committee's work appeared in 1927.[2] A

---

[1] U.S. Bureau of Education, *Report of the Committee on Uniform Records and Reports*, Bulletin No. 3 (1912), p. 471.

[2] National Education Association, Research Division, *School Records and Reports, Research Bulletin*, V, No. 5 (1927).

new committee appointed in January 1948 by the Commissioner of Education was to work with the Office of Education in planning and carrying out a three- to five-year study of the cumulative record.

The National Association of Secondary School Principals has attempted to standardize the information on cumulative records of pupils in secondary schools through the development and publication of forms made available to principals at small cost. This effort was prompted by the desire to simplify the work of preparing admission blanks for graduates seeking to enter institutions of higher learning. The forms have passed through several revisions, the latest in the 1960s.

Variations in Cumulative Records

A study[3] of the nature and use of the cumulative record in 177 school systems sheds considerable light on the size of the problem of office bookkeeping involved in preparing and keeping cumulative records for pupils at all levels of public schooling. (See Table 17.) No single item of information was collected by all the elementary schools and only one item, namely, scholarship as revealed through marks, was collected and recorded by all the junior and senior high schools. The analysis of the cards shows that seventeen different types of information with varying degrees of frequency were found in permanent cumulative records in the schools. The collection of these items was generally provided for on administrative forms which were often discarded after the data was transcribed to the permanent record. The task of transcribing was usually assigned to a clerk in schools that have clerical assistance, or in schools without clerical aid, the task could be performed by a teacher, by the principal, or by different members of the school staff. Whatever method is used, the greatest care should be observed to avoid errors in transcription.

Justification for Adequate Records

The office work required to assemble and make available in accessible form the cumulative school record of each student can be justified by (1) the administrative necessity of giving the parent an accounting of school progress; (2) the professional responsibility of school administrators for the student guidance; and (3) the need for factual evidence concerning student progress in the study of problems of curricular and extracurricular organization and internal school management. Since the principal of a school can scarcely function effectively in these respects without comprehensive cumulative records of the progress of his student personnel, office bookkeeping and administration must necessarily make heavy demands on

---

[3]David Segel, *Nature and Use of the Cumulative Record*, Bulletin No. 3, U.S. Office of Education (1938).

Table 17

PERCENTAGES OF FREQUENCY WITH
WHICH ITEMS OF INFORMATION WERE
FOUND IN THE CUMULATIVE RECORD
FORMS OF ELEMENTARY SCHOOLS,
JUNIOR HIGH SCHOOLS, AND SENIOR
HIGH SCHOOLS IN 177 SCHOOL SYSTEMS

Items of Information	Percentage of Frequency in the Cumulative Forms of		
	113 Elementary Schools	87 Junior High Schools	136 Senior High Schools
Scholarship (marks)	96	100	100
School progress	80	92	79
Attendance	86	85	77
Entrance and withdrawal	71	86	79
Home conditions and family history	70	71	69
Intelligence test results	58	77	71
Social and character ratings	73	71	63
Health	65	64	56
Space for notes	58	63	57
Achievement test results	51	56	49
Extracurriculum activities	19	64	63
Vocational and educational plans	17	45	44
Residence record	38	26	21
College or vocation entered after leaving school	15	34	33
Special abilities	14	23	16
Photograph	7	23	16
Out-of-school employment	5	20	18

the principal's time. Because all members of the school staff must also be conversant with the cumulative records of students with whom they are concerned, the records should be filed for convenient use as well as for protection from misplacement or loss. The storage most frequently adopted for permanent cumulative records is some kind of visible file which permits inspection without removing the record.

A satisfactory visible record form could contain all the personal information considered necessary to deal intelligently with the student. More extensive information could be available in the cumulative folder. The extracurricular record should also be included on the forms, since both employers and college admission officers are concerned with such data. A photograph of the student could be attached to the form when the student enters the school and again when he graduates. Some forms provide for a complete record of the student in the high school and a graphic portrayal of his test results in percentile ranks as well as the test scores themselves. Such a record is invaluable in student guidance. Some other forms provide space for additional notes or for a record of items of significance abstracted from the cumulative folder. The American Council on Education recommends a four-page cumulative record folder which includes all the data we have discussed.

Cumulative Pocket-File Folders

The rapid multiplication of record materials regarding the progress of students in all types of schools has created a problem of filing and recording in the offices of many principals. The record material available is too great to be transcribed, yet the material is too valuable to be discarded or destroyed while the student is in school. The solution proposed for the problem is an individual pocket-file folder in which the various records of a pupil may be placed without recording the information on any forms. These folders are especially valuable in counseling pupils and in dealing with cases of maladjustment.

Entire school systems in some cities have adopted the cumulative folder as a means of reducing the work of transcribing data onto forms. Filing cases and pocket-file folders are supplied for local school offices, and in some instances for each classroom. Although recent evidence indicates that only about 40 percent of secondary schools use pocket-file folders, this practice has become practically universal in large urban school systems in elementary as well as secondary schools. The adoption of this method of preserving student information in an accessible form is justified by the value of the materials and the small amount of labor involved in this system of filing.

Methods of Filing

In some schools a plain manila folder with the cumulative form printed on the inner pages and the miscellaneous record materials filed inside is used for student cumulative records. The cost of the plan is less than that of providing both cumulative record cards in visible filing cabinets and regular letter files for folders. The disadvantage is in the necessity for handling both the folder and its contents when information from just the record form is desired.

In secondary schools the cumulative folder has a slightly greater frequency of use than visible records. But the answer to the question of the best kind of cumulative record does not appear to be a choice between a cumulative record in a visible file and a cumulative folder, but rather the wise use of both devices. A permanent record card containing items of frequently used information should be kept in easily accessible form for the convenience of the principal and his office assistants. Likewise, a cumulative folder should be provided for each student in which other materials for the use of teachers, advisers, and administrative officers in the diagnostic study of the student and in the evaluation of his progress are filed.

The cumulative folder is an excellent device for use in schools that desire to engage in extensive student evaluative studies. Laboratory schools of departments of education in universities and in teacher training institutions which are interested in the mental and physical growth of children, their progress in the school subjects, social development, and personal characteristics will find the individual cumulative folder valuable for preserving a great variety of materials that cannot be transcribed onto record cards. Other schools which desire to study similar topics as the basis of student guidance and for making improvements in curriculum materials and in teaching methods will find the cumulative folder indispensable.

Material Included in Folders

Generally speaking, the following kinds of material should be considered appropriate for cumulative folders:

1. Manuscripts of achievement tests and examinations
2. Manuscripts of intelligence tests
3. Interest questionnaires
4. Anecdotal records
5. Personality ratings
6. Autobiographical material prepared by pupils
7. Records of recreational reading
8. Memoranda of interviews with pupils or parents by teachers, advisers, and administrative officers
9. Records of participation in extracurricular activities
10. Outstanding examples of creative work
11. Physical and health examinations and records
12. Records of absence, tardiness, and disciplinary cases

Periodic Reports to Parents

The school's periodic report to parents regarding the progress of students is a time-honored practice in all types of schools at all levels of instruction. The nature and the form of this report may vary greatly from school to school, but the bookkeeping involved in the preparation of the records from which the reports are made and the clerical effort involved in making the reports are much the same. True, some kinds of records and reports involve a greater amount of labor per student than others. But the clerical processes of collecting and checking records, of transcribing data from records to reports, and of distributing the reports to the recipients vary only slightly in degree. The main concern is that the reports be clearly understood by parents and students; this is best accomplished through the definition of the symbols used in the evaluation of pupil progress.

Purpose of Reports

It is generally agreed that the main objectives of the periodic reports to parents are (1) improvement in the educational progress of students, (2) improvement in the professional knowledge and skill of the teacher through student appraisal, and (3) improvement in the confidence of parents and the general public in the school and its work. The sole function of such reports is to convey helpful information about the child and his work from the teacher to the parents.

Many students of education have tried to improve these reports so that they serve their function better. The reforms have been centered chiefly around the kinds of information reported to parents on the cards and the symbols used in reporting the evaluation. Analysis of seventy-three such cards revealed a total of thirty-seven items of information reported to parents. The number of items on a single card ranged from eight to twenty-three; the average for the seventy-three cards was fifteen. The items appearing on two-thirds or more of the cards are shown in Table 18. The evaluation of scholastic progress on seventy-one cards was given by three methods: (1) letters (47.9 percent), (2) descriptive remarks (42.4 percent), and (3) percentage estimates (6.8 percent). The trend in evaluation appears to be in the direction of letters and descriptive comments rather than percentage estimates.

The forms for periodic report cards have usually been designed by administrative officers who assumed that the items of information reported were the items parents wanted to know. Recently many report cards have undergone revision by committees of teachers advised by committees of parents. As a result, most school systems have departed greatly from the old-fashioned monthly type of report card which gave percentage marks designed to inform parents of the progress made by their children in school subjects. The newer reports are intended to indicate to parents the nature and character of their children's growth and the problems encountered by the teachers in their work with the children. The report is essentially intended to serve as a basis for a conference between the teacher and parent if student progress is not satisfactory.

In the 1960s, over 75 percent of urban school districts used a com-

Table 18

ITEMS OF INFORMATION APPEARING ON
TWO-THIRDS OR MORE OF 73 PERIODIC
REPORT CARDS USED BY PRINCIPALS IN
REPORTING PUPIL PROGRESS TO PARENTS

Item of Information	Percentage of Frequency
Name of school	100.0
Name of pupil	100.0
Attendance	95.8
Request for parent's signature	95.8
Grade or room	94.5
Term or year of report	93.1
Teacher's name	89.0
Key to scholarship rating	87.6
Statement or explanation to parents	83.5
Reports covering one year	69.8
Average for term or year	65.7
Notice of promotion	64.3
Deportment, conduct, or behavior	63.0
Character traits, citizenship	52.0
Scholarship rating by letter	47.9
Notice of promotion signed by teacher	46.5
Scholarship rating by remarks	42.4
Health, health habits	35.6
Date of notice of promotion	31.5
Notice of promotion signed by principal	30.1
Effort	27.3
Reports covering one term	27.3
Teacher's remarks	16.4
Scholarship by per cent	6.8
Mental health	4.1
Parent's remarks	4.1
Pupil's rank	4.1
Report of homework	4.1
Rating on standard tests	4.1
Date of pupil's birth	1.3
Extra-class activities	1.3
Name and occupation of parent	1.3
Notice of P.T.A.	1.3
Physical defects	1.3
Report of vaccination	1.3
Report of Regents' Examination	1.3
Time of first entrance	1.3

bination of report cards and parent conferences at the elementary level; 22 percent used a report card only; and one percent, parent conferences only. At the junior high school level, approximately half the districts used a combination of report cards and parent conferences, and the remainder used report cards only. For senior high schools, 42 percent used a combination of parent conferences and report cards, while 58 percent used only report cards.[4] Apparently, the parent-teacher conference has not penetrated deeply into secondary schools.

Frequency of Reports

In urban school districts of all sizes, pupil progress reports are issued either four times a year or more than five times. In elementary schools, these two practices are encountered to almost the same extent and together account for almost 90 percent of the districts in the U.S. In junior and senior high schools, they account for approximately 93 percent of the practices. And while in 44.2 percent of the districts, elementary schools report to parents more than five times per year, 55.7 percent of the junior high schools and to 58.6 percent of the senior high schools report to parents more than five times a year. Accompanying this tendency is the decrease in the only two or three reports a year practice.[5]

Parent-Teacher Conferences

In some school systems, periodic conferences between teachers and parents are replacing report cards. The plan was first developed in the kindergarten, where teachers found it difficult to evaluate children in terms of report card criteria. The kindergarten teachers found the conference more informative for the parents than the formal reports, and also more productive of information significant for the teachers.

Using Data Processing

Many schools are now making use of automatic data processing equipment. Although first introduced into the school business offices, the equipment has been adapted to serve many educational purposes. The professional personnel department often uses such equipment to store information concerning staff members, while those concerned with pupil personnel also use it in many ways. The forms required depend upon the capabilities

---

[4]National Education Association, Research Division, "What Do You Know About Today's Schools?" *Research Bulletin* 39 (February 1961), 24–25.

[5]National Education Association, Research Division, "Reporting to Parents," *Research Bulletin*, 39 (February 1961), 26–31.

of the machines available. Some schools have not only automated the preparation of a master schedule and individual pupil schedules in multiple copies, but attendance records as well. It is also possible to maintain permanent records and issue periodic reports on student progress with such equipment.

When automatic data processing is used, it is the principal's responsibility to assess the capabilities of the equipment and make the greatest possible use of it. Most members of the staff need specific instructions in providing materials to be computerized; they must realize that the data provided by the machinery are not better than the data submitted to it. Provision should be made to help parents understand how to interpret reports that come as a result of automatic data processing. And data processing should not become master of providing information needed in the general operation of the school. In other words, when it is impossible to program the machine to provide needed information, other means must be developed to obtain it.

The administrator who has the benefit of automatic data processing should be reminded that an efficient programmer is needed to make the system work effectively. Few administrators are competent enough in this area to do it themselves. Administrators should remember too that automated machinery is intolerant of error and will repeat or multiply mistakes. Training faculty members to use proper techniques in using the forms needed for the collection of data is another important responsibility of the administrator.

Using Information

From what we have said concerning the school's collection of records and reports, it is evident that the school has extensive information concerning its pupils. Some of the information in the climate of today's society could represent an invasion of privacy. While the school has the obligation to explore all legitimate means of obtaining information necessary to facilitate the educational progress of all pupils, some information should not be placed on permanent records and some should never be made available to the general public or even to the professional staff without the consent of the pupil and his parents. Serious problems have resulted when information has been collected and used without consent.

A conference, convened by the Russell Sage Foundation, has dealt with this matter in depth.[6] Among the suggestions made to avoid problems

---

[6]*Guidelines for the Collection, Maintenance, and Dissemination of Pupil Records,* Russell Sage Foundation (Hartford, Conn.: Connecticut Printers, Inc., 1970), pp. 20–22.

is that of classifying data into three categories. The first would include official records that provide minimum data necessary for the proper operation of the school system, and would remain a part of the permanent record. The second category would contain data helpful to the child, but would not be absolutely necessary to the school. Family background material and aptitude test scores would fall within this classification. The third category would include information of immediate importance but of little value for the future. Information collected in dealing with disciplinary cases and personality test results would fall in this category, and this type of information would be kept in the record only with the consent of the persons involved.

The report also offers guidelines for collecting, maintaining, and disseminating pupil records and represents a valuable source of information for administrators and the staff of the pupil personnel department.

Because the type and use of information collected should be governed by the rules and regulations of the board of education, the rules should be specific and easily interpreted. Some state departments offer both guidelines on the length of time certain information should be kept and outline proper procedures for disposal of records when they are no longer required. Floyd A. Vanderpool has offered some suggestions with respect to keeping records and getting rid of them.[7] He suggests that (1) records should be made of all releases of information concerning pupils; (2) information of a restricted nature should not be released by telephone; (3) during any inspection of school records, the custodian of the records should be present; (4) schools should not release any information that has not been collected by them; (5) information given for research should not identify individual pupils; and (6) only those working directly with a child should have access to his record.

Official Reports of Principals

The school principal has a considerable number of local official reports to make during a school year, some of which are periodic and some occasional. The ease or the difficulty involved in making such reports is conditioned by the status of the records in the principal's office. If attendance records are properly kept, for example, the monthly, bimonthly, mid-semester, or semester reports on attendance can be made with little effort by the person charged with attendance. Errors in records will be checked each day. As a result, the periodic reports can be quickly made

---

[7]Vanderpool, Floyd A., Jr., "A Guide for Keeping Student Records and Getting Rid of Them," *The American School Board Journal*, 158, No. 10 (April, 1971), 25–27.

by totaling the data which are usually summarized at weekly and monthly intervals. In a like manner, the periodic supervisory reports occasion little difficulty if records are made and filed properly.

State and County Reports

The school principal is required to make annual reports of a statistical character to the state and county in which his school is located. These reports are usually staggered throughout the school year, and require information on faculty, nonacademic staff, enrollment, attendance, and expenditures for certain purposes. Special reports are required on pupil transportation, education of exceptional pupils, and vocational education. All these reports necessitate keeping accurate records and require considerable time.

Reports to Accrediting Associations

Certain other types of official reports are more extensive in character than those previously mentioned. An example of such reports is the annual report made to accrediting associations by secondary schools. These reports, which in the past have made heavy demands on the time and attention of the school principal, are now less onerous because of the criteria developed by the National Study of Secondary School Evaluation.[8]

Probably the greatest benefit to be derived from using the *Evaluative Criteria* is the stimulus to improvement which they furnish to faculty members. In several states, committees of principals have been organized to work with local principals who wish to evaluate their schools to insure some degree of uniformity. If such a committee is to be of assistance, the local staff must allow ample time, certainly not less than a month, to compile and analyze data before the committee calls. The committee then checks over the analyses, inquires into some additional matters, and revises or approves the local analyses.

Evaluation of the type described is necessary not only for reports which are required if a school is to obtain or to continue accredited standing, but also as a means of stimulating the entire staff to constructive improvement. The preparation of reports to accrediting associations should therefore be regarded as the task of the entire staff. All should participate in collecting data for the records, and all should share in the process of data evaluation. The compiling of the report in its final form is the duty of the principal alone or of his designated assistant.

There is a growing feeling that permanent records should not be

---

[8]American Council on Education, *Evaluative Criteria* (Washington, D.C.: The Council, 1969).

| PUPIL'S PERMANENT RECORD | SHELDON HIGH SCHOOL, 2455 WILLAKENZIE ROAD | EUGENE, OREGON |

GRADUATION REQUIREMENTS: 15 UNITS ABOVE 9TH GRADE

TEST RECORD   UNIT: 36 WEEKS OF DAILY RECITATION. GRADING SYSTEM: ABCD PASSING F FAILURE   8 CLASS PERIODS—40 MIN.
ACCREDITED BY NOTRHWEST ASSOCIATION OF SECONDARY AND HIGHER SCHOOLS

paste-on data processing information

| RANK | OF | STUDENTS GRADUATED | JUNE | 19 | G.P.A. | TOTAL SENIOR HIGH UNITS EARNED → |

TRANSCRIPTS	COMMENTS
SENT TO/DATE	
EXTRA CURRICULAR RECORD	HONORS

| SUMMER SCHOOL OR CORRESPONDENCE COURSES | | GRADES | | UNITS EARNED |
| YEAR | COURSE | 1ST SEM | 2ND SEM | |

| 9TH GRADE | 10TH GRADE | 11TH GRADE | 12TH GRADE |

paste-on information

personnel data deleted (court cases)

| | | TARDIES | | | TARDIES | | | TARDIES | | | TARDIES |

SEX	BIRTHDATE	BIRTHPLACE		FATHER'S NAME	OCCUPATION
ENTERED FROM		DATE		MOTHER'S NAME	OCCUPATION
WITHDRAWN TO		DATE		GUARDIAN'S NAME	OCCUPATION
NAME	LAST	FIRST	MIDDLE	ADDRESS	PHONE

Fig. 19. One type of senior high permanent record form.

voluminous, but in some schools "incidents" are recorded. If they are, they should not be a part of the permanent record and should be destroyed when the person graduates or terminates his course. Records can be subpoenaed by the court and, "incidents" which may be rumors could be produced in court without a truthful foundation.

A satisfactory permanent record is produced for examination purposes and as a sample of a satisfactory record in Fig. 19.

Selected References

ALSPAUGH, J., "Utilization of Computing and Data Processing in Education," *Clearing House*, 43 (April 1969), 455–57.

AUSTIN, ALEXANDER, and ROBERT BORICH, "A Link System for Assuring Confidentiality of Research Data in Longitudinal Studies," *ACE Research Reports*, 5, No. 3 (February 1970).

BROOKS, A. F., "Reporting Pupil Progress to Parents," *National Association of Secondary School Principals Bulletin*, 45 (May 1961), 160–62.

Bureau of Pupil Personnel, "Statewide Conference on the Professional, Ethical, and Legal Responsibilities of School Guidance Counselors in Maintaining, Using, and Releasing Student Records," *Conference Report* (June 1968).

BUSHNELL, D. D., and D. W. ALLEN, *The Computer in American Education*. New York: John Wiley & Sons, Inc., 1967.

DALMAN, H., and K. E. MICHAEL, "What Are Some New Trends in Reporting Student Growth and Achievement to Parents?" *National Association of Secondary School Principals Bulletin*, 44 (April 1960), 146–49.

ELLIS, G. G., "Pupil Information and Records Systems," *National Association of Secondary School Principals Bulletin*, 52 (January 1968), 99–109.

GODDARD, W., "Computer Technology for the Whole School," *Journal of Educational Data Processing*, 6 (Spring 1969), 108–20.

GOODLAD, J. I., F. J. O'TOOLE, JR., and LAWRENCE L. TYLER, *Computers and Information Systems in Education*. New York: Harcourt, Brace & World, Inc., 1966.

GROSSMAN, ALVIN, and R. L. HOWE, *Data Processing for Education*. Chicago: Educational Methods Company, 1965.

HAGA, ENOCH, *Automated Educational Systems*. Elmhurst, Ill.: Business Press, 1967.

JANSEN, V. H., *Marking and Reporting Procedures in the Secondary Schools of Texas*. Austin, Texas: Texas Study of Secondary Education, 1960.

LEVENSTEEN, SIDNEY, "Ethical and Legal Considerations of Release of Information Relating to Students," *EDRS* (January 1969).

LEWIS, R., and D. McCREA, "Three Around the Conference Table," *Elementary School Journal*, 61 (November 1960), 72–50.

Musso, B., "Are Student Records Public?" *Education,* 87 (August 1967), 488–90.

National Education Association, "Reporting Pupil Progress." *NEA Research Bulletin,* 47 (October 1969), 75–76.

National Education Association, Research Division, *Reports on Pupil Progress and Elementary School Promotion Policies,* Research Memo 1960–36. Washington, D.C.: The Association, 1960.

Neumann, R. A., and R. W. Marker, *Educational Data Processing: New Dimensions and Prospects.* Boston: Houghton Mifflin Co., 1967.

Patton, Stanley R., "A Suggested Pupil Requirements File: Educational Data Processing Planning Study #1," Willis Educational Services, Inc., Chicago, Ill., Sponsoring Agency Educational Development Cooperative, Homewood, Illinois (June 1969).

Phillips, Beeman N., "Characteristics of High School Report Cards," *National Association of Secondary School Principals Bulletin,* 40 (September 1956), 63–67.

Prince, J. D., and Renan Richmond, "Electronic Data Processing for the Small School District," *National Association of Secondary School Principals Bulletin,* 54 (February 1970), 48–58.

Putnam, J. F., "Accounting for Every Pupil," *School Life,* 47 (December 1964), 31–33.

Rothney, J. W. M., *Evaluating and Reporting Pupil Progress.* Washington, D.C.: National Education Association, 1955.

"Salaries Paid Employees of State Departments of Education 1969–70," *NEA Research Bulletin,* 48, No. 3 (October 1970), 67–81.

Smith, A. E., "Innovations in Attendance Processing," *Balance Sheet,* 48 (December 1966), 164ff.

Smitter, F., "Report Cards: Problems and Possibilities," *National Elementary Principal,* 40 (September 1960), 166–71.

Terhune, V., "How to Maintain More Records in the Same Space," *School Management,* 9 (May 1965), 154–55.

Terwilliger, J. S., "Marking Practices and Policies," *National Association of Secondary School Principals Bulletin,* 50 (March 1966), 5–37.

Tompkins, E., and W. Gaumnitz, "The Carnegie Unit: Its Origin, Status, and Trends," *National Association of Secondary School Principals Bulletin,* 48 (January 1964), 1–72.

Trump, J. L., and D. F. Miller, *Secondary School Curriculum Improvement.* Boston: Allyn & Bacon, Inc., 1968, pp. 351–61.

Whigham, E. L., "What Should Report Cards Report?" *School Executive,* 77 (1958), 21–23.

Wilson, E. S., et al., " Rrank in Class," *National Association of Secondary School Principals Bulletin,* 50 (November 1966), 76–82.

18

Business Functions
of Principals

The school is obviously an educational enterprise, and as its manager the principal is responsible for its total operation. This means that he has business functions to perform as well as educational functions. The educational functions, of course, exceed in importance the duties which are managerial in nature, yet without the efficient performance of the managerial tasks, the school as an educational enterprise operates under serious handicaps.

Supplies and Equipment

Supplies and equipment are essential to the school enterprise. Indeed, the difference between an efficient and an inefficient school might depend on a difference in the quantity and quality of the supplies and equipment provided.

Nearly all schools furnish some supplies, while many furnish all. The tendency of schools today is to furnish more than formerly, and therefore it may be expected that schools will ultimately furnish all supplies. The problem of administering, requisitioning, storing, and preparing the budget for supplies becomes increasingly important for the head of the local school as the amount and variety of supplies and equipment increase. Even in schools which furnish no supplies to children, it is customary to provide towels, soap, chalk, erasers, and janitorial supplies. These supplies may or may not be requisitioned by the principal depending on local policy, warehouse facilities, and the relation of the educational and custodial staffs.

415

In any case, the principal should know what constitutes proper procedure in obtaining the necessary supplies and equipment for a school. In large cities he will find that requisitioning, storing, and distributing educational supplies is an arduous task unless the procedures for doing so are systematized. And since the trend is toward furnishing school supplies more widely through the school budget rather than through individual purchase, the efficient performance of administrative duties with respect to such supplies and equipment becomes increasingly important in all school offices.

Classification of Supplies

If supplies are to be used efficiently, they must be classified according to their function so that both professional and nonprofessional employees may refer to such materials without confusion. For example, materials may be classified as library supplies, industrial arts supplies, home economics supplies, kindergarten supplies, music supplies, janitorial supplies, and so forth.

Progressive theories of school administration recommend that both teachers and principals participate in selecting supplies. Such participation imposes an obligation on the teachers to consider carefully what is needed and requires the principal to harmonize the requests of his spendthrift and parsimonious teachers. Records of supply needs of former years may help in evaluating teachers' requests.

Large city systems usually employ a purchasing agent to do all school purchasing, but in smaller schools the purchasing is usually done by the superintendent of schools, and frequently by the secretary of the board. If the supplies delivered to the school are inferior to those requested— no matter who ordered them—and if the inferior product will in any way interfere with good results in the school, the local principal must bring the matter courteously but firmly to the attention of his administrative superior without making it in any sense a personal issue.

The problem of inferior supplies is less likely to occur in schools having a standardized supply list—a practice common both in large business and in large school systems, and one that should be much more widely used in schools generally. Again, teachers should have a share in preparing the standard list so that they will not be dissatisfied with supplies furnished.

The use of standardized lists will also result in savings to the public funds when all or some supplies are furnished to pupils. But the standardized list is recommended whether educational supplies are furnished by the school district or purchased by the pupils or their parents. The use of a standardized supply list should not preclude the purchase of special instructional supplies such as those necessary for a special class project. A reserve sum—a nominal amount—should be set aside for this purpose.

Requisitioning Supplies

There is a growing tendency for school systems to maintain a central warehouse where supplies purchased in quantity are stored for the school year. Large cities are more likely to have special warehouse facilities than are smaller cities. When a warehouse is maintained, both educational and maintenance supplies are distributed to local schools by employees of the board of education, using a truck furnished for that purpose.

A strong argument for the use of a central warehouse for educational supplies in medium and large city systems is that the plan prompts efficiency of administration and accounting, and the supplies stored in this way are less subject to losses such as destruction by rodents or water damage. Supplies can be cared for more economically in a warehouse than when the supplies are decentralized. When supply control is centralized, the supplies can be issued only on written requisition; this is almost universal practice.

In large systems the days of the month on which requisitions may be received are staggered so that the requisitions do not accumulate in the central warehouse to such an extent that they cannot be cared for efficiently. The principal should likewise have a regular time during which he receives requisitions from teachers. Unless this is done, the principal's time will be taken up with so much routine that he will not have time for more important duties.

Handling Requisitions

Requisitions are usually printed forms, although some systems use mimeographed forms, and are generally issued in triplicate. The principal keeps one copy and sends two to the central office, where they are approved or cut, depending on the care with which the requisitions have been prepared by the principal. Requests which fall within budget appropriations should be approved without question and sent to the warehouse for prompt delivery to the local school. Careful preparation of requisitions facilitates prompt delivery and avoids the petty frictions which can so easily creep into relations between professional and nonprofessional employees.

Drawing requisitions is a clerical task and should be delegated to clerks; the principal should approve or reject the teachers' requisitions after the requests have been received and organized by the clerk.

Accounting for Supplies

It is general practice in city school administration to keep an account of the supplies furnished to each school. Such accounting is essential to the evaluation of the uses made of the supplies. Well-managed central stock rooms also have a perpetual inventory to show the amount of stock on hand in order to prevent either overstocking or handicapping due to lack of supplies.

In the local school, some method of handling supplies must also be arranged so that supply administration makes only a reasonable demand on the principal's time, and does not prevent him from giving adequate attention to his most important duty, the improvement of instruction. Requests from teachers for supplies should be received on a regular form similar to the one on which the principal makes requisition to the central office, though somewhat less detailed. In no instance should requisitioning be permitted to deteriorate into hastily scrawled notes on different sizes of blank paper. When the supplies have been received, they can be distributed to the teachers by a custodian or student monitor on the basis of the teachers' requests.

Storage space for supplies must be provided in the local school. Such space may be in the basement or in an unused room with shelving or bins to facilitate classification of supplies. In some school systems a permanent inventory may be necessary, though it is not generally kept by the local school. A record of the amount of supplies requisitioned and used by each teacher should be kept so that careless or overzealous teachers do not use a disproportionate share of the materials. Inspection of rooms at irregular intervals will quickly indicate which rooms or teachers are wasteful of educational supplies. A cumulative folder of original requisitions for each teacher kept in the office and brought up to date after the custodian has issued the regular monthly requisitions will supply objective information on use of school supplies.

Special classes obviously require special supplies. Consequently, the principal should familiarize himself with such special needs so that he can facilitate instruction in these areas. Supplies are especially needed in industrial arts, home arts, physical education, and ungraded classes. A principal who does not familiarize himself with the needs of these areas may easily provide too little or too much if he relies solely on teacher requisitions for supply information.

At times it may be necessary to present emergency requisitions because of increased enrollment or other unforeseen problems. Such requests —and they should not be many—should be presented to the superintendent with an oral or written supporting statement of the reasons why the supplies above those regularly allotted are necessary. The principal must also have some accounting system so that he knows how he is conforming to the budget allowance.

School Equipment

The principal has no less responsibility for equipment than for supplies, although he ordinarily is much less likely to be consulted in selection of equipment. The responsibility of the principal with respect to supplies is a recurrent one, but his responsibility for equipment is to see that it is in good condition, that it is protected from abuse or loss, and occasionally to recommend new equipment to replace the old.

When a principal is new to his position, he must often forego requesting additional equipment until he is well-oriented, or at least until he is doubly sure that he can demonstrate the indispensability of the particular equipment which he desires to requisition. Even then it may be impossible to secure needed equipment, because well-organized schools operate on a budget, and unless provision was made for particular equipment in the budget, it is frequently impossible to release the necessary funds until another budget is prepared.

The Importance of Equipment

Proper equipment is essential for the orderly and efficient operation of a school. Even a superior school building is of little use without teaching equipment, whereas an old building, though inadequate, may serve its purpose if properly equipped.

In order to economize, some schools have equipped new buildings with old equipment, only to find that the old is not suitable and does not fit into its new surroundings. Equipment for a new school should be requested at the time the new building is planned. Building plans should show the location of all furniture and equipment drawn to scale. Suitable outlets for electricity, water, sewage, and gas should be indicated on the floor plans.

Classification of Equipment

Equipment is often classified as to status: permanent or movable. Permanent equipment refers to articles that are part of the building: electric light fixtures, heating and ventilation fixtures, toilet fixtures, blackboards, and any other materials permanently fastened in the building. Permanent equipment is generally moved only upon requisition by the principal, and then only for unusually good cause. Permanent equipment or buildings may be marred by such readjustments. For instance, permanent hangers for maps are often provided to prevent marring the woodwork or walls with nails. Teachers and principals sometimes resent such restrictions, but they must realize that the building must be kept unmarred as far as possible; reasonable restrictions are necessary for this purpose.

Movable equipment refers to chairs, office furniture, projection instruments, portable radios, books, duplicating machines, and so forth. Equipment may also be classified according to its function—seating, visual aid, cafeteria, home economics, industrial arts, music, and athletics.

Restrictions are rarely placed on the rearrangement of movable equipment within a room or from room to room at the discretion of the principal and teachers, since such rearrangements usually do not conflict with sound instructional procedures or provisions for proper hygienic conditions.

When antiquated or obsolete equipment is to be withdrawn from service, it is usually done at the end of the year so that replacements can be made during the summer recess at the convenience of the workmen and without disrupting the school program. This takes place only if the principal has requested the replacement of equipment and provided for it in the annual budget.

The Principal's Responsibility for Equipment

The principal has always been expected to organize his school so that equipment is cared for with a minimum of effort. Proper morale in the school prevents wanton equipment damage; accidental damage or vandalism by a few must be dealt with individually. Accidental damage of equipment through use in schools is to be expected; monetary reimbursement should not be expected in such cases. Children are not always competent, and the equipment is for their use under the guidance of the teachers. Damage due to accidents is a normal operating cost which the school must assume.

In the case of perverse destruction of equipment, the principal should attempt to collect for the damage as a moral rather than as a legal claim; school authorities should rarely undertake collection through the courts. Punishment of the student, whether corporal or not, for damage to equipment might conceivably result in a suit against the principal for unreasonable severity. Whether a suit is decided for or against him, it does not help the school's public image.

Student cooperation is necessary in protecting school property, but such help cannot be secured through admonition or preachment. It is necessary to develop pride in the local school so that the students will feel a sense of participation in ownership. Such a sense of partnership may be developed through group guidance discussions that show the cost of school property to the community and that indicate each pupil's responsibility for considerate use of supplies and equipment.

Keeping a Record of Equipment

Many school systems keep an inventory of movable equipment, but this practice is not followed universally, nor is there any universal way of taking school inventories. Some inventories are periodic, others are perpetual; the form in use varies with the opinion of the administrator who prepares it. Inventories conducted on a periodic basis are usually made annually, while perpetual inventories are kept up to date as new equipment is added or old equipment removed. The new principal who assumes the responsibility for a school should ascertain whether an inventory is being kept. If there is none, he should take steps to make some sort of an inventory immediately. Any previous inventories should be checked for accuracy, so that missing equipment may be charged against the administration which lost or misplaced it.

The inventory also offers an objective and reliable basis for estimating the needs of the school when the budget is being prepared. It may also aid in preventing theft or misplacing equipment, and it forms an accurate basis for estimating insurance needs or claims in case of loss.

Inventories are most likely to be usable if they are taken for each room or department which contains movable equipment, such as the industrial arts, physical education, interscholastic athletics, and home economics departments. The form used need not be elaborate, but it should furnish enough information to be of value. If the school system does not have a form for this use, the form in Fig. 20 may provide suggestions.

The form may provide space for listing the articles in alphabetical order and for recording the number of items added during the year, the deductions for obsolescence or retirement, the total on hand, and the value. An inventory which shows the amount and condition of equipment in a room or department for a series of years is preferable to one which does not.

When equipment is issued to students for use, a record should also be kept as a means of preventing loss to the school. An inventory is also helpful in determining what equipment is in need of repair. Even though the custodial staff has delegated to it the responsibility for requisitioning and keeping in repair certain types of equipment, the principal as head of the school is responsible for much of the equipment and the nature of its use.

ATHLETIC EQUIPMENT INVENTORY (Name of School) 197_ – 197_							
Article	No. Last Inventory	No. Discarded	No. Added	Total No.	Cost Per Item	Date of Purchase	Date of Inventory	Present Value
Football —								
Helmets								
Hip pads								
Jerseys								
Pants								
Shoes								
Shoulder pads								
Socks								
Sweat shirts								
Thigh guards								

Fig. 20. Inventory form for athletic equipment.

Modern Trends in Equipment

Every school principal should keep abreast of developments in the school equipment field. The companies which manufacture equipment are always eager to inform school principals of new developments. Books and articles on school administration and attendance at the major educational meetings furnish any additional information. It is unnecessary to determine whether one company's movable seating is better than another company's until a purchase is actually contemplated, but it is necessary to know that the trend in school seating is toward movable equipment and light-colored furniture. The growing importance of the auditorium makes it imperative that the principal know something of stage scenery and lighting so that requests for such equipment can be made intelligently. Similarly, the principal should know that radio equipment is more widely used and that centralized systems are preferred over individual classroom sets.

Many communities have both radio and television stations which may have some free time available for the schools if the schools can make creditable use of the time. Central office policy should recognize the importance of making proper use of these public facilities in the cultivation of wholesome school and community relations. The principal should inform his teachers when opportunities for presenting school activities and classroom work are available, and he should obtain consultative assistance for them which is necessary in preparing such presentations.

New developments in instruction result in the development of new equipment to meet these developments. Three such developments—the teaching machine, television, and the language laboratory—merit the attention of the principal, for they are likely to become as common in the next decade as other equipment has in the past. With the increased emphasis on greater efficiency in educational methods, economy of teacher time, and acceleration of the more able pupils, schools will be expected to provide equipment which will most likely contribute to accomplishment of these things.

Many different types of teaching machines are already on the market and more will come. They range from a simple form, which is little more than a mechanized workbook, to those which approach the complexity of an electronic computer. As for television, a vast area in the North Central states is now being covered by educational television broadcasts from an airplane, with many different types of television sets available for receiving such programs. Due to the impetus given to the study of foreign languages by the National Defense Education Act of 1957, many schools have installed sound equipment for language laboratories.

It will be the principal's added responsibility to inform himself on the merits and deficiencies of the various kinds of equipment offered in these three new areas not only so that available money may be spent wisely, but also so that the greatest possible value may come to the school's instructional program.

Free Textbooks

Principal's Responsibility for Textbooks

There is a growing sentiment that school districts should furnish textbooks free to students. Proponents argue that the total cost to the community is less if books are purchased directly by the school from the publishers rather than by the students or their parents from local tradesmen. Another contention is that when pupils are required to purchase books, the pressure of public opinion to retain an adopted text after its period of usefulness is almost inevitable. Free textbooks remove such pressure because books may be retired from service after the normal period of use—three to five years—depending on the extent of use and the sturdiness of manufacture.

More than two-thirds of the states provide free textbooks for the elementary grades, but only about half of them provide free texts for high school pupils. Free texts at the secondary level have met opposition in several states, because opponents say that not only are high school pupils old enough to work and earn the money to buy their books, but also that they will take better care of the books if they own them. Actually many individuals only oppose the free high school texts because such a provision represents another expenditure from tax funds and is likely to increase the school budget. Such a position or belief is probably based on the fact that free secondary education for all has not yet become universally accepted.

Some schools have tried to compromise the two positions by purchasing books and renting them to the pupils, particularly at the secondary school level. Although this plan furnishes textbooks at less cost to parents and allows freedom from public pressure in the selection of books, it is not recommended if free books can be provided. Where the rental plan is adopted, it is usually a compromise measure which will eventually be replaced by free books.

Modern methods of teaching involve large numbers of books in either the classroom library or the central library for use with certain classroom units. This fact makes it necessary for the school district rather than the individual pupil to purchase the books. In many cases no basic text is used, but rather a series of books. Furnishing books in such quantities places a responsibility on the principal both for selection and administration. Quite generally in city systems, committees of teachers are appointed to choose textbooks, and often a principal is placed on a city-wide committee with the same function. The members examine books, listen to salesmen, and make their selections. It is almost universal practice for the district to accept the recommendations of the textbook committee.

When free textbooks are furnished, they may be stored centrally and requisitioned annually, although this procedure involves a large amount of hauling. Better practice is to retain a reasonable number in each school and transfer them by requisition on the basis of enrollment at the beginning of each term. The surplus, which would require much less storage space, could be kept in the central warehouse where further supplies could be requisitioned by principals. In order to prevent the ambitious and aggressive principals from securing more than a just allotment of textbooks, some schools have found it desirable to allot books on the basis of enrollment.

Accounting for Textbooks

Textbooks are not usually accessioned through the library, but they must be housed in the local school. Probably the best storage plan is to put them in a central book room, where they may be conveniently arranged and from which they may be requisitioned by teachers. Textbooks should be returned to the central book room at the end of the year, where they can be checked with the inventory of the previous year. At this time, provisions should be made for replacement and repairs. During the year, someone in the principal's office, preferably a clerk, should issue the books on requisition and keep the accounting of the book room up to date.

All textbooks should be labeled as property of the school district and numbered as such. In addition, the name of the school district is frequently stamped on the top and bottom edges to prevent books from finding their way into private book collections or secondhand stores.

Because the teacher must keep a book record for each student, Fig. 21 will serve as an example. The record prevents the loss of books, since each book is numbered and charged to a certain student. Experience indicates little difficulty in administering such a system and very little unwarranted wear or loss for the books.

The principal also needs a control form for the book room from which he can determine the number on hand at any time. A satisfactory example is shown in Fig. 22.

Every principal encounters the problem of dealing with lost or misused books. If fines are to be collected, they should be dealt with as moral rather than legal obligations. As was pointed out in connection with broken equipment, it is doubtful that such claims could be collected legally from

TEXTBOOK LOAN RECORD

(Name of School)

197_ – 197_

Name of Teacher .... Textbook ....

Pupil's Name	Book No.	Condition		Fine	Pupil's Name	Book No.	Condition		Fine
		at Issue	on Return				at Issue	on Return	

Fig. 21. Teacher's record of textbooks lent to class.

Title of Book	Total	Issued to Teachers				Lost	Unfit	Re-mainder
		(Name and Number)						

PRINCIPAL'S RECORD OF TEXTBOOKS

(Name of School)

197__ – 197__

Fig. 22. Principal's record of textbooks issued to teachers.

the parents even though the claims might be large enough to warrant court action. Fortunately, the number of lost or misused books is very small, and most parents pay fines as moral obligations if not as legal claims. Because it is inevitable that loss will occur in the distribution of free textbooks, the principal must hold the loss as low as possible.

Pupil Transportation

Pupil transportation is largely a school system problem; that is, whether or not pupils are transported and the regulations pertaining to methods and schedules are system-wide decisions. The local school principal's problems involve meshing the dismissal schedule with that of the bus schedule and the pupils to be transported. The control of children on buses to and from school often presents aggravating problems. The driver, although in control of the bus, is usually too busy to give close supervision to his passengers, but he can and should report unruly students to the school principal who has authority over students en route to and from school.

In some school systems which transport large numbers of students, student government polices the situation. Each bus has student officers in control who are responsible to the school principal for the behavior of students on their buses. The principal's problem is one of careful planning for the student organization of each bus and close supervision as it functions. This method of control has worked so well that it probably represents a pattern of management which may become general practice in the future.

School Lunch Program

In many parts of the country the school lunch program has become an important part of the business responsibility of the principal. In some communities more meals are served in school lunchrooms than in the restaurants. With the subsidies provided by the federal government in cash and surplus commodities, the school lunch program has been greatly stimulated in the years since World War II. From 645 million school lunches served in 1947, the number has increased to over 1,712,000,000.[1] Figures for 1969 reveal that more than 20 million children were served 3,400,000,000 meals in elementary and secondary schools through the federally assisted school lunch program.[2] In 1970, more than 1½ billion dollars of federal, state, and local funds were expended for the school lunch program. The increased availability of money to high school pupils through work opportunities and increased family incomes, the greater distances they live from school, the increased transportation of pupils, and the increase in the number of working mothers of younger children have all contributed to greater patronage of the school lunch program.

Most principals have found it advantageous to employ a capable head cook or lunchroom manager and turn over to him or her complete responsibility for the day-to-day operation of the lunch program. The old system of assigning the cafeteria to a home economics teacher as an extracurricular duty is hardly defensible today because of the increased demands on teacher time for instructional purposes. A few principals may still try to manage the lunchroom themselves, but this practice is even less defensible than assigning it to a teacher.

Breakfast at School

Many children come to school without breakfast. Since the federal government recognizes that a child cannot learn effectively when he is hungry, it has made fiscal provision for poor children to receive breakfast

---

[1]United States Department of Agriculture, *School Lunch Programs in Elementary and Secondary Schools in the United States,* Marketing Research Report No. 262, (Washington, D.C.: Government Printing Office), p. 5.

[2]Senate Committee on Agriculture and Forestry, *Hearings on School Lunch and Child Nutrition Program,* 91st Cong., 1st sess., 1969 (Washington, D.C.: Government Printing Office, 1970), p. 74.

at school. Although local districts furnish a minimal amount of the total cost, very few schools have availed themselves of this assistance to poor children. Most of the money available through the state department is not used but is returned to the federal government.

Problems of School Finance

Budget Responsibilities

It is generally recognized that a carefully made and well-administered budget, based on educational needs, is necessary to the efficient management of a school system. The principal's responsibility varies with the size of the school system and the theory of school administration held by the board of education and the superintendent. In general, the tendency to delegate to the principal greater responsibilities in preparing and administering a budget is much desired. If the individual school is made the unit of preparation and administration of the budget—a practice in many school systems—the principal must participate. And if the principal is to administer the budget, he and his faculty should share in its construction. Usually this participation takes the form of compiling requests for supplies, equipment, and books which are revised by the central office and returned to the principal for review before the budget is presented for final approval or revision by the reviewing body.

In much the same way, maintenance and repair budgets are submitted, revised, and reviewed. The principal has some responsibility for teachers' salaries through formal evaluation of teachers. If formal ratings are not required, salary recommendations based on sound educational reasons are expected. These duties, which do not include preparation of the salary schedule, are ordinarily concluded well in advance of the date when the budget is submitted for approval. The preparation of other budget items, such as fixed charges, capital outlay, debt service, or estimation of income, is not the responsibility of the principal.

After the budget has been adopted, the responsibilities of the principal are limited to the administration of his school's allotment for supplies and equipment. When budget allotments have been made, they should be adhered to except in unusual cases, such as an unexpected increase in enrollment. In such cases special arrangements between the principal and the superintendent make sure that sufficient supplies, books, and equipment will be available. Requests to transfer funds from one account to another should be made infrequently, if at all, and then only for extraordinary educational reasons. The budget, if well-made, should provide for all regular or anticipated needs; requests for major transfers usually indicate carelessness in planning or inefficiency in administration.

If the principal is to administer a budget, he must know the amounts in each account which are already spent, committed but unspent, or unallocated in order to avoid embarrassment to himself and his superior officers. Some schools send to the principals monthly financial statements showing the amount allocated to the budget, amount spent to date, and the amount available for expenditure. These reports enable the principal to keep within budget appropriations. If such reports are not made, the principal should set up a series of memorandum accounts in his office which will give sufficient information to make intelligent administration of the budget possible. Such an account should be kept for each heading of the school budget for which the principal is responsible and should show the amount appropriated, amount expended, commitments which must be paid but have not yet been received, and unallocated balance. A satisfactory form, if one does not exist in the system, is provided in Fig. 23.

Memorandum accounts are not official and should be reconciled with the central office accounts periodically. They serve as a satisfactory working control for each major account for which a principal is responsible, and they prevent the embarrassment which results from overdrawn accounts or from careless administration. If the principal wishes to determine costs per room or by department, the account should have supplementary columnar distribution sheets where the clerk may enter headings from the controlling account. These distributions make possible any cost studies the principal may wish.

BUDGET ACCOUNTS

(Name of School)

197_ – 197_

Name of Account ....

Amount and Date of Appropriation	Goods Received	Commitments Not Yet Received	Unexpended Balance

Fig. 23. Record form for budget accounts.

Memorandum accounts do not always agree fully with official accounts, because small sums which were not recommended or approved by the principal will inevitably and justifiably appear in the central office records from time to time. These corrections, which are usually not large, should be made from time to time to reconcile the memorandum accounts with the official books.

Keeping accounts facilitates studies of school costs within the building. Such studies may be made to compare costs among the various grades or departments as to teachers' salaries, pupil enrollment, and supplies.

Petty Cash and Financial Accounting

In every school small sums from book fines, sales to students, or petty cash funds from the central office must be accounted for. Unless there is a school store, the greatest problems in bookkeeping will ordinarily arise from the sale of materials such as industrial arts or home economic supplies, which are used by pupils in making articles which become their property. Such supplies are not likely to be furnished without cost no matter how generously the school provides supplies and equipment, nor is there any reason why these articles should be furnished at public expense.

It becomes the duty of the individual instructor to collect the cost of the materials, issue a receipt in duplicate for them, and account for the transactions to the principal. The principal or his clerk should issue a receipt in duplicate to the teacher and send the money to the central office, where it can be credited to stores or to the revolving account. The principal's office should also remit book fines to the central office, although receipts are not issued. The office should retain the teachers' forms showing the conditions of books returned and fines levied until probability of possible reference to them has passed. Ordinarily these accounts will be sufficient records. If the school keeps petty cash, receipts must be secured for every expenditure so that the sums may be accounted for in a businesslike way. Public funds are a public trust, and accounting for them is an obligation which any principal must perform with meticulous care.

The School Store

For the many articles needed by students which are not furnished by the board of education, the school store has been found to be desirable in some communities, particularly at the secondary level, to provide for the convenience of the students and to standardize the merchandise available for purchase. Some schools sell textbooks and other necessary articles such as pencils, ink, paper, and notebooks. Other schools have gone further and have stocked art supplies, music supplies, suits to be worn in physical education classes, gymnasium shoes, and other supplies which students may need.

Reasons for the School Store

The reasons usually given by principals for establishing the school stores are (1) convenience to the students, (2) economy for the students, (3) standardization of supplies, and (4) elimination of satellite stores. Although the last one is not advanced frequently, it is recognized as a pertinent reason by all who have struggled with the problem of undesirable fringe stores.

The primary reason for the establishment of the store, convenience to the pupils, is well-justified since many schools are frequently located a considerable distance from the community's business district. The second reason, economy for the pupil, is also a good reason, because by patronizing the school store, the student can save as much as 20 percent of the cost price in retail stores—the school purchases direct from the jobber, does not pay rent for the store, and is not interested in profit.

Local merchants almost unanimously consider school stores unfair competition, since the school store does not pay rent or local property taxes. Unless the principal can show that the store is a real convenience for the students, it is unwise to open it; local merchants may attempt to close it and may succeed.

Articles Sold

The supplies sold in school stores can be classified into three groups: (1) general supplies used in many different classrooms, such as pencils, inexpensive ball-point pens, theme paper, ink, and erasers; (2) special supplies used in one or a few courses, such as stenographer notebooks, art supplies, or mechanical drawing paper; (3) noneducational articles, such as candy, soft drinks, peanuts, chewing gum, and fruit.

Operation of the Store

The operating capital of school stores is secured chiefly from four sources: (1) the small profit which accrues from operating the store; (2) money appropriated by the board of education for the original capital outlay; (3) payments for goods out of the income of the store by staggering payments bills from jobbers; and (4) general student body funds. By all odds, the second source is best, because funds from the board place the official stamp of approval on the venture.

Stores are usually managed by the principal or his office clerk, but he apparently only acts as personal manager in smaller schools; in the larger schools, some other adult is assigned the duty. Most schools also use some paid student help.

The store can be justified only as a service to students, but even this reason should not be acceptable to a board of education if the school principal allows his time to be monopolized in its operation. He is employed as a school leader and administrator, not an operator of petty business. If the school is to operate a store, the principal must arrange for its operation in an efficient manner, restricting the scope of activities to services approved by the board of education. A wise principal never allows the school store to be his hobby. The financing of the store must be in harmony with sound business methods and its accounts must be subject to the same periodic auditing as all school accounts. The nearer an approach can be made to complete operation by students under faculty guidance and supervision, the greater the educational value of the venture.

Extracurricular Finance

We have already stated that in many schools athletics present problems of considerable financial responsibility. In an even greater number of schools, the entire extracurricular program may involve large expenditures. Even a small high school, through its student council or other means of control, may run thousands of dollars through its accounts in the course of a year. In a large school, sums in excess of $100,000 a year are not unusual. Some schools carry such large reserves that they invest a part of them in government bonds or other securities.

The Necessity for Financial Accounting

Because these sums are comparable to the current operating expense of a small school system, expenditure of the funds must be accounted for carefully. Any school administrator who does not do so soon forfeits public confidence. The accounting obligation would be no less imperative if the extracurricular funds were no greater than $50 for an entire year.

Instances can be found in which treasurers of school organizations have misappropriated funds or in which the staff of a publication which has shown a profit for the year has distributed the proceeds among its members. (The latter arrangement still exists in some higher institutions.) Many school systems account for all extracurricular funds carefully, but others do not. It is a rare school which has complete financial records going back ten or fifteen years. Even when there are such records, it is doubtful that adequate audits cover the entire period.

Unless accounting is centralized and carefully supervised, organizations with funds left in their accounts will logically wish to spend them before the end of the school year. Organizations that have overspent will forget the deficit, which will plague the sponsor and the administrative officer during the summer and perhaps throughout the following year. Such occurrences cause irritation and unnecessarily complicate the problem of school administration.

In nearly all cases where financial records of extracurricular activities are incomplete or inadequate, the oversight is due to carelessness or lack of awareness as to the necessity of keeping records, rather than deliberate neglect on the part of school principals. That boards of education have at times allowed extracurricular funds to be accounted for inadequately can be explained only by their ignorance of the sums which are handled. Fortunately many school administrators now see the necessity of caring for funds.

The system of accounting recommended here for extracurricular funds is to have the responsibility for all accounts centralized in one adult —principal, secretary, teacher of commercial subjects, or special person hired to supervise all extracurricular funds. Decentralized accounting will inevitably lead to confusion, inaccuracy, and misappropriation of funds. The minimum which can be accepted in accounting for funds in an individual school is:[3]

a. Official receipts should be issued for all money received.

b. All money received should be deposited in a bank.

c. All money expended should be expended by check except for small cash purchases paid from petty cash.

d. Supporting documents should be kept for all expenditures made.

e. Bank reconciliation statements should be made each month.

f. Monthly and yearly financial statements should be prepared.

g. An audit should be made each year and copies of the audit should be filed with persons having administrative authority for the school.

Suggested Accounting Procedure

The procedure proposed here is simple, provides all information that is necessary, and has both the sanction of competent school authorities and successful practice to recommend it.

Each organization treasurer deposits with the school treasurer regularly all funds which come to his hands. The school treasurer issues a

---

[3]*Financial Accounting for School Activities*, U.S. Department of Health, Education, and Welfare, Office of Education Bulletin No. 21, (Washington, D.C.: Government Printing Office, 1959), p. 12.

receipt in duplicate. One copy is kept in the school treasurer's files, the other is kept by the organization treasurer. There can never be any doubt as to the amount of money deposited by an organization, because the matter can be checked. A sample of such a receipt, on a three-by-five-inch card, is shown in Fig. 24. Such forms are in current use in most schools.

Purchase Order or Requisition Blank

When any organization wishes to make a purchase, it should fill out a blank similar to the one shown in Fig. 25. This blank is signed by the treasurer and the representative of the organization, and certified by the school treasurer that there are sufficient funds to pay the bill.

The purchase request is filled out in triplicate. One copy goes to the vendor, one to the organization treasurer, and one remains with the school treasurer. It is necessary to impress on tradesmen with whom the school does business, on student officers, and on sponsors that no goods may be ordered or charged against the school account unless a requisition is obtained first. Unless this is done, unexpected bills and invoices may arrive which cannot be met because funds may not be available for payment. Unauthorized purchasing constitutes a very real problem, especially in small schools.

Controlling Accounts and Subsidiary Accounts

All school accounts, from whatever source, should be kept in one account at a bank and a controlling account showing the balance for all ac-

---

TREASURER'S RECEIPT

(Name of School)

Date . . . .   No. . . . .

Received of . . . . the sum of

. . . . for . . . . organization.

. . . .
School Treasurer

Fig. 24. Activity receipt issued to school treasurer.

```
┌─────────────────────────────────────────────────────────┐
│                    PURCHASE REQUEST                       │
│                                                           │
│                    (Name of School)                       │
│                                                           │
│                                    No............         │
│                                                           │
│                                                           │
│                              Date...................      │
│                                                           │
│  Name of firm .........................................   │
│                                                           │
│  Address ..............................................   │
│                                                           │
│  Purchase .............................................   │
│                                                           │
│  ......................................................   │
│                                                           │
│                                                           │
│                   Organization .....................      │
│                                                           │
│  Amount           Treasurer ........................      │
│                                                           │
│  $ ............   Faculty Sponsor ..................      │
│                                                           │
│                                                           │
│                   School Treasurer .................      │
└─────────────────────────────────────────────────────────┘
```

Fig. 25. Activity purchase order form.

counts should be kept by the school treasurer. The controlling account may be kept on a single sheet punched for a loose-leaf notebook, and should show receipts, total receipts, date, item entered, number of the check used for each payment, disbursements, the total amount disbursed, and the bank balance. Each subsidiary account should have a similar sheet which shows its balance. The total of all subsidiary accounts must balance with the total in the controlling account, which must be checked with monthly bank statements.

Payment of Bills

No bills should be paid until an invoice has been received from the vendor and the sponsor of the organization or the treasurer has checked it. An order for payment may then be issued, as shown in Fig. 26.

Such an order for payment, in duplicate, should then be signed by the sponsor and treasurer of the organization, attached to the invoices for goods received, and sent to the school treasurer, who checks to see that the order corresponds to the requisition. The treasurer should fill in the check number, keep the original and the invoices, and give the duplicate to the organization treasurer. The check is then issued and sent to the vendor with a form showing the date and number of the tradesman's invoice (see Fig. 27). The proper entries are made in the controlling and subsidiary accounts. This is a common practice in all well-managed schools.

When the check returns from the bank at the end of the month, it is attached to the invoice, original requisition, and order for payment, and all of it is filed numerically by check number. It is then easy to refer to the transaction at any time in case invoices are presented a second time, or if some error has occurred in the transaction.

At regular intervals, probably once a month, the school treasurer

---

TREASURER'S ORDER

(Name of School)

No.........

Pay to the order of .... for

invoices attached and goods received, the sum of $ ....

Sponsor ....

Check No. .... Treasurer ....

Date .... School Treasurer ....

Fig. 26. Form used as treasurer's order for payment.

NOTICE OF PAYMENT

(Name of School)

Enclosed is our check No. · in payment of

your invoices numbered · , covering our

requisitions numbered ·

Very truly yours,

· ·
School Treasurer

Date ·

Fig. 27. Form used as notice of payment.

should issue a statement of the condition of each of the funds for which he is responsible. These statements should go to each sponsor, organization treasurer, and the principal. In some schools it is the practice for all organization treasurers to meet with the school treasurer early in the year to receive systematic instruction in proper methods of keeping accounts. Following the period of instruction they should meet with the school treasurer regularly, probably once a month, to check their accounts with his. But there is no value in having pupils keep accounts unless the accounting is properly done.

The condition of the entire fund should be published annually with the certificate of audit which should be made by a competent disinterested auditor, preferably a certified public accountant.

The school treasurer should be bonded with a surety company for the largest amount of money for which he is likely to be responsible at any one time. The cost of a bond is negligible, and bonding protects both the school and the person responsible for the funds. The cost of bonding may be charged to the general account of the school or divided proportionately among the subsidiary accounts.

To facilitate orderly business practice, all goods and invoices should be delivered to the school treasurer, who in turn should distribute them to the proper organizations or individuals for checking before the payment order is made out.

The system described here is simple and workable. A school that desires a more comprehensive plan can easily secure one from a commercial supply house or find one described in the writings on school administration.

The General School Fund

It is desirable to have a general fund from which purchases of benefit to the entire school—outside the scope of any organization—may be made. The source of this fund varies. In a few schools it is customary to impose a tax of 10 percent on the net receipts of all the major revenue-producing activities, such as athletic games and dramatic performances. The theory on which this tax is based is that the activities thrive because of their connection with the school; it is, therefore, reasonable that part of the receipts should benefit the entire student body.

In other schools, bazaars, carnivals, and other entertainments furnish the funds for the general school fund. Such a fund is the responsibility of the student council in schools where the council is allowed financial responsibility. From the general fund may be purchased paintings, trophy cases, motion picture projectors, and other equipment which cannot be secured through regular board of education appropriations. The fund may also help worthy but nonrevenue-producing activities in the school. In the high school in Austin, Minnesota, the general fund was used to purchase a pipe organ for the auditorium, sound motion picture equipment, musical instruments, and other needed equipment.

A note of caution should be added. Purchasing equipment which is properly the responsibility of the board of education may set a precedent difficult to break. But despite this precedent, the general fund is a desirable practice which many schools should adopt. In large schools the general account may reach such proportions that part of it may be deposited at interest until it is needed for purchase or expenditure.

Methods of Securing Funds

The main source of funds for extracurricular activities is from the sale of tickets for individual events, but other sources include dues from pupils, receipts from special activities, season tickets, tag days, profits on sales in the school store or at school functions, and social events. Some schools sell season tickets to football games or other events which occur in series. This practice tends to insure the school against low receipts because of a poor season, unfavorable weather conditions, or other unforeseen factors. In other schools an activity ticket is sold which admits pupils to all events —athletic and nonathletic—and often includes a small fee for student body membership.

Many schools use some form of installment payment to enable all students to subscribe for activity tickets. Usually a large percentage of the student body supports such a plan and continues installments throughout the year. The plan insures good attendance at all events and enables more students to attend school functions. If such a plan is adopted, it is necessary to have events well-distributed throughout the year and to have a highly prized token such as the annual or yearbook distributed after the last payment on the activity ticket has been made.

Schools which have tried the plan are enthusiastic about it. Drives for each activity are no longer necessary, attendance increases, and sufficient revenue is available to operate the activities. After the amount to be received has been determined, it can be allocated to the activities early in the year so that each organization knows what its resources are and can plan its expenditures accordingly. Selling an activity ticket which admits students to all school events is much more businesslike and dignified than having tag days, bazaars, or benefit performances. The latter two are particularly likely to disrupt the entire school with preparation for them. Even though the sum realized from such events may be considerable, it is extremely unlikely that the results can be justified in the light of the loss of time.

When ticket sales are held, they should be carefully supervised. All tickets should be numbered and a record of the numbers issued to each seller should be kept. Students should realize that losing tickets is a personal liability that they must assume just as they assume liability for their own money. Those who lose tickets may reasonably be held accountable for those presented for admission. If the numbered tickets are not presented, there is no reason why the student who lost them should reimburse the school; it has suffered no loss.

Even when an activity is used as the basis for student admission, it is necessary to sell admission tickets to adults. Such selling should be carefully supervised and receipts checked with tickets. To fail to do so, particularly if students are allowed to sell tickets, offers the possibility for fraud. The principal may delegate the responsibility for selling to the activity sponsor and the treasurer of the organization presenting a public performance, with the provision that an accurate report of sales will be furnished promptly after the sale of tickets is concluded.

Responsibility for Finance

The student council may assume responsibility for allocating extra-curricular funds to the various activities on the basis of need and within the limits of the funds available. Such a practice may well be one of the most vital experiences that comes to students.

In large councils a committee under faculty sponsorship may more conveniently consider all budget requests and recommend to the council, which in turn accepts or rejects the recommendations. Such recommendations are, of course, subject to the principal's approval, as are all other acts of the council.

If pupils are to participate in the school government, which implies management of extracurricular activities, they should participate in the allocation of the funds necessary for the operation of the activities. Such a student committee is especially necessary when all moneys are placed in a general school fund, and from which funds are disbursed to activities—irrespective of which activities helped raise the funds.

Methods of management of the fiscal affairs of the school activity program have improved greatly during the past two decades. Purchase by requisition is now the general practice in most schools. Payments for goods and services are made by check and on invoice only. The annual audit, recommended by most authorities, is used more widely than before, but less extensively than is desirable. Complete security for school activity funds can not be attained until all schools have an annual audit of their accounts. This should be made by a person licensed to make municipal audits, should preferably be employed by the board of education, and should make his report to the board.

The making of the budget for extracurricular activities may vary, from a simple allocation to each activity to carefully worked out plans under which each activity receives a percentage of the total budget. No matter what plan is used, the budget should form the financial chart for the year, from which deviation should not be made except for emergencies. As a backlog for such contingencies, a reserve fund should be set up, or part of the expected annual receipts should be kept in the general fund for such emergencies.

The council or its finance committee need not handle funds or do the bookkeeping; legislative bodies, whether Congress or a student council, allocate rather than administer funds. Fiscal administration should be reserved for a bonded adult treasurer who reports regularly to the council the condition of all funds. The school treasurer should be a member of the finance committee—in fact he might be the sponsor for the group.

Pupils should learn that public funds such as those used in extracurricular activities must be supervised carefully, that expenditures should be made according to a budget plan, and that expenditures must be accounted for according to approved business practice. If pupils in school are taught to handle public funds in a careful manner, they will be more likely to insist on similar careful handling of public funds outside the school. To foster such a desire on the part of pupils is one of the school's obligations.

A Word of Caution

The rapid increase in school size and the changed conditions under which schools operate today have greatly increased the business responsibilities of school principals. Many schools enroll more pupils than the population of towns and small cities. The efficient operation of these schools as communities makes heavy demands on the business competency of the principal. Job analysis of the business functions required of school principals runs into hundreds of duties and it is highly important that principals and persons aspiring to be principals take courses in school administration in institutions of higher learning dealing with the nature of the business aspects of school administration. It is also essential that they keep up with the current literature on school organization and administration. Sufficient clerical help must be provided, too, so that the principal does not become a clerk. The tendency of all this is to make the principal business-minded, but important as it is that school principals become efficient managers of their school enterprises, it is imperative that they not lose their perspective as educators. In the final analysis they will be evaluated by the quality of their leadership as educators rather than by their acumen as business functionaries.

Selected References

BEACH, F. F., and G. G. TANKARD, JR., "Standard Accounting for School Activities," *School Life*, 42 (November 1959), 26–27.

"Business Management: Practices and Problems," (Special Report), *Nation's Schools*, (Summer 1966), 53–80.

CAHALL, T. WILSON, *The Hagerstown Project, A Preliminary Report*, International Television Seminar (Boston: Boston University, 1958), pp. 1–43.

CARLSON, W. H., "The Principal and the Textbook," *National Elementary Principal*, 38 (October 1958), 29–32.

CARROLL, JOSEPH M., "School Lunch From Pail to Plate," *The School Executive*, 78 (December 1958), 37–38.

DAUM, HENRY F., and MARGARETTA PLEWES, "Paying for Food Services," *The School Executive*, 78 (December 1958), 38–39.

DEBERNARDIS, AMO, VICTOR DOHERTY, ERRETT HUMMELL, and CHARLES W.

BRUCBACKER, *Planning Schools for New Media*, U.S. Office of Education (Washington, D.C.: Government Printing Office, 1961), pp. 1–71.

FORSYTH, RALPH A., and LELAND A. THOMPSON, "Criteria for Centralized Warehousing Procedures in Public School Districts," *Summary Report* (Denver, Colorado: Denver University, 1968), 59 pp.

GABLE, MARTHA A., "Educational TV—Catastrophe or Opportunity?" *American Association of University Women Journal*, 53 (May 1960), 213–16.

GLASPEY, J. L., "Can Modern Management Techniques Be Applied to Education?" *Association of School Business Officials Proceedings*, 53 (1967), 254–65.

GRAHAM, ALVIN D., "Buying for the School Store," *Clearing House*, 35 (October 1960), 77–78.

GUBA, EGON GOTTHOLD, "Evaluation and the Airborne Television Project," *Educational Research Bulletin*, 39 (October 1960), 179–93.

HARTMAN, A. S., "Saving Money Through Better Business Practices," *School Management*, 14 (December 1970), 25–26.

ISENBERG, ROBERT M., "The Bus Can Be an Instructional Facility," *Nation's Schools*, 65 (May 1960), 80–81.

KENNEDY, ROBERT H., "Profits From Our School Store," *School Activities*, 31 (December 1959), 99–100.

KNEZEVICH, STEPHEN J., and JOHN GUY FOWLKES, *Business Management of Local School Systems*. New York: Harper & Row, Publishers, 1960. See especially Chapter 5, "The Purchasing and Management of School Supplies and Equipment"; Chapter 11, "Managing and Accounting for Student Body Activities"; and Chapter 16, "Management of School Transportation and School Food Services."

LOPEZ, PAUL, "More Than a Feeding Program," *American School Board Journal*, 141 (September 1960), 22–23.

POWELL, RUTH, "School Lunch Evaluation: An Aid to Administrators," *School Executive*, 78 (July 1959), 65–66.

SAMUELSON, EVERETT V., "Financial Accounting for School Activities," *National Association of Secondary School Principals Bulletin*, 44 (April 1960), 269–72.

STICKEL, WERNER E., "How Effective is Teaching by Television?" *The Instructor*, 69 (January 1960), 4, 48.

TRACY, G. S., and M. J. NORMAN, "A Computerized System for School Bus Routing." Toronto: Ontario Institute for Studies in Education (1970), p. 291.

WALLACE, C. E., "Teacher Responsibility for Student Funds," *National Association of Secondary School Principals Bulletin*, 42 (September 1958), 138–41.

WALLACE, GERALD R., "Six Ways to Safer Transportation," *Nation's Schools*, 65 (May 1960), 75–76.

"Will Industry Run Our Ghetto Schools?" *Nation's Schools*, (January 1970), 85ff.

19

Supervising Noninstructional Personnel

Selecting and supervising noninstructional personnel has not received the attention from educators that the selection and supervision of instructional personnel has. This is often defended on the grounds that noninstructional personnel do not have the direct contact with students that the instructional staff does, but this is only partially true.

The only contact that a person often has with the school is a telephone call. If the secretary who answers the call is a well-informed individual, has a pleasing voice, and is helpful (giving information which is accurate and within her responsibility to give, or referring the caller to an appropriate individual), then the caller immediately has a favorable impression of the school.

Today approximately one-third of the people on the school payroll are noninstructional personnel. In small districts, the principal has prime responsibility for supervising their activities; in larger districts, this responsibility is delegated. Regardless of the size of district, such supervision is an important responsibility. This chapter is concerned with suggesting broad guidelines for supervision and evaluation in several of the more important service areas in the school.

Jeanette Bragin, chairman of the research committee in office management of the Association of School Business Officials[1] suggests some guidelines for developing an effective program for noncertified school personnel.

---

[1]Jeanette Bragin, chairman, *Guiding Principles and Practices in Office Management: A Handbook for School Business Officials*, Research Bulletin No. 4, (Chicago: Research Corporation of the Association of School Business Officials, 1969), pp. 27–31.

1. *Develop a description for each job.* This description should include a definition which clearly outlines the job; gives some typical duties that the job entails; indicates competencies, both in knowledge and skills, required; and outlines the necessary educational background for the job.

2. *Check each job description.* Once the description has been written, it should be tested under actual working conditions. Tests should be made upon or with persons having long periods of employment in the school system so that the job description can relate specifically to the functions and activities of a particular job.

3. *Establish a program of employee recruitment.* Several suggested sources of recruitment are local and state employment agencies, placement services, advertisement, local radio and TV broadcasts, and dissemination of information about job openings through school staff and parent groups.

4. *Develop a system of internship or apprentice experience.* On-the-job training under the direction of an experienced employee should be used as an opportunity for checking abilities and fitness of the probationary employee. It is an opportunity to observe not only job competency, but the adaptability of the employee in working with children, parents, and teachers.

5. *Establish inservice training programs.* For the new employee, the inservice training program develops competency and teaches good practice. For the experienced employee, the inservice training program refreshes and/or retrains him. A newssheet or administrative newsletter issued on a regular basis helps keep employees informed of good practices. Training sessions can also be scheduled by bringing in personnel speakers, and using films and materials from all areas of the school system in order to acquaint the noncertified personnel with the operation of the entire school program.

6. *Establish work schedules.* Schedules ensure that the employee knows exactly what is expected of him, when he is to do it, and under what conditions he is to work. It also provides the supervisor with a specific outline of duties which makes his job of supervision easier by pinpointing the responsibilities of the noninstructional personnel. Teachers also find these schedules valuable so that they know when service personnel are available to them.

7. *Plan a program for improving relationships between teachers and noncertified personnel.* Periodic joint meetings between the teaching and nonteaching staff help to develop mutual understanding of the problems in each area. Examples of appropriate topics for such joint meetings might be availability of group insurance plans, medical insurance plans, vacation schedules, and working hours. Such meetings help to foster a working team spirit.

8. *Develop personnel policies and procedures.* A simple, readable handbook of pertinent information on regulations, policies, and procedures

should be developed, adopted by the board of education, and distributed to all employees concerned. Such a handbook should include salary schedules, promotion policies and procedures, procedures for transfers, retirement plans, leave possibilities, development of tenure status, procedure for submitting grievances or complaints, procedures that apply to assignment or appointment of personnel, means of recognition of service, fringe benefits, organizational charts, and procedures for the dismissal of employees whose performance is unsatisfactory.

9. *Schedule staff conferences.* These should be scheduled on a regular basis so that the information can be shared, troublesome problems discussed, and courses of action outlined.

10. *Emphasize and practice good human relations.* Organizations are composed of human beings who are individuals and who expect to be treated as individuals. People perform best when they know what is expected of them and know that their supervisor is aware of what they are doing. People who are more motivated by encouragement and job satisfaction than by fear, who want to succeed on the job, and who need to feel that they play an important part in the institutional program do a better job. And those who want to know the ground rules under which they are working, and who know that the opportunity for promotion and salary increases are open to them if they are worthy, make a better working team.

Supervising Custodians

In large systems, principals receive assistance in rating the performance of custodians from the man directly involved with plant operations—the head custodian. In all systems regardless of size, the custodial staff must be supervised and evaluated. A written checklist is helpful, and it also serves as a standard against which the custodian can rate himself and his performance. The checklist should contain such items as personal appearance; personality traits; relationship with staff, students, and public; quality of cleaning (the normal areas of the school should be rated independently, such as general traffic area, classrooms, restrooms, shower rooms, office area, grounds); and knowledge of materials used. After the checklist has been completed by the principal or the head custodian, the rating should be discussed with the individual custodian.

Custodians should be selected with care. Some qualifications which should be considered when hiring a custodian are whether he has a genuine liking for children (evidence of this trait might be gained both through conversation and observation of his contacts with pupils during a preliminary tour before he is hired); a pleasant personality; a good physical appearance; decent moral standards and good habits; an interest in the job he will do; and information about his technical skills in heating, carpentry, plumbing, and electrical maintenance and repair.

The Broward County Board of Public Instruction indicates the following as a work schedule for custodial trainees:[2]

First four days
1. Clean sixteen classrooms.
2. Help scrub and wax one of these rooms.

Fifth through eighth days
1. Clean twelve classrooms.
2. Help scrub and wax one of these rooms.
3. Help sweep and mop cafeteria.
4. Clean two master toilets.

Ninth and tenth days
1. Clean eight primary classrooms.
2. Clean eight small toilets.
3. Help clean administration suite.
4. Help clean library.
5. Help clean cafeteria.
6. Help mop and wax one of the above classrooms.

This school district also indicated the training program for full-time maids:[3]

1. Work hours: 7:00 A.M. through 4:00 P.M. with one hour for lunch (12:00 to 1:00).
2. Report for work promptly, having previously studied the printed instructions for the training program. The area to be cleaned will be explained in detail by the head custodian, using the instructions as a guide.
3. Assemble all equipment and materials necessary to complete the assigned job.
4. Check condition of the administration office, performing any tasks needed.
5. Repeat above operations in deans' offices and clinics.
6. Check condition of all girls' toilets; service dispensers as needed.
7. Wash all drinking fountains.
8. Sweep loggias.
9. Wash glass in doors.
10. Service all girls' restrooms.
11. Clean homemaking department.
12. Clean other offices.

---

[2]*In-Service Training Program for Custodians* (Fort Lauderdale, Fla.: Broward County Board of Public Instruction, 1965).
[3]*In-Service Training*, p. 6.

13. Clean one standard classroom.
14. Daily mop or machine scrub one classroom or area.
15. Daily wax or refinish floors.
16. Daily clean master restroom.

In supervising the custodial staff, the principal is responsible for:

1. Reporting to the central office the maintenance needs of the school building.
2. Orientation of new custodians to their tasks.
3. Making clear building regulations and procedures which affect the work of the custodian.
4. Introducing the new custodian to the staff members and to instructional personnel.
5. Requisitioning supplies and equipment within the limitations of the budget.
6. Securing the cooperation of teachers and pupils so that the work of the custodian can be more effective.
7. Observing daily the general appearance of the building, hallways, restrooms, classrooms, plants, and grounds. If a good job has been done, the custodian should be complimented; if the job is poorly done or not done at all, it should be called to the attention of the custodian and a program to correct the deficiencies should be instituted.
8. Instituting procedures for the safety of the building, including clearing hallways of obstruction; locking doors when the school is not in session; making sure that trash, sweeping compounds, rags, and mops are not stored in such a fashion as to create a fire hazard.
9. Inspecting the building at intervals with the custodian, and discussing with him existing conditions.

Supervising Secretarial and Clerical Personnel

For supervising the performance of secretarial and clerical personnel, guidelines are also required. A job description should be written out carefully for each position, indicating the specific skills that are required. For example, typing (indicating both speed and accuracy); filing; record keeping; telephone techniques; procedures for receiving and handling all types of office visitors; description of the school business forms which will be used; responsibility for originating responses to correspondence; procedures for accepting, securing, and disbursing cash; use and repair of machines; and personal qualities should all be clearly defined. Care should be taken that clerical personnel both understand and follow approved policies and procedures as well as understand the full range of the principal's responsibilities and authority.

Also to be considered in hiring clerical personnel is the efficiency with which the prospect arranges your appointments and prepares background information for such appointments; the consistency with which she meets deadlines; and the extent to which she is friendly, courteous, and respectful to school visitors. The school office is a business office and not a place for extended social conversations. In her relationships with the instructional staff, there should be mutual respect and support. Instructional staff who accept the secretary greet her pleasantly in the morning, during the day, and upon leaving school.

The principal must make sure that he understands his personal goals. He must be certain that his office workers, too, understand the dimensions of their roles and responsibilities. They are not professional educators, and should respond only to routine questions which they are qualified to answer. The secretary often views herself as a second principal and can very quickly alienate the instructional staff by assuming authority for which she does not have an adequate background. The school office is no place for a "little Caesar."

The principal should also consider in choosing personnel the extent to which they show initiative in solving problems that fall within their areas of responsibility, and the extent to which they can be trusted with confidential information. Because an office seems to operate on paper flow, the principal must ask, Does this prospective employee know how to keep correspondence flowing smoothly, or will she perhaps let it pile up on her desk or mine? And finally he must evaluate: the suggestions she makes for the improvement of office procedure; her interest in the school's program (Does she show pride in the school? In the students? In the instructional staff? In the achievements of the school?); the program which she has outlined for her own self-improvement; and her general health and emotional stability, personal appearance, punctuality, accuracy, ability to follow instructions, oral expression, spelling, handwriting, and good general office housekeeping.

As we mentioned previously, the secretary is often the only contact that a caller, on the telephone or in person, might have with the school. On the basis of this contact, he may form an impression about the school. The secretary is truly an image-maker for the school.

Pupil Transportation Staff

The number of staff needed in the transportation system of course varies with the size of the district. *The School Executive's Guide,*[4] in dis-

---

[4] *The School Executive's Guide.* Prepared by the Prentice-Hall editorial staff and a board of 46 contributors. (Englewood Cliffs, N.J.: Prentice-Hall, Inc., 1964), p. 171.

cussing the criteria for determining the number of positions and jobs needed for pupil transportation programs, indicates that if a transportation program utilizes twenty or more units of equipment, the district should usually employ a transportation supervisor who is accountable to the superintendent of schools in the moderate size district, or to the assistant superintendent of business affairs in the larger districts. In addition to a supervisor, most schools systems operating a transportation system also find it advisable to employ a chief mechanic. A full-time mechanic can adequately maintain an average of fifteen vehicles, but the age and condition of the equipment will determine the mechanic-vehicle ratio more than any other factor.

The transportation supervisor responsibilities include (1) being familiar with all of the duties associated with the position; (2) enforcing school board policies governing the transportation system; (3) planning bus routes; (4) checking to see that the transportation service is running on schedule; (5) supervising the employees who are responsible for the maintenance of the school's vehicles; and (6) holding regular conferences with the school principals on matters relating to the conduct of pupils on the buses.[5]

This school bus safety check-list may help in supervising transportation facilities.

Do all of the vehicles used in your district, both school-owned and/or contracted, meet state and national minimum standards for school bus construction?

Are the vehicles used by your district, both school-owned and/or contracted, inspected periodically (at least monthly)?

Does your district require that all vehicles be given a thorough checkup annually?

Does your district thoroughly investigate all new school bus drivers, those employed by the school district or by private contractors, prior to employment in regard to their experience and previous driving record, character, and other personal qualities?

Does your district require a complete physical examination for all new drivers prior to employment—and an examination at least annually for all drivers?

Does your district require all new drivers to undergo a training program that includes both classroom and driving instruction?

Are all drivers required to take part periodically, both prior to and during the school year, in some type of inservice training conducted by qualified personnel?

Are the responsibilities and obligations of all persons concerned

---

[5]*The School Executive's Guide,* p. 985.

with children's safety—the parent, the student, the driver, the teacher, and the administrative staff—clearly stated in board policy statements and regulations? Do all concerned understand fully?

Does your district cooperate with local civic organizations such as the P.T.A. in planning safety meetings?

Does your district have a planned program for teaching pupils sound school bus safety practices through various classroom activities, demonstrations, and emergency drills?

Does your district utilize school patrols in heavily urbanized areas to provide protection for pupils at busy intersections—or in rural areas to assist in maintaining order when children enter, leave, and ride buses?[6]

The principal, of course, is not normally responsible for close supervision of the transportation system as indicated on this check-list, but he should be familiar with procedure in providing such transportation services. He is usually the spokesman for the local school, and must be able to answer parents' questions about the transportation system accurately.

The principal can read some of the selected references included at the end of this chapter for a more detailed and profitable examination of supervisory techniques and approaches.

Selected References

BRAGIN, JEANETTE, chairman, *Guiding Principles and Practices in Office Management: A Handbook for School Business Officials,* Research Bulletin No. 4. Chicago: Research Corporation of the Association of School Business Officials, 1969.

In-Service Training Program for Custodians. Fort Lauderdale, Fla.: Broward County Board of Public Instruction, 1965.

Minimum Standards for School Buses, rev. ed. Recommendations of the National Conference on School Transportation. Washington, D.C.: National Education Association, 1964.

Selection, Instruction, and Supervision of School Bus Drivers, rev. ed. Recommendations of National Conference on School Transportation. Washington, D.C.: National Education Association, 1964.

---

[6]*The School Executive's Guide,* p. 1005.

20

The Principal in the Community

Schools belong to the communities in which they are located, even though they are theoretically state institutions. In most states the local community still bears a major share of the costs of school construction and operation. For several years, the taxpayer has been asked to provide additional facilities for a growing population, and, in keeping pace with new methods of teaching, there have been additional demands for instructional materials and educational hardware. For the most part, the taxpayer has met these demands. But increased tax burdens at all levels have created a condition where there is some resistance to increase the local tax burden any further. The failure of tax rate referendums and bond issues is evidence that support may be more difficult to muster in the future.

The school principal has continued to be a positive force in building good relationships within the community. He has made contacts with parent groups, church organizations, civic clubs, service groups, and labor-management organizations. Through such contacts in the community he has developed faith in the local schools, but there is some evidence that this task may become more difficult in the future. There have been attacks upon the schools because some have sincerely believed that the schools should be more effective. Others have attacked the schools as a means of developing a force to keep taxes at a low level, or for the purpose of seeking personal publicity and political power.

The school principal must therefore acquaint himself with the necessity for carrying on an intelligent program of school-community relations so that he can meet such attacks and plan a sound policy for informing the public about the philosophy and the operation of the school. Some

451

large systems have the benefits of a well-organized public relations program, but smaller schools usually do not have such services. In any case, the responsibility for school interpretation to the public rests largely with the principal.

As long as the great majority of the people believe in the public school and its program, sporadic attacks from hostile groups in the community have less success in defeating the educational program or even parts of it. Schools which have carried on a program to keep the public enlightened have not been subjected to serious curtailments when demands are made for reduction. In some communities where programs have been developed without adequate explanations to parents, progress has been retarded and changes forced on the schools because of opposition from uninformed groups. Attacks on so-called "fads and frills" are often successful because the public has not been sufficiently enlightened regarding the merits of such activities. Interpretation should not be deferred until a crisis occurs. Some school systems have resorted to whirlwind or high-pressure campaigns when new buildings were needed and have said nothing about the schools between times. This is unsound and perhaps dangerous practice.

Most efforts toward interpretation of school programs in former years were carried on largely by the central office, but in recent years there has been an increasing realization of the importance of the principal as the local interpreter of the district's educational policies. The duties of the chief administrator have become so complex that he has found it necessary to share this responsibility with the principals. In most large cities, the superintendent meets regularly with the principals to consider and explain policies at such length that all of the principals can interpret the policies to the teachers and the community.

Time Spent in Community Activities

In a study that analyzed the amount of time principals spent in various activities (previously mentioned in another chapter), the data indicate that those who participated in the survey spent some time with laymen, either as individuals or groups. The percentage of time spent by junior high school principals was as follows: 18 percent spent no time, 65 percent spent from 1 to 3 percent of their time, 12 percent spent from 4 to 6 percent, and 4 percent spent from 7 to 15 percent of their time with laymen.[1] Figures for senior high school principals were as follows:[2] 22 per-

---

[1] *The Junior High-School Principalship* (Washington, D.C.: The National Association of Secondary School Principals, 1966), p. 54.

[2] *The Senior High-School Principalship* (Washington, D.C.: The National Association of Secondary School Principals, 1965), p. 84.

cent of the principals indicated that they spent no time with individuals or groups outside the school, 71 percent spent 1 to 6 percent, 5 percent spent from 7 to 12 percent, and 1 percent indicated an allotment to this activity of more than 12 percent of their time.

The figures seem to indicate that some principals have realized the importance of this activity while others have given it little consideration. If the principal's work week consists of fifty hours, the figures indicate that the average principal spends no more than three hours per week in this activity. It is doubtful whether that amount of time is sufficient to build community support for the school program.

Organization for School Interpretation

A number of school systems have provided a public relations program headed by a director who is a staff officer in the superintendent's office. Where this officer exists, the principal has the responsibility to work in close cooperation with the director both to promote the interpretation program for the system as a whole and also to carry it out in the individual school.

It is more effective to follow plans which have been successful than to rely on an individual's opinion of the best methods of school-community relations procedure. The National School Public Relations Association, a department of the National Education Association, is a valuable organization dedicated to assist in developing programs to keep the public informed. Other agencies offer assistance as well. The Pennsylvania Department of Education has published a booklet helpful to administrators which describes the duties and qualifications for a staff specialist in communications for the North Penn School District. Key duties described are: (1) to disseminate information to the public in a systematic fashion, (2) to disseminate information to the staff of the school district, (3) to process requests for use of school facilities by community groups, and (4) to edit curriculum publications.

The key duties of informing the public in a systematic fashion as to school programs and activities include:

a. Preparing news releases for radio and the press and newsletters on school activities, events, and programs
b. Collecting information from building sources, district administrators, and the board of education in a systematic fashion
c. Coordinating the schedules of school personnel with requests for speakers from community organizations
d. Preparing brochures describing the school district and available positions for use in personnel recruitment

  e. Preparing brochures describing the school program for distribution through the chamber of commerce, realtors, and local industries
  f. Preparing interpretative sound/film presentations for service clubs, P.T.A., and other community organizations[3]

When the school system does not have specialized personnel for this area of the school's operation, the duties must be assigned to other personnel. The local principal may secure the assistance from teachers in the English department or journalism classes. Guidelines are necessary for operation of information dissemination; these should be developed to implement rules and regulations of the board of education that pertain to this responsibility.

Newspaper Publicity

Although newspapers in most communities provide generous space for reporting school news, much of this news deals with school activities, particularly athletics. While the interest in this type of school news continues to persist, there appears to be a growing tendency to devote more attention to other aspects of the educational program. Although *The Twenty-Eighth Yearbook of The American Association of School Administrators* was published in 1950, the "ten priorities for publicity" are as valid today as they were then. Priorities listed are:[4]

  1. Pupil Progress and Welfare
  2. Instructional Program
  3. Guidance and Health Services
  4. Attendance and Discipline
  5. Enrollment Trends
  6. School Staff Members and Alumni
  7. Building Program
  8. Administration and Finance
  9. Parent-Teacher Association
  10. Student Activities

These so-called priorities represent practically all the facets of an educational program such as school progress, curriculum, child development, health of pupils, and building plans. A principal who sensitizes the

---

[3] *Guidelines for Public School Communication* (Harrisburg, Pa.: Office of Information and Publications, Pennsylvania Department of Education, 1970), pp. 11–12.

[4] American Association of School Administrators, *Public Relations for America's Schools, Twenty-Eighth Yearbook* (Washington, D.C.: The Association, 1950), p. 278.

faculty to the desirability of collecting worthwhile news items concerning these and other phases of the school has made an important step toward a good interpretation of his school.

From our experience, we suggest that principals consider the following guidelines in establishing good working relations with the media.

1. Responsibility for preparing news releases should be assigned to one individual. Some schools view this as a service for which extra pay is provided. The journalism sponsor is one possible choice, while a member of the English department with special skills in writing is another.

2. News releases should be disseminated on a regular basis to all media. Releases should be written in reportorial manner. Many local papers appreciate material that does not require further editorial preparation.

3. Representatives of all media should receive invitations to all types of school functions. This provides an opportunity for them to become acquainted with the breadth of learning experiences in the school.

4. There should be no attempts to conceal facts from the media. When incidents and shortcomings exist, there should be a frank discussion of the matters involved. Representatives of the media are not amateurs, but experts at discovering facts. The quickest way to alienate the press is to be evasive or dishonest in giving accounts of events.

5. The media should not be expected to become enthusiastic about every school endeavor. The media has many publics, and although most educational efforts, including innovations, are worthy of support, some burden of proof rests with the proponents.

6. Crash programs for school publicity are never successful. It is a mistake to assume that continuous neglect concerning news releases can be corrected by a sudden all-out effort. Scarcely a day passes in any school without at least one newsworthy item occurring.

7. Representatives of the media should be contacted for suggestions with respect to evaluating the school's efforts in the area of public relations and news reporting. They are experts in the field and are usually willing to share their expertise when invited to do so.

The local newspaper is an important medium of interpretation. In some cases the newspaper allots a specified amount of space to school news. Others use material as considered appropriate. Whether a reporter is assigned to make definite calls upon school officials or the newspaper is contacted by the school are matters to be considered locally. It is important that the principal avoid personal prominence and that he stress the school, individual teachers, or pupils who constitute the news. The principal's name is unimportant; if the people in the community believe in the school, they will quickly learn the principal's name if they do not know it already. But if they do not believe in the school, the principal's name will add no weight to the news or to the school.

Radio and Television

Both radio and television may be used in interpreting the schools to the public. Principals should welcome the opportunity to make radio and television appearances concerning educational topics when invited to do so. Students too can be used to develop programs of interest to youth. Local stations should be informed of a school's interest and willingness to participate in worthwhile programs. Many schools also use closed-circuit television and operate ham radio stations. Students in such schools are experienced performers and could make impressive appearances.

Annual Reports

Many school superintendents furnish annual reports to the patrons of the district, and individual schools are often highlighted in these reports. The school principal is usually called upon to furnish material for the report which usually features such matters as enrollment, finance, activities, future plans, areas of concern, school achievements, and so forth. Some communities have used the secondary school yearbook as a source for pictures to enhance the report.

Communication to the Homes

School news is sent to many homes through the school newspaper. A well-edited school paper, explaining changes in the services offered by the schools, describing the curriculum and extracurricular activities, noting honors or awards which have been earned by pupils, and listing professional staff activities has been very effective in the program of school interpretation. In addition it provides an effective way of developing school spirit within the student body.

Many schools send bulletins to the pupils' homes at regular intervals, while in other cases, bulletins or letters are sent as needed. Such communications may be printed or mimeographed, depending on the purposes to be served. The general purpose is to acquaint the school patrons with the school's methods and practices and to enlist their cooperation in providing for the needs of the boys and girls in the school.

One example of a letter to school patrons at the secondary level is as follows:

Suburbia High School
Suburbia, Any State
Any Day, Month, and Year

Dear Parents of Juniors and Seniors in Suburbia High School:

For several years it has been our practice to send a letter to those parents whose sons and daughters are eligible to attend the high school Prom. Our purpose in doing so has been to suggest what we feel are good practices to be observed while attending social activities which are incident to the graduation season. The following suggestions, therefore, we hope will be helpful not only to parents but also to the students involved. There is no attempt upon the part of anyone connected with the high school to dictate to parents, but it is our duty as parents and teachers to take every precaution to make the graduation season a happy time for all concerned.

It is our desire to make this year's Prom one of the best ever. One of our main objectives is that it be well attended. Because there are always many disappointments for those who are not invited, we feel that parents may be of assistance in encouraging students to participate in this event. Of prime importance is our desire to establish standards which will prove helpful in making the affair a success in every way. The following specific suggestions are made for your thoughtful consideration.

1. We should like as many as possible of our students who are members of the junior and senior classes to attend. Outside guests who are juniors or seniors in another high school may be invited by a junior or senior in Suburbia High School.

2. We are trying to keep the costs within moderation. Girls wear formal dresses, and boys dress formally or informally, as they choose. Again, we hope that costs for the evening will be kept appropriate to high school students.

3. The Prom closes at 12:00 A.M., midnight. It takes at least thirty minutes to clear the gymnasium following the closing. It is generally customary for students to go some place for refreshments afterwards. If your son or daughter follows that practice, it would be difficult for him to be home before 2:30 A.M., so you should not expect them before that time. The important thing is that plans be discussed beforehand with your son or daughter and that there be a definite time set when parents may expect their young people to be home. If something should happen to make it impossible for the schedule to be met, the young man or woman should call the parents and notify them of the situation.

4. There are a few people who may have the attitude that "a Prom happens only once in a lifetime," so anything goes. This attitude is dangerous and should not be tolerated. The school faculty feels that liquor or drugs have no place at the Prom, and we hope that parents feel that they have no place at home parties preceding or following the

Prom. People who have indulged in liquor or drugs at pre-Prom parties are not welcome at the Prom. If this general rule is followed by everyone, we would not then need to fear the unfavorable publicity that arises from indiscretion.

5. If parents are holding an open house, definite invitations should be extended to those who are expected to be guests. Homes which permit indiscriminate crashing subject themselves to many difficulties. At open houses, parents should naturally be present. If students tell you that parents are not present at the other homes they are to visit, you may be sure that they are going to the wrong homes. Naturally, the standards you set for your children are your concern, but the situations in which other students are placed are the concern of the school and society in general. One further difficulty often accompanying the practice of party crashing is the matter of drinking which takes place between crashes. Each parent might well remind his son or daughter that crashing a party is not in good taste.

6. Prior arrangements should be made by both the boy and the girl as to the hour when each is expected to be home. The boy should never make his date uncomfortable by objecting to a girl's wishes in this matter.

7. We suggest that parents of all boys who are driving cars on the night of the Prom caution them to drive responsibly. No one wants our memories of this occasion marred by any tragedy.

If all concerned make adequate advance plans for the high school Prom, it should prove to be a happy affair for everyone. In the interest of the school and community, the foregoing suggestions are offered for your consideration. We hope these remarks may be accepted in the spirit in which they are sent.

Sincerely yours,

Square John, Principal

The chief purpose of such communications is to secure cooperation in creating a better situation for young people. Further, it is an indication of the willingness of the school to accept parents as partners in solving educational and activity problems.

Bringing Patrons to the School

School Exhibits

One of the most effective and frequently used methods of interpreting the schools to the patrons is the school exhibit. Schools may display their work in specially built cases in the corridors of the building. Such exhibits, changed at regular intervals, usually show the more spectacular results attained in fine arts, home economics, and industrial arts. In addition to display cases, many schools have permanent or temporary exhibits in the show windows of stores in the community, at public fairs, or at other places where they may attract the attention of large groups of people. In some communities pupils secure permission from merchants to display school work in show windows. Such exhibits are more effective when also reported in the local press, or on the radio. Some cities have sponsored contests in which pupils were allowed to use their artistic talents in the decorations of show windows themselves.

Science fairs have also become increasingly popular, and science exhibits are usually worthy student projects. Parents and school personnel outside the science departments are given the opportunity to see the quality of work done by pupils. This technique has been so successful that some schools now sponsor humanities and art fairs. Competition in these events should not be stressed to the point where students are tempted to exhibit projects not of their own making.

Open House

Open houses have tended to supersede exhibits. At such affairs in secondary schools, various members of the faculty give talks concerning such topics as college entrance, new curriculum provisions, extracurricular opportunities, the social program, guidance, and so on. In some cases students may make an open house presentation in which narrators show slides prepared by the school's photography club. Elementary schools likewise use the open house to describe a new marking system, interest the parents in a cooperative study of child development, explain provisions for physical and for mental health, and so forth.

School Visitation

If parents can be brought to see the school in operation, they will better understand what it is attempting to do. It is generally recognized that parents, especially mothers, visit the regular sessions of schools during the elementary school period but that the practice is less frequent at the secondary level. The reason, no doubt, is in part the unwillingness of adolescents to have their parents participate in activities. Such action conceivably might result in being considered immature by his peers. And parents try to respect the wishes of their children.

In an effort to get a large number of parents to visit the school, some principals hold night sessions of the regularly scheduled daytime classes.

An excellent example of this practice takes the form of an evening re-enactment of the entire school day with each class period shortened to approximately fifteen or twenty minutes. Each parent who comes is asked to attend the classes in which his child is enrolled. School principals who have tried the plan are enthusiastic about the numbers of parents who attend and their sincere interest and keen appreciation of the opportunity. A difficulty often encountered is that the classrooms cannot accommodate the visitors.

Parents and patrons are almost always interested in the more spectacular school activities such as the band, the shops, and the laboratories. Opportunity for inspection of these activities, with pupil interpreters, can be valuable and informative. Showing educational pictures, if the school possesses audio-visual equipment, or a concert by the musical organizations can form a fitting climax to what should prove to be an important experience for the school and the community.

Education Week

Evening sessions are frequently held during American Education Week in the fall, although any other time of year is equally satisfactory. If Education Week is to be used to exhibit school work, the program should be planned well in advance to allow enough time for proper newspaper publicity or for preparation of posters announcing the events of the various days of the week. Special entertainments in the evening may also be planned during Education Week. In all probability programs in which children participate are more effective than those with adult speakers, no matter how effective they may be. And it is more effective when groups participate rather than individual children, regardless of how competent the individuals are. This does not mean, for example, that individual soloists should not be used on musical programs, but it does mean that the entire program should not be made up of individual numbers. Emphasizing group activity rather than individual excellence develops good feeling in the community and averts the bitterness which is sometimes created by a discussion of the relative merits of the individuals who appear on the program.

Parent Organizations

During the latter years of the nineteenth century, the parent-teacher association was organized as an outgrowth of mothers' clubs. The movement gained strength as it widened its scope of activity and at present its membership is in the millions. Although the organization has national policies which it attempts to promote, local associations have considerable freedom in their activities as long as these do not conflict with national policy.

These associations render valuable services to schools. Many of them are busy with money-raising activities to support school services. Some have supplied dishes for the cafeteria, lunch for poor children, audio-visual equipment, and so forth. It is questionable whether these types of expenditures should be the responsibility of a parent organization, because such items represent a possible legitimate expenditure by the board of education from tax funds. If the organization desires to present something to the school, it should be something that might not be furnished by the school board.

Some principals have not been enthusiastic about parent organizations, and they have, in some cases, proved troublesome. But that is the exception and not the rule. The organization has usually been viewed as a vital force in interpreting the school to the community.

For some people, the parent-teacher organization represents an important social contact, but for all parents it offers an opportunity to become acquainted with their children's present or prospective teachers. From this kind of understanding, the organization can go on to interpret what is being done, answer questions of concern to parents, and interpret the entire school system. A wise principal works unobtrusively with the program committee to suggest topics or demonstrations that will enlighten parents. Outside speakers may be used on some occasions, but demonstrations of new methods of teaching or explanations of school policy or finance will ordinarily be more effective.

The best parent-teacher associations are those that work for intelligent, cooperative relations between the home and the school. Situations where associations are impotent or unusually belligerent are almost without exception the result of a lack of leadership and poorly planned or unbalanced programs. Leadership does not mean that the principal or his teachers should strive to be elected to an office. It is usually better for the professional staff to serve in an advisory capacity.

In some communities, particularly at the secondary level, the parent-teacher association is not successful. The diversity and number of the population prevent the feeling of homogeneity so often present in elementary schools. As a result some schools have developed homeroom groups, mothers' and fathers' clubs, band parents, school improvement councils, and other organizations with similar purposes to draw interest groups together. The smaller groups provide the homogeneity which is necessary for success. The sort of organization that will best serve a local school must be decided locally, and except where a parent-teacher group has failed miserably, a forward-looking principal will see to it that cooperation exists.

Parent Workshops

Some schools have been instrumental in forming workshops for specific purposes. Teachers and administrators work with parents in planning such groups and in deciding upon the topics to be discussed. Problems such as health habits, new mathematics, child growth and development, and study techniques are subjects in which parents of elementary pupils have vital interest. At the secondary level matters such as drugs, alcohol, boy and girl relationships, vocational information, and preparation for college can be considered in workshop discussions.

Workshops of this nature should involve both parents and school personnel in planning and should be arranged at a time when both mothers and fathers may attend. Schools with parent-teacher organizations may use this group to plan the workshop.

Lay Advisory Committees

Some principals have formed lay advisory committees to assist in evaluating the school's operation and in planning future developments. The chief function of such a committee is to provide a technique for developing a so-called "grass roots" relationship, to offer the principal an opportunity to get parent opinion in a small and informal group. He may describe any innovations or changes which he feels are desirable to the group. Their reaction can render valuable assistance and support in his planning.

When a committee is formed, it should be fairly representative of the community, not a hand-picked elite. Furthermore, to avoid embarrassing developments, the members of the committee should be informed of its purpose. They should understand completely and clearly that the committee serves in an advisory capacity only. If this is not emphasized, the group may feel that it is empowered to make final decisions, creating a difficult situation.

At the secondary level, advisory committees are often formed to assist in evaluating the various vocational programs available. Representatives from business and industry could make up the membership of the various committees, and assist the school in evaluating curriculum materials and appraising the equipment being used in vocational classes. They could also provide continuous contact for the vocational teacher. The value of these committees is obvious.

School Performances

In all schools, particularly at the secondary level, there will be public events, such as dramatic productions, athletic events, and concerts, where school patrons will be present and from which they will form opinions about the school. At dramatic performances it is a simple matter to have a well-drilled and courteous group of pupils do the ushering under the direction of an adult. Such a service may be one of the duties performed by a committee responsible to the student council. Athletic games may also have student ushers.

At most contests, and especially at night football games, some sort of policing is necessary if spectators are to be directed effectively and confusion prevented. Parking automobiles adjacent to a football playing field and their orderly exit is a problem which can best be handled by uniformed city police if the latter can be secured. If not, the problem can be handled by adults, either men teachers or custodians, but in no cases where large student groups congregate should students do the policing. Regular city police in uniform detailed for policing athletic contests which draw several hundred or thousand spectators is highly desirable. Using experts to direct people at events to which the public is invited is no more prevalent than may reasonably be expected, but it is by no means a universal practice. When tickets are sold for such events, the box office and, if necessary, several suboffices should be opened early enough to reduce waiting to a minimum. If reserved seats are to be available, they should be on sale at places in the community convenient for patrons. The orderly handling of crowds assembled for school activities can by no stretch of the imagination be considered informing-patrons-about-the-school category. Rather it may be classified as a means of creating favorable public opinion by promoting the orderly assembly and management of crowds.

Relations in the School Community

Schools Exist Within Communities

A community is made up of a variety of people who have different points of view. Various methods are used to bring all these views before the school principal, and most principals recognize the complexity of this responsibility. Since every effective school principal hopes to gain strong support for his school, he plans his efforts so that he will get community backing. He knows that he cannot please every group, but that his standards must be high and his ultimate aim to create a situation which permits the best possible learning environment in the school. He should support constructive movements and oppose those that detract from the school's major objectives.

Demands by Pressure Groups

In a study conducted by the National Association of Secondary School Principals, principals were asked to report incidents when pressure was exerted on the school.[5] Most pressure reported was exerted by citizen or parent groups other than the P.T.A. Athletic-minded persons comprised the group exerting the second major source of pressure. Almost 46 percent of the principals reported that colleges and universities had exerted influence. Other sources of influence were listed as follows: religious groups (noted by 35 percent of the principals), those concerned with testing programs (31 percent); "local labor organizations" exerted the least pressure—5 percent.

Principals were also asked about public accusations of anti-Americanism or lack of patriotism on the part of staff members. The study showed that only one out of ten principals had experienced any difficulties in that matter. But the study indicated that a total of more than one thousand incidents had been reported within a two-year span. About one out of five principals reported incidents of citizen apprehension over books or reading assignments.

In dealing with outside influences, the principal should be guided by a well-defined policy developed by the staff and approved by the general administration and board of education. When policy has been developed, the principal is relieved of dealing with such matters as an emergency situation.

Local business and economic groups sometimes bring pressure on the schools by insisting that school supplies be purchased locally. Others seek to obtain names and addresses of students, while others wish to use the school for advertising purposes. The practice of buying the best educational supplies for the least amount of money should be a board of education policy, which eventually takes care of pressure that may be created. It is also wise to buy upon a bid basis.

The direct activities of economic groups, usually the only ones that affect the school principal and the local school, are easy to detect and not difficult to deal with. They usually include giving samples, prizes, or free educational supplies and they often have direct teaching value. A general policy which permits the school to appraise the products and accept what it can use is sufficient. These and similar problems can be handled uniformly if the principal is provided a set of official rules and regulations from the board of education.

The policy developed and approved for use in the situations described should have as its central purpose protecting young people from exploitation. Exploitation may range all the way from trying to require every pupil to write a particular theme, to having pupils solicit or engage in spelling bees, to hobby shows, athletic contests, or other activities which the pressure group wishes to promote. The principal can solve the problem by making it a practice to follow established policy.

---

[5]*The Senior High School Principalship*, pp. 86–89.

Coordinating Councils

A recent form of organization which many principals have found effective in interpreting the school to the community and in assisting youth is the coordinating council. Other names sometimes used are youth council or community council. In such organizations many groups such as the parent-teacher organization, scout group leaders, labor, Red Cross, Y.M.C.A., and other organizations in the community participate. The purpose of the council is to coordinate all agencies in the community concerned with the welfare of young people. The principal should find it an excellent medium for developing the school as a community agency. If there is no council, the principal may wish to help organize one, unless the functions to be served are cared for adequately through some other agency.

Service Clubs

Service clubs such as Rotary, Kiwanis, and Lions seek the leaders in the community as members. Their avowed purpose is to work for the common good of the community and the welfare of their fellow men. They are particularly interested in youth, and frequently do considerable good for the disadvantaged children in the community. Some people deride service clubs because of their supposed good fellowship, which is in some instances forced. But there can be little doubt that the principal's membership in such groups affords contact with civic leaders, offers an unusual opportunity to interpret the schools to these community leaders casually and directly, and often affords a social contact for the somewhat cloistered school executive.

Some of these organizations sponsor their junior counterparts in the local school. This provides additional contact for the adult members and a wholesome relationship for youth. Service clubs should understand that their sponsorship must be in keeping with the established rules and policy of the school.

Involving Teachers and Other School Employees

Many principals have adopted a policy of informing teachers, clerks, and custodians about the purposes and policies of the schools so that they may possess accurate information and may disseminate it in conversation whenever schools are the subject of discussion. Information about the budget, charts or graphs showing how the local tax dollar is apportioned to the various governmental agencies in the community, as well as a discussion of school policies, may well be the basis of some teachers' meetings.

The custodial staff and the clerical workers ordinarily have a circle of friends who are just as desirous of accurate information as any other group in the community. Because of this, some school systems plan meetings for clerical and janitorial workers where the policies of the schools are explained. In school systems where the noninstructional staff information meeting policies are in force, it will be necessary for the principal to carry out instructions from the central office. Where such policies do not exist, he may furnish information to the clerks and custodians in a regular but informal manner. Such information should yield dividends in community understanding.

Incidentally the character of custodial care given the building, the courtesy extended to visitors in the school by the clerks, and the neatness of the written work which comes from the principal's office have a cumulative effect in the community's interpretation of the schools. Slovenly work or careless treatment reflects an attitude of indifference on the part of the principal that cannot help but lower public confidence in the school.

Some school principals have adopted a plan of preparing a periodic bulletin to all members of the teaching and noninstructional staff. This presents an opportunity to comment on current issues, to furnish directions needed in carrying on administrative business, and to prepare the entire staff for future events.

Interpreting the School to the Pupils

No matter how seriously and conscientiously the school is interpreted by radio, newspaper, or home visits, the most constant means of obtaining good public relations is furnished by the pupils. Casual conversation by children about school matters at the dinner table or during a lull in the radio or TV program is responsible in large part for the opinions that parents form regarding the school. Furthermore, pupils will soon be adult members of the community who should be informed of what the schools cost, what the schools are trying to accomplish, and what may reasonably be expected. The ease with which pupils may be instructed in such matters has up to now been overlooked—perhaps because schools expect that they absorb the information without direct teaching.

One way pupils can help interpret the schools is through information in social science classes on educational topics and problems. Pupils who understand the program and purposes of the school may be influential in conveying such information to their parents and interpreting education generally. A number of schools have attempted to interpret the schools through the guidance system or by homeroom discussion. Certainly instruction in the homeroom is preferable to none, but there appears to be no reason why a study of schools and education should not be included in the social science course. A study of the school system may be properly included in the study of social science, for it is a curriculum matter more than it is a problem of pupil personnel or guidance. Such instruction could be more vital than many of the topics ordinarily included in the social studies, and it offers an excellent opportunity to relate local policies.

Another topic that may have a place in the school curriculum is the cost of schools locally and nationally. This leads to a study of taxation—a topic on which children should be instructed carefully so that they see it as a method of securing cooperatively that which could not be secured individually. The effects of long-term borrowing, the necessity for careful budgetary procedure, and the relations among various types of governmental and nongovernmental expenditures should be taught to the young people at some point in public schools.

Attention to Problems of Social Concern

In today's society there are countless problems facing almost every community. Biracial communities have experienced serious trouble in developing harmonious relationships. The schools are often centers in which difficulties occur, even though the difficulties usually originate outside the school. Community agencies formed to study human relations and to recommend community action encourage cooperation between different ethnic and socioeconomic levels. Young people, particularly those of secondary school age, should be involved in discussing such matters, and their advice should be sought in attempting to arrive at constructive solutions. The principal can be effective in establishing avenues of cooperation.

There are other matters of societal concern such as pollution in which youth have an interest. Many schools have organized campaigns to enlist support in community beautification and park preservation, as well as in clearing pollution from streams. These are all problems where young people can provide leadership and service. The end results may be increased appreciation for the effectiveness of the school and the students.

Another project which had both social and educational significance was initiated in the schools of Thornton Township, Cook County, Illinois, during the time one of the authors was serving as superintendent of the township. The idea for the project began through the interest of teachers who were interested in developing a program for students below average in ability. Many of the students were potential dropouts. A school-sponsored work program was suggested in which students would attend classes part-time and spend the rest of their time working in clothing renovation, arts, and crafts. The idea gained the support of the administration and board of education.

An unused residence owned by the district was remodeled to provide a workshop where students made a variety of saleable articles and established a salesroom. After a year's operation, a larger building within the area of the business district was made available and the project was broadened. Money from the sales was used to purchase materials, and profits were made available to the students. The new facilities provided equipment for painting cars, printing, bookbinding, ceramics, and leather-work. This project operated under the name *Pilot* (Program in Limited Occupational Training). The Vocational Division of Vocational Rehabilitation of the State of Illinois has supported both the idea and the development of the program.

In the initial stages of *Pilot* there was generous cooperation from interested citizens including housewives and representatives of business and labor. The community's interest and concern was most rewarding. The project demonstrated a high degree of cooperation among faculty, board of education, administration, and staff, but credit for it belongs to the members of the teaching staff who developed the idea. For its interest and support the board of education received an award from the National Education Association.

Another development within the same district was the establishment of an adjustment program for students unable to make proper adjustment to the normal school program. When a student had reached the stage where expulsion seemed imminent, he was given the alternative of enrolling in evening classes to pursue his school program. These classes were tutorial in nature, and the focus was on academic matters and personal adjustment. Teachers especially interested in this type of student volunteered their services. Many students who would have been pushed out or expelled made satisfactory progress and were readmitted to the regular day-school program.

Community Education

Traditionally the school has operated during the regular school day. It opened for students in the morning and closed its doors in the afternoon when they returned to their homes. Most schools were not used in the evening and few were utilized over the weekend. While many activities were scheduled for students on Saturdays and Sundays and some adult education programs were developed, the full potential of both buildings and staff were never fully realized in the "regular" school.

School administrators have realized that it is a waste to allow excellent facilities to remain idle for large segments of time, particularly during evenings, weekends, and summers. They have also realized that every community has citizens who are interested in self improvement through additional education, increased recreation, more opportunities for interaction and socialization. In addition there are talented people who are interested and willing to share their skills and knowledge with others. Community education is a process of mobilizing the community to render the broadest kind of service to meet both individual and community needs. The Mott Foundation of Flint, Michigan, has long been interested in this concept and has made generous contribution to its development in many areas.

In commenting on community education, V. M. Kerensky said that

> community education at its best educates *all* and mobilizes *all* in the educational process. Its distinguishing characteristic is that it goes all out —it does everything that can be done—it places at the disposal of each child, each person the sum total of human knowledge, and human service. It leaves no stone unturned in an effort to see that every human being has the optimum climate for growth.[6]

Community schools not only serve children and adolescents during the day, but should be a community center in the late afternoon and evening. Some schools have for years offered academic training for those who wish to become citizens or to study in certain subjects offered by adult education. They have broadened the program to provide other services such as supervised play for children who have no place to play except the street. Such wholesome activity not only reduces juvenile delinquency, but it is also a service to children who may have all too little play and happiness otherwise.

But the school can do far more than furnish after-school play for children, desirable as that activity is. With shorter work weeks, more leisure, and more social awareness, adults should have the opportunities for educational, social, and recreational development. Both children and adults should be involved in developing the programs.

If the activities that are provided are to be worthwhile, there must be competent instruction and leadership. In some cases this requires regular teachers, but in many instances the necessary personnel are available in the community. It is essential that such services are furnished without cost, or at least at a very nominal cost, if they are to reach those who need and desire the activities the most but are unable to pay.

In organizing the community education program, the principal also has a major role in encouraging its development, although he need not personally direct it if there is someone else who is acceptable. The best solution to the leadership problem is to establish a Community School Director who cooperates with the principal in developing the program. The director may be a member of the regular faculty who accepts the

---

[6]V. M. Kerensky, "Community Education," *NCSEA News*, May 1971, p. 3.

directorship as an extra responsibility. In such cases, it is important to realize that his load as a teacher should be lightened considerably to allow adequate time for the position.

The community activities of the principal represent an important part of his responsibilities. They may not require more than a few hours each week, but that time should be made as productive as possible. Ordinarily it is assumed that the principal is the key to a successful program of interpretation in the community. His activities within the community demonstrate his interest in the welfare of the citizens as well as the school's students. He may initiate some community activities and be a part of many others, but he should maintain close contact with the superintendent and report the results of his efforts. Few principals will be recognized as successful if they fail in their community duties. The principal's prime objective should be to create an our school concept—a school which citizens, teachers, and pupils identify as their school.

Selected References

ALEXANDER, WILLIAM M., ed., *The High School of the Future: A Memorial to Kimball Wiles*. Columbus, Ohio: Charles E. Merrill Publishing Company, 1970.

CARTER, BOYD, and TED DE VRIES, "Ten Commandments of Successful School Tax Campaigns," *The Clearing House*, 42 (December 1967), 210–12.

Communication Ideas in Action. Washington, D.C.: National School Public Relations Association of the National Education Association, 1970.

DAPPER, GLORIA, *Public Relations for Educators*. New York: The Macmillan Company, 1964.

DARROW, RICHARD W., DAN J. FORRESTAL, and AUDREY O. COOKMAN, *Public Relations Handbook*. Chicago: Dartnell Press, 1967.

FREY, GEORGE T., "Improving School-Community Relations," *Today's Education*, 60 (January 1971), 14–17.

FOLK, CHRIS, "Interpreting the Secondary School," *The High School Journal*, 58 (January 1965), 257–61.

FUSCO, GENE C., *Improving Your School Community Relations Program*. Englewood Cliffs, N.J.: Prentice-Hall, Inc., 1967.

HEFFERNAN, HELEN, and VIVIAN E. TODD, *Elementary Teacher's Guide to Working with Parents*. West Nyack, N.Y.: Parker Publishing Company, 1969.

HOLDER, ROBERT, *A Complete Guide to Successful School Publications*. Englewood Cliffs, N.J.: Prentice-Hall, Inc., 1967.

JACKSON, RONALD B., "Schools and Communities: A Necessary Relevance," *The Clearing House*, 44 (April 1970), 488–90.

JOHNSON, DAVID W., and LINDA B. JOHNSON, "Intervention Within Uncrystallized Groups," *Educational Leadership*, 27 (October 1969), 39–43.

JOHNSON, W. R., "Parent-Teacher Conferences," *National Elementary Principal*, 47 (May 1966), 48–50.

KROLL, ARTHUR M., ed., *Issues in American Education*. New York: Oxford University Press, 1970.

LURIE, ELLEN, *How to Change the Schools: A Parent's Action Handbook on How to Fight the System*. New York: Random House, Inc., 1970.

National Education Association, *The Elementary School Principalship in 1968 —A Research Study*. Washington, D.C.: Department of Elementary School Principals, April 1968.

NORTON, M. SCOTT, "School-Community Relations—New Issues, New Trends," *The Clearing House*, 44 (May 1970), 538–40.

Public Relations Goldmine. Washington, D.C.: National School Public Relations of the Department of the National Education Association, 1968.

SMITH, FREDERICK R., and R. BRUCE McQUIGG, *Secondary Schools Today: Readings for Educators*. (2nd ed.), Boston: Houghton Mifflin Company, 1969.

SUMPTION, MERLE R., and YVONNE ENGSTROM, *School-Community Relations: A New Approach*. New York: McGraw-Hill Book Company, 1966.

ZIMMERMAN, HERBERT M., "The Community and the Schools: Who Are the Decision-Makers?" *National Association of Secondary School Principals Bulletin*, 53 (May 1969), 169–75.

21

School Media Center

The principal has long been recognized as the instructional leader in the school. While he has many duties, none is more important than improving instruction and facilitating the learning process. At one time the school library represented the chief source for augmenting the materials used in the traditional classroom. While the library is still the focus of many instructional activities, it is only a part of the instructional materials center. The center makes its full contribution to instruction only when it has the active and enthusiastic support of the school principal.

The modern media center, with its listening and viewing devices, its open stacks of books and informal, often homelike atmosphere, is in pleasant contrast to the institution described in the Old Librarian's Almanac:

> Keep your Books behind stout Gratings and in no wise let any Person come at them to take them from the Shelf except yourself. Have in mind the Counsel of Master Enoch (that most Worthy Librarian) who says: "It were better that no Person enter the Library (save the Librarian Himself) and that the Books be kept in Safety, than that one Book be lost, or others Misplaced." Guard well your Books—this is always your foremost Duty.... So far as your Authority will permit of it, exercise great Discrimination as to which Persons shall be admitted to the use of the Library. For the Treasure House of Literature is no more to be thrown open to the ravages of the unreasoning Mob, than is a fair Garden to be laid unprotected at the Mercy of a Swarm of Beasts.[1]

---

[1] L. F. Fargo, "Training High School Students in the Use of the Library," *Journal of Proceedings and Addresses of the National Education Association*, LI (1913), 756.

And the librarian today has a different conception of his role in the instructional process. In many areas the head librarian has become the media specialist.

The trend in recent years has been to set aside a portion of the school plant to serve as a media center. (The terms instructional services center, audio-visual center, materials service center, and multimedia center are also used by some school systems.) For purposes of consistency and clarification, The American Library Association uses the term *media center*.[2]

Historical Perspective

The first library was a classroom library, often consisting of a few books lent by the public library to the teacher, who re-lent them to pupils. This plan acquainted the pupils and the teacher with the resources of the public library, but it did not have a sufficient variety of materials and placed additional burdens upon the teacher.

Later on, in some cases, the public library established a branch in the local school. Schools, particularly in small districts, were thus provided with an immediate source of books at little expense. There appears to be no effort to continue this practice today, although many school libraries have established excellent working relations with public libraries in the community.

Next came the establishment of a school library within the school. Because at first the location depended on the availability of unused classrooms, in many cases, these rooms were ill-suited for library purposes. They were frequently located in unattractive, isolated areas and were generally not very accessible to teachers or students. This development was usually accompanied by designation of a teacher-librarian for part-time service.

A further step toward full facilities was the development of a school library in a central room planned specifically for that purpose with a full-time, trained school librarian in charge. Under this plan, the library became the principal source for reading materials and trained librarians became available to both students and the professional staff for research projects and curriculum development.

A final development has been the establishment of the media center. In addition to housing the materials usually associated with the traditional library, the complex is also likely to include large and small rooms for

---

[2]*Standards for School Media Programs* (Chicago: American Library Association), 1969, p. XI.

group meetings equipped for visual aids, storage areas for hardware, and individual study carrels where the student may do research, listen to tapes or recordings, and view film strips, films, slides, or TV.

Media Center Facilities

Modern techniques in teaching and learning are greatly complemented by the resources and services of the media center: The location and the environment of the center should be considered in planning it. The following are suggested guidelines for those who will be working with architects in the construction of new buildings or the remodelling of existing facilities. (1) The area set aside for the media center should be decided upon first, and enough space allotted to allow fulfillment of the center's purposes. (2) The center should be located to attract maximum use by students and professional staff. This implies a central location within the learning areas. In communities with strong community school programs, an area might be provided that can be opened without providing access to other building areas. (3) There should be good lighting and effective acoustics so that a proper climate for learning may be preserved. Most schools now use carpeting to improve the appearance and to reduce the noise. (4) There should be adequate office space for the staff and sufficient work space for storage and the repair and construction of classroom learning aids.

The facilities provided for the media center necessarily depend on the type of school to be served and the established objectives. Needs vary according to whether a school is elementary, middle, secondary, or a combination of the three. Vocational-technical libraries require facilities that may differ from those of a more generalized type. The principal should involve the media specialist in planning new construction or remodelling existing facilities.

Since many traditional libraries have been expanded to perform the functions of the instructional materials or media center, the facilities must be adapted to carry out the center's objectives. In addition to housing magazines, books, and pictorial materials, it must be equipped for the use of slides, films, filmstrips, tapes, and recordings. It therefore becomes necessary to have such equipment as portable radios and television sets, slide projectors, and tape recorders. This also implies a need for viewing rooms, conference rooms, and individual study carrels equipped with outlets to permit the use of various machines and other hardware. The American Library Association and the National Education Association have established standards for most items of the modern media center. In addition, it recommends that 6 percent of the annual per pupil operational cost be spent to maintain the center's supplies and equipment.[3]

In recommending basic collections for media centers for schools of two hundred fifty or more students, the ALA suggested: (1) at least 6,600–10,000 titles or twenty volumes per student, whichever is greater; (2) 40 to 50 periodicals for kindergarten through sixth grade, 50 to 75 periodical titles for kindergarten through eighth grade, 100 to 125 periodical titles for the junior high school, and 125 to 175 for secondary schools; (3) three to six newspapers for the elementary, six to ten for the junior high school, and the same number for the secondary school; (4) 500 to 1,000 filmstrip titles or three prints per pupil, whichever is greater. In addition, the association provides quantitative standards for other materials such as films, tape and disc recordings.[4]

These standards recommended do tend to border on the ideal, but they represent an excellent guide for administrators and media specialists. The standards should be adapted to conform to the needs of the school in the local setting.

Some school systems have equipped their schools for closed-circuit television. Since the use of many materials in the media center is required to make television productions possible, the television studio should be located in or near the center. Such cases require planning so that individual and group work in or near the area is undisturbed. The apparent success of teaching by closed-circuit television should convince the principal to make provision for its inclusion in the media center.

Functions of the Media Center

The traditional school library was considered the learning laboratory of an effective school, and the media center serves in the same capacity. When properly organized and managed the center provides not only a place where the student may read, but also where he may see, listen, and perform. In describing the extent of the services to be provided, the American Library Association suggests (1) providing consultant services to improve learning and instruction; (2) improving learning through the use of printed and audio-visual materials; (3) making information available on new educational development; (4) creating and producing new materials for students and teachers; (5) providing materials for classes and individuals doing investigation and exploration; (6) making available working areas

---

[3]*School Media Programs*, pp. 29–49.
[4]*School Media Programs*, pp. 30–33.

for media staff, teachers, and students; and (7) providing equipment to convey materials to student and teacher.[5]

The current emphasis on individualized learning creates a need for increased services and facilities in the media center such as additional materials in the form of books, pamphlets, magazines, cassettes, films, slides, and so on. Under proper management, the media center can contribute materially to fulfilling the concept of individualized teaching and learning.

The Use of School Media Centers

Accessibility of the Media Center

Maximum use of the center is possible only when the pupils and members of the professional staff are thoroughly familiar with the available resources. One important consideration is the time when the center is open for use. The traditional library's hours usually coincided with the hours during which the entire school was in operation. The library was open shortly before classes began and closed soon after classes were dismissed. Under such an arrangement there was little time for either students or teachers to take advantage of the resources.

A recent study by the National Education Research Division made to determine the attitudes of teachers with respect to library hours[6] disclosed that more than half the responding teachers felt that school libraries should be open before or after school, but only three in ten reported that their libraries were open at either of these times. Further, more than two out of ten teachers believed that libraries should be open evenings during the week. More teachers felt that the library should be open on Saturdays.

The study also pointed out that more secondary teachers than elementary teachers believe that the library should be open during after-school hours. However, the results showed similar views with respect to libraries being open on Saturday. Most of those in favor of extended hours suggested one or more hours before school and one or two hours after school. They also suggested two or three hours in the evening on school days and a half-day on Saturday.

It is apparent that most media centers have not been open long enough to serve the needs of most teachers and students. Consideration should be given to expanding the service to meet the needs. In communities where community education programs have been developed, there is an even greater need for more flexibility and expansion of the time schedule.

---

[5]*School Media Programs*, p. 4.
[6]National Education Association, *NEA Research Bulletin*, 49, No. 1 (March 1971), 23–24.

Teaching Pupils to Use the Resources

Maximum use of the media center is possible only when the pupils and the members of the professional staff are familiar with what services are offered and their uses. Regular instruction should be given pupils on use of the resources, but the manner in which such instruction should be given is not agreed upon. The least satisfactory method leaves instruction to incidental teaching.

The media specialist and the regular teacher should share in the instruction. In some cases, a member of the media staff may plan regular visits to the class with appropriate follow-up by the regular teacher. The advantage of this plan is that it acquaints students with a member of the media staff and motivates teachers to stimulate pupils to make wide use of the services and facilities.

Use of Books

While the book collections and other reading materials are only a part of the center, they comprise a most important part. Any unit dealing with the use of reading materials should include instruction in: (1) arrangement of resources, appropriate behavior, and loan procedures; (2) book classification; (3) use of the card catalog; (4) periodicals and periodical indexes; (5) dictionaries, encyclopedias, yearbooks, and almanacs; (6) atlases, gazeteers, use of maps; (7) special reference books and indexes for biography, social studies, languages, literature, and science; and (8) recreational materials and items of personal interest.

Any unit of instruction should teach appreciation and proper care of reading materials. The loss of books and other materials is a persistent problem. While it is true that the professional staff is responsible for safeguarding the center and its materials, rules for its use must not be so drastic as to discourage student use of the materials. The availability of copying devices may further reduce loss of materials.

Use of Audio-Visual Materials

The use of audio-visual materials has become an increasingly important part of teaching. Likewise, with the new emphasis on individualized learning and student research, students should be taught to utilize these resources properly. Because many teachers have not received training in the proper use of these materials, it becomes necessary for the audio-visual specialist to assist teachers and students use both machines and materials correctly. Any instruction should cover: (1) location of film projectors, slide projectors, and recorders; (2) location of slides, films, and tapes;

(3) identification and use of electrical outlets in listening and viewing rooms; (4) use and care of machines; (5) film splicing and minor repair of machines and materials; (6) use of microphones; (7) use of video tape recorders, tape recorders, and cassettes; and (8) orientation to services offered.

Most students are interested in the use of machines to improve learning. Most equipment, though complicated in construction, is simple to operate. A majority of students and teachers can use the available equipment if the audio-visual specialist organizes effective instruction and contributes specific directions for their use.

Stimulating Use of Resources

The use of books can be stimulated by the activities of the staff as well as by the classroom teacher. During the days when the library was used as a combination library and study hall, almost all students became acquainted with the resources and services available. Since this combination is impractical in today's schools, other means must be employed.

There are several ways in which students may be motivated to make extensive use of the media centers. The following suggestions may be useful: (1) visit to individual classrooms by a member of the professional staff to assist in research studies and individualized learning programs; (2) preparation of special racks for display of new materials and to highlight special seasons of the year; (3) school assemblies featuring the media center and facilities; (4) periodic bulletins announcing materials and equipment; (5) use of facilities for special occasions such as open house and meetings of special groups and clubs. Perhaps the most effective way to stimulate use of the media center is to provide the kind of materials and services that will provide students with rewarding experiences.

The Media Center Staff

The size of the staff recommended for a school media center has been based almost entirely on the size of the school's enrollment. In former years, small schools used the services of a part-time teacher who had been trained in library services. With school reorganization and the development of new theories in learning, the part-time librarian is no longer practical. An ideal arrangement suggested by the American Library Association is that the media center have one full-time media specialist for every 250 students, or major fraction thereof.[7] This type of staffing makes it possible to serve pupils and staff adequately and permits enough diversification that

---

[7]*School Media Programs*, p. 12.

the many needs of the media center can be met. Division of labor can be effected for dealing with written materials and audio-visual resources.

The Professional Staff

The work load which the media specialist carries is more important but not as easily measured as enrollment. In schools with only one specialist, the difficulties are numerous. The traditional librarian specialized in an area involving largely printed materials, but current needs require a knowledge of electronic and computerized processes, projectors of all types, and machines for programmed instruction. Inservice training programs, workshops, and university centers are useful in producing well-rounded programs to train and retrain personnel. An additional difficulty is that various grade levels require different programs. Elementary schools require one set of skills and knowledge, while middle and secondary schools demand additional ones. Some degree of specialization with respect to level seems necessary.

In large schools, it is possible to build a professional staff to accommodate a wide variety of needs. If the head of the center has specialized in printed materials, the assistants may be chosen because of their qualifications in television or other areas of the audio-visual field. Centers that are staffed with a number of professional people find it necessary to delineate the duties and coordinate the efforts. The principal of the school is obligated to assist in coordinating these activities and services.

The Use of Media Technicians

The demands of modern media centers are such that they cannot be met by a professional staff alone. It is uneconomical to use highly trained personnel to perform tasks that can be done by competent technicians. The school's objectives are the determining factors in developing the staff. A modern staff should include the following: (1) clerical workers; (2) graphics specialists; (3) photographic personnel; (4) television technicians; and (5) repair personnel.

In spite of the need for additional personnel, it is probably true that most centers cannot provide for all the services needed in most schools. A recent study made of emerging media centers indicates that staff organizations do not employ paraprofessional assistants, assistant librarians, technicians, media specialists, photographic technicians, and so forth.[8] The needs of students and teachers demand a variety of services and

[8]Mary V. Gaver, *Patterns of Development in Elementary School Libraries Today. A Five Year Report on Emerging Media Centers* (Chicago: Encyclopedia Britannica, Inc., 1969), pp. 1–76.

materials from the media center, and these needs can be met only when the professional staff is given proper assistance. The American Library Association has suggested that one media technician and one media aid be employed to support each media specialist in schools of 2,000 or fewer students. The association has further suggested that a technician with graphics abilities be available in each school.[9]

The Use of Pupil Assistants

It is common practice to use students as assistants in the media center. In some cases the assistants supplement an inadequate staff, but in many schools pupils volunteer their services as a method of serving the school or securing extra credit in one of their academic courses. In other institutions student assistants are paid by the school to expand the school's services. Among the duties that pupils perform are returning books to the shelves, filing charging slips, assisting at the charge desk, arranging bulletin boards, delivering audio-visual materials, filing films and slides, doing minor repair, and assisting with general housekeeping.

The experience pupil assistants gain can be most worthwhile, but it is necessary that they be given competent supervision in planning the work and arranging the tasks that will contribute to their educational development. Routine tasks soon lose their challenge unless variety is added. There should be some attempt to assist the pupils in developing work habits and utilizing the social values of the experience. It is entirely possible that these experiences may result in a number of future media specialists. Only through proper training and systematic planning is it possible to make effective use of pupil assistants.

The Media Center of the Future

Recent educational innovations indicate that resources outside the classroom will play an ever increasing part in learning activities. School construction in many school systems is planned to create an arrangement where a learning resource center occupies the central area of the complex. The center provides areas for book shelving, large and small group areas, conference rooms, study carrels, preview rooms, dark rooms, television studios, work rooms, listening areas, and storage rooms. Many libraries are also using retrieval systems and computers to assist them in serving the school. The administrator must understand the importance of the con-

---

[9]*School Media Programs*, pp. 16–17.

tributions and innovations that can be made, and he must be active in supporting their development.

The most modern center achieves its purposes only when it is staffed by professional personnel and paraprofessional assistants. The media specialist must be trained specifically in the broad framework of the various kinds of media, in human relations, communication, educational methods, curriculum, and research. Even pupils at the elementary level are motivated to do research and all individual learning programs are receiving increasing emphasis. The media specialist must not only be a qualified teacher, but also a teacher of teachers. The effective school of the future will have a media center with adequate facilities staffed by a highly trained professional and paraprofessional staff.

In addition to satisfying the needs of students, the members of the teaching staff must be served as well. The principal and the media specialist plan the resources around such objectives as (1) a sufficient number and variety of volumes pertaining to child growth and development; (2) references to serve as source materials in curriculum development and teaching techniques; (3) procurement of special materials from other organizations or institutions upon a loan basis; and (4) providing books and periodicals of a general nature that will contribute to further professionalization of teachers. Such materials should be procured with the advice and assistance of those who need and will use the resources. This implies an effective working relationship between media staff, teachers, and administrators.

Selected References

BREWER, MARGARET L., and SHARON O. WILLIS, *The Elementary School Library*. Hamden, Conn.: Shoe String Press, 1970.

BROWN, WALTER L., ed., *Selected Readings in Educational Media*. New York: Simon & Schuster, Inc., 1969.

GAVER, MARY V., *Patterns of Development in Elementary School Libraries Today: A Five Year Report on Emerging Media Centers*. Chicago: Encyclopedia Britannica, Inc., 1969.

Greensboro Public Schools, *Centralized Ordering, Cataloging and Processing of Library Materials: An Outline*. Greensboro, N.C.: Greensboro Public Schools, 1969.

HICKS, WARREN B., and ALMA TILLIN, *Developing Multi-Media Libraries*. New York: R. R. Bowker, Co., 1970.

KELLEY, GAYLEN B., "Technological Advances Affecting School Instructional Media Centers," *Audiovisual Instruction*, 14 (September 1969), 42–48.

NEAGLEY, ROSS L., N. DEAN EVANS, and CLARENCE A. LYMAN, JR., *The School Administrator and Learning Resources: A Handbook for Effective Action*. Englewood Cliffs, N.J.: Prentice-Hall, Inc., 1969.

NEWCOMB, RUTH BECKER, "Role Expectations of the School Library Supervisor as a Function of the Distance Between Expected and Perceived Fulfillment," *Educational Leadership*, 26 (March 1971), 637–40.

NORBERG, KENNETH, "The Challenge of the New Media Center," *Audiovisual Instruction*, 14 (September 1969), 21–23.

POWELL, JUDITH, "From Library to Media Center," *National Association of Secondary School Principals Bulletin*, 55 (March 1971), 79–85.

RAMAGE, VIVIAN, *Instructional Materials Center Manual*. Hinsdale, Illinois: Philosophy and Procedures of Hinsdale Public Schools, 1970.

SAUNDERS, HELEN E., *The Modern School Library: Its Administration as a Materials Center*. Metuchen, N.J.: Scarecrow Press, 1968.

SHIREY, LAURIE, and KATHLEEN RYAN, *The Audio-Visual Equipment Directory*. (14th ed.) Washington, D.C.: National Audio-Visual Association, Inc., 1968.

U.S. Department of Health, Education, and Welfare, *Emphasis on Excellence in School Media Programs*. Washington: U.S. Government Printing Office, 1969.

VAN MONDFRANS, ADRIAN, and RONALD L. HOUSER, "Selecting Media to Present Basic Concepts," *Educational Technology*, X (December 1970), 40–44.

WEISGERBER, ROBERT A., ed., *Instructional Process and Media Innovation*. Chicago: Rand McNally and Company, 1968.

Index